Environmental Literature

Environmental Literature

*An Encyclopedia of Works,
Authors, and Themes*

Patricia D. Netzley

ABC-CLIO

Santa Barbara, California
Denver, Colorado
Oxford, England

Library of Congress Cataloging-in-Publication Data
Environmental literature : an encyclopedia of works, authors, and
    themes / [compiled by] Patricia D. Netzley.
        p.   cm.
    Includes bibliographical references (p.) and index.
    ISBN 1-57607-000-X (alk. paper)
    1. Environmental literature—Encyclopedias.   2. Environmental
literature—Bibliography.   I. Netzley, Patricia D.
GE35.E58   1999
333.7'2.—dc21   99-35271
                                                           CIP

05 04 03 02 01 00 99   10 9 8 7 6 5 4 3 2 1

ABC-CLIO, Inc.
130 Cremona Drive, P.O. Box 1911
Santa Barbara, California 93116-1911

This book is printed on acid-free paper ∞ .

Manufactured in the United States of America

CONTENTS

Entries by Category, ix
Preface, xiii

ENVIRONMENTAL LITERATURE:
AN ENCYCLOPEDIA OF WORKS, AUTHORS, AND THEMES

ENTRIES BY CATEGORY

Authors

Abbey, Edward
Abrahamson, Dean Edwin
Ackerman, Diane
Adamson, Joy
Agassiz, (Jean) Louis
  (Rodolphe)
Agricola, Georgius
Albertus Magnus, Saint
Allee, Warder Clyde
Anderson, Ray
Aridjis, Homero
Aristotle
Asimov, Isaac
Attenborough, Sir David
Audubon, John James
Austin, Mary
Bailey, Florence Augusta
  Merriam
Bailey, Liberty Hyde
Bailey, Ronald
Barron, T. A.
Bartram, John and William
Bass, Rick
Berry, Thomas Mary
Berry, Wendell
Bookchin, Murray
Botkin, Daniel B.
Boulle, Pierre
Brand, Stewart
Brooks, Paul
Buffon, Georges Louis Leclerc
Bulloch, David K.
Burroughs, Edgar Rice
Burroughs, John
Butler, Samuel
Caldicott, Helen
Caldwell, Lynton K.
Callicott, J. Baird
Candolle, Augustin de
Carr, Archie
Carrighar, Sally
Carson, Rachel Louise

Catlin, George
Catton, William
Caufield, Catherine
Chambers, Robert
Chase, Alston
Cherry, Lynn
Clare, John
Clements, Frederick E.
Club of Rome, The
Coleridge, Samuel Taylor
Commoner, Barry
Comstock, Anna Botsford
Cousteau, Jacques-Yves
Crèvecoeur, J. Hector St. John
Crichton, Michael
Cuvier, Georges
Dana, James Dwight
Darwin, Charles Robert
Darwin, Erasmus
Devall, Bill
Dillard, Annie
Dinesen, Isak
Dioscordides, Pedanius
Douglas, William O.
Dowie, Mark
Doyle, Arthur Conan
Easterbrook, Gregg
Eckholm, Erik P.
Ehrlich, Gretel
Ehrlich, Paul and Anne
Eiseley, Loren
Emerson, Ralph Waldo
Evelyn, John
Fabre, Jean-Henri
Finch, Robert
Flavin, Christopher
Foreman, Dave
Forster, Johann Reingold
Fossey, Dian
Foster, John Bellamy
Fouts, Roger
Fritsch, Albert J.
Fuller, R. Buckminster

Fumento, Michael
Gesner, Conrad
Goodall, Jane
Gore Jr., Albert
Gottlieb, Robert
Gould, Stephen Jay
Grew, Nehemiah
Guzzo, Lou
Haeckel, Ernst
Haines, John
Hales, Stephen
Hamilton, Alice
Hardin, Garrett
Harr, Jonathan
Harrison, Harry
Hasselstrom, Linda
Hawken, Paul
Hawkes, Jacquetta
Hay, John
Hearne, Vicki
Helvarg, David
Hoagland, Edward
Hogan, Linda
Hooke, Robert
Howard, Ebenezer
Hubbell, Sue
Hudson, William Henry
Hughes, Ted
Humboldt, Alexander Von
Huxley, Thomas Henry
Ibsen, Henrik
Ingenhousz, Jan
Irving, Washington
Ishimure, Michiko
Jefferies, (John) Richard
Jeffers, (John) Robinson
Jevons, William Stanley
Kaufman, Wallace
Kent, Rockwell
Krutch, Joseph Wood
Lamarck, Jean-Baptiste
Lawrence, D. H.
Leakey, Louis

PREFACE

Environmental Literature: An Encyclopedia of Works, Authors, and Themes presents the works of explorers, scientists, environmentalists, ecologists, conservationists, and nature writers throughout history who have sought not only to impart information about the earth and its creatures but also to influence the way people view the natural world. This qualification— that the writing must advance knowledge and change the reader's perception of the environment—is important, because it separates environmental literature from travel writing that aims merely to report on the author's adventures in a known place.

Although some nature writers do engage in such reportage, they also typically encourage an emotional response to the environment. As scholar Thomas J. Lyon explains in *This Incomperable Lande,* the goal of nature writing is "to turn our attention outward to the activity of nature.... The literary record time and again displays the claim that there is a lifting and a clarifying of perception inherent in this refocusing, which opens up something like a new world.... This sense of wonder conveyed ... may eventually be seen as a more important discovery beyond the finding of new lands." (Lyon 1989, 7) Some environmental fiction and poetry does this as well. For example, Karen Tei Yamashita and Edgar Rice Burroughs have created novels set in the natural world that make people think about the interconnection between the human spirit and the environment. Ted Hughes has created poems that elicit the same response.

Even though such writings influence the reader's views of nature in a subtle way, other forms of environmental literature can be far less subtle. For example, the works of scientists like Charles Darwin and Stephen Schneider, who address important controversies (evolution and global warming, respectively), have openly attempted to sway public opinion on scientific issues; likewise, the writings of ecologists like Arne Naess and Wendell Berry argue in favor of lifestyle changes that benefit the land. Similarly, conservationists such as John Muir and Farley Mowat advocate an appreciation of wilderness habitats and animals, and environmentalists like Rachel Carson, Dave Foreman, and Mark Dowie talk about environmental issues in an attempt to alter the way the public addresses these issues.

Works of environmental fiction have also displayed this desire to influence public opinion. For example, Edward Abbey's *The Monkey Wrench Gang* was in part an attempt to justify the actions of radical environmentalists and make them acceptable. Frederik Pohl's *Chernobyl* depicted the risks of nuclear power, and the novels of Kurt Vonnegut and John Wyndham offered scenarios in which nature runs amok, thereby warning of an environmental apocalypse unless people become more concerned about their antienvironmental behavior.

Many short stories present similar views. However, *Environmental Literature* focuses on book-length rather than short works. Therefore, it excludes individual stories, essays, articles, and poems, although it includes collections of such writings. It also excludes works that have not been translated into English, as well as works that are extremely difficult to obtain, in order to facilitate further study.

Exploring environmental literature in depth is a worthwhile pursuit. It provides information about important discoveries, theories, and controversies in the environmental sciences from ancient times to the present. It also shows the ways in which human beings have interacted with the environment, offering insights into how people view their place in the world. This view has changed dramatically throughout history, in part because of the efforts of environmental authors and their works.

Patricia D. Netzley

Abbey, Edward

Environmental activist Edward Abbey is the author of more than a dozen fiction and non-fiction books, but he is best known for *The Monkey Wrench Gang*. Published in 1975, this novel had a profound influence on the American environmental movement, because it promoted a new form of environmental activism.

The Monkey Wrench Gang is about a band of activists who use environmental sabotage, or ecotage, to protest desert development in the American Southwest. Six years after the book's publication, a newly formed environmental group called Earth First! decided to adopt the same tactics. As Philip Shabecoff explains in *A Fierce Green Fire:*

> These radicals . . . choose instead to defend the natural world by direct action, civil disobedience, and the kind of ecosabotage romanticized by the novelist Edward Abbey as "monkeywrenching." Earth First!ers, some of them remnants of the back-to-the-land movement of the 1960s, have thrown themselves in front of logging trucks, pulled up survey stakes for an oil exploration project, chained themselves to the upper branches of centuries-old trees marked for the chain saw by timber companies, and driven iron spikes into

trees to make it dangerous for loggers to cut into the wood. (Shabecoff 1993, p. 123)

Dave Foreman, one of the founders of Earth First!, convinced Abbey to join the group and be present at its first major media event, the "cracking" of the Glen Canyon Dam in 1981. In *The Monkey Wrench Gang,* the characters had advocated the dam's destruction; Earth First! accomplished it symbolically, unfurling a "crack" of black plastic over the face of the dam. According to Susan Zakin in *Coyotes and Town Dogs,* Abbey watched the event from a nearby bridge, shouting "Earth First!" and "Free the Colorado!" (Zakin 1993; 150)

For Abbey, radical politics were nothing new. Born on January 29, 1927, in Home, Pennsylvania, he was the son of an avowed anarchist, Paul Revere Abbey, and his wife, Mildred. At age 17 Edward Abbey hitchhiked west and fell in love with the American Desert. That same year, he was drafted into the U.S. Army; after receiving an honorable discharge in 1946 he actively protested the draft. He also began attending the University of New Mexico, where he received his B.A. in 1951 and a Masters in Philosophy in 1956. His thesis was entitled "Anarchism and the Morality of Violence."

While in college he wrote his first novel, the largely autobiographical *Jonathan Troy*. It was published in 1954 but soon went out of print, and Abbey considered it so bad that he refused to allow its republication years later. Nonetheless, in 1957 Abbey received a writing fellowship to Stanford University in California. By this time he had married one woman, divorced her, and married another; he was to have five wives and several children during his lifetime.

From 1956 to 1971, Abbey spent his summers working for the National Park Service, as park ranger and fire watcher, at a succession of desert locations. He also continued his writing. His second novel, *The Brave Cowboy*, was published in 1956 and later made into a movie. It focuses on two characters, a cowboy and an intellectual, both of whom are anarchists who suffer government persecution for their political views. According to Zakin, Abbey himself was investigated by the U.S. Federal Bureau of Investigation because of his draft protests. She says:

> The McCarthyesque repression that hammered down on Abbey's fictional [characters] in *The Brave Cowboy* is more dramatic than what Abbey experienced—in Abbey's case, the FBI's busiest period was ten months of scrambling after him while he was working as a clerk-typist for the U.S. Geological Survey in 1952, supporting himself while he finished *Jonathan Troy*. The FBI kept trying to find out if he was a communist but failed to turn up enough evidence to get him fired. . . . The FBI says its investigation of Abbey ended in 1967, when Abbey was working in Death Valley as a school-bus driver. (303)

Abbey's third novel, *Fire on the Mountain* (1962), also contains political elements, as does his nonfiction book *Desert Solitaire*, published in 1968. *Desert Solitaire* is the first-person account of Abbey's experiences as a ranger at Arches National Monument (now a national park) in Utah, and in it he bemoans the negative effects of "industrial tourism" on desert land. He also criticizes the National Park Service. His next book, the novel *Black Sun* (1971), was a love story between a young woman and a park ranger.

With the publication of *The Monkey Wrench Gang* in 1975, Abbey became a cult hero to environmentalists. He not only became involved in Earth First! but also increasingly spoke out against the ravages of technology. For example, Zakin quotes Abbey as saying:

> I take a dim view of dams; I find it hard to learn to love cement; I am poorly impressed by concrete aggregates and statistics in the cubic tons. But in this weakness I am not alone, for I belong to that ever-growing number of Americans, probably a good majority now, who have become aware that a fully industrialized, thoroughly urbanized, elegantly computerized social system is not suitable for human habitation. Great for the machines, yes. But unfit for people. (167)

Abbey also continued to write essays, as well as newspaper columns and letters to the editor, expressing his views on a wide range of subjects. In January 1989 he contracted a fatal illness and died two months later, on March 14, 1989, at his home in Tucson, Arizona. He left behind the following instructions, as quoted by Zakin:

> *Funeral instructions:* transported in bed of pickup truck and body to be buried as soon as possible after death, in a hole dug on our private property somewhere. . . . No undertakers wanted; no embalming (for godsake!); no coffin. Just a plain pine box hammered together by a friend; or an old sleeping-bag, or tarp, will do. If site selected is too rocky for burial, then pile on sand and a pile of stones sufficient to keep the coyotes from dismembering and scattering my bones. Wrap body in my anarchist flag. But bury if possible; I want my body to help fertilize the growth of a cactus, or cliffrose, or sagebrush, or tree, etc. . . . (313)

He was buried in the desert in accordance with his wishes.

(Abbey 1975; Glotfelty and Fromm 1996; Shabecoff 1993; Zakin 1993)

See also Deep Ecology Movement; *Desert Solitaire;* Environmental Activism; Environmental Fiction; Environmental Groups; Environmental Movement; Foreman, Dave; *Monkey Wrench Gang, The.*

Abrahamson, Dean Edwin

Board member of the National Resources Defense Council (NRDC), an environmental group, Dean Edwin Abrahamson edited *The Challenge of Global Warming*, published by the NRDC in 1989. This book, a collection of chapters written by different authors, focuses on the impact of environmental damage to the earth's climate, and it is representative of many works published by environmental groups during the 1980s. Abrahamson actively studied global warming, also known as the greenhouse effect, before editing *The Challenge of Global Warming*. At the time of its publication, he was a university professor of public affairs, specializing in energy policies and environmental quality. He holds degrees in physics, medicine, and biology. (Abrahamson 1989)

See also *Challenge of Global Warming, The;* Climate Changes.

Ackerman, Diane

New York author and naturalist Diane Ackerman has written books, essays, articles, and poems on a range of subjects, including environmentalism. Her work is well known for making environmental issues accessible to the general public.

Ackerman's 1995 book, *The Rarest of the Rare,* is a collection of essays, some of which first appeared in such magazines as *Life* and *National Geographic,* on endangered species and ecosystems. *The Moon by Whale Light,* published in 1992, discusses research into the habits and habitats of bats, penguins, crocodilians, and whales. She has also written children's books, including the 1997 *Bats: Shadows in the Night,* which includes photographs by bat expert and conservationist Merlin Tut-

tle documenting bat behavior at Big Bend National Park in Texas. In addition to her environmental work, Ackerman is the author of *A Natural History of the Senses*. Published in 1990, this book is a collection of essays on smell, touch, vision, hearing, and taste; it was the basis of the PBS television series *Mystery of the Senses*. (Ackerman 1995)

See also Habitat Protection; *Rarest of the Rare, The;* Wildlife Conservation.

Adam's Ancestors

Published in May 1934, *Adam's Ancestors* was the first book by anthropologist Louis Leakey, who was responsible for many important discoveries related to evolution and early humans. It was written for nonscientists and did much to further laypeople's understanding of evolution, particularly in regard to Leakey's significant discoveries in the field.

The book is a summation of all known research from early times to its publication. It addresses the prehistoric environment, offering information about climate, geography, and geology, and discusses earlier work on the subject, such as the writings of geologist Charles Lyell. It describes prehistoric humans and their cultures, artwork, and tools; it provides black-and-white photographs of human fossils. The book also acknowledges that new research will continue to shed light on these subjects, saying:

> The study of human evolution is still in its infancy. . . . We still have a great deal to learn and many more facts to unearth before we can be certain of the line followed by human evolution or of the stages through which man passed. We may also have to revise our ideas form time to time as to where the 'cradle of mankind' is to be found. This was once commonly believed to lie in Central Asia, since that region had yielded more fossil evidence that had a bearing on the subject than any other continent. Now the pendulum has swung to Africa. . . . (Leakey 171)

Throughout *Adam's Ancestors,* Leakey focuses on the fossil evidence and his own

Joy Adamson with Elsa the lion, April 1965 (Express Newspapers/Archive Photos)

interpretation of it. He does not discuss those who rejected the theory of evolution, either when his book was published or in earlier years. In fact he says: "Most educated people believe in evolution in the animal and plant kingdoms, and consequently are more than usually interested in any light that can be thrown on the stages of evolution of man himself." (1) Not everyone accepted Leakey's work, and the book met with some controversy. (Leakey 1953)

See also Evolution; Leakey, Louis; Lyell, Charles.

Adamson, Joy

As the wife of an African game warden, Joy Adamson (born in Austria as Friederike Victoria Gessner) wrote three books about her experiences with lions in the African wilderness. Entitled *Born Free* (1960), *Living Free* (1961), and *Forever Free* (1963), they were international best-sellers and inspired several film projects, including the movie *Born Free* (1966), the movie *Living Free* (1971), the doc-

umentary *The Lions Are Free* (1970), and the television series *Born Free* (1975). Along with Adamson's books, these films brought massive public attention to wildlife conservation issues and environmental problems in Africa.

The book *Born Free* is based on material provided by Adamson's husband, George, including some of his letters. Therefore, Adamson acknowledges that *Born Free* is "partly his book as well as mine." (Adamson 1960, p. 6) Nonetheless, the two had a stormy relationship. Adamson first met George, a naturalist, in 1942. Their marriage was her third.

The two lived in the small town of Isiolo, in northern Kenya, Africa, where Adamson sketched and painted flowers and plants. In 1947 London's Royal Horticultural Society awarded her its Grenfell Gold Medal for her artwork and held an exhibition of her paintings. In 1949 the British government hired her to paint portraits of representatives from twenty of Kenya's native tribes.

Adamson was also an accomplished photographer. Her most famous photographs were of a lioness named Elsa, an orphaned cub George found in 1956. Adamson bottle-fed the animal and taught her to behave well around humans before realizing that Elsa belonged in the wild. She and George set out to teach the lioness how to hunt, and after their efforts were successful, Adamson wrote *Born Free* to document their experience. The book includes many of Adamson's photographs (as do the sequels *Living Free* and *Forever Free*).

Adamson used the money she earned from her work to establish a nonprofit organization, the Elsa Wild Animal Appeal, which supports African wildlife conservation. Opposed to zoos, she once wrote: "My personal ideal would be that zoos should only acquire animals born in captivity, and thus leave the wild animals, born in freedom, where they belong. Forgive me if I trespass with my ideas, but I am at a loss to see how the often inadequate conditions in zoos can be changed, unless the public is more aware of what goes on behind the curtain." (Adamson 1986, p. 256)

Rewarded by her experiences with Elsa, Adamson dedicated herself to the idea of returning other captive animals, particularly lions, cheetahs, and leopards, to the wild. She continued writing books on Africa and its wildlife, including *The People of Kenya* (1967), *The Spotted Sphinx* (1969), *Pippa: The Cheetah and Her Cubs* (1970), and *Joy Adamson's Africa* (1972), which reproduced many of her paintings and sketches, as well as an autobiography, *The Searching Spirit* (1979).

George shared his wife's enthusiasm for releasing captive animals into the wild. Nonetheless, the marriage deteriorated, and they began living in separate camps. While on her own, Adamson raised a leopard cub, which she named Penny, and taught it to live in the wild. She photographed and filmed her experiences, but before she could publish her work, someone stole her film and cameras. More thefts followed. On January 3, 1980, Adamson was discovered dead. At first police thought she had been attacked by a lion, but later they determined that she had been murdered, and eventually a disgruntled former employee confessed to the crime. George dis-

cusses his wife's murder in his autobiography, *My Pride and Joy* (1986). After her death he continued to live in Africa and work with lions until his own murder by poachers. (Adamson 1960; Adamson, 1986; Adamson 1988)

See also Animal Behavior; *Born Free;* Conservationism; *Forever Free; Living Free;* Wildlife Conservation.

Afoot in England

Published in 1909, *Afoot in England* is British naturalist William Henry Hudson's description of the English countryside. The book is significant because it took the guidebook genre, which was very popular at the time, to a new level, not only describing places but also encouraging others to explore these settings themselves as amateur naturalists. As Hudson himself explains in the introduction to *Afoot in England:*

> Guide-books are very important to us, and . . . there is little or no fault to be found with them, since even the worst give some guidance and enable us in after times mentally to revisit distant places. . . . It is, however, possible to make an injudicious use of these books, and by so doing to miss the fine point of many a pleasure. The very fact that these books are guides to us and invaluable, and that we readily acquire the habit of taking them about with us and consulting them at frequent intervals, comes between us and that rarest and most exquisite enjoyment to be experienced amidst novel scenes. . . . But if pleasure be the main object, it will only be experienced in the highest degree by him who goes without book and discovers . . . the "observables" for himself. There will be no mental pictures previously formed; consequently what is found will not disappoint. (Hudson 1922, 10–12)

Hudson was a well-known novelist when he turned to writing guidebooks in his later years. These books were widely read, and they increased interest in naturalism among the British population. In fact Hudson's work is often credited with inspiring the naturalist movement that gained force in England during the 1920s and 1930s. (Hudson 1922)

See also Animal Ecology; Hudson, William Henry

African Silences

Published in 1991, *African Silences* discusses author Peter Matthiessen's expeditions to Africa in 1978 and 1986. Like Matthiessen's earlier work, *Wildlife in America,* this book helped focus public attention on wildlife conservation issues. It is written in the conversational style typical of modern environmental literature that documents a specific naturalist experience.

Matthiessen accompanied primatologist Gilbert Boese on a wildlife survey in West Africa in 1978, and in 1986 he went to Central Africa with ecologist David Western to study an elephant population. *African Silences* describes these journeys in great detail. The book also discusses African conservationism. For example, Matthiessen says:

> In his years at Amboseli [an African national park], Jonah [the nickname of Dr. David Western] worked continually with Africans, in particular the Masai, whose cattle competed with the wild animals for the scarce grass, and he is convinced that conservation that does not cooperate with the local people is of limited value, confining the preservation of animals to the artificial limits imposed by the boundaries of a national park. "Putting a boundary around Amboseli did not protect it. If you work with the people, show them the benefits that may come to them, show them the compatibility of human use and conservation, they will support what you are doing, even help with antipoaching. This way, wildlife conservation can extend beyond park boundaries. . . . Things still go wrong, of course. . . . Nevertheless, cooperation with the other interests, with the farmers or pastoralists, or with the foresters, is far more effective in the long run than fighting everyone as Dian Fossey did." (Matthiessen 1991, 151)

Western is referring to Dian Fossey, the gorilla researcher who was murdered while fighting poaching at her study center. (Matthiessen 1991)

See also Fossey, Dian; Matthiessen, Peter; Wildlife Conservation.

Agassiz, (Jean) Louis (Rodolphe)

Author of *Studies on Glaciers* (1840), naturalist and geologist Louis Agassiz was the first person to identify the ice ages. He also developed new teaching methods for the natural sciences, encouraging students to rely on direct contact with the environment rather than on facts gathered from books. In discussing Agassiz's influence on scientific study, scholar Hans Huth writes:

> Distinguished in the field of scientific research, Agassiz was also a great teacher. Indeed, he became the greatest teachers' teacher in the nation as far as science was concerned; the period between 1840 and 1870 has been called the age of Agassiz. It was he who made science fashionable. He imbued students . . . and future teachers with his enthusiasm and imparted to them his meticulous method of exploring nature. In an age when public lectures, institutes, and summer schools were the vogue, Agassiz was able to influence a far wider public than the circle of his Harvard students. Instead of giving his pupils lessons to learn, he advised them to "read Nature." Very much in Emerson's spirit, Agassiz asserted that it was his duty to open eyes which "cannot see" to the wonders of God's creation. (Huth 1972, 90)

Agassiz was born on May 28, 1807, in Motier, Switzerland. Educated in Europe, he first began studying glaciers in 1836 while a professor of natural history at the College of Neuchatel, Switzerland. He also wrote a five-volume book, *Studies on Fossilized Fish* (1833–1844), to describe more than 1,700 fish species. In 1846 he moved to the United States and became a professor at Harvard, where he helped found the National Academy of Sciences in 1863. He also established Harvard's Museum of Comparative Zoology and did much to support the establishment of museums elsewhere. During his later years, Agassiz was a vocal opponent of Charles Darwin's theory of evolution, arguing that environment could not cause an organism to change its nature. He died on December 14, 1873. (Huth 1972; Lurie 1960)

See also Climate Changes; Darwin, Charles Robert; Emerson, Ralph Waldo; Evolution; Geological Research; *Studies on Glaciers.*

Agricola, Georgius

Born on March 24, 1494, in Clauchau, Saxony, Georgius Agricola is considered the father of mineralogy, because he identified and classified many new minerals and wrote extensively on the subjects of mineralogy and mining. His greatest work, the 12-volume *De Re Metallica,* was published posthumously in 1556.

Agricola did not set out to be a scientist. As a young man he studied philosophy and the classics, and after graduating from the University of Leipzig in 1518 he became a teacher of Latin and Greek. In 1522 he decided to study medicine and the natural sciences, first in Leipzig and later at various universities in Italy, where he first became interested in mineralogy. In 1527 he became a physician in a Saxon mining town, which enabled him to practice medicine while also studying minerals and mining. In 1530 he published his first book on mining, *Bermannus; sive, de re metallica.* Many others followed, including *De natura fossilium,* which is considered the first mineralogy textbook. Despite achieving success as a mineralogist, Agricola remained a physician until his death on November 21, 1555. (Boynton 1948)

See also Geological Research; Species Identification and Classification.

Agriculture

Agriculture, or farming, can have serious impacts to the environment. Sometimes agriculture destroys natural prairies and wilderness, threatening endemic (native) species that inhabit those places. Agriculture also alters the underlying soil, whether by simply disturbing it or by changing its chemical composition through the use of fertilizers that can eventually pollute water sources. Consequently, agriculture has been the focus of a great deal of environmental literature from ancient times to the present.

One of the earliest works to address the subject was *Critias,* written sometime before 347 B.C. by the Greek philosopher Plato. It criticizes farmers for destroying forests in order to provide more agricultural land, reporting that soil erosion on Greek hillsides has become so severe that "what now remains compared with what then existed is like the skeleton of a sick man, all the fat and soft earth having wasted away, and only the bare framework of the land being left." (Ponting 1991, 76)

For centuries after Plato's warning, the human population remained relatively small and did not inhabit a large area of the planet; it wasn't until modern times that agricultural began to cause wider damage to the earth. Consequently, the largest body of literature expressing concerns about soil management is from the 19th and 20th centuries, after exploration, colonization, and dramatic increases in population had left their mark upon the land. Among the best-known works are those of Paul and Anne Ehrlich, who raise fears that poor agricultural practices will eventually destroy humankind. In *The Stork and the Plow* (1995), for example, they state that "no human activity causes as much direct environmental damage as agriculture" and suggest that overfarming has led to soil erosion and other problems that might eventually make the earth completely uninhabitable. (Ehrlich and Ehrlich 1995, 6) In an earlier work (*Extinction,* 1981), the Ehrlichs argue that for the health of the planet no new farmland or grazing areas should be created.

The exhaustion of the land's productivity was also a matter of concern for botanist Frederick E. Clements. His 1905 book, *Research Methods in Ecology,* is one of the earliest

A farmer in Iowa with a stunted soybean crop during the drought of 1988 (U.S. Department of Agriculture)

modern scientific discussions of the subject. Clements argued that farming interfered with the health of the earth, but he was convinced that the land, if left alone, would quickly revert to its natural state. In contrast, Fairfield Osborn's 1948 book, *Our Plundered Planet,* suggests that the damage done by overfarming might never be reversed. Osborn writes that vast areas of farmland have "been so misused by man that they have lost their productive capacity" and berates mankind for allowing "the life-giving soils for his crops to wash into the oceans." (Osborn 1948, 36 and 31)

Many authors have attributed water pollution in part to poor agricultural practices, particularly those involving the misuse of fertilizers and pesticides. For example, Rachel Carson's *Silent Spring,* considered one of the most important books of the environmental movement, is an argument against the use of agricultural pesticides and other chemicals. Similarly, Marc Reisner's 1986 book, *Cadillac Desert,* blames water pollution largely on "the

untreated runoff of hundreds and thousands of cows . . . and pesticides and fertilizers washing in from thousands and thousands of areas of intensively farmed land." (Reisner 1986, 446)

Others authors have written about agriculture in terms of land preservation rather than health risks. For example, George Perkins Marsh, in his 1864 book, *Man and Nature,* advocated protecting wilderness areas, particularly forests, from farming and grazing. Conservationist John Muir also argued in favor of protecting forests from destruction. Aldo Leopold wrote about the need for mankind to develop a "land ethic" to curtail the exploitation of wilderness areas, and in his 1949 book, *A Sand County Almanac,* he complains: "We abuse land because we regard it as a commodity belonging to us. When we see land as a community to which we belong, we may begin to use it with love and respect." (Leopold 1966, x) Similarly, in his 1977 book, *The Unsettling of America,* Wendell Berry states that there are two ways to use the land, as an exploiter or as a nurturer. Berry is an ecologist and a farmer and, consequently, has written extensively on the relationship between agriculture and environmentalism. (Ehrlich and Ehrlich 1981, 1995; Leopold 1966; Osborn 1948; Ponting 1991; Reisner 1986)

See also Berry, Wendell; *Cadillac Desert;* Clements, Frederick E.; Ehrlich, Paul and Anne; *Extinction;* Habitat Protection; Human Ecology; Leopold, Aldo; *Man and Nature;* Marsh, George Perkins; Muir, John; *Our Plundered Planet;* Pesticides and Chemicals; Reisner, Marc; *Sand County Almanac, A; Stork and the Plow, The; Unsettling of America, The;* Water Pollution; Wildlife Conservation.

Air Pollution

Air pollution is caused when foreign substances, or pollutants, are released into the air. The most common pollutants are carbon monoxide, hydrocarbons, nitrogen compounds, particulate matter, and sulfur dioxide. They are primarily generated by automobiles and other vehicles, as well as the burning of coal and oil (though there are other sources).

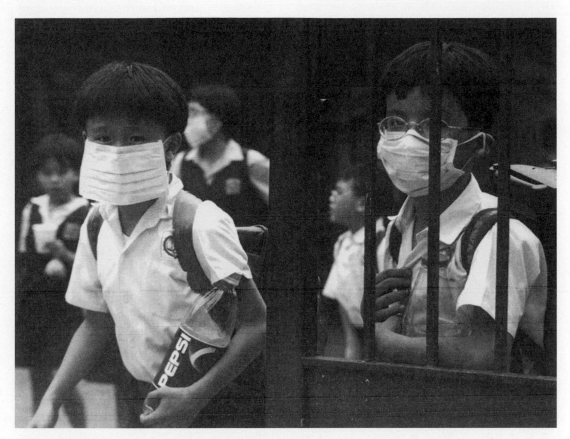

School children don masks for protection against the haze in Kuala Lumpur as the air pollution index reaches a very unhealthy level, September 19, 1997 (Reuters/David Loh/Archive Photos)

One of the earliest environmental books to address air pollution was William Jevons's *The Coal Question,* published in England in 1885. At that time, the people of London were dependent on coal as a source of heat and energy, and Jevons was concerned about the consequent air pollution. Of all the fossil fuels, coal is the dirtiest when burned, and it produces the largest amount of carbon dioxide. It causes a visible reduction in the quality of air.

Since Jevons's time, many other environmentalists have addressed the issue of air pollution. However, modern environmental literature discusses the impact of pollution not only on human health but also on ecosystems and global climate. Two examples of such works are Erik Eckholm's *Down to Earth* and Isaac Asimov and Frederik Pohl's *Our Angry Earth.* The former reports on a major environmental conference that examined air pollution in terms of other environmental prob-

lems; the latter, an example of apocalyptic literature, warns that air pollution is threatening to destroy mankind.

See also Asimov, Isaac; *Coal Question, The; Down to Earth;* Eckholm, Erik P.; Environmental Apocalypse; Environmental Fiction; Jevons, William Stanley; *Our Angry Earth;* Pohl, Frederik.

Albertus Magnus, Saint

In 1941 the Catholic Church declared Dominican Bishop Albertus Magnus to be the patron saint of all students of the natural sciences. Born in Lauingen an der Donau, Germany, in approximately 1200, Albertus was a well-educated theologian, philosopher, and teacher who first became interested in the sciences while studying the works of the Greek philosopher Aristotle. Aristotle's writings included material on species identification and classification, and Albertus began adding to these classifications. He produced several volumes of observations, including *De Mineralibus et Rebus Metallicis* (On Minerals and Metals), *De Animalibus* (On Animals), and *De Vegetabilibus et Plantis* (On Vegetables and Plants), before his death on November 15, 1280. (Bowler 1993)

See also Aristotle; *De Animalibus; De Mineralibus et Rebus Metallicis; De Vegetabilibus et Plantis.*

Allee, Warder Clyde

During the 1930s and 1940s ecologist Warder Clyde Allee directed studies on animal behavior at the University of Chicago. In 1931 he published *Animal Aggregations: A Study in General Sociology,* which discusses the way animals within a social group cooperate with one another. Allee believed that his studies applied to human behavior as well, and in expressing this view he influenced subsequent research in the environmental sciences.

In 1949, in conjunction with colleagues Alfred Emerson, Orlando Park, Thomas Park, and Karl Schmidt, he published *Principles of Animal Ecology,* which further expressed the importance of cooperation within animal and human groups. According to Peter J. Bowler in *The Norton History of the Environmental Sciences,* Allee and his associates "worked actively to promote co-operation as a model for international relations and social reform." (Bowler 1993, 528) However, Bowler says that their work lost its focus after the onset of World War II. Born on June 5, 1885, Allee retired from the University of Chicago in 1950 and died on March 18, 1955. (Bowler 1993)

See also Animal Behavior; Human Ecology; *Principles of Animal Ecology.*

Almanac for Moderns, An

Published in 1935, *An Almanac for Moderns* by Donald Culross Peattie (1898–1964) is a daily almanac with 365 short essays on various aspects of nature, combining personal observations with general commentaries. As an example, Peattie's essay for March 21 says in part:

On this chill uncertain spring day, toward

twilight, I have heard the first frog quaver from the marsh. . . . It always seems to me that no sooner do I hear the first frog trill than I find the first cloud of frog's eggs in a wayside pool, so swiftly does the emergent creature pour out the libation of its cool fertility. There is life where before there was none. It is as repulsive as it is beautiful, as silvery-black as it is slimy. Life, in short, raw and exciting, life almost in primordial form, irreducible element. (Finch and Elder 1990, 451–450)

Peattie also talks about those who have influenced the study of nature, particularly Aristotle. He explains that the Greek philosopher believed that all living things could be ordered "from the tidal ooze up to man, the plants placed below the animals, the animals ranged in order of increasing intelligence. Beyond man nothing could be imagined but God, the supreme intelligence. God was all spirit; the lifeless rock was all matter. Living beings on this earth were spirit infusing matter." (453) He expresses respect for Aristotle's philosophy before stating:

Unlike many of the more timid or less gifted investigators of today, Aristotle could not help coming to conclusions [about the origin and nature of life]. . . . But as it was Aristotle himself who taught us to observe, investigate, deduce what facts compel us to deduce, so we must concede that it is Nature herself, century after century—day after day, indeed, in the whirlwind progress of science—that propels us farther and farther away from Aristotelian beliefs. (456)

Peattie discusses other ancient beliefs as well, mentioning nature-related material in mythology and the Bible. He also recalls old almanacs, which included "weather-wisdom" and predictions based on astrology, a belief system "not more dead, for the modern mind, than the Nature philosophy of a generation ago." (451) Peattie once worked as a government botanist and approaches his material not only as a naturalist but as a scientist. (Finch and Elder 1990)

See also Aristotle.

Almanac of the Dead

Published in 1991, *Almanac of the Dead* is a complex, lengthy novel by Leslie Marmon Silko, a poetess of Native American heritage who grew up on a reservation in New Mexico. Her work expresses a respect for the earth, suggesting that this attitude is important for the human spirit. It is therefore not a coincidence that the many depraved characters in the novel have lost touch with ancient ways of relating to the earth. As Gregory Salyer explains in his essay "*Almanac of the Dead:* The Politics of Time":

> *Almanac* judges Euro-American culture by its own standards, and that culture falls tragically short. At the same time, Native American values gradually emerge from their entanglement with colonial culture to offer some sense of hope for anyone who loves and respects the earth. *Almanac of the Dead* is a moral statement as much as anything else, and it calls us to judge the society that we all have made through greed and ecological apathy. (Salyer 1997, 99)

In Silko's view, technology is also to blame for many problems in modern society. However, she does not believe it needs to be rejected entirely. Instead, she suggests that technology can be a helpful tool rather than a destructive force. Salyer explains:

> In *Almanac* Euro-American culture is unraveling thread by thread in both its spirituality and its technology. In Native cultures, on the other hand, technology is used both to thwart the otherness of Euro-American culture and to spin a web of stories that offers Native peoples all over the world a way to see how land, history, and technology all cohere into a reconstituted world where Native people take back their lands from Alaska to Chile.

An Alaskan medicine woman in *Almanac* . . . aptly represents how storytelling and technology weave a web that overcomes witchery and destruction. A satellite television is installed in her . . . village, and most of the villagers ignore it or fall asleep in front of it. The woman has a pelt that is sacred to her and becomes the channel she uses to lock in on the spirits of the ancestors. The television enhances the power of the pelt by the appropriation of the satellite signals. . . . The old . . . woman uses her pelt, her stories, and a weather map on the television screen successfully to crash an airplane that is carrying surveyors and equipment from American oil companies. (115)

By the end of *Almanac,* the Native people have begun the process of reclaiming their land as well as their ancient heritage. (Salyer 1997)

American Natural History

Published in 1826, *American Natural History* is the major work of Dr. John D. Godman, who dissected animals and wrote about their anatomy. The work not only describes the physical characteristics of American mammals but also includes commentary on nature-related subjects. For this reason, scholars have called it an ecological treatise as well as a scientific study. For example, in *This Incomperable Lande,* professor Thomas Lyon says:

> *American Natural History* is in good part a philosophical text, and may be seen as an important American continuation of the line established in England by John Ray. In Ray's view, science—the study of nature—promotes an expansion and naturalizing of our view of things, particularly our ethical sense. (Lyon 1989, 46)

As an example of such thinking, Lyon quotes Godman's description of feline predators, which shows an understanding of the animals' relationship to their environment: "We must not rashly contend that these animals are an evil unattended by any utility or good.

They are designed by nature to occupy regions where animal life is most likely to increase in undue proportion, and it is their province to keep this increase from becoming excessive." (Lyon 46)

In addition to *American Natural History,* Godman wrote 12 nature essays for a weekly periodical, *The Friend,* in 1828. These writings, which were published in an 1833 collection entitled *Rambles of a Naturalist,* describe Godman's experiences on short nature walks and are considered among the earliest works of their type. The author died of tuberculosis shortly after finishing his essays, an event that Lyon calls "a loss both to natural history and literature." (Lyon 47)

See also Ray, John.

American Ornithology

Alexander Wilson's *American Ornithology* (published between 1808 and 1813) was the first major work on birds of the United States. It presented information on 262 species, including 30 that were unknown before the author identified them. It also included Wilson's own illustrations of his subjects, as well as some comments on how important it was to preserve them. For this reason, Wilson is considered one of America's earliest conservationists.

The author originally intended his book to be 10 volumes, but he died while working on the eighth in 1813. Shortly after the first volume was published in 1808, Wilson began selling subscriptions to the entire work as he traveled the country to study birds. The total cost of the *American Ornithology* series was $120; among the first subscribers were Thomas Jefferson and James Monroe. (Cox 1971)

See also Species Identification and Classification; Wilson, Alexander.

Anatomy of Plants, The

The Anatomy of Plants is significant because it was the first work to suggest that plants have male and female sex organs. Published in 1682, it offers detailed descriptions and drawings of plant species and their parts. The book's author, Nehemiah Grew, is considered one of the founders of plant anatomy. (Boynton 1948)

See also Grew, Nehemiah; Species Identification and Classification.

Anderson, Ray

Ray Anderson is the author of *Mid-Course Correction: Toward a Sustainable Enterprise* (1999), which discusses business practices in terms of environmentalism. The founder and CEO of a major carpet manufacturing company, he became aware of environmental issues and decided to make his business more ecologically sound. He often lectures on waste issues and sustainable development.

Animal Behavior

Some environmental authors focus on *animal ecology,* which concerns the relationship of an animal to its environment, whereas others focus primarily on *animal behavior.* The latter might mention animal habitats yet are more interested in the way that animals of a particular species relate to one another and/or to humans rather than the way they relate to their surroundings. Books on animal behavior are often popular and increase public sympathy for the animal subjects. Accordingly, these books promote wildlife conservation efforts for those species.

One of the most prominent examples of this type of environmental literature is Joy Adamson's *Born Free,* which documents her efforts to raise a lion cub and return it to the wild. After the book was published, donations to lion conservation efforts in Africa increased dramatically. Similarly, Dian Fossey's book *Gorillas in the Mist* brought public attention to the plight of mountain gorillas in Africa, and Jane Goodall's *In the Shadow of Man* piqued public interest in chimpanzee research. The works of Canadian naturalist Farley Mowat also promoted animal conservation efforts. His *A Whale for the Killing* helped convince people that killer whales were not to be hated and wantonly destroyed; *Never Cry Wolf* did the same for the gray wolf.

See also Adamson, Joy; Animal Ecology; *Born Free;* Fossey, Dian; Goodall, Jane; *Gorillas in the Mist; In the Shadow of Man;* Mowat, Farley; *Never Cry Wolf; Whale for the Killing, A.*

Animal Ecology

Ecology is the study of how all the parts of an environment interact. *Animal ecology* focuses on how animals are affected by these interactions and therefore includes issues like species endangerment and habitat destruction. In contrast, *human ecology* concerns how humans are affected by their environment, as well as health risks caused by such problems as pesticide use and pollution.

The first textbook on animal ecology, *The Principles of Animal Ecology* by ecologist Warder C. Allee was published in 1949, though some authors addressed the subject before then. For example, in 1881 Karl Semper's *Animal Life as Affected by the Natural Conditions of Existence* discussed the relationship between predators and prey, as well as man's interference with that relationship; in the early 1900s British ecologist Arthur Tansley developed the term "ecosystem" to discuss the relationship between animals and their environment. However, most environmental literature on animal ecology has been published in modern times. Some of these books, such as Diane Ackerman's *The Rarest of the Rare* and Edward O. Wilson's *The Diversity of Life,* discuss specific endangered species in their habitats throughout the world. Others, such as John Muir's *Our National Parks,* discuss a broad range of species within a single habitat. In addition, there are many books that discuss animal ecology in terms of human attitudes. For example, Alston Chase's *Playing God in Yellowstone* criticizes the way people have sought to control animal populations in Yellowstone National Park, and Gary Snyder's *Practice of the Wild* talks about the need for human beings to feel more connected to animals and the wild.

See also Ackerman, Diane; Allee, Warder Clyde; *Animal Life as Affected by the Natural Conditions of Existence;* Chase, Alston; *Diversity of Life, The;* Muir, John; *Our National Parks; Practice of the Wild, The; Principles of Animal Ecology; Rarest of the Rare, The;* Semper, Karl; Snyder, Gary; Tansley, Arthur G.; Wilson, Edward O.

Animal Life as Affected by the Natural Conditions of Existence

Published in 1881, *Animal Life as Affected by the Natural Conditions of Existence* by Karl Semper was the first book to present the relationship between animal predators and prey as a hierarchy, or food chain. Moreover, because it talks about individual animals in terms of their environment, it is considered one of the earliest works on animal ecology. Semper argues that there is an optimal predator-to-prey ratio; if this ratio is altered in favor of the predator, the delicate animal community will be destroyed. His work therefore foreshadowed the modern discussions on balanced ecosystems. (Bowler 1993)

See also Animal Behavior; Animal Ecology; Balanced Ecosystems.

Antienvironmentalism

During the 1960s and 1970s, the environmental movement gained strength in the United States, and as American environmental groups gained political power they were able to influence public policy. Consequently, the government created many new laws to restrict air and water pollution and to protect endangered species and habitats. However, many of these laws were economically expensive to enact, and they often required people to change their habits or business practices. For example, in *Environmental Overkill,* Dixy Lee Ray reports that the cost of protecting the northern spotted owl population in 1992 was $9.7 million. Moreover, property owners could not build on their land if an owl was present.

As a result of environmentalism's growing expense and inconvenience, during the late 1980s and early 1990s people began to question whether such stringent laws were really necessary. Dixy Lee Ray and Lou Guzzo, for example, wrote *Environmental Overkill* to suggest that America's environmental movement had gone too far. Others proposed that environmental groups might be falsely reporting new environmental threats in order to gain support for new laws or to promote their fundraising efforts. During the 1990s, several works of environmental literature were published to express this view, including Michael Fumento's *Science Under Siege* and Ronald Bailey's *Eco-Scam*.

The climate of antienvironmentalism in the United States also inspired some environmentalists to examine their philosophies and groups more carefully. For example, during the 1990s environmentalists Wallace Kaufman, Gregg Easterbrook, and Mark Dowie all wrote books critical of environmentalism. Kaufman's *No Turning Back* expresses his dissatisfaction with the modern environmental movement, Easterbrook's *A Moment on the Earth* criticizes the pessimism of environmental groups, and Dowie's *Losing Ground* examines the activities of environmental groups and suggests that they need to change their approach to environmentalism. Antienvironmentalism is also briefly discussed in books on environmental history and politics, as in Robert Gottlieb's *Forcing the Spring* and Philip Shabecoff's *A Fierce Green Fire;* it is the sole focus of David Helvarg's 1994 book, *The War Against the Greens,* which was published by an environmental group.

> See also Bailey, Ronald; Dowie, Mark; Easterbrook, Gregg; *Eco-Scam;* Environmental Groups; Environmental Movement; *Environmental Overkill;* Environmental Politics; *Fierce Green Fire, A; Forcing the Spring;* Fumento, Michael; Gottlieb, Robert; Guzzo, Lou; Helvarg, David; Kaufman, Wallace; *Losing Ground; Moment on the Earth, A; No Turning Back;* Ray, Dixy Lee; *Science Under Siege; War Against the Greens, The.*

Aridjis, Homero

Mexican poet Homero Aridjis often writes about the land, not only in poems but also in articles such as "The Silence of the Whales" (1995), which appeared in *Reforma* magazine. This piece expressed opposition to the construction of the world's largest saltworks at Baja California's Laguna San Ignacio, an important birthing ground for the gray whale. The industrialization project was opposed by the Group of 100 (Grupo de los Cien), an organization of writers and activists fighting to preserve the Mexican environment; Aridjis and his wife, Betty, helped found the organi-

zation and remain active in it today. Ardjis's poetry books include *Los espacios azules* (1968), *Antologia* (1976), *Antologia poetica, 1960–1994* (1994), and *Tiempo de angeles* (Time of Angels, 1997).

Aristotle

Aristotle, an ancient Greek philosopher, did much to advance scientific thinking. Born in Stagira, Macedonia, in 384 B.C., he traveled to Athens at age 17 to study with the philosopher Plato. His association with Plato's Academy continued until 347 B.C., when Plato died. He left Athens, eventually moving to Pella in Macedonia, where he spent seven years tutoring the son of King Philip II— Alexander the Great. When Alexander became king in 335 B.C. he gave Aristotle money to set up his own school in Athens. Aristotle taught there until his retirement in 323 B.C. He died in 322 B.C.

Most of Aristotle's writings have been lost to history. However, his lecture notes remain intact and have been published in book form. They include *Historia Anamalium,* in which he identifies and classifies many animal species. (Bowler 1993)

> See also *Historia Anamalium;* Species Identification and Classification.

Asimov, Isaac

Isaac Asimov was a prolific author, writing hundreds of books, short stories, and articles. He is perhaps best known for his award-winning science fiction novels, but he also wrote many critically acclaimed nonfiction books, including *The Intelligent Man's Guide to Science* (1960), *Asimov's New Guide to Science* (revised in 1984), and *Our Angry Earth* (1991), written with Frederik Pohl. *Our Angry Earth* discusses a variety of environmental problems in a clear and concise manner, and because of Asimov's popularity as a novelist it was widely read.

Asimov was born in Petrovichi, Russia, on January 2, 1920, but moved to America three years later. He grew up in Brooklyn, New York, and at age 18 he sold his first science fiction story to *Amazing Stories* magazine. Despite this early success as a writer, he decided

Isaac Asimov (Frank Capri/Saga/Archive Photos)

to study science at Columbia University, and in 1949 he became a biochemistry teacher at Boston University. He continued to write. In 1950 his first science fiction novels, *Pebble in the Sky* and *I Robot,* were published; subsequent novels include *The Gods Themselves* (1972), *Foundation's Edge* (1982), and *Nemesis* (1989). Eventually Asimov abandoned teaching, but he continued to educate people through his numerous nonfiction books, both for children and adults. In them he wrote about such diverse topics as dinosaurs, microwaves, germs, physics, the environment, and biblical studies. Asimov died on April 6, 1992, in New York City. (Asimov and Pohl 1991)

See also *Our Angry Earth;* Pohl, Frederik.

Attenborough, Sir David

Born on May 8, 1926, zoologist David Attenborough joined the British Broadcasting Company (BBC) as a writer and broadcaster in 1952. Two years later he created *Zoo Quest,* a popular television series that offered filmed footage of animals in a variety of settings.

From 1969 to 1972 he was programming director for the BBC, and during the 1970s and 1980s he created several more television series, including *Life on Earth* in 1979, as well as books to accompany the series. These television programs and books helped further the public's interest in naturalism and environmental issues throughout the world. Attenborough was knighted for his work in 1985. (Attenborough 1979)

See also Animal Behavior; Conservationism; *Life on Earth;* Wildlife Conservation.

Audubon, John James

Between 1827 and 1838, artist John James Audubon published a 435-print collection of realistic crayon-and-watercolor paintings representing 1,065 different types of birds. From 1840 to 1844 these paintings were reprinted in his seven-volume *Birds of America,* which included descriptive text about bird behavior. Both versions of Audubon's work increased public interest in bird-watching and conservation, and in 1886 the Audubon Society, a group dedicated to the preservation of birds, was founded in his honor.

Audubon was born in Les Cayes, Santo Domingo (now Haiti), on April 26, 1785, at his father's sugar plantation. He was raised in France, where he first began to sketch birds; at age 18 John was sent to Philadelphia by his father to manage a family-owned plantation. Audubon proved unsuited for the task. After marrying Lucy Bakewell in 1808, he moved to Kentucky and tried a series of jobs, including clerk, merchant, and miller. He failed at all of them, primarily because he preferred sketching birds to doing work. Meanwhile, his wife supported him by teaching school. In 1823 she started her own school, and Audubon began teaching drawing there. By this time he had collected a large portfolio of work, and within a year he decided to look for an art patron. After exhausting his connections in the United States, he traveled to London and found a publisher there willing to print *Birds of America.* After the first volume was published in 1827, Audubon traveled through the United States promoting his

Painting of white egret (snowy heron) from Birds of America *(Corbis)*

book, which was sold by subscription, and working on future volumes. In this regard he gathered specimens, killed them, and posed them for drawing. He also studied bird behavior and habitats.

In later years, Audubon painted animals as well as birds, and eventually he decided to produce a book on mammals entitled *The Viviparous Quadrupeds of North America* (volume one published in 1845). The following year he became mentally ill. He died on January 27, 1851. One hundred years later, President Harry Truman honored him through a special proclamation naming 1951 the Audubon Centennial Year. In his speech Truman said: "Audubon was a forerunner of the movement for the conservation of wildlife in America, and his work continued to stimulate appreciation for the wealth and beauty of America's natural resources, serving as a con-

stant inspiration in the continuing endeavor to preserve our birds and other wildlife from extinction." (Cox 24) (Cox 1971; Fitter 1959; Glotfelty and Fromm 1996)

> See also *Birds of America;* Conservationism; Environmental Groups; Species Identification and Classification; Wildlife Conservation.

Austin, Mary

Mary Austin was a novelist and essayist who wrote not only about nature but also about Native American issues. Born Mary Hunter on September 9, 1868, in Carlinville, Illinois, Austin attended college in her hometown and taught there for a brief time before moving West with her mother and brother. The trio homesteaded property near the desert community of Bakersfield, California.

In 1892, after marrying Stafford Austin, Mary Austin moved to Owens Valley, also in the California desert. There she explored the terrain and became friends with local Native Americans. Out of these experiences came her first book, *The Land of Little Rain* (1903), which brought her much acclaim. Her other nature works were *The Flock* (1906), which deals with sheep-raising in the American Southwest, *California: The Land of the Sun* (1914), and *The Land of Journey's Ending* (1924). The latter two describe Austin's deep relationship with the American Southwest.

Austin also wrote two short-story collections, *The Basket Woman* (1904) and *Lost Borders* (1909), as well as a play, *The Arrow Maker* (1911). However, the bulk of her work addressed social problems, particularly among Native Americans, and she wrote approximately 200 articles dealing with important issues such as socialism and feminism. Austin died in Santa Fe, New Mexico, on August 13, 1934.

B

Bailey, Florence Augusta Merriam

Florence Augusta Merriam Bailey was one of the most important female naturalists in America during the early 19th century. Her ornithological guidebooks, which include *Handbook of Birds of the Western United States* (1902), *Birds of New Mexico* (1928), and *Among the Birds in the Grand Canyon Country* (1939), were immensely popular and helped interest the general public in bird-watching. Polly Wells Kaufman, in *National Parks and the Woman's Voice*, explains the significance of Bailey's work:

> Bailey transcends the role of naturalist: she became an environmentalist dedicated to protecting habitats in advance of male ornithologists caught up in collecting trophies. Unlike botany, a field long open to women, ornithology began as a male occupation: bird identification was competitive and depended on shooting birds and collecting skins. When binoculars replaced the gun as the accepted tool for bird study late in the nineteenth century, women quickly entered the field. Bird-watchers called "snapshooters" used cameras instead of guns. Women bird-watchers became bird protectors as they joined the campaign, often as leaders, to outlaw killing birds for their feathers, used to decorate women's hats. Bailey's guides were detailed descriptions of a bird's habitat and behavior over a period of time and not designed simply for quick bird identification. She drew the reader into the pleasures of bird study and the need to preserve habitats. (Kaufman 1996, 67)

Bailey was born on August 8, 1863, in Locust Grove, New York. She began writing about birds while attending Smith College in Massachusetts from 1882 to 1886. Her first book appeared in 1889. Entitled *Birds Through an Opera Glass* (1889), it was a collection of essays on bird-watching with binoculars. Bailey continued to publish books throughout her lifetime. She also became involved in politics and promoted the Audubon Society. In 1889 she married a fellow naturalist who worked for the federal government. Bailey died on September 22, 1948, in Washington, D.C. (Kaufman 1996)

See also Audubon, John James; Conservationism.

Bailey, Liberty Hyde

Botanist Liberty Hyde Bailey wrote 700 scientific papers and 66 books on botanical and agricultural subjects. He also addressed issues related to the relationship between humans and the land. In fact many scholars consider him to be one of the earliest deep ecologists.

Bailey was born on March 15, 1858, near South Haven, Michigan. From 1882 to 1884 he worked as an assistant to Asa Gray, a botanist at Harvard University. From 1884 to 1888 he was a professor of horticulture and landscape gardening at Michigan State Agricultural College, which is now Michigan State University. There he set up the first American laboratory to focus exclusively on horticultural studies.

In 1888 Bailey became a professor of botany and horticulture at Cornell University in Ithaca, New York, a position he retained until 1903, when he became dean of Cornell's New York State College of Agriculture. In 1935 he established the Bailey Hortorium, which was originally independent but is now a division of the state college; he served as director until retiring in 1951.

Bailey died in Ithaca on December 25, 1954. His works include *Cyclopedia of American Horticulture* (four volumes, 1900–1902), *The Manual of Cultivated Plants* (1923), and *The Holy Earth* (1915), which expresses his deep-ecology philosophy.

See also *Holy Earth, The.*

Bailey, Ronald

Ronald Bailey is noted for his 1993 book, *Eco-Scam: The False Prophets of Ecological Apocalypse,* which is highly critical of the modern environmental movement. In it he argues that environmentalists have been misleading the American public about the status of global environmental problems. The work is extremely controversial and is frequently cited by environmentalists as well as antienvironmentalists.

In addition to *Eco-Scam,* Bailey has written articles about science for *Forbes* magazine and once worked as a producer for the Public Broadcasting System. He is currently an analyst for the Cato Institute, a conservative think tank, where he has expressed support for the antienvironmental movement. (R. Bailey 1993)

See also Antienvironmentalism; *Eco-Scam.*

Balanced Ecosystems

The term "ecosystem" was first used by British ecologist-writer Arthur G. Tansley during the early 1900s. It refers to both the living and nonliving components of a region designated by the person studying it, as well as to the way in which those components relate to and interact with one another. A *balanced ecosystem* is one that is stable, which often means that it is not subject to human interference.

Aside from Tansley, one of the earliest authors to discuss balanced ecosystems was Alexander von Humboldt, whose 1845 work, *Kosmos,* argued that the relationship between animals and their environment is delicate and should not be interfered with by humans. For this reason, Humboldt is considered by some to be the first true ecologist. Another 19th-century writer to address the subject of balanced ecosystems is Karl Semper, the first person to analyze the relationship between predator and prey in terms of a hierarchical food chain. In his 1881 book, *Animal Life as Affected by the Natural Conditions of the Existence,* Semper, like Humboldt, argues that animal communities can be harmed by human interference.

Modern environmental authors continue to warn that humans can damage ecosystems.

Baron von Humboldt (Archive Photos)

Some, like Wendell Berry and Paul and Anne Ehrlich, focus on land devastation caused by agricultural practices. Others are more interested in forestry issues (for example, Catherine Caufield's *In the Rainforest,* on rainforest destruction worldwide; John Muir's *Our National Parks,* on U.S. forestry practice; and Alston Chase's *Playing God in Yellowstone,* on the management of Yellowstone National Park). The ocean habitat is also a frequent topic for advocates of balanced ecosystems. One of the most influential works of environmental literature ever written, Rachel Carson's *The Sea Around Us,* warns about practices that threaten the health of the ocean, as does David Bulloch's *The Wasted Ocean.* Roger Stone's *The Voyage of the Sanderling* also addresses the ocean ecosystem, although he primarily discusses its marine life, as does Farley Mowat's *Sea of Slaughter.* Similarly, Diane Ackerman's *The Rarest of the Rare* discusses ecosystems in the context of endangered species.

See also Ackerman, Diane; Berry, Wendell; Bulloch, David K.; Carson, Rachel Louise; Caufield, Catherine; Chase, Alston; Ehrlich, Paul and Anne; Humboldt, Alexander von; *In the Rainforest; Kosmos;* Mowat, Farley; Muir, John; *Our National Parks; Playing God in Yellowstone; Rarest of the Rare, The; Sea Around Us, The; Sea of Slaughter;* Stone, Roger D.; Tansley, Arthur G.; *Voyage of the Sanderling, The; Wasted Ocean, The.*

Barron, T. A.

T. A. Barron is the coauthor of *To Walk in the Wilderness: A Rocky Mountain Journal* (1993), with photographer John Fielder. A collection of prose and poetry about nature in the Rocky Mountains, the book is the result of a month the two men spent hiking in the Snowmass–Maroon Bells Wilderness area of Colorado. They traveled more than 200 miles, using llamas to carry their gear, and Fielder documented their experience with breathtaking photographs. Barron has lived in Colorado as an adult since 1990, but he also grew up on a Colorado ranch as a boy. He attended Princeton University before becoming a Rhodes scholar at Oxford University in London. He currently serves on the board of several major

environmental groups and often lectures on environmentalism at schools and businesses. He is also the author of a children's book series about Merlin, as well as several novels.

Bartram, John and William

John Bartram (1699–1777) and son William Bartram (1739–1823) were naturalists and explorers who traveled extensively throughout Florida, the Carolinas, and other parts of North America. Born in Pennsylvania, John Bartram first worked as a botanist, reporting his discoveries in the American colonies to England's King George III. He also experimented with plant hybridization and exported seeds to European botanists. William Bartram wrote a book about his travels entitled *Travels Through North and South Carolina, Georgia, East and West Florida, the Cherokee Country, the Extensive Territories of the Muscogulges, or Creek Confederacy, and the Country of the Choctaws* (1791; more commonly reprinted as *The Travels of William Bartram*).

See also *Travels of William Bartram, The.*

Bass, Rick

Conservationist Rick Bass has contributed hundreds of articles and essays to magazines such as *Sierra* and *Audubon.* He has also written numerous books about nature, including *Wild to the Heart* (1987), *Winter: Notes from Montana* (1991), *Platte River* (1994), *The Lost Grizzlies: A Search for Survivors in the Wilderness of Colorado* (1995), *The Sky, the Stars, the Wilderness* (1997), and *Where the Sea Used to Be* (1998). Born in 1958 in Fort Worth, Texas, Bass attended Utah State University and later worked as an oil and gas geologist before becoming a writer of both fiction and nonfiction. He currently lives in Montana.

Berry, Thomas Mary

Theologian Thomas Mary Barry often writes about environmental issues, expressing the view that animal extinctions will eventually lead to human extinction. His works include *The Dream of the Earth* (1988), *Befriending the Earth: A Theology of Reconciliation between Humans and the Earth* (1991), and *Creative*

Energy: Bearing Witness for the Earth (1996), which updates *The Dream of the Earth*. Both the *Dream of the Earth* and *Creative Energy* discuss the spiritual aspects of environmentalism. Berry also wrote a book about Buddhism in 1996.

Berry, Wendell

Wendell Berry is a farmer, poet, and essayist whose writings about ecology and agriculture are among the best known in the American environmental movement. Moreover, he often discusses these subjects in terms of Christianity, which leads Phillip Shabecoff, in *A Fierce Green Fire,* to refer to Berry as a Christian ecologist. In addition, Shabecoff cites Berry's work as "evidence that environmentalism is causing an upheaval in Judeo-Christian thought." (Shabecoff 127).

Born in 1934 in Henry County, Kentucky, Berry attended the University of Kentucky, then California's Stanford University. He began teaching at New York University, and in 1960 he published a novel, *Nathan Coulter.* In 1964 he returned to his native land, buying a farm along the Kentucky River. He worked it organically, even to the point of using draft horses rather than tractors and other machinery to plow and plant. He also taught at the University of Kentucky and began to write poetry and essays related to ecology. His work from this period includes a 1972 essay collection entitled *A Continuous Harmony: Essays Cultural and Agricultural,* which was well received.

In 1977 Berry resigned his position at the university to write full-time. That same year brought the publication of perhaps his most widely read collection of environmental essays, *The Unsettling of America.* This work expresses many opinions regarding the relationship between environmental problems and changes in agricultural practices. In subsequent years he continued to express his views in essay collections such as *The Gift of Good Land* (1981) as well as in poetry collections like *Openings* (1968) and *To What Listens* (1975). His 1983 novel, *A Place on Earth,* concerns country life in Kentucky and has been classified as pastoral fiction.

Berry has also used his writing to speak out on local environmental issues. For example, in 1971 he wrote *The Unforeseen Wilderness: An Essay on Kentucky's Red River Gorge* in an attempt to stop the building of a dam on the Red River. However, as he typically does in his works, he addresses the particular while commenting on the general, saying of the proposed dam's recreation area:

Modern Americans, as we all know, are crowded and stifled in the cities, and are therefore most excruciatingly in need of recreation. And what is to be the form of this recreation? Why, it is to be crowded and stifled in the country. Relief from the suburbs of brick and Bedford stone is to be found in suburbs of canvas and aluminum. Relief from traffic in the streets is to be sought amid traffic on a lake. The harried city dweller, who has for fifty weeks coveted his neighbor's house and his neighbor's wife, may now soothe his nerves for two weeks in coveting his neighbor's trailer and his neighbor's boat—also in putting up with this neighbor's children, listening to his neighbor's radio, breathing his neighbor's smoke, walking on his neighbor's broken bottles. While he is doing all these things he is surrounded by "the beauty of nature," which is a big item in recreation. . . . Why be satisfied with mere yards of natural beauty when you can have *miles* of it? (Trimble 229)

Berry continues to write about ecological issues while living on his Kentucky farm. Over the years he has received numerous writing awards, including one from the National Institute and Academy of Arts and Letters. He is also a former fellow of the Guggenheim Foundation and the Rockefeller Foundation. (Slovic 1992; Trimble 1995)

See also Agriculture; *Continuous Harmony, A; Unsettling of America, The.*

Biodiversity

The term "biodiversity" refers to maintaining a wide variety of biological life on earth. Biodiversity is often mentioned in concert with endangered or extinct plant and animal species, because when species are lost, so is biodiversity. Moreover, when a particular habitat or ecosystem loses its biodiversity, it can collapse. Certain species are more likely to cause this collapse upon their removal than others; they are called "keystone species."

Literature that discusses endangered species and habitat protection therefore also typically discusses biodiversity. For example, Diane Ackerman's *The Rarest of the Rare* concerns endangered species, but it also stresses the importance of biodiversity. Similarly, Catherine Caufield's *In the Rainforest* warns that rainforest destruction will cause a loss of biodiversity. Works on evolution also talk about biodiversity, because throughout history the extinction of some species has allowed others to evolve. Edward O. Wilson talks about this in *The Diversity of Life,* as do Richard Leakey and Roger Lewin in *The Sixth Extinction: Patterns of Life and the Future of Humankind* and Paul and Anne Ehrlich in *Extinction: The Causes and Consequences of the Disappearance of Species.*

> **See also** Ackerman, Diane; Caufield, Catherine; *Diversity of Life, The;* Ehrlich, Paul and Anne; *Extinction; In the Rainforest;* Leakey, Richard; *Rarest of the Rare, The; Sixth Extinction, The;* Wilson, Edward O.

Birds of America

John James Audubon's *Birds of America* helped to interest the American public in naturalist activities, thereby furthering early conservationism. Published between 1827 and 1838 by Robert Havell of London, the four-volume work includes 435 hand-colored plates illustrating the birds known in North America at the time. A companion work, the five-volume *Ornithological Biography* (1831–1839), offered text descriptions of the birds; Audubon wrote it with the help of William MacGillivray. In 1839 *A Synopsis of the Birds of North America,* a single-volume index of *Birds of America,* was published. Between 1840 and 1844, Audubon created a smaller-format, seven-volume *Birds of America* that was immensely popular. Many

bird-watchers carried one of Audubon's volumes with them as they explored their own naturalist interests.

Philip Shabecoff discusses the importance of Audubon's work in his history of the environmental movement, *A Fierce Green Fire.* He explains:

> Audubon was not a conservationist or environmentalist as we would define them today. He generally shot the birds that were his subjects so he could sketch them at leisure. But he was something of a naturalist as well as an artist. His paintings in *The Birds of America* . . . called the attention of his contemporaries to the wonders of nature. . . . He combined a frontiersman's ardor for travel and adventure with an almost scientific keenness of observation and an artist's aesthetic appreciation of the beautiful wildlife he painted. . . . While he did not condemn the juggernaut of westward settlement, he did express deep regret over the destruction of the forest: "The greedy mills," he wrote in an essay, "told the sad tale, that in a century the noble forests . . . should exist no more." (Shabecoff 44)

In this way, Audubon inspired in the public not only an appreciation for the wilderness but a concern that this wilderness might not exist forever.

> **See also** Audubon, John James; Conservationism; Species Identification and Classification.

Blueprint for a Green Economy

Published in 1989, *Blueprint for a Green Economy* was written by economists David Pearce, Anil Markandya, and Edward B. Barbier, who based their book on a report they made for the British government. The work is significant because it is representative of early attempts to place a monetary value on the environment. Its authors explain:

> One of the central themes of environmental economics . . . is the need to place proper values on the services provided by natural environments. The central prob-

lem is that many of these services are provided "free." They have a zero price simply because no market place exists in which their true values can be revealed through the acts of buying and selling. Examples might be a fine view, the water purification and storm protection functions of coastal wetlands, or the biological diversity within a tropical forest. The elementary theory of supply and demand tells us that if something is provided at a zero price, more of it will be demanded than if there was a positive price. Very simply, the cheaper it is the more will be demanded. The danger is that this greater level of demand will be unrelated to the capacity of the relevant natural environments to meet the demand. For example, by treating the ozone layer as a resource with a zero price there never was any incentive to protect it. . . . The important principle is that resources and environments serve economic functions and have positive value. To treat them as if they had zero value is seriously to risk overusing the resource. (Pearce, Markandya, and Barbier 1989, 5–6)

However, the authors add that "this does not mean we should automatically introduce actual, positive prices for environmental functions wherever we can." (6) Instead, "we should try, as best we can, to record the economic values that natural environments provide." (6) The book discusses issues related to such valuation in depth. It also suggests environmental taxes that, in effect, "make the user pay." (6) For example, it talks about pollution taxes that make polluters economically responsible for maintaining environmental quality. In particular, the authors mention a tax on carbon fuels, which would vary depending on the environmental damage caused by each type of fuel. Under this system, "coal would attract a higher tax than oil which in turn would attract a higher tax than natural gas. Electricity would not be taxed directly but would pay the taxes on the carbon fuels. In this way the electricity sector would alter its fuel mix to a less carbon-polluting form." (164–165) Such taxes encour-

age consumers to reduce their use of these products. However, the authors acknowledge that energy taxes do not affect all sectors of the population equally and that "new taxes tend to be treated with suspicion." (165) Accordingly, they recognize that enacting such taxes will be difficult yet believe they are necessary to end practices that harm the environment. (Pearce, Markandya, and Barbier 1989)

Blueprint for Survival

Blueprint for Survival was cowritten by American environmentalist Edward Goldsmith, founder and editor of *The Ecologist* magazine, with his editorial board. When it was published in 1972, the book was lauded by several prominent scientists and economists, and its ideas influenced later authors who addressed the impacts human societies have on the environment.

The main argument of *Blueprint for Survival* is that in order to improve the health of the planet human societies must be completely restructured. Among its recommendations is that societies be decentralized so that people live in small, self-contained, easily sustainable communities and have no need to travel to obtain goods or services. The authors offer four reasons in support. First, they argue that it is too difficult to enforce moral behavior in a large community:

> In communities small enough for the general will to be worked out and expressed by individuals confident of themselves and their fellows as individuals, 'us and them' situations are less likely to occur—people having learned the limits of a stable society would be free to order their own lives within them as they wished, and would therefore accept the restraints of the stable society as necessary and desirable and not as some arbitrary restriction imposed by a remote and unsympathetic government. (Goldsmith et al.1972, 50)

Second, agricultural and business practices are more likely to be ecologically sound in smaller communities, because in industry, as with agriculture, it will be important to maintain a vigorous feedback between supply and demand in order to avoid waste, overproduction, or production of goods which the community does not really want, thereby eliminating the needless expense of time, energy and money in attempts to persuade it that it does. If an industry is an integral part of a community, it is much more likely to encourage product innovation because people clearly want qualitative improvements in a given field, rather than because expansion is necessary for that industry's survival or because there is otherwise insufficient work for its research and development section. (50–51)

Third, the authors insist that people feel more fulfilled in smaller communities because "only in the small community can a man or woman be an individual," adding that in a small community people "enjoy the rewards of . . . knowing and being known, of an intensity of relationships with a few, rather than urban man's variety of innumerable, superficial relationships." (51–52) This enriches the human experience and decreases materialism, thereby decreasing waste and pollution.

Finally, the authors argue that reducing an area's human population reduces its environmental damage: "The actual urban superstructure required per inhabitant goes up radically as the size of the town increases beyond a certain point." (52) For example, "if everybody lived in villages the need for sewage treatment plants would be somewhat reduced, while in an entirely urban society they are essential, and the cost of treatment is high. Broadly speaking, it is only by decentralization that we can increase self-sufficiency—and self-sufficiency is vital if we are to minimize the burden of social systems on the ecosystems that support them." (52–53)

The authors also offer a recommendation regarding community size. The exact size, however, is not as important as the general attitudes that smallness evokes:

We have no hard and fast views on the size of the proposed communities, but for the moment we suggest neighbourhoods of 500, represented in communities of 5,000, in regions of 500,000, represented nationally, which in turn as today should be represented globally. We emphasize that our goal should be to create *community feeling* and *global awareness,* rather than that dangerous and sterile compromise which is nationalism. (53)

In stressing the connection between environmentalism and quality of human life, *Blueprint for Survival* expresses a common attitude within the environmental movement. Its advocacy of community restructuring is echoed in many other works of the period, including *Small Is Beautiful,* by economist Fritz Schumacher. (Goldsmith et al. 1972)

See also *Small Is Beautiful.*

Bookchin, Murray

Murray Bookchin is credited with introducing the concept of social ecology, which in part blames capitalism and urbanization for environmental problems. Social ecologists suggest that society be restructured so that large cities are replaced with relatively small, cooperative, economically independent communities that rely on environmentally friendly practices and technologies.

During the 1930s and 1940s Bookchin was a trade-union activist; using the pseudonym Lewis Herber, he began writing about environmental issues in 1951. His early environmental essays include "The Problem of Chemicals in Food" (1952), which argues against the use of pesticides. This subject was also the focus of his 1962 book, *Our Synthetic Environment.* However, it never achieved the fame of another 1962 book on the same subject, Rachel Carson's *Silent Spring.*

In 1965 Bookchin again warned of disaster in *The Crisis of the Cities.* This time, he focused on the relationship between pollution and urbanization. Bookchin continued to write about environmental, political, and social issues

Virginia McKenna and Bill Travers with three lion cubs in the 1966 British film Born Free *(Archive Photos)*

throughout the 1970s and 1980s, when he was also involved in antinuclear activities. Two of his most important works from this period are *Toward an Ecological Society* (1980) and *The Ecology of Freedom* (1982), which he also discusses in his 1994 collection of essays *Which Way for the Ecology Movement?* His later works include essays on social anarchism. Bookchin formed the Vermont-based Institute for Social Ecology, which is active in environmental politics. (Bookchin 1994; Gottlieb 1993)

> See also Environmental Movement; *Our Synthetic Environment;* Social Ecology; *Toward an Ecological Society; Which Way for the Ecology Movement?*

Born Free

Born Free is the true account of author Joy Adamson's experiences raising an orphaned lioness cub named Elsa, eventually released into the wild; it includes several black-and-white Adamson photographs of Elsa. The work is often credited with being the first to bring public attention to African conservation issues, because it engendered great sympathy for lions and great enmity against poachers.

Published in 1960, the book was an immediate international best-seller. As Adamson's husband, George, says in his autobiography *My Pride and Joy:* "All over [Great Britain] the orders came in and the edition sold out. We were told that people were unwrapping their books on the pavements to gaze at the pictures. Very soon the success in Britain and Europe was repeated in America, Japan and even in Russia." (Adamson 1988, p. 94)

Adamson wrote two sequels to *Born Free,* entitled *Living Free* (1961) and *Forever Free* (1962). There was also a movie version of *Born Free* (1966), a 1970 documentary called *The Lions Are Free,* a 1971 movie version of *Living Free,* a 1975 television series based on *Born Free,* and many other book and film projects based on Adamson's work. All of these projects furthered public interest in wildlife conservation issues.

The book *Born Free* tells the story of the lioness's life from 1956 to 1959. The story begins when Adamson's husband, a game warden in what is now the country of Kenya, brings three female cubs home to his wife. George had been forced to shoot the cubs' mother when she charged him in the wild. Adamson immediately takes over the care of the infants, who are only a few weeks old, and the trio thrives. As the cubs grow bigger, however, Adamson realizes she cannot continue to handle all of them, and she sends Elsa's sisters to the Blydorp Zoo in Rotterdam, Holland.

Elsa is a family pet until, at 23 months, she becomes interested in some nearby wild lions and starts spending more and more time away from camp. Adamson realizes that Elsa is becoming wild yet doesn't know how to feed herself. She and George decide to try to retrain the lioness for life on her own. This proves difficult. Adamson writes that after releasing Elsa at one distant site: "We now left Elsa alone for two or three days at a time, hoping that hunger would make her kill. But when we came back we always found her waiting for us and hungry. It was heartbreaking. . . ." (Adamson 1960, 96) George intermittently brings Elsa meat; nonetheless, the weakened lioness becomes ill with parasites and a virus. After three months Adamson takes Elsa back to camp and nurses her back to health. She and George then release her at another site, where she gradually begins to hunt for herself. At last, after three years of being cared for by humans, Elsa is on her own.

Adamson includes a postscript to her story: a series of letters that George wrote to her while she was away in London. In them he describes Elsa's successful adaptation to living in the wild. In one he writes that Elsa has found a mate and is pregnant; the story of her cubs is continued in *Living Free*. (Adamson 1960; Adamson 1988)

See also Adamson, Joy; Animal Behavior; *Forever Free; Living Free;* Wildlife Conservation.

Botkin, Daniel B.

Environmental scientist Daniel B. Botkin has written more than a hundred books and articles on environmental issues and related subjects. A professor of biology at George Mason University, he has also served as the president of the Center for the Study of the Environment in Santa Barbara, California, and conducted many research projects on environmental problems. His 1995 book, *Our Natural History,* summarizes much of that work and "represents the products of many specific research projects." (Botkin 1995, x) It expands on concepts he presented in an earlier work, *Discordant Harmony: A New Ecology for the Twenty-first Century* (1990). Botkin holds a doctorate degree in biology from Rutgers University in New Brunswick, New Jersey, a master's degree from the University of Wisconsin at Madison, and a bachelor's degree from the University of Rochester in New York.

See also *Our Natural History.*

Boulle, Pierre

Born on February 20, 1912, French novelist Pierre Boulle wrote numerous works based on his experiences as a soldier. His most famous novel is *The Bridge Over the River Kwai,* published in French in 1952 and in English in 1954. However, Boulle also addressed the consequences of war in his apocalyptic science fiction novel *Planet of the Apes,* published in 1963. The book depicts the aftermath of a global nuclear war, showing its effects on the environment and on evolution. It was one of the first works of modern fiction to predict a doomsday caused by environmental destruction. Boulle's other novels include *The Executioner* (1954), *The Ears of the Jungle* (1972), *The Good Leviathan* (1978), and *Le Professeur Mortimer* (1988). He died on January 30, 1994, in Paris. (Becker 1996)

See also *Planet of the Apes.*

Brand, Stewart

Environmentalist Stewart Brand is the founding editor of the *Whole Earth Catalogue,* which first appeared in 1968 and has become synonymous with the early environmental movement. It has been called "a bible for the back-to-the-land movement." According to friend Stephanie Mills, Brand's intent in presenting his collection of environmental products "was simply to be useful to his brave contemporaries, many of whom were starting from scratch out in the sticks." (Mills 1989, 84)

When he established the catalog Brand was editor of an environmental magazine, *CoEvolution Quarterly,* and wanted to express his opposition to modern technological society. Mills reports that he was a nonconformist, even among fellow environmentalists. She says: "*Whole Earth Catalogue* has been associated in the public mind with the ecology movement from the beginning. . . . [Therefore] members of the ecology movement felt, rightly or wrongly, that the *Catalogue* and *Quarterly* should be toeing some standard environmental line. . . . So over the years when ecology types promoted a definition of political correctness, Stewart responded with annoyance, period." (86)

Brand published the catalog throughout the 1970s and 1980s, revising it several times to add new information about helpful tools, products, and books related to simple living and environmentalism. A 1972 edition of the work, *The Last Whole Earth Catalogue,* received the National Book Award. More recently, Brand helped found the WELL, an early Internet bulletin board that developed into a prototypical online community. He advocates the sensible use of technology to limit the use of paper, consumer goods, and energy. (Mills 1989)

See also *Whole Earth Catalogue.*

Brazil-Maru

Published in 1992, the novel *Brazil-Maru* by Karen Tei Yamashita concerns a group of Christian Japanese who emigrate to Brazil in 1925 to become farmers. Several characters narrate the story, telling of the many hardships faced while building a new life in a new land.

The work is significant for its descriptions of the South American rain forest and the consequences of settlement for the environment. For example, when the immigrants reach their new home they burn the forest to clear land for farming. One narrator says:

> Looking out on these endless fields of pasture and planted land today, it is hard to imagine this land as it was then, known only to the wild animals and the Indians. In those days, we thought that the forest was so wide and so deep that it would never end, that carving out our small piece of it wouldn't make such a great difference to something so immense. Besides, we had come to create a new world, and starting on new land was a special and sacred gift given only to a chosen few. Perhaps it was a great sin to destroy the forest in this way. Ever since, we have tried to replace the forest with a new life—growth, sustenance, call it what you will. I have lived here a mere lifetime, but the forest had peacefully existed here for many centuries. What we have taken from the earth will, I think, take many more lifetimes to return in kind. When my father talked of the sin of the immigrant, I believe he meant this sin of clearing the forest away forever. (Yamashita 1992, 22)

In time, one of the immigrants, Kantaro, realizes that the richness of the land has been depleted: "Until now, we have occupied ourselves in the great task of clearing the virgin forest. We have used the land, planted coffee, rice and cotton. In a matter of years, we've become guilty of depleting the soil of its natural fertility. Many Japanese have left the land and gone off to the city. We must find a way to keep people on the land. The answer is simple: restore the land's fertility." (77)

Kantaro develops a plan to create compost through widespread chicken farming, and by the end of World War II he is the leader of a large commune with 10 poultry barns and 5,000 laying hens. However, he is also in debt, and eventually he loses everything. Several years later, he dies in a plane crash in the forest. Meanwhile, his descendants continue farming. As one character reports: "The Japanese have origins in the land. And having settled virgin soil, our responsibility to the land is great; farming is our contribution." (248) (Yamashita 1992)

Brooks, Paul

Naturalist Paul Brooks is the author of several books about the relationship between humans and nature, including *The People of Concord: One Year in the Flowering of New England* (1990), *The Pursuit of Wilderness* (1971), and *The View from Lincoln Hill: Man and the Land in a New England Town* (1976). He has also written extensively about environmental literature and nature writers in such books as *The House of Life: Rachel Carson at Work* (1972) and *Speaking for Nature: How Literary Naturalists from Henry Thoreau to Rachel Carson Have Shaped America* (1980).

See also Carson, Rachel Louise; Thoreau, Henry David.

Buffon, Georges Louis Leclerc, Comte de

French naturalist George Louis Buffon wrote one of the first histories of earth based on science rather than religion. Called *Histoire naturelle* (Natural History), it was published in 44 volumes from 1749 to 1789. Buffon was born in Montbard, France, on September 7, 1707; in 1739 he began working as director of Jardin du Roi, the royal botanical gardens. King Louis XV made him a count in 1753. The Comte de Buffon continued working on *Histoire naturelle* until his death on April 16, 1788. (Bowler 1993)

See also Geological Research; *Natural History.*

Bulloch, David K.

Industrial chemist David K. Bulloch writes about marine conservation issues. He is a member and past president of the American Littoral Society, a nonprofit organization dedicated to preserving the littoral zone, the region where the sea meets the land. His best-known book is *The Wasted Ocean* (1989), but he is also the author of *The Underwater Naturalist* (1991), *The American Littoral Society*

Handbook for the Marine Naturalist (1991), and *The Whale-Watchers Handbook* (1993).

See also Habitat Protection; *Wasted Ocean, The;* Water Pollution

Burroughs, Edgar Rice

Edgar Rice Burroughs wrote novels set in the natural world. He is best known for the *Tarzan of the Jungle* books, but he also authored of one of the earliest popular novels to feature evolutionary theory: *The Land That Time Forgot* (1908).

Burroughs was born in Chicago on September 1, 1875. As a young man he had trouble settling on a career, and in 1911 he decided to write fiction. That year, his first adventure story, "Under the Moon of Mars," was published in *All-Story* magazine. His first Tarzan story, about a man raised by apes, was published in 1912, and his first Tarzan book in 1914. Burroughs wrote 68 novels including 25 Tarzan books during his lifetime. He also worked as a news correspondent during World War II. He died on March 19, 1950, in Encino, California. (Burroughs 1946; Holtsmark 1986)

See also Evolution; *Land That Time Forgot, The.*

Burroughs, John

John Burroughs wrote extensively on nature and conservation issues. Born near Roxbury, New York, on April 3, 1837, he grew up enjoying bird-watching and hiking. In 1854 he became a schoolteacher. Six years later he sent an essay called "From the Back Country" to *Atlantic Monthly* magazine. It was his first publication and led to many others in the same magazine, including "With the Birds" (1865), which some scholars consider to be the first true nature essay. In 1863 Burroughs moved to Washington, D.C., to become a clerk in an office of the U.S. Treasury; he continued his writing. In addition to essays, he published a book to honor friend Walt Whitman (*Notes on Walt Whitman as Poet and Person,* 1867). In 1871 he published *Wake Robin,* the first of several books on birds.

In 1873 Burroughs decided to quit his job,

buy a farm, and live off his writing income. He became successful and spent his free time camping with friends such as John Muir and Theodore Roosevelt, two legendary conservationists. Burroughs's subsequent works include *Birds and Poets* (1877), *Locusts and Wild Honey* (1879), *Ways of Nature* (1905), *Camping and Tramping with Roosevelt* (1907), *The Summit of the Years* (1914), *Field and Study* (1919), and *The Last Harvest* (1922).

In much of his nature writing, Burroughs comments on the topic of conservationism. In *Field and Study* he says:

> In my boyhood the vast armies of the passenger pigeons were one of the most notable spring tokens. . . .The last great flight of them that I ever beheld was on the 10th of April, 1875, when, for the greater part of the day, one could not at any moment look skyward above the Hudson River Valley without seeing several flocks, great and small, of the migrating birds. But that spectacle was never repeated as it had been for generations before. The pigeons . . .were pursued from State to State by professional pothunters and netters, and the numbers so reduced and their flocking instinct so disorganized that their vast migrating bands disappeared, and they were seen only in loosely scattered and diminishing flocks in different parts of the West during the remainder of the century. . . . The last time that my eyes beheld a passenger pigeon was in the fall of 1876 when I was out for grouse. I saw a solitary cock sitting in a tree. I killed it, little dreaming that, so far as I was concerned, I was killing the last pigeon. (Wiley 1967, 213)

Like many early conservationists, Burroughs was a hunter who wanted to preserve species for reasons of sport. At the same time, he deeply appreciated nature, and his writings encouraged others to enjoy it as well—not necessarily as hunters but as naturalists. However, scholar Hans Huth, in *Nature and the American,* suggests that it was not really the wilderness that attracted Burroughs but its relationship to human beings. Quoting from various writings of Burroughs, Huth explains:

> Among the many photographs of Burroughs, the most characteristic are those which show him kneeling to examine some flower growing in his path, or watching birds and clouds while looking at the sky from his lodge. Burroughs did not really care for these phenomena as such, but rather was interested in the way they were correlated and the manner in which they fitted into the universe. Man in harmony with nature was Burroughs' concern; in fact, he believed that "man can have but one interest in nature, namely, to see himself reflected or interpreted there." Bound to the universe, "every creature must take its chance, and man is no exception." Burroughs achieved the apogee of nature writing. He was more successful than anyone else had been in capturing the minds of the public and injecting into them deep affection for nature seasoned by genuine understanding. He knew well that a part of his success was based on his putting "personal feelings and attractions into subjects of universal interest." (Huth 1972, 103)

After Burroughs's death on March 29, 1921, the John Burroughs Association was established in his honor. It is a society dedicated to the encouragement of writings on natural science. (Cox 1971; Huth 1972; Wiley 1967)

See also Conservationism; Muir, John; Nature Writing.

Butler, Samuel

Born on December 4, 1835, in Nottinghamshire, England, novelist and essayist Samuel Butler became involved in the debate surrounding Charles Darwin's theory of evolution. Butler presented some of his views regarding evolution in his first novel, *Erewhon* (1872), a satirical work that portrayed a utopian society. In 1901 he wrote a sequel to *Erewhon* entitled *Erewhon Revisited*.

Samuel Butler (Archive Photos)

Butler did not plan to be a novelist. His father, the Reverend Thomas Butler, wanted his son to become a clergyman, but after graduating from Cambridge University in 1858 Samuel decided to move to New Zealand and take up sheep farming. Shortly thereafter he read Darwin's *Origin of Species* (1859) and became a supporter, renouncing Christianity in favor of Darwin's view of creation. But he was uncomfortable with this decision, and he began to question many aspects of Darwinian theory. He wrote several articles critical of Darwinism; two of these would later be revised for inclusion in *Erewhon*.

In 1864 he returned to England, where he became a painter and a music composer as well as a writer. He made little money from his work, which included an essay on evolution called *Life and Habit: An Essay After a Completer View of Evolution* (1878) and a series of books on evolutionary theory (*Evolution, Old and New,* 1849; *Unconscious Memory,* 1880; and *Luck or Cunning as the Main Means of Organic Modification?,* 1887). Butler died on June 18, 1902; a year later his most famous book was published. Entitled *The Way of All Flesh,* it was a semiautobiographical novel featuring a young man who questions the moral rigidity of his parents. (Furbank 1976; Harris 1977; Holt 1964)

See also Darwin, Charles Robert; *Erewhon;* Evolution.

C

Cadillac Desert

Published in 1986, *Cadillac Desert: The American West and Its Disappearing Water* is an example of environmental literature that offers a historical survey and in-depth discussion of a single issue. In this case, the issue is water use and conservation in the western United States. *Cadillac Desert* is considered one of the most thorough treatments of the subject.

The book's author, Marc Reisner, began his journalism career writing for the National Resources Defense Council, a group concerned with environmental politics. He conducted the research for *Cadillac Desert* with the help of a journalism fellowship. It is a lengthy work, with 12 substantial chapters, an epilogue, and an extensive bibliography. The book begins with a first-person narrative in which Reisner reveals his own environmental sensibilities. For example:

> Confronted by the desert, the first thing Americans want to do is change it. People say that they "love" the desert, but few of them love it enough to live there. I mean in the real desert, not in a make-believe city like Phoenix with exotic palms and golf-course lawns and a five-hundred-foot fountain and an artificial surf. Most people "love" the desert by driving through it in air-conditioned cars, "experiencing" its grandeur. That may be some kind of experience, but it is living in a fool's paradise. To *really* experience the desert you have to march right into its white bowl of sky and shape-contorting heat with your mind on your canteen as if it were your last gallon of gas and you were being chased by a carload of escaped murderers. You have to imagine what it would be like to drink blood from a lizard or, in the grip of dementia, claw bare-handed through sand and rock for the vestigial moisture beneath a dry wash (Reisner 4–5)

Reisner connects his own feelings about the desert with the challenges related to its lack of water, saying "One does not really conquer a place like this. One inhabits it like an uneasy truce with it. . . . The only way to make the region over is to irrigate it. But there is too little water to begin with, and water in rivers is phenomenally expensive to move. And even if you succeeded in moving every drop, it wouldn't make much of a difference." (Reisner 4–5)

Reisner traces the history of development in the western United States, particularly California. He talks about several powerful men in Los Angeles who, during the early 1900s, began to look outside of California for water to support the region's growing population. He explores various controversies over water rights, laws, dam and aqueduct construction, and other water-use issues. He also discusses the environmental impact of water use in the West. For example, of one water reservoir he says:

It would quickly turn into a fetid, grossly polluted agricultural sump. Between the partially treated sewage of nearly two million people, the untreated runoff of hundreds of thousands of cows (some of them defecating right in the river), and pesticides and fertilizers washing in from thousands and thousands of acres of intensively farmed land—between this, and the fact that the reservoir would be shallow and warm, with an evaporation rate of four feet a year, the water quality was going to be absolutely awful. The EPA [U.S. Environmental Protection Agency] was suggesting that it would not be fit for *contact*, which meant no swimming or water skiing without a waterproof covering over every inch of one's body. (445–446)

In addition to such facts, Reisner offers quotes from a variety of environmental scientists, politicians, and others who have studied Western water-use issues. His work on the subject is exhaustive. It is also highly critical of the way water has been exploited for political and financial gain, suggesting that many public officials have little interest in protecting the environment. (Reisner 1986)

See also Agriculture; Reisner, Marc; Water Pollution.

Caldicott, Helen

Born in Australia in 1938, pediatrician Helen Caldicott is an environmental activist who has written several books about the medical hazards of nuclear energy. She helped found Physicians for Social Responsibility (PSR), a group concerned with environmental and human health issues, and Women's Action for Nuclear Disarmament (WAND). PSR received a Nobel Peace Prize in 1985 and Caldicott was nominated for one as well. Her

life has been the subject of several movies, including the 1983 Academy Award–winning documentary *If You Love This Planet*. Her books include *Environment: A Challenge to Modern Society* (1970), *In Defense of the Earth: International Protection of the Biosphere* (1972), *Nuclear Madness: What You Can Do* (1979), *Missile Envy: The Arms Race and Nuclear War* (1984), *If You Love This Planet: A Plan to Heal the Earth* (1992), and *A Desperate Passion: An Autobiography* (1996).

Caldwell, Lynton K.

Lynton K. Caldwell is a professor of political science and environmental affairs. He has written several books on environmental policies, including *Man and His Environment: Policy and Administration* (1975), *International Environmental Policy: Emergence and Dimensions* (1984), *Biocracy: Public Policy and the Life Sciences* (1987), and *Policy for Land: Law and Ethics* (1993).

Callicott, J. Baird

J. Baird Callicott is a professor of philosophy at the University of North Texas who has written extensively on environmental ethics. His books include *Earth's Insights: A Survey of Ecological Ethics from the Mediterranean Basin to the Australian Outback* (1994) and *In Defense of the Land Ethic: Essays in Environmental Philosophy* (1989). Callicott has also edited or coedited several environmental books, such as *Companion to A Sand County Almanac: Interpretive and Critical Essays* (1987), *Nature in Asian Traditions of Thought: Essays in Environmental Philosophy* (1989), *Environmental Philosophy: From Animal Rights to Social Ecology* (1993), and *The Great New Wilderness Debate* (1997).

Candolle, Augustin de

Swiss botanist Augustin de Candolle developed an important system of plant classification that was based on plant anatomy. He published several works on the subject, including *Theorie elementaire de la botanique* (Elementary Theory of Botany, 1813) and the two-volume *Regni Vegetabilis Systema Naturale*

(Natural Classification for the Plant Kingdom, 1818–1821). Born on February 4, 1778, in Geneva, Switzerland, he went to Paris in 1796 and befriended scientists Georges Cuvier and Jean-Baptiste de Lamarck, eventually working for both. In 1808 he became a professor of botany at the University of Montpellier. He also conducted government studies on botany and agriculture. In 1817 he became a professor of natural history at the Universite de Geneve in Switzerland. In addition, he traveled extensively to study the botany of Brazil, India, and China. He died in Geneva on September 9, 1841.

See also Cuvier, Georges; Lamarck, Jean-Baptiste.

Carr, Archie

Marine biologist Archie Carr was an expert on the plight of endangered sea turtles throughout the world. His works include *So Excellent A Fishe: A Natural History of Sea Turtles* (1967) and *The Windward Road: Adventures of a Naturalist on Remote Caribbean Shores* (1957), the latter of which is a first-person account of his experiences studying turtles and other animals in the Caribbean. Born in Mobile, Alabama, in 1909, Carr was a professor of biology at the University of Florida. He died in 1987.

Carrighar, Sally

Sally Carrighar is the author of two popular nature books of the late 1970s: *One Day at Beetle Rock* (1978) and *One Day on Teton Marsh* (1979). Both are written from the perspective of animals; *Beetle Rock* describes a day in Sequoia National Park, *Teton Marsh* a day in the wilderness near Jackson, Wyoming. Carrighar also wrote *Icebound Summer* (1991), a natural history of Alaska, and *The Twilight Seas* (1975), a children's book about the life of a blue whale.

Carson, Rachel Louise

Conservationist Rachel Carson is often credited with inspiring the American environmental movement of the 1960s and 1970s. Her book *Silent Spring* (1962), which discusses the impact of pesticide use on public health, triggered a government study that eventually resulted in the banning of several pesticides in 1970.

Silent Spring was influential not only because of the information it imparted but also for Carson's writing style. Philip Shabecoff explains in *A Fierce Green Fire:*

Carson did not do much of the research that showed the dangers of [pesticides]. She was not even the first to cry the alarm—[environmentalist Murray] Bookchin, the naturalist Edwin Way Teale, and a number of others had already sounded public warnings.

What Carson did in *Silent Spring*, however, was to present the scientific evidence in clear, poetic, and moving prose that demonstrated how the destruction of nature and the threat to human health from pollution were completely intertwined. She showed how all life, including human life, was affected by misguided technology. The book synthesized many of the concerns of earlier conservationists and preservationists with the warnings of newer environmentalists who worried about pollution and public health. It made frighteningly clear that they were all skeins of a large web of environmental evil settling over the nation and the world. . . . She combined a transcendentalist's passion for nature and wildlife with the cool analytical mind of a trained scientist and the contained anger of a political activist. She touched an exposed wound. (Shabecoff 1993, 109–110)

Carson was a scientist as well as a writer. Born on May 27, 1907, in Springdale, Pennsylvania, she received a bachelor's degree in biology from the Pennsylvania College for Women in 1929 and a master's degree from Johns Hopkins University in 1932. From 1936 to 1952 she worked as an aquatic biologist for the U.S. Fish and Wildlife Service. She also began writing about nature and ecology.

Rachel Carson, April 27, 1963 (Archive Photos)

In 1941 she wrote *Under the Sea Wind* and in 1951 *The Sea Around Us;* both books discuss the ecology of the ocean. *The Sea Around Us* was an immediate best-seller and won the National Book Award. Carson's subsequent nature and environmental books, including *Silent Spring,* were similarly well received.

Carson remained active in environmental causes until her death on April 14, 1964. One year later, Rachel Carson Council, Inc., was founded to carry on her crusade against pesticides. This nonprofit scientific and environmental corporation studies and disseminates information about chemical contamination of the environment and its effects on human health. (Carson 1961; Carson 1962; Cox 1971; Glotfelty and Fromm 1996; Shabecoff 1993)

See also Bookchin, Murray; Environmental Movement; Human Ecology; Pesticides and Chemicals; *Sea Around Us, The; Silent Spring.*

Cat's Cradle

Kurt Vonnegut's 1963 novel, *Cat's Cradle,* does not directly address the subject of environmentalism. However, it uses an environmental threat as a plot device and concludes with an environmental apocalypse; thus it can be classified as a form of environmental fiction. Because Vonnegut was an extremely popular author at the beginning of the environmental movement, particularly with young people interested in environmental activism, his fictional portrayal of environmental disaster is perhaps more significant than most others of the period.

Cat's Cradle concerns the efforts of a writer, the first-person narrator of the story, to research the life of the late Dr. Felix Hoenikker, one of the scientists who created the atomic bomb. The writer soon discovers that Hoenikker created a substance called ice-nine, which could harden water. When Hoenikker died, his three children broke the chunk of ice-nine into pieces to share. Using gloves and tongs, they placed it into Thermos bottles for safekeeping. However, during the process, some of it dropped on the floor; the dog ate it, turned solid, and died.

When the narrator encounters Hoenikker's children, he soon learns the power of ice-nine. Felix Hoenikker's oldest son, Frank, has allied with an island dictator, who keeps the ice-nine in a vial around his neck. When the dictator learns he is going to die a painful death, he eats the ice-nine to commit suicide. Unfortunately, anyone who touches his body and then touches his own lips dies too. Moreover, when the body is accidentally plunged into the ocean, the entire earth becomes ice-nine. According to the narrator, "All the sea was *ice-nine*. The moist green earth was a blue-white pearl. . . . The sky was filled with worms. The worms were tornadoes." (Vonnegut 1963, 211)

The narrator and his new fiancée take refuge from the disaster in a stone cellar. When they come out, the weather has settled down but the earth is still ice-nine, and most everyone is gone. It is apparent that many committed suicide by putting chunks of ice-nine to their lips. The narrator's fiancée does the same. The narrator, however, perseveres until he encounters a man who says: "If I were a younger man, I would write a history of human stupidity; and I would climb to the top of Mount McCabe and lie down on my back with my history for a pillow; and I would take from the ground some of the blue-white poison that makes statues of men; and I would make a statue of myself, lying on my back, grinning horribly, and thumbing my nose at You Know Who." (231) This is where the story ends, with the implication that the narrator followed this suggestion. (Vonnegut 1961)

See also Environmental Apocalypse; Environmental Fiction; Vonnegut, Kurt.

Catlin, George

Nineteenth-century artist George Catlin wrote and illustrated several books about his travels throughout North America. In one of them, the 1841 *North American Indians: Being Letters and Notes on their Manners, Customs, and Conditions, Written during Eight Years' Travel Amongst the Wildest Tribes in North America, 1832–1839*, he became the first American to suggest that wilderness areas be preserved for public enjoyment, thereby creating the concept of the national park. He wrote:

It is a melancholy contemplation for one who has travelled as I have, through these realms, and seen this noble animal [the buffalo] in all its pride and glory, to contemplate it so rapidly wasting from the world. . . .And what a splendid contemplation too, when one (who has travelled these realms, and can duly appreciate them) imagines them as they *might* in future be seen (by some great protecting policy of government) preserved in their pristine beauty and wildness, in a *magnificent* park. . . .What a beautiful and thrilling specimen for America to preserve and hold up to the view of her refined citizens and the world, in future ages! A *nation's Park,* containing man and beast, in all the wild and freshness of their nature's beauty! (Nash 1976, 8–9)

Catlin was born on July 26, 1796, in Wilkes-Barre, Pennsylvania. A lawyer by trade, in 1823 he became a full-time portrait painter. Six years later he set out to paint portraits of Native Americans from various tribes, particularly in the Great Plains. In 1837 he began exhibiting his work. Shortly thereafter he also began writing books that featured his illustrations. They include *Catlin's North American Indian Portfolio: Hunting Scenes and Amusements of the Rocky Mountains and Prairies of America* (1845) and *Life Amongst the Indians* (1867). Catlin died on December 23, 1872, in Jersey City, New Jersey. (Haverstock 1973; Nash 1976)

See also Conservationism.

Catton, William

American sociologist William Catton is the author of *Overshoot: The Ecological Basis of Revolutionary Change* (1980). The work discusses the dynamics of human population and its effect on the environment, reporting on the fate of various species and population groups to illustrate why overpopulation is a matter of concern.

Caufield, Catherine

An American journalist living in London, Catherine Caufield is the author of *In the Rainforest,* a first-person account of her investigations into the destruction of rain forests throughout the world. She has written many newspaper and magazine articles, as well as a 1981 book, *The Emperor of the United States of America and Other Magnificent British Eccentrics.* Her work is representative of most modern naturalist writings, in which observations on plants and animals are combined with commentary regarding environmental destruction. (Caufield 1989)

> **See also** Balanced Ecosystems; Forest Management; Habitat Protection; *In the Rainforest.*

Ceremony

The 1977 novel *Ceremony* by Leslie Marmon Silko concerns a Native American, Tayo, who became ill while serving in World War II. The work's significance for environmental literature is its emphasis on the relationship between man's inner and outer landscape. Not only is Tayo sick, but the land around him is suffering from severe drought. Once Tayo is healed—not just physically, but spiritually—the rain returns. As Gregory Salyer explains in his essay "*Ceremony:* Healing with Stories": "The 'benefits' of the war are transitory and illusory because they are made of nothing; it is all just a trick. Sustenance for physical and emotional life comes not from money or people who have power but from the source of life, the earth." (Salyer 1997, 41)

Salyer points out that Silko wrote *Ceremony* while living in Alaska, far from her native home in the desert of the American Southwest. Consequently, the work "was a product of her struggles with the changes of climate, both physical and emotional." (6) (Salyer 1997)

Challenge of Global Warming, The

Published in 1989 by the National Resources Defense Council (NRDC) and edited by an NRDC board member, *The Challenge of Global Warming* is a compilation of scientific articles discussing how environmental destruction impacts the world's climate. The work is representative of many other books published by environmental groups during the early environmental movement. Its contributors include chemists, biologists, climatologists, geophysicists, and environmentalists, all of whom offer detailed discussions of issues related to global warming, also known as the "greenhouse effect."

The collected articles offer many statistics and scientific citations and are often accompanied by numerical tables and charts. According to editor Dean Edwin Abrahamson, however, the work "is intended for the nonscientist—the policy analyst, the legislative staff member, the advocate of environmental values, the student." (Abrahamson 1989, xi) The book is thus an important work for those interested in learning more about environmental politics. Yet *The Challenge of Global Warming* generated the same criticism directed at many other books published by environmental groups: bias. Opponents of the modern environmental movement believe that global warming does not exist and often condemn books like this for creating a nonexistent controversy.

Nonetheless, Abrahamson offers a variety of in-depth articles on global warming. He divided the book into five parts. The first introduces the problem of global warming. The second discusses its impact on biological life, the third its impact on physical systems such as soil and water, and the fourth its impact on the earth's atmosphere. The fifth and final part, "Policy Responses," discusses political aspects. Abrahamson explains that "each part opens with a chapter written especially for this book by a recognized expert, followed by chapters, previously published elsewhere, which focus more narrowly on some aspect of climatic change. Considerable use has been made of recent congressional testimony, as it represents what is in many cases the only material written by leading scientists for a nonscientific audience." (xi)

Abrahamson believes that "limiting global heating and climatic change is the central environmental challenge of our time," because "fossil fuel burning, deforestation, and the release of industrial chemicals are rapidly heating the earth to temperatures not experienced in human memory." (xi) Therefore, *The Challenge of Global Warming* includes no articles on the theory that global warming might be a natural rather than man-made phenomenon. (Abrahamson 1989) This is a continuing controversy between environmentalists and antienvironmentalists.

See also Abrahamson, Dean Edwin; Climate Changes.

Chambers, Robert

Born on July 10, 1802, in Peebles, Scotland, amateur naturalist Robert Chambers wrote books on history, geology, and evolution. Many of them were based on his own research. His most controversial work was *Vestiges of the Natural History of Creation,* which he published anonymously in 1844. It argued that creatures evolve over time and that humans are descended from animals. However, unlike later evolutionary theorists, such as Charles Darwin, Chambers saw evolution not as a scientific process but as something preordained by God.

Chambers began his publishing career in 1818, working as a bookseller in Edinburgh, Scotland. In 1832 he and his brother, William, founded their own publishing company, W. and R. Chambers, Ltd., and produced *Chambers's Encyclopedia.* He remained active in the firm until his death on March 17, 1871. (Bowler 1993; Chambers 1994)

See also Darwin, Charles Robert; Evolution; *Vestiges of the Natural History of Creation.*

Chase, Alston

Alston Chase writes about forestry issues and national park management and is considered one of the foremost experts on the subject. His best-known work is *Playing God in Yellowstone: The Destruction of America's First National Park* (1987), which criticizes environmentalists' attempts to manage Yellowstone. Chase was once chair of the park's Library and Museum Association, which publishes books on Yellowstone and sponsors a summer education program called the Yellowstone Institute. His newest book, *In a Dark Wood: The Fight Over Forests and the Rising Tyranny of Ecology* (1995), is also critical of American environmentalists. (Chase 1986; Glotfelty and Fromm 1996)

See also Antienvironmentalism; Forest Management; Habitat Protection; *Playing God in Yellowstone;* Wildlife Conservation.

Chernobyl

Like Edward Abbey's 1975 novel, *The Monkey Wrench Gang,* the 1987 novel *Chernobyl: A Novel* by science fiction writer Frederik Pohl is based on real-life people and events related to an environmental issue. Whereas Abbey's work concerns environmental activists working to sabotage development, Pohl's book is about the Chernobyl nuclear disaster in the former Soviet Union. The novel follows the daily lives of several fictional characters to portray events leading up to the Russian power plant's explosion and the subsequent evacuation and cleanup efforts. It also offers detailed information about Chernobyl in particular and nuclear reactions in general. For example, Pohl summarizes the explosion thus:

What went wrong at 1:23 a.m. on that Saturday morning in Chernobyl occurred in four separate stages, but they followed so closely on each other that they were only seconds from beginning to end. First, there was the power surge in one little corner of the vast graphite and uranium core. Although the reactor had been throttled back almost to extinction, a small section went critical; that was the atomic explosion. The second stage was steam. The nuclear blast blew the caps off the 1,661 steam tubes. . . . The steam explosion shattered the containment vessel. At that point the disaster was completely out of control and everything that followed was inevitable. . . . The terrible heat and pressure caused the steam from the ruptured pipes to break down into its gaseous elements. . . . That produced a hydrogen-oxygen explosion . . . Fiercely radioactive

Chernobyl workers' town evacuated after the disaster at the nuclear plant (Corbis)

material was thrown in all directions. Anything nearby that could burn was ignited. . . . All the fires together produced a vertical hurricane of hot gases that carried along with it a soup of fragmentary particles and even ions of everything nearby . . . including the radionuclides of the core. . . . It was the fire that carried the calamity over a million square miles. (Pohl 1987, 63–64)

Pohl explains the danger to human health caused by this disaster: "Without exception, all radioactive elements are harmful to living things—every living thing, from fungi to human beings. High doses of radiation kill quickly. Lower doses take more time." (120) Many of *Chernobyl*'s characters die of radiation poisoning, and although the nuclear reactor's radiation is ultimately contained, the novel suggests that the area will always be dangerous to human life.

When one character, a plant engineer named Sheranchuk, asks how the plant is doing after the disaster, an expert from Russia's Ministry of Nuclear Energy explains that the core, which has been sealed with concrete slabs and steel doors, will have to remain a "sarcophagus" forever, adding: "What 'forever' means is *forever*. Through all the rest of your lifetime, and your children's, and your children's children's, for perhaps hundreds of years. Long after the rest of the Chernobyl Nuclear Power Station is decommissioned and torn down and carted away, that sarcophagus will remain." (326) The expert then says that people will forever be "watching the instruments inside to make sure that nothing is going wrong. Always. Forever." (326) Through such statements, *Chernobyl* expresses antinuclear sentiments in an effective style. Pohl has written on this and other environmental issues in nonfiction works, including *Our Angry Earth,* which he coauthored with Isaac Asimov. (Pohl 1987)

See also Abbey, Edward; Asimov, Isaac; Environmental Apocalypse; Environmental Fiction; Environmental Politics; Human Ecology; *Monkey Wrench Gang, The;* Nuclear Energy; *Our Angry Earth;* Pohl, Frederik.

Cherry, Lynn

Lynn Cherry is a children's book author and illustrator who works to promote environmentalism among young people as the founder and director of the Center for Children's Environmental Literature. Her works include *A River Ran Wild: An Environmental History* (1992), *The Great Kapok Tree: A Tale of the Amazon Rain Forest* (1994), *The Armadillo from Amarillo* (1994), and *Flute's Journey: The Life of a Wood Thrush* (1997). She maintains homes in Cleveland Park in Washington, D.C., in Woods Hole on Cape Cod, and in the Catoctin Mountains in Maryland, changing locations as an artist-in-residence for writing and nature-related programs.

Clare, John

Born in 1793 in Northamptonshire, England, John Clare was a poet who wrote about rural life. A collection of his verse, *Poems Descriptive of Rural Life and Scenery,* published in 1820 made him famous. However, with fame came mental illness. Clare was committed to an asylum in 1837 and remained there until his death in 1864. In addition to poems, his work includes detailed notebooks of his experiences in nature, which appear in *The Natural History Prose Writings of John Clare,* edited by Margaret Grainger (1983).

Clements, Frederick E.

Botanist Frederick E. Clements (1874–1926) was a pioneer ecologist. His *Research Methods in Ecology* (1905) is the first textbook on ecology as a science. In addition, he developed many theories regarding ecological communities and had many supporters. Nonetheless, fellow botanist Arthur Tansley was an outspoken opponent of his work.

Clements's particular field of interest was the study of grasslands. He developed a way to scientifically examine grasslands by sectioning them into quadrants. Then, he identified and removed each plant in the quadrant and studied regrowth. Using this method, he could discover which forms of vegetation were truly natural to an area; he could also determine the exact range and distribution of each plant species.

Based on this work Clements suggested that farming was a destructive activity that interfered with the health of the land. Yet he also believed land could be quickly restored simply by leaving it alone for a time. In addition, Clements proposed the idea that a plant community is actually a single, complex organism. In this respect his work is similar to the Gaia hypothesis developed during the late 1970s and 1980s. (Bowler 1993)

See also Agriculture; Animal Ecology; Gaia Hypothesis; Tansley, Arthur G.

Climate and Evolution

Paleontologist William Diller Matthew published *Climate and Evolution* in 1914. It proposed several new views regarding evolution and mammalian paleontology. For example, many scientists had believed that the point of origin for a species was where its primitive forms could be found; in contrast, Matthew argued that the opposite as true. He felt that the most highly evolved members of a species would remain concentrated in their original territory; as they migrated, they would force lesser-evolved members to move farther and farther away from that central location. Therefore, he says:

> In considering the evidence from extinct species as to the center of dispersal of a race, it has frequently been assumed that the region where the most primitive member of a race has been found should be regarded as the source of the race, although in some instances more advanced species of the same race were living at the same time in other regions. The discovery of very primitive sirenians in Egypt while at the same time much more advanced sirenians were living in Europe has been regarded as evidence that Africa was the center of dispersal of this order. It is to my mind good evidence that it was not. (Matthew 1939, 10)

For the same reason, Matthew argues that even though many primitive humans live in Australia, "it is not in Australia that we should look for the ancestry of man, but in Asia." (10) He states that the prevailing notion that evolution is caused by environment supports this theory. He explains:

> The chief arguments advanced in support of [the idea that the location of primitive forms indicates a point of origin for a species] appear to be that the modification of a race is due to the changes in its environment and that the primitive species are altered more and more as they spread out or migrate into a new environment; but, assuming that a species is the product of its environment, the conclusions drawn would only hold true if the environment remained constant. This is assuredly not the case, and if it were there would be no cause left for the species to change its range. In fact, it is the environment itself, biotic as well as physical, that migrates, and the primitive species are those which have followed it, while those which remained have had to adapt themselves to a new environment and become altered thereby. (11)

In discussing species migration, Matthew rejects the prevailing theory that land bridges once existed to link continents: "The numerous hypothetical land bridges in temperate tropical and southern regions, connecting continents now separated by deep oceans, which have been advocated by various authors, are improbable and unnecessary to explain geographic distribution." (3) *Climate and Evolution* thus offers a thorough discussion of geographic distribution, addressing animal dispersal patterns on a species-by-species basis. (Bowler 1993; Matthew 1939)

See also Climate Changes; Evolution; Geological Research; Matthew, William Diller.

Climate Changes

The issue of global climate has attracted the attention of scientists throughout history. Ancient scholars such as the Roman philosopher Lucretius wrote about weather phenomena like thunder and lightning. Others speculated on the connection between weather and geology. In 1837 Swiss naturalist and geologist Louis Agassiz was the first to suggest that the earth once experienced an ice age that covered it with glaciers.

Writings on climate change, as opposed to merely climate, were often based on the experiences of early explorers, who first noted the relationship between weather changes and geography. One such author was German naturalist Johann Reinhold Forster. Forster traveled with British explorer Captain James Cook, and in his 1778 book, *Observations Made During a Voyage Round the World,* he reported on climate changes he witnessed while venturing from frigid to tropical zones. More importantly, he discussed the impacts of climate on the types and numbers of plant and animal species in a given region.

Forster was one of the first to theorize that climate affects the development of living things; the idea that evolution is related to environment thus grew over the years. During the 1800s many books on evolution, including the works of Charles Darwin, discussed evolution partially in terms of the environment, and in 1914 paleontologist William Diller Matthew thoroughly explored the subject in *Climate and Evolution.* Matthew supported the idea that "the modification of a race is due to the changes in its environment." (Matthew 1939, 11)

Discussions over climate shifted focus during the mid-1900s, however, as many scientists became concerned more with the overall health of the planet. Those in the environmental movement increasingly supported the theory of global warming, which holds that carbon monoxide emissions and other air pollutants cause a "greenhouse effect," increasing the planet's surface temperature. Many scientists suggest that deforestation also causes global warming and predict dramatic climate changes in the future. The concept of global warming has been well covered in the environmental literature, most notably in Stephen Schneider's *Global Warming* and Dean Edwin Abrahamson's *The Challenge of Global Warming.* Global warming is also frequently mentioned in books that warn of a future environmental apocalypse, such as Carl Sagan's *A Path Where No Man Thought,* Richard Leakey's *The Sixth Extinction,* Paul and Anne Ehrlich's *The Stork and the Plow,* and Bill McKibben's *The End of Nature.* For antienvironmentalist arguments against the concept of global warming, see Ronald Bailey's *Eco-Scam.*

See also Abrahamson, Dean Edwin; Agassiz, (Jean) Louis (Rodolphe); Bailey, Ronald; *Challenge of Global Warming, The; Climate and Evolution;* Darwin, Charles Robert; *Eco-Scam;* Ehrlich, Paul and Anne; *End of Nature, The;* Environmental Apocalypse; Evolution; Forster, Johann Reingold; *Global Warming;* Leakey, Richard; Lucretius; Matthew, William Diller; McKibben, Bill; *Observations Made During a Voyage Round the World; Path Where No Man Thought, A;* Sagan, Carl; Schneider, Stephen H.; *Sixth Extinction, The.*

Closing Circle, The

Published in 1971, *The Closing Circle* was one of the first books to discuss the relationship between technological progress and environmental destruction. Its author, scientist and environmentalist Barry Commoner, outlines the work as follows:

It begins with the ecosphere, the setting in which civilization has done its great—and terrible—deeds. Then it moves to a description of some of the damage we have done to the ecosphere—to the air, the water, the soil. However, by now such horror stories of environmental destruction are familiar, even tiresome. Much less clear is what we need to learn from them, and so I have chosen less to shed tears for our past mistakes than to try to understand them. . . . I trace the environmental crisis from its overt manifestations in the ecosphere to the ecological stresses which they reflect, to the faults in productive technology—and in its scientific background—that generate these stresses, and finally to the economic, social, and political forces which have driven us down this self-destructive course. All this in the hope—and expectation—that once we understand

the origins of the environmental crisis, we can begin to manage the huge undertaking of surviving it. (Commoner 1971, 13)

To this end, Commoner urges society to re-examine its dependence on technology. He believes that "the environmental crisis is somber evidence of an insidious fraud hidden in the vaunted productivity and wealth of modern, technology based society." He continues: "This wealth has been gained by rapid short-term exploitation of the environmental system, but it has blindly accumulated a debt to nature (in the form of environmental destruction in developing countries and of population pressure in developing ones)—a debt so large and so pervasive that in the next generation it may, if unpaid, wipe out most of the wealth it has gained us." (295) Commoner also suggests that changes in technology will occur only if industry is no longer controlled by private corporations.

Commoner argues that the environmental crisis "is not the product of man's *biological* capabilities . . . but of his *social* actions." (299) He therefore suggests that the way to resolve this crisis is to promote social reform. He calls for "sweeping social change":

Human beings have broken out of the circle of life, driven not by biological need, but by the social organization which they have devised to "conquer" nature: means of gaining wealth that are governed by requirements conflicting with those which govern nature. The end result is the environmental crisis, a crisis of survival. . . . [T]o survive, we must close the circle. We must learn how to restore to nature the wealth that we borrow from it. (300)

In *A Fierce Green Fire,* Philip Shabecoff explains that Commoner's call for social change separated him from other environmentalists of the period:

Commoner's insistence that socialism . . . was the road to ecological salvation opened a wide gulf between him and the

Environmental activist Barry Commoner speaks to protestors outside the Exxon stockholder meeting about the Exxon Valdez *oil spill, May 18, 1989 (Reuters/Ray Stubblebine/Archive Photos)*

mainstream national environmental groups, to whom he was a perpetual gadfly. For his part, Commoner was convinced that the established environmentalists were only nibbling at the edges of the problem rather than working at its roots. He had even less respect for the efforts of the federal, state, and local regulatory agencies to address the toxification of the environment. (Shabecoff 1993, 99)

Yet Shabecoff considers *The Closing Circle* to be one of the most important books of the environmental movement. He says: "*The Closing Circle,* along with [Commoner's] other writings and many lecturers and often acerbic speeches, did as much to awaken the country to the rapidly worsening environmental crisis as any other effort by a contemporary writer or scientist—save Rachel Carson. Across the country there are many men and women who will recall that they first began to march in the environmental crusade when they heard the sharp tattoo of Barry Commoner's drum." (300) (Commoner 1971; Glotfelty and Fromm 1996; Shabecoff 1993)

See also Carson, Rachel Louise; Commoner, Barry; Environmental Movement; Social Ecology.

Club of Rome, The
Formed in 1968, this group of influential scientists and businessmen gained notoriety throughout the environmental community when, in 1972, it published *The Limits to Growth.* Using mathematical models developed at the Massachusetts Institute of Technology, *The Limits to Growth* presents the idea that as a result of overpopulation the earth is running out of natural resources.

According to Clive Ponting in *A Green History of the World:* "The computer models on which the study was based, and the assumption of continued exponential growth in production, have proved to be unreliable." (Ponting 1991, p. 402) Nonetheless, the group's theories regarding the relationship between population growth and environmental depletion gained widespread recognition, earning the Club of Rome an important place within the American environmental movement. Today the group continues to meet and discuss environmental issues as they relate to natural resources, climate, and demography. It continues to publish books on these issues. (Ponting 1991; Shabecoff 1993)

See also Climate Changes; Environmental Groups; Environmental Movement; Human Ecology; *Limits to Growth, The.*

Coal Question, The
The Coal Question (1865), written by British economist William Stanley Jevons, drew attention to energy problems during the nineteenth century. At that time, England was dependent on coal. As Jevons explains:

Day by day it becomes more evident that the Coal we happily possess in excellent quality and abundance is the mainspring of modern material civilization. As the source of fire, it is the source at once of mechanical motion and of chemical change. Accordingly it is the chief agent in almost every improvement or discovery in the arts which the present age brings force. It is to us indispensable for domestic purposes. . . . And as the source especially of steam and iron, coal is all powerful. This age has been called the Iron Age, and it is true that iron is the material of most great novelties. . . . But coal alone can command in sufficient abundance either the iron or the steam; and coal, therefore, commands this age—the Age of Coal. (Jevons 1906, 1–2)

Jevons estimated that coal, a nonrenewable natural resource, would eventually run out given the current rates of coal consumption and population growth. Geologists had already warned that new sources of coal were becoming scarce, and after *The Coal Question* came off the press the British government grew concerned as well. It appointed two royal commissions, one in 1866 and another in 1901, to examine the problem. Both commissions decided that Jevons's calculations were incorrect. As Peter J. Bowler (1992) explains in *The Norton History of the Environmental Sciences:*

Jevons used exaggerated estimates of the rate at which consumption would increase in the future, and Royal Commissions . . . dismissed his arguments as alarmist. The supply of coal seemed so vast that no one was willing to concede the possibility of exhaustion in the near future, and in the

An unreclaimed coal strip mine in Garrett County, near Westernport, Maryland (NASA)

twentieth century oil began to offer a new source of energy that the scientists and engineers of Jevons' time had not anticipated. As yet, no one was prepared to worry about what might happen in the *distant* future. For all the warnings of the conservationists, the late nineteenth and early twentieth centuries were a period of unparalleled expansion in the consumption of resources. (Bowler 1993, 323)

Nonetheless, *The Coal Question* brought Jevons public recognition, and his subsequent works on economic theory were given more credibility. (Bowler 1993; Jevons 1906)

See also Air Pollution; Conservationism; Jevons, William Stanley.

Coleridge, Samuel Taylor

Poet, philosopher, and literary and social critic, Englishman Samuel Taylor Coleridge produced an extensive body of work, much of it expressing a deep respect for nature. In one of his most widely known poems, "The Rime of the Ancient Mariner," a sailor who kills an albatross suffers physical and mental torment for violating the natural world.

Coleridge also wrote about his love of nature in journals published posthumously. In one prose collection (*Animae Poetae*, 1895), he says:

The love of nature is ever returned double to us, not only the delighter in our delight, but by linking our sweetest, but of themselves perishable feelings to distinct and vivid images, which we ourselves, at times, and which a thousand casual recollections, recall to our memory. She is the preserver, the treasurer of our joys. Even in sickness and nervous diseases, she has peopled our imagination with lovely forms which have sometimes overpowered the inward pain and brought with them their odd sensations. (Finch and Elder 1990, 98)

Coleridge was born on October 21, 1772, in Ottery St. Mary, Devonshire, England, where his father was a school headmaster. Upon his father's death in 1781, Coleridge was sent to school in London. He attended Cambridge University but left twice, first to join the dragoons and then, after being returned to school by his brothers, to promote a new community based on revolutionary social concepts that Coleridge developed with poet Robert Southey. When Southey abandoned the idea, Coleridge did as well. He turned to writing, encouraged by friend and poet William Wordsworth.

Coleridge's first poetry collection, *Lyrical Ballads,* was published in 1798. He continued to write poetry over the next few years, despite poor health, a deteriorating marriage, difficulties with a mistress, and a growing opium addiction. During 1809–1810 he published a periodical, *The Friend,* and during 1811–1812 he gave a series of lectures on literature. In 1813 his play *Remorse* was performed for the first time; another drama, *Zapolya,* was published in 1817. That same year, Coleridge produced a collection of poems, *Sibylline Leaves,* and a complex work entitled *Biographia Literaria,* part autobiography, part philosophical discussion, and part criticism of Wordsworth's poems. In 1824 Coleridge was elected to the Royal Society of Literature. He died on July 25, 1834.

See also Wordsworth, William.

Commoner, Barry

During the early environmental movement, biologist Barry Commoner raised public awareness of the environmental consequences of technological growth. Born in Brooklyn, New York, on May 28, 1917, he joined the faculty of Washington University in St. Louis, Missouri, in 1947. He remained for 34 years as a specialist in cellular physiology, studying viral function and performing cellular research related to cancer growth.

During the early 1950s Commoner grew concerned that above-ground nuclear testing was threatening human health. Consequently, he founded the St. Louis Committee for Nuclear Information, a group of scientists and civic leaders that promoted studies on the dangers of nuclear radiation and encouraged the passage of the Nuclear Test Ban Treaty in 1963. In 1966 Commoner established the Center for Biology of Natural Systems (CBNS), which studies the relationship between human beings and their environment. Commoner has written extensively on environmental issues; his books include *The Closing Circle: Nature, Man, and Technology* (1971), *The Politics of Energy* (1979), and *Making Peace with the Planet* (1993). He is currently a professor at Queens College in New York and continues to support CBNS. (Commoner 1971; Dashefsky 1993; Glotfelty and Fromm 1996; Shabecoff 1993)

See also *Closing Circle, The;* Environmental Movement; Human Ecology; Nuclear Energy; Social Ecology.

Comstock, Anna Botsford

Anna Botsford Comstock was one of the foremost female naturalists of the early 20th century. She was part of a trend that Polly Welts Kaufman, in *National Parks and the Woman's Voice,* labeled the "nature study movement," which "first offered wide-scale employment to women naturalists as nature study teachers in public schools." (Kaufman 1996, 68) Kaufman calls Comstock "the most widely-recognized leader" of this movement. (68)

Comstock was born on September 1, 1854, in Otto, New York. After marrying an entomologist in 1878, she began drawing illustrations of insects. In 1895 she developed her first nature-study course and began working with the American Nature Study Society and American Nature Association to promote nature education in public schools. In 1897 she and her husband collaborated on a book, *Insect Life.* Their *Ways of the Six-Footed* appeared in 1903. Comstock was the sole author of her most famous work, *Handbook of Nature Study* (1911). Six years later she became editor of *Nature-Study Review,* a position she held until 1923. Comstock died on August 24, 1930, in Ithaca, New York. (Kaufman 1996)

See also *Handbook of Nature Study.*

Confessions of an Eco-Warrior

Confessions of an Eco-Warrior (1991) is one of the most important works on radical environmentalism. Its author, Dave Foreman, was a leader of the radical environmental movement, and *Confessions* describes his participation therein. Foreman cofounded the environmental group Earth First!, which uses ecological sabotage (known as "ecotage" or "monkeywrenching") and other illegal tactics to stop wilderness destruction. His book was an attempt to justify ecotage as a way to fight antienvironmentalism. However, when the book was published, a majority of Americans disapproved of ecotage, and members of mainstream environmental groups feared that *Confessions of an Eco-Warrior* would give all environmentalists a bad reputation.

Foreman begins his work by explaining how he came to establish Earth First!. He also discusses a variety of wilderness-related environmental problems and defends his beliefs regarding monkeywrenching. Although Foreman's critics insist that monkeywrenching is a violent activity (sabotaged saws and trees have injured loggers), he says: "Contrary to the demagogues' claims, no one has been injured in any monkeywrenching operation carried out by preservationists." (Foreman 1991, 124) Moreover, he states:

> The true ecoterrorists are the planet-despoilers: Those in the Forest Service and the timber industry who are annihilating thousand-year-old forests for paper bags and picnic tables. Ranchers and employees of the Department of Agriculture's Animal Damage Control unit who have exterminated predators . . . and continue to slaughter them in their remnant ranges. The calculator-rational engineers and pork-barrel politicians who want to plug every free-flowing river with dams. The thrill-seeking dirt bikers who terrify wildlife and scar delicate watersheds with mindless play. Japanese and Icelandic whalers who are hounding the last great whales to the ends of the Earth, despite international agreements against whaling.

The heads of Exxon and other giant oil companies who cut back on safety measures to save a few pennies and thereby cause disasters like the Prince William Sound oil-tanker wreck. . . . The list of ecoterrorists is endless—but it does not include the brave and conscientious individuals who are defending threatened wild areas by placing a monkeywrench into the gears of the machine. (124–125)

Foreman argues that radical environmentalism is more effective than conservative environmentalism, because "many of the people who work for environmental groups today are not conservationists but technicians." (201) In addition, "many people working for environmental groups today have a higher loyalty to the political process than to conservation." (203) Foreman criticizes many aspects of conventional environmentalism. He also expresses pride in Earth First!'s accomplishments.

However, in his conclusion, Foreman admits that he is no longer a part of Earth First!, saying that he disassociated himself from the group largely because of "external harassment by the FBI." (219) In her book on Earth First!, entitled *Coyotes and Town Dogs: Earth First! and the Environmental Movement,* journalist Susan Zakin explains that Foreman was arrested for conspiring to destroy nuclear power plants and that as part of a plea bargain he agreed to stop espousing monkeywrenching. Nonetheless, Foreman says that Earth First! "cannot be stamped out even if it ceases to exist as a distinct entity," because there will always be "gutsy, never-say-die tree climbers and bulldozer blockaders; there will continue to be biocentric, activist biologists working for other species; there will be increasing numbers of stronger, bolder, less compromising mainstream activists; and there will be even more anonymous ecodefenders messing around with big yellow machines in the dark of the new moon." (220)

Foreman's name continues to be associated with radical environmentalism, and his writings are often cited by antienvironmentalists discussing violence within the movement. (Foreman 1991; Zakin 1993)

> **See also** Abbey, Edward; *Coyotes and Town Dogs;* Environmental Activism; Environmental Groups; Environmental Movement; Environmental Politics; Foreman, Dave; *Monkey Wrench Gang, The;* Zakin, Susan.

Conservationism

In general terms, conservationism advocates the "wise use" of natural resources, which typically include fossil fuels, minerals, game animals, timber, and similar commodities; in a larger sense, natural resources can also include entire habitats such as forests, wilderness areas, lakes, even oceans. In either case, conservationists argue that natural resources must be carefully managed in order to prevent their permanent destruction.

The earliest conservationists were farmers, who were concerned with preventing soil erosion and maximizing crop yield. Ancient writings, including the Bible, advocate the wise use of agricultural land, yet abuses continued down through the ages. As early as 347 B.C. the Greek philosopher Plato wrote of soil erosion on Greek hillsides due to poor agricultural practices and forest decimation.

As the human population increased, forests were destroyed to clear agricultural land and to provide wood for building, heating, and cooking. This led European experts like John Evelyn, who wrote during the 17th century, to promote better forest management. During the 19th century the issue of forest conservation was instrumental in triggering the American conservation movement, which inspired the establishment of the National Park System and prompted many new laws devoted to preserving wilderness areas. The conservation movement increases general awareness of conservation issues, primarily through literature. Authors such as John Muir, Gifford Pinchot, George Perkins Marsh, William O. Douglas, John Burroughs, and John James Audubon wrote about the need to protect the earth's plants and animals for future use and enjoyment.

At the time, conservationists viewed wilderness as separate from humankind, something that needed to be preserved for its own sake. During the early 1900s that attitude began to change as conservationists increasingly spoke of humankind's interconnectedness with nature. The work of Aldo Leopold illustrates this shift. In 1933 he wrote a textbook on game management; in 1948 he wrote a book on the personal enjoyment of wilderness areas and their importance to human existence. By the 1950s conservationists had begun to think more deeply about the relationship between people and nature, pondering the effects environmental destruction might have for human health. Authors like Rachel Carson and Murray Bookchin warned that pesticides and other pollutants might well threaten the existence of humankind. This new focus of conservationism—that preserving the environment was necessary to the survival of human beings—marked the beginning of the environmental movement. (Netzley 1998)

> **See also** Agriculture; Audubon, John James; Bookchin, Murray; Burroughs, John; Carson, Rachel Louise; Douglas, William O.; Environmental Movement; Evelyn, John; Forest Management; Habitat Protection; Leopold, Aldo; Muir, John; Pesticides and Chemicals; Pinchot, Gifford; Plato.

Continuous Harmony, A

Published in 1972, *A Continuous Harmony* is a collection of essays on agriculture and ecology. The author, noted conservationist Wendell Berry, has been an outspoken supporter of simple living as a way to solve environmental problems; *A Continuous Harmony* was one of his earliest expressions of that philosophy. It argues against materialism and advocates a return to a more primitive lifestyle:

> If you are concerned about air pollution, help push for government controls, but drive your car less, use less fuel in your home. If you are worried about the damming of wilderness rivers, . . . write to the government, but turn off the lights you're not using, don't install an air conditioner, don't be a sucker for electrical

gadgets, don't waste water. In other words, if you are fearful of the destruction of the environment, then learn to quit being an environmental parasite. We all are, in one way or another, and the remedies are not always obvious, though they certainly will always be difficult. They require a new kind of life—harder, more laborious, poorer in luxuries and gadgets, but also, I am certain, richer in meaning and more abundant in real pleasure. To have a healthy environment, we will also have to give up things we like; we may even have to give up things we have come to think of as necessities. (Berry 1972, 80–83)

Berry himself practiced simple living, going so far as to use primitive agricultural tools on his farmland, and he believes that the earth would benefit if others did the same: "Odd as I am sure it will appear to some, I can think of no better form of personal involvement in the cure of the environment than that of gardening." (Berry 82) He calls for people to reconsider their relationship to the land, explaining:

A person who undertakes to grow a garden at home, by practices that will preserve rather than exploit the economy of the soil, has set his mind decisively against what is wrong with us. He is helping himself in a way that dignifies him and that is rich in meaning and pleasure. But he is doing something else that is more important: he is making vital contact with the soil and the weather on which his life depends. He will no longer look upon rain as an impediment of traffic, or upon the sun as a holiday decoration. And his sense of man's dependence on the world will have grown precise enough, one would hope, to be clarifying and useful.

Berry believes that deepening people's connection to the land will also solve a variety of global problems. He continues:

What I am saying is that if we apply our minds directly and competently to the needs of the earth, then we will have begun to make fundamental and necessary changes in our minds. We will begin to understand and to mistrust *and to change* our wasteful economy, which markets not just the produce of the earth, but also the earth's ability to produce. We will see that beauty and utility are alike dependent upon the health of the world. But we will also see through the fads and the fashions of protest. We will see that war and oppression and pollution are not separate issues, but are aspects of the same issue.

Berry further suggests that this change of attititude has a spiritual quality:

But the change of mind I am talking about involves not just a change of knowledge, but also a change of attitude toward our essential ignorance, a change in our bearing in the face of mystery. The principle of ecology, if we will take it to heart, should keep us aware that our lives depend upon other lives and upon processes and energies in an interlocking system that, though we can destroy it, we can neither fully understand nor fully control. And our great dangerousness is that, locked in our selfish and myopic economics, we have been willing to change or destroy far beyond our power to understand. We are not humble or reverent enough. (Berry 1972, 83–85)

Berry also examines the importance of agriculture throughout history. He reports that "intensive, organic agriculture kept the farms of the Orient thriving for thousands of years, whereas extensive—which is to say, exploitive or extractive—agriculture has critically reduced the fertility of American farmlands in a few centuries or even a few decades." (83) In addition, he says that "we appear to be facing the possibility of widespread famine" and suggests that personal gardens will be the key to a family's survival in the future. (83–84) In this respect Berry's work is similar to that of overpopulation experts Paul and Anne Ehrlich, who also warn about the possibility of famine in the context of agriculture and the environment. (Berry 1972)

See also Agriculture; Berry, Wendell; Ehrlich, Paul and Anne; Simple Living Movement.

Control of Nature, The

The Control of Nature (1989) by journalist John McPhee represents an example of modern naturalist writing. Whereas early naturalists often analyzed the environment in terms of its beauty and restorative effect for humans, contemporary writers often address the struggle to live in society without causing the environment too much harm. McPhee is the author of many such books. In The Control of Nature, he reports several cases of people trying to contain natural forces, for example, attempts to redirect rivers, cool lava, prevent landslides, and suppress the growth of vegetation and naturally caused wildfires. For example, he explains that mountain erosion in Los Angeles, California, is causing soil debris to flow into people's homes:

At least one family has experienced so many debris flows coming through their back yard that they long ago installed over-head doors in the rear end of their built-in garage. To guide the flows, they put deflection walls in their back yard. Now when the boulders come they open both ends of their garage, and the debris goes through to the street. (McPhee 1989, p. 189)

Although The Control of Nature is McPhee's first-person account of his investigations into such incidents, the author offers little personal commentary. He focuses on facts, and his book provides no introduction or conclusion. (McPhee 1989)

See also Environmental Politics; Habitat Protection; McPhee, John.

Cousteau, Jacques-Yves

Ocean explorer Jacques-Yves Cousteau did a great deal to popularize oceanography. He wrote several books on ocean research and exploration, including The Silent World (1953), The Living Sea (1963), and Jacques Cousteau: The Ocean World (1985). Even more significant were his many movies and television programs, which introduced an entire generation to ocean conservation issues. His popular television series, The Undersea World of Jacques Cousteau, began in 1968 and won many awards.

Jacques Cousteau in The Cousteau Odyssey (Photofest)

Cousteau was born in Saint-Andre-de-Cubzac, France, on June 11, 1910; he lived in New York for two years as a child. During the early 1930s he joined the French Navy, and during World War II he began developing the Aqua-Lung, a breathing device that enabled divers to swim underwater for long periods; it became available to the public in 1946. In 1948 Cousteau advanced to the rank of captain, but two years later he left naval service and became president of the French Oceanographic Campaigns. In that capacity he commanded *Calypso,* a converted minesweeper that achieved recognition in its own right thanks to Cousteau's work.

Cousteau headed many ocean research projects and helped develop new techniques in underwater photography, particularly for television. He also began experimenting with underwater habitats for people. During the 1970s he became increasingly involved in environmentalism. In 1974 he founded the Cousteau Society, dedicated to marine conservation; often he spoke against ocean dumping and coral reef destruction. Cousteau died on June 25, 1997. (Munson 1989)

See also *Living Sea, The.*

Coyotes and Town Dogs

Susan Zakin's *Coyotes and Town Dogs: Earth First! and the Environmental Movement* (1993) traces the development of the radical environmental group Earth First! and is considered one of the most thorough books on America's radical environmental movement. Zakin interviewed many of the group's early participants, including cofounder Dave Foreman; she includes biographical as well as historical information.

Zakin reports that Earth First! began in 1980, inspired by environmentalist Edward Abbey's 1975 novel, *The Monkey Wrench Gang.* Abbey's monkeywrenchers used ecological sabotage, or ecotage, to thwart wilderness development. Earth First! adopted the same tactics (which included burning bulldozers and destroying survey stakes), using them to gain media attention for environmental causes. According to Zakin:

By the late 1980s, the self-proclaimed anarchist "non-organization" boasted more than five thousand subscribers to its newspaper, the closest thing the group had to a membership roster. . . . Taking the term *photo opportunity* to lengths previously unknown in the environmental movement, they were doing everything from bicycle-locking their necks to bulldozers . . . to parading down Wall Street dressed as spotted owls. And all around the country, there were quiet acts of sabotage. (Zakin 1993, 8)

Zakin reveals the inner workings of the group and follows its story until Foreman's exodus from Earth First! in 1991. She explains that he agreed to disassociate himself from monkeywrenching as part of a plea bargain with the FBI, which had arrested him for conspiring to destroy nuclear power plants. Other founding members subsequently left the group as well. However, Zakin adds that the "lone, wild wolves of environmentalism were not about to be deterred by a plea bargain or even by the breakup of the old Earth First!." (442) She reports that after a short period of turmoil the group experienced a revival. Earth First! and its monkeywrenching activities continue today. (Zakin 1993)

See also Environmental Activism; Environmental Groups; Environmental Politics; Foreman, Dave; Zakin, Susan.

Crèvecoeur, J. Hector St. John

French naturalist J. Hector St. John Crèvecoeur, the pseudonym of Michel-Guillaume-Jean de Crèvecoeur, has been called the 18th-century Thoreau because of his essays about life in rural America. He published 12 essays in 1782 as *Letters from an American Farmer.* Born on January 31, 1735, in Caen, France, de Crèvecoeur spent some time in Canada before becoming a surveyor in America in 1759. In 1764 he became a naturalized U.S. citizen, living first in Ohio and then in New York, and in 1769 he married. He and his wife, who eventually had three children, settled on a farm in Orange County, New

York, where de Crèvecoeur wrote his essays on rural life.

During the American Revolution, de Crèvecoeur fled to Europe with his oldest son, leaving his wife and two other children behind. He ended up in London. There he published *Letters,* and its widespread success brought him a change in fortune. He not only received the patronage of a well-known naturalist, the Comte de Buffon, but also earned an appointment as a French consul to the United States. He returned to America in 1784, only to find that his wife had died and his house had been destroyed in the war. However, his children had survived; after tracking them down he remained in America for six years, working as a consul and writing about agriculture.

By this time de Crèvecoeur had added to *Letters;* he republished the work in two volumes in 1784. He published another book, *Travels in Upper Pennsylvania and New York,* in 1801. De Crèvecoeur died in Sarcelles, France, on November 12, 1813. More than a century later, someone discovered additional essays in a French attic. They were published in 1925 as *Sketches of Eighteenth Century America, or More Letters from an American Farmer.* (de Crèvecoeur 1957)

See also Buffon, Georges Louis Leclerc, Comte de; *Letters from an American Farmer;* Thoreau, Henry David.

Crichton, Michael

Michael Crichton is the author of the 1990 novel *Jurassic Park,* the most popular modern treatment of the subject of evolution. His work typifies the way contemporary authors address the environmental sciences, that is, by suggesting that nature is too easily exploited for monetary gain, and warning that technology can lead to the destruction of the natural world.

Crichton was born in Chicago on October 23, 1942. He attended Harvard University intending to become a writer, but after receiving poor grades in his English classes he switched his major to anthropology and eventually entered Harvard Medical School. He received his medical degree in 1969. By this time, he

was already a successful author, having sold his first novel while a student. In addition to *Jurassic Park,* his novels include *The Andromeda Strain* (1969), *The Terminal Man* (1972), *The Great Train Robbery* (1972), *Congo* (1980), *Sphere* (1987), *Rising Sun* (1992), and *The Lost World* (1995). (Greenberg 1997)

See also Evolution; *Jurassic Park.*

Cuvier, Georges

Georges-Leopold-Cretien-Frederic-Dagobert Cuvier, or Baron Cuvier, was the first scientist to compare the anatomical structure of an animal's organs and to recognize that organ function was related to the environment in which the animal lived. He used this material to develop his own species classification system that took into account each animal's physical structure. In addition, he conducted detailed studies of fossils and is credited with founding the science of paleontology.

Cuvier was born on August 23, 1769, in Montbeliard, France. From 1784 to 1788 he studied science in Germany, and in 1789 he became a tutor. As a hobby he began to study marine animals. He sent information about his work to the Museum of Natural History in Paris, and in 1795 the museum directors asked him to join the staff. He subsequently began researching mammal anatomy.

In 1797 Cuvier published some of his results as *Tableau elementaire de l'histoire naturelle des animaux* (Elementary Survey of the Natural History of Animals). A more thorough discussion of his theories on comparative anatomy appears in his *Leçons d'anatomie comparee* (Lessons on Comparative Anatomy, 1800–1805). As Cuvier continued to study anatomy, he developed his own animal classification system, which he discussed in his *Le Regne animal distribue diapres son organisation* (The Animal Kingdom, Distributed According to Its Organization, 1817). By this time, Cuvier had begun to study fossils, and he realized that many represented animals that had become extinct. He wrote about these fossils in his 1812 essay, *Recherches sur les ossements fossiles de quadrupedes* (Researches on the Bones of Fossil Vertebrates), which was later included in his 1825 book, *Discours sur les revolutions de la surface du globe* (Discourse on the Revolutions of the Globe). This work also discussed the geologic history of the earth.

Many of Cuvier's theories were controversial, and in 1830 he participated in a public debate with a scientist who disagreed with his method of classifying species. Cuvier was also at odds with Jean-Baptiste Lamarck, who believed in evolution, whereas Cuvier did not. Despite such disagreements, Cuvier was one of the most respected scientists of his day. He died in Paris on May 13, 1832. (Spangenburg and Moser 1993)

See also Evolution; Geological Research; Lamarck, Jean-Baptiste; Species Identification and Classification.

D

Dana, James Dwight

James D. Dana was a 19th-century geologist who made important discoveries on the creation of mountains and volcanoes. Three written works, *A System of Mineralogy* (1837), *Manual of Geology* (1862), and *A Text-book of Geology* (1864), were considered classics by contemporaries in the field of geology.

Dana was born on February 12, 1813, in Utica, New York. He graduated from Yale in 1833 and became a teacher, first of mathematics and later of chemistry and mineralogy. He also went on a research expedition to the South Seas from 1838 to 1842. When he returned, he developed a new classification system for minerals that relied on chemistry and physics. His work brought recognition, and he was asked to become a regular contributor to *American Journal of Science,* which subsequently published much of his work in geology.

In 1859 Dana became a professor of natural history at Yale, but he found the position too stressful. He retreated to his studies and began to consider evolutionary theory as well as geology. He eventually accepted Charles Darwin's position on evolution and included information about it in later editions of his *Manual of Mineralogy.* Dana died in New Haven, Connecticut, on April 14, 1895. (Bowler 1993)

See also Evolution; Geological Research.

Darwin, Charles Robert

Born in Shrewsbury, England, on February 19, 1809, Charles Robert Darwin developed one of the most important theories in environmental science. He proposed that animal species evolve through a process called "natural selection," in which traits that enhance an individual animal's chances for survival are passed on to subsequent generations and gradually become dominant in a population.

Darwin was the son of a prominent physician. His grandfather, Erasmus Darwin, also a physician, was the author of his own work on animal species (*Zoonomia, or the Laws of Organic Life,* 1794–1796). Charles Darwin was therefore exposed to the sciences as a young man, and at age 16 he attended the University of Edinburgh to study medicine. Much to his family's dismay, he quickly decided he did not want to be a physician after all, and in 1827 he left Edinburgh to study divinity at the University of Cambridge. There he met several scientists who encouraged him to pursue his passion for science. Consequently, in 1831, after reading Alexander von Humboldt's writings on scientific exploration, he accepted an unpaid position as a naturalist on an expedition to South America and the Pacific Islands.

Charles Darwin (Library of Congress)

During his five-year voyage on HMS *Beagle,* Darwin collected scientific specimens and kept careful records of his observations. He also read Charles Lyell's *Principles of Geology,* which led him to accept the idea that the earth changed over time through slow geologic processes rather than sudden events. This concept later influenced his views on species evolution. Darwin wrote and edited several books based on his *Beagle* experience, including *The Voyage of the Beagle* (1839), *Journal of Researches into the Geology and Natural History of the Various Countries Visited by H.M.S. Beagle* (1839), and *Zoology of the Voyage of H.M.S. Beagle* (1839–1843).

After returning home from his expedition, Darwin made detailed notes on the specimens he had gathered and began to formulate theories regarding the variations he discovered about individual species. In this he was influenced by Thomas Malthus's *An Essay on the Principle of Population,* which discusses species' intense competition for food. The concept led Darwin to conclude that only the fittest individuals within a species would survive to pass on its traits to the next generation.

However, he was hesitant to publish his ideas on the subject. Then, in June 1858 he read a paper by naturalist Alfred Russel Wallace that presented views similar to his own. Through the help of friends, he contacted Wallace, and the two collaborated on a paper that in July 1858 was presented to the Linnean Society of London, a scientific group.

The following year Darwin published a more thorough discussion of his theories. Entitled *On the Origin of Species by Means of Natural Selection, or the Preservation of Favoured Races in the Struggle for Life,* it was well received by most scientists and the general public but was opposed by the religious community. The clergy argued that evolutionary theory was sacrilegious, and the resulting controversy inspired heated public debate, which continues to this day.

Meanwhile, Darwin kept at his writing on evolution. In 1868 he published *The Variation of Animals and Plants Under Domestication,* which discusses heredity and animal husbandry, and in 1871 he published *The Descent of Man, and Selection in Relation to Sex,* which focuses on human evolution. The latter was as controversial as *Origin of Species,* primarily because it emphasized man's connection to apes. Darwin then turned his attention to human emotion and decided that animals display evidence of experiencing emotion as well. He expressed this view in *The Expression of the Emotions in Man and Animals* (1872).

In later years Darwin wrote several books on botany, applying his evolutionary theories to the study of plants and flowers. He also raised a large family. Married to his wealthy first cousin in 1839, he produced 10 children in all, although two died as infants and one at age 10. Three of his five sons became well-known scientists in their own right; another became a prominent engineer. The Darwin children grew up surrounded by scientific experiments when their father was at home; otherwise he was traveling through England and abroad to lecture on his theories. However, he had experienced ill health off and on since returning from the South America expedition;

he lived to the age of 73, dying on April 19, 1882. (Bowler 1996; Mayr and Mayr 1985; Ridley 1996)

See also Darwin, Erasmus; *Descent of Man, The; Essay on the Principle of Population, An;* Evolution; Lyell, Charles; Malthus, Thomas Robert; *Origin of Species, The; Principles of Geology; Voyage of the Beagle, The; Zoonomia.*

Darwin, Erasmus

Grandfather of evolutionary theorist Charles Darwin, Erasmus Darwin was an English physician and poet who developed his own theory about how life evolved. In *Zoonomia, or the Laws of Organic Life* (1794–1796), he expressed the views that individual organisms adapted to a changing environment with deliberate purpose and that each generation built upon the advances of the last. A similar view was later expressed by French naturalist Jean Baptiste Lamarck in *Philosophie zoologique* (1809).

Erasmus Darwin was born in Nottinghamshire, England, on December 12, 1731, and educated at both Cambridge and Edinburgh. After graduating in 1756 he opened a medical practice in Lichfield, England, where he developed an excellent reputation and made the acquaintance of many prominent men. In 1781 he founded a philosophical society in Derby, England; although he continued to practice medicine, he devoted increasing time to his writing.

In addition to *Zoonomia,* Darwin wrote *A Plan for the Conduct of Female Education in Boarding Schools* (1797), *Phytologia, or the Philosophy of Agriculture and Gardening* (1800), and other prose works. However, during his lifetime he was best known for his verse, in which he often presented opinions and scientific theories. His works of poetry include *The Botanic Garden* (1794–1795) and *The Temple of Nature, or the Origin of Society* (1803). Darwin died in Derby on April 18, 1802. (Hassler 1973)

See also Agriculture; Darwin, Charles Robert; Evolution; Lamarck, Jean-Baptiste; Species Identification and Classification; *Zoonomia.*

Day of the Triffids

John Wyndham's *Day of the Triffids* (1951) reflects the impact that modern environmentalism had on fiction writing during the 1950s. The novel concerns a scientifically created new plant species—the triffid; its seeds are accidentally released into the air when a spy's airplane is shot down. When triffids start to grow, they appear as a common garden weed. However, they soon display unusual traits. When mature, they can pull their roots from the ground and "walk," and they have stinging tentacles that kill human beings. Triffids are carnivorous—and humans are their preferred food.

Scientists are able to control these strange plants until a cosmic light show suddenly renders most people in the world blind. The triffids quickly take advantage and threaten to become the dominant species on earth. The main character of the novel, a biologist-biochemist named Bill Masen, fights the triffid advance. He and wife Josella retain their sight, and in the end they join an island colony dedicated to researching and destroying triffids.

In this way, *Day of the Triffids* suggests that even though science caused the natural order of the world to become unbalanced, science will once again balance it. The work also depicts man's alienation from nature, using metaphors to emphasize the risks of being blinded to environmental problems. At one point, Bill realizes just how far from nature modern man has gone. A city-dweller now thrown into a primitive world, he says:

I was endeavouring to learn the a-b-c of farming. It is not the kind of thing that is easily learnt from books. For one thing, it had never occurred to any writer on the subject that any potential farmer could be starting from absolute zero. I found, therefore, that all works began, as it were, in the middle, taking for granted both a basis and a vocabulary that I did not have. My specialized biological knowledge was all but useless to me in the face of practical problems. Much of the theory called for materials and substances which were either unavailable to me, or unrecognizable by me if I could find them. I began to see quite soon that by the time I had dismissed the things that would shortly be unprocurable such as chemical fertilizers, imported feeding-stuffs, and all but the simpler kinds of machinery there was going to be much expenditure of sweat for problematical returns. (Wyndham 1964, 168)

Only by reconnecting to the land and understanding its creatures can people survive. (Wyndham 1964)

See also Environmental Fiction; Wyndham, John.

De Animalibus

De Animalibus (On Animals) is one of the earliest books on animal species. As such, it not only expanded human knowledge regarding animal behavior but also formed the basis of future works on the subject. However, *De Animalibus* was not entirely original. Its author, 13th-century German scholar Albertus Magnus, based his writings on those of the ancient Greek philosopher Aristotle, who discussed animal classification and described a variety of species in his *Historia Animalium*. Magnus followed Aristotle's classification scheme, grouping animals according to how they reproduce. But unlike Aristotle, Magnus decided to classify whales and dolphins as fish even though they bear live young. He also included information regarding animal species discovered since Aristotle's time. (Bowler 1993)

See also Albertus Magnus, Saint; Aristotle; *Historia Animalium;* Species Identification and Classification.

De Mineralibus et Rebus Metallicis

De Mineralibus et Rebus Metallicis (On Minerals and Metals) is one of the earliest books on mineralogy. Written during the 13th century by the German scholar Albertus Magnus, it discusses the physical properties of various minerals and metals and supports a 10th-century Persian theory that fossils are mineralized plant and animal remains. However, the book also includes erroneous speculations and non-scientific information. For example, it upholds the theory of the Greek philosopher Aristotle that volcanoes are caused by underground winds and explains how minerals can enhance the practice of magic. (Bowler 1993)

See also Albertus Magnus, Saint; Aristotle; Geological Research.

De re metallica

De re metallica (On Metals) is the greatest work of German physician Georgius Agricola, considered to be the father of mineralogy. Its 12 volumes were published after Agricola's death in 1555 and were immediately acclaimed by scholars. The book mentions the writings of Aristotle and Albertus Magnus, discusses past and present mining practices, and carefully explains subjects related to metallurgy, mineralogy, and geology. It presents many of these subjects not just as individual components of the earth but in terms of how they relate to the environment as a whole. For example, it describes the formation of mountains by discussing their relationship to air, water, and fire, saying:

Hills and mountains are produced by two forces, one of which is the power of water, and the other the strength of the wind. There are three forces which loosen and demolish the mountains, for in this case, to the power of the water and the strength of the wind we must add the fire in the interior of the earth. Now we can plainly see that a great abundance of water produces mountains, for the torrents first of all, wash out the soft earth, next carry away the harder earth, and then roll down the rocks, and thus in a few years they excavate the plains or slopes to a considerable depth; this may be noticed in mountainous regions even by unskilled observers. By such excavation to a great depth through many ages, there rises an immense eminence on each side. When an eminence has thus arisen, the earth rolls down, loosened by constant rain and split away by frost, and the rocks, unless they are exceedingly firm, since their seams are similarly softened by the damp, roll down into the excavations below. This continues until the steep eminence is changed into a slope. (Boynton 1948, 348)

See also Agricola, Georgius; Geological Research; Species Identification and Classification.

De Rerum Natura

De Rerum Natura (On the Nature of Things) is a long poem by the ancient Roman philosopher Lucretius (ca. 95 B.C.–54 B.C.). It is divided into several parts. The first two establish various principles of the atomic universe. The third discusses the atomic structure of the soul. The fourth describes the senses and various other functions of the human body. The fifth addresses the creation of the world and the evolution of life, and the sixth discusses phenomena of the earth and sky, particularly thunder and lightning. The work ends with a description of the plague in Athens.

In *The Environmental Sciences,* Peter J. Bowler suggests that the most important aspect of *De Rerum Natura* (which he refers to as *De Natura Rerum,* translated as "On the Nature of the Universe") lies in its discussion of evolutionary theory. According to Bowler, Lucretius did not believe that God created life but instead thought that animals were spontaneously generated from the earth's soil. Bowler quotes him as saying: "Even now multitudes of [small] animals are formed out of the earth with the aid of showers and the sun's genial warmth. So it is not surprising if more and bigger ones took shape and developed . . . when the earth and ether were young. . . . There was a great superfluity of heat and moisture in the soil. So, whenever a suitable spot occurred, there grew up wombs, clinging to the earth by roots. These, when the time was ripe, were burst open by the maturation of the embryos, rejecting moisture now and struggling for air." (Bowler 1993, 42) In addition, Bowler reports that Lucretius believed the earth would eventually "grow old and die" and "appealed to the evidence of weathering

and erosion to show that the surface of the land was subject to decay." (42) (Bowler 1993; Lucretius 1975; Sikes 1971)

See also Evolution; Lucretius.

De Vegetabilibus et Plantis

De Vegetabilibus et Plantis (On Vegetables and Plants) is one of the earliest books on plant structure and classification. Written in the 13th century by German scholar Albertus Magnus, it added to the body of observations made by earlier scholars, particularly the ancient Greek scholar Theophrastus. (Bowler 1993)

See also Albertus Magnus, Saint; Theophrastus.

Deep Ecology

Published in 1985, *Deep Ecology: Living as If Nature Mattered* was the first North American book on deep ecology, an environment-centered philosophy originated by Norwegian philosopher Arne Naess. The book helped define the deep ecology movement in the United States. Its authors, sociologist Bill Devall and ecophilosopher George Sessions, did not merely report on Naess's work; instead they developed their own interpretation of it.

In the book's introduction, the authors explain that deep ecology is "a way of developing a new balance and harmony between individual, communities and all of nature. It can potentially satisfy our deepest yearnings: faith and trust in our most basic intuitions; courage to take direct action; joyous confidence to dance with sensuous harmonies discovered through the spontaneous, playful intercourse with the rhythm of our bodies, the rhythms of flowing water, changes in the weather and the seasons, and the overall process of life on Earth." (Devall and Sessions 1985, 7)

In this regard, Devall and Sessions talk about spirituality as well as environmental concerns. They state that the only way to become a deep ecologist is to develop the Self, which they explain in Zen terms. They believe that "to study the self is to forget the self" and "to forget the self is to be enlightened by all things." This enlightenment eliminates "the barrier between one's self and others," so that there is no separation between man and nature. (11)

Deep Ecology emphasizes the need to become a part of nature in order to achieve a deeper consciousness: "Spiritual growth, or unfolding, begins when we cease to understand or see ourselves as isolated and narrow competing egos." (67) To accomplish this, Devall and Sessions suggest returning to a more simple lifestyle and rejecting many aspects of modern society. They view primitive societies as being more conducive to "cultivating ecological consciousness." (18)

The authors discuss primitive traditions at length. They also include a great many quotations in their book from spiritual leaders, philosophers, and environmentalists. The latter include Gary Snyder, Murray Bookchin, Paul Ehrlich, John Muir, Aldo Leopold, and Rachel Carson. (Devall and Sessions 1985)

See also Bookchin, Murray; Carson, Rachel Louise; Deep Ecology Movement; Devall, Bill; Ehrlich, Paul and Anne; Leopold, Aldo; Muir, John; Naess, Arne; Sessions, George; Snyder, Gary.

Deep Ecology Movement

The philosophy of deep ecology is based on the concept that humans are not separate from nature but are instead an integral part of it. Out of this concept, deep ecologists have developed a set of precepts for living an ecologically sound life, as well as recommendations for changes in the world's social and political systems. For example, deep ecologists believe that human overpopulation threatens the balance of nature and therefore argue that people should limit reproduction. They also oppose materialism and wastefulness in modern society.

The basic principles of deep ecology were first outlined by Norwegian philosopher Arne Naess in *Ecology, Community, and Lifestyle* (1976). This work was eventually translated into English by David Rothenberg, who also published a book on his conversations with Naess (*Is It Painful to Think?,* 1992).

As Naess's ideas became known in the United States, ecologists and philosophers began to expand on the philosophy, and today the American deep ecology movement remains somewhat different from its European counterpart. The American movement has largely been shaped by the writings of sociologist Bill Devall and ecophilosopher George Sessions, whose 1985 book, *Deep Ecology: Living as If Nature Mattered,* did much to increase public awareness of deep ecology. Deep ecology has also gained adherents because of the simple living movement, a modern back-to-nature movement to reduce people's dependence on technology. (Naess 1989; Rothenberg 1993)

See also *Deep Ecology;* Devall, Bill; *Ecology, Community, and Lifestyle; Is It Painful to Think?;* Naess, Arne; Rothenberg, David; Sessions, George; Simple Living Movement.

Descent of Man, The

The Descent of Man and Selection in Relation to Sex by noted evolutionary theorist Charles Darwin was first published in 1871 in two volumes. It expands on the ideas presented in his previous work, *Origin of Species,* proposing that human beings were subject to the same evolutionary principles as animals and therefore descended from apes. This concept was not mentioned in *Origin of Species* but could be inferred from some of Darwin's comments therein. Accordingly, *The Descent of Man* was not as controversial as it might have been had *Origin of Species* not been published beforehand.

The Descent of Man connects human evolution to animal evolution by comparing humans to lesser life forms. As Darwin explains: "He who wishes to decide whether man is the modified descendant of some pre-existing form, would probably first enquire whether man varies, however slightly, in bodily structure and in mental faculties; and if so, whether the variations are transmitted to his offspring in accordance with the laws which prevail with the lower animals." (Bates and Humphrey 1957, 271)

The book outlines the physical, developmental, and behavioral similarities between humans and animals. It also discusses emotions and morality, arguing that "the difference in mind between man and the higher animals, great as it is, certainly is one of degree and not of kind. We have seen that the senses and intuitions, the various emotions and faculties, such as love, memory, attention, curiosity, imitation, reason, &c., of which man boasts, may be found in an incipient, or even sometimes in a well-developed condition, in the lower animals. They are also capable of some inherited improvement, as we see in the domestic dog compared to the wolf or jackal." (294)

Darwin then examines the variety among human beings and the processes by which the differences between races might have evolved. In this regard he talks about natural selection, which he explains at length in *Origin of Species,* and sexual selection, which concerns the physical traits that make males distinct from females and help them attract mates. Darwin introduces this topic by discussing sexual selection among birds, then moves to human beings. He believes that sexual selection accounts for the diversity of humans:

It has . . . been shewn that the races of man differ from each other and from their nearest allies, in certain characters which are of no service to them in their daily habits of life, and which it is extremely probable would have been modified through sexual selection. We have seen that with the lowest savages the people of each tribe admire their own characteristic qualities,—the shape of the head and face, the squareness of the cheek-bones, the prominence or depression of the nose, the colour of the skin, the length of the hair on the head, the absence of hair on the face and body, or the presence of a great beard, and so forth. Hence these and other such points could hardly fail to be slowly and gradually exaggerated, from the more powerful and able men in each tribe, who would succeed in rearing the largest number of offspring, having selected during many generations for their wives the most strongly characterised and therefore most attractive women. (355)

In the concluding chapter of *The Descent of Man,* Darwin summarizes his theories on human evolution, natural selection, and sexual selection, acknowledging that some of his work will be controversial:

The main conclusion arrived at in this work, namely, that man is descended from some lowly organised form, will, I regret to think, be highly distasteful to many. But there can hardly be a doubt that we are descended from barbarians. The astonishment which I felt on first seeing a party of Fuegians [a primitive people] on a wild and broken shore will never be forgotten by me, for the reflection at once rushed into my mind—such were our ancestors. These men were absolutely naked and bedaubed with paint, their long hair was tangled, their mouths frothed with excitement, and their expression was wild, startled, and distrustful. . . . He who has seen a savage in his native land will not feel much shame, if forced to acknowledge that the blood of some more humble creature flows in his veins. For my own part I would as soon be descended from [a pet monkey or baboon] . . . as from a savage who delights to torture his enemies, offers up bloody sacrifices, practises infanticide without remorse, treats his wives like slaves, knows no decency, and is haunted by the grossest superstitions. (365)

(Bates and Humphrey 1957; Bowler 1996; Mayr and Mayr 1985; Ridley 1996)

See also Darwin, Charles Robert; Evolution; *Origin of Species, The.*

Desert Solitaire

Desert Solitaire is a collection of first-person essays related to environmental activist Edward Abbey's experiences as a park ranger at Utah's Arches National Monument (now a national park). The book describes the beauty of the desert, telling of Abbey's emotional reaction to the place. However, when it was published in 1968, *Desert Solitaire* was

Delicate Arch at Arches National Park, Utah (Corbis)

markedly different from earlier nature writing. As Susan Zakin explains in *Coyotes and Town Dogs:*

> [Abbey] created a new kind of nature writing. . . . By the time *Desert Solitaire* was published in 1968, [nature writer] John Muir's . . . [work] seemed hopelessly sugarcoated, only most nature writers hadn't figured it out yet. Abbey almost single-handedly made it impossible for nature writing to lapse back into babbling brooks and heavenly birdsong. In his books, real people made love, got mad, and threw beer cans out of car windows. They did it all in the midst of devastating natural beauty, which was under siege by . . . developers and, invariably, the United States government. . . . Ponderous and poetic mawkishness, the bane of most nature writing, were completely foreign to Abbey. (Zakin 1993, p. 136)

Abbey originally intended the title of *Desert Solitaire* to be *Desert Solecism* (the definition of *solecism* being a breech of etiquette or a deviation from normal behavior); Abbey's book points out the ways in which human beings affront the natural world. It opens with an introduction lamenting the death of the desert Abbey once knew:

> Do not jump into your automobile next June and rush out to the canyon country hoping to see some of that which I have attempted to evoke in these pages. In the first place you can't see *anything* from a car; you've got to get out of the . . . contraption and walk, better yet crawl, on hands and knees, over the sandstone and through the thornbush and cactus. When traces of blood begin to mark your trail you'll see something, maybe. Probably not. In the second place most of what I write about in this book is already gone or

going under fast. This is not a travel guide but an elegy. A memorial. (Abbey 1968, xiv)

Throughout the book Abbey criticizes America's environmental policies and offers suggestions to improve wilderness management. But he particularly condemns so-called industrial tourism, which brings people into the desert at the expense of its environmental health. For example, he says:

Industrial Tourism is a big business. It means money. It includes the motel and restaurant owners, the gasoline retailers, the oil corporations, the road-building contractors, the heavy equipment manufacturers, the state and federal engineering agencies and the sovereign, all-powerful automotive industry. . . . When a new national park, national monument, national seashore, or whatever it may be called is set up, the various forces of Industrial Tourism, on all levels, immediately expect action—meaning specifically a road-building program. Where trails or primitive dirt roads already exist, the Industry expects . . . that these be developed into modern paved highways. (49–50)

Abbey concludes that industrial tourism is a threat to national parks, remarking: "But the chief victims of the system are the motorized tourists. They are being robbed and robbing themselves. So long as they are unwilling to crawl out of their cars they will not discover the treasures of the national parks and will never escape the stress and turmoil of those urban-suburban complexes which they had hoped, presumably, to leave behind for a while." (51) (Abbey 1968; Zakin 1993)

See also Abbey, Edward; Environmental Politics; Habitat Protection.

Devall, Bill

With George Sessions, William Devall coauthored the 1985 book, *Deep Ecology: Living as If Nature Mattered,* which expands on the views of Norwegian philosopher Arne Naess.

The book helped define the deep ecology movement in the United States, which emphasizes the need to become a part of nature in order to achieve a deeper consciousness. Devall is currently a professor of sociology at Humboldt State University and remains active in the environmental movement.

See also *Deep Ecology;* Deep Ecology Movement; Naess, Arne; Sessions, George.

Diamond, Jared

A professor of evolution at the University of California–Los Angeles Jared Diamond has written several books about environment and evolution. He believes that the environment has had a significant impact on human development. His works include *Ecology and Evolution of Communities* (1975) and *The Third Chimpanzee: The Evolution and Future of the Human Animal* (1992).

Dillard, Annie

Annie Dillard is one of the best-known nature writers of the modern era. However, as is typical of modern nature writing, her work is also an expression of her environmentalism. For example, *Teaching a Stone to Talk* (1982) mentions human destruction of the environment, as well as research related to biology, evolution, and other environmental sciences. Dillard's most famous work is *Pilgrim at Tinker Creek* (1974), which won the Pulitzer Prize; it describes a year of Dillard's naturalist experiences in Virginia's Blue Ridge Mountains.

Dillard was born on April 30, 1945, in Pittsburgh, Pennsylvania; she attended college in Virginia. She has written several nonfiction books, including an autobiography entitled *An American Childhood* (1987), as well as a novel, *The Living* (1992). She lives in Middletown, Connecticut, and is a writer-in-residence at Wesleyan University. (Dillard 1974; Dillard 1982)

See also Nature Writing; *Pilgrim at Tinker Creek; Teaching a Stone to Talk.*

Dinesen, Isak

Isak Dinesen is the pseudonym of Karen Christence Dinesen, Baroness Blixen-Finecke, a Danish author who recorded her experiences in Kenya, in *Den Afrikanske farm* (Out of Africa, 1937). Born on April 17, 1885, in Rungsted, Denmark, Dinesen traveled to Africa with her husband in 1914. The couple owned a coffee plantation, which they worked together until their divorce in 1921. Dinesen managed the plantation herself until 1931, when drought and financial difficulties forced her return to Denmark. Her other works include *Syv fantastiske fortoellinger* (Seven Gothic Tales, 1934), *Vinter-eventyr* (Winter's Tales, 1942), and *Letters from Africa, 1914–1931* (published posthumously in 1981). Dinesen died on September 7, 1962, in Rungsted.

See also *Out of Africa*.

Dioscordides, Pedanius

Pedanius Dioscordides (ca. 40 A.D.–90 A.D.) was a Greek military physician. His five-volume *De Materia Medica* (ca. 77 A.D.) offered detailed descriptions of some 600 plants with medicinal properties, providing information on more than 1,000 drugs. This work was translated into several languages and remained the most important pharmacological reference book in the world until the early 16th century. It also created many botanical terms still in use today. However, Dioscorides's writings did not remain in their original form over time. Copyists often changed his words, either through carelessness or out of a mistaken belief that they could improve upon his work. (Spangenburg and Moser 1993)

See also Species Identification and Classification.

Discourse of Earthquakes

Discourse of Earthquakes was written in 1668 by scientist Robert Hooke, who published the work in 1705. It was the first book to recognize that fossils were evidence of prehistoric life. Hooke considered fossils to be "truly Authentick Antiquity, not to be counterfeited, the Stamps and Impressions, and Characters of Nature that are beyond the Reach and Powers of Humane Wit and Invention, and are true universal Characters legible to all rational Men." (Bowler 1993, 118) In contrast, most of his contemporaries thought that fossils were supernatural items or strange rocks, perhaps the remains of a great flood mentioned in the Bible. Hooke therefore did much to further studies related to geology, ancient life, and species evolution.

See also Evolution; Geological Research; Hooke, Robert.

Diversity of Life, The

The Diversity of Life was written by Edward O. Wilson, considered to be one of the foremost evolutionary theorists since Charles Darwin. Published in 1992, the book discusses evolution and extinction yet stresses the importance of species diversity:

Biodiversity is our most valuable but least appreciated resource. . . . We need to reclassify environmental problems in a way that more accurately reflects reality. There are two major categories, and two only. One is alteration of the physical environment to a state uncongenial to life, the now familiar syndrome of toxic pollution, loss of the ozone layer, climatic warming by the greenhouse effect, and depletion of arable land and aquifers—all accelerated by the continued growth of human populations. These trends can be reversed if we have the will. . . . The second category is the loss of biological diversity. Its root cause is the despoliation of the physical environment, but is otherwise radically different in quality. Although the loss cannot be redeemed, its rate can be slowed to the barely perceptible levels of prehistory. If what is left is a lesser biotic world than the one humanity inherited, at least an equilibrium will have been reattained in the birth and death of species. (E. Wilson 1992, 281–282)

Wilson believes that it is dangerous to be complacent about species loss:

Why should we care [about species loss]? What difference does it make if some species are extinguished, if even half of all the species on earth disappear? Let me count the ways. New sources of scientific information will be lost. Vast potential biological wealth will be destroyed. Still undeveloped medicines, crops, pharmaceuticals, timber, fibers, pulp, soil-restoring vegetation, petroleum substitutes, and other products and amenities will never come to light. It is fashionable in some quarters to wave aside the small and obscure, the bugs and weeds, forgetting that an obscure moth from Latin America saved Australia's pastureland from overgrowth by cactus, that the rosy periwinkle provided the cure for Hodgkin's disease and childhood lymphocytic leukemia, that the bark of the Pacific yew offers hope for victims of ovarian and breast cancer, that a chemical from the saliva of leeches dissolves blood clots during surgery, and so on down a roster already grown long and illustrious despite the limited research addressed to it. (347)

Wilson also argues that the loss of enough individual species could threaten the health of the entire planet:

If we were to dismantle an ecosystem gradually, removing one species after another, the exact consequences at each step would be impossible to predict, but one general result seems certain: at some point the ecosystem would suffer a collapse. Most communities of organisms are held together by redundancies in the system. In many cases two or more ecologically similar species live in the same area, and any one can fill the niches of others extinguished, more or less. But inevitably the resiliency would be sapped, efficiency of the food webs would drop, nutrient flow would decline, and eventually one of the elements deleted would prove to be a keystone species. Its extinction would bring down other species with it, possibly so extensively as to alter the physical structure of the habitat itself. Because ecology is still

a primitive science, no one is sure of the identity of most keystone species. (309)

In discussing earth's ecosystems, Wilson dismisses James Lovelock's Gaia hypothesis, which suggests that earth is a single living organism, saying: "Mother Earth, lately called Gaia, is no more than the commonality of organisms and the physical environment they maintain with each passing moment, an environment that will destabilize and turn lethal if the organisms are disturbed too much." (347) Wilson contends that regardless of one's beliefs on Gaia and the creation of earth and its species, more must be done to safeguard biodiversity. He states:

The evidence of swift environmental change calls for an ethic uncoupled from other systems of belief. Those committed by religion to believe that life was put on earth in one divine stroke will recognize that we are destroying the Creation, and those who perceive biodiversity to be the product of blind evolution will agree. Across the other great philosophical divide, it does not matter whether species have independent rights or, conversely, that moral reasoning is uniquely a human concern. . . . The stewardship of environment is a domain on the near side of metaphysics where all reflective persons can surely find common ground. . . . An enduring environmental ethic will aim to preserve not only the health and freedom of our species, but access to the world in which the human spirit was born. (351)

(E. Wilson 1992)

See also Animal Ecology; Biodiversity; Darwin, Charles Robert; Evolution; Gaia Hypothesis; Habitat Protection; Lovelock, James.

Douglas, William O.

William Orville Douglas served as a justice of the U.S. Supreme Court for 36 years; he was an active conservationist who believed that jurists needed to protect wilderness areas. He promoted his beliefs in several essays and books on conservation issues, including *A Wilderness Bill of Rights* (1965); he profiled the lives of early conservationists in *Of Men and Mountains* (1950).

Douglas was born on October 16, 1898, in Maine, Minnesota, but grew up in Yakima, Washington. Raised by his widowed mother, he contracted polio as a boy and recovered with the help of daily exercise and fresh air. This instilled in him a life-long love for the outdoors. He went hiking and camping often, and as an adult he even went on a Himalayan expedition.

Douglas studied law at Columbia University, graduating in 1925 to join a New York law firm. He quit his job a year later to begin teaching law, first at Columbia and then at Yale University. He remained at Yale until 1936, when he became a member of the Securities and Exchange Commission (SEC); he was named SEC chair in 1937.

During his three years with the SEC, Douglas did many things to improve stock exchanges and protect investors. He also advised President Franklin D. Roosevelt regularly on related issues. Consequently, in 1936 Roosevelt nominated Douglas to replace retiring U.S. Supreme Court Justice Louis Brandeis. Douglas was quickly confirmed and took his seat on the Court in April 1939, at age 40. He soon became a passionate defender of civil liberties, particularly free speech, and continued to write and speak on conservation issues, both officially and informally. Douglas served until November 1975, when the after-effects of a stroke and other health problems forced his retirement. He died on January 19, 1980, in Washington, D.C. (McHenry 1972)

See also *Wilderness Bill of Rights, A.*

Dowie, Mark

Journalist Mark Dowie writes extensively on environmental issues as well as health and safety risks. He was a former editor of *Mother Jones* magazine and also worked for InterNation, a feature syndicate based in New York; he is the recipient of several prestigious journalism awards. His book *Losing Ground: American Environmentalism at the Close of the Twentieth Century* (1995) is considered one of the most comprehensive examinations of the history of environmentalism and the movement's current controversies. Its most controversial aspect is its analysis of internal problems within modern environmental groups. (Dowie 1995)

See also Antienvironmentalism; Environmental Movement; Environmental Politics; *Losing Ground.*

Down to Earth

Down to Earth (1982) was written to commemorate the 10th anniversary of the 1972 United Nations Conference on the Human Environment, or the Stockholm Conference; the book is typical of works derived from environmental meetings. The Stockholm Conference was the first major international discussion of global environmental issues. The author of *Down to Earth,* Erik P. Eckholm, was a visiting fellow of the International Institute for Environment and Development at the time of its writing, and his work was funded by the UN Environment Programme; the book is therefore not unbiased.

At the beginning of *Down to Earth,* Eckholm explains that the Stockholm Conference was a turning point in environmental awareness, particularly in Third World countries:

A decade back many Third World leaders were openly dubious about the relevance of environmental issues to their countries' development struggles. Today such doubts are rarely heard, though it would be an exaggeration to say that all such feelings have been dispelled. Brazil, for example, some of whose representatives at Stockholm characterized the hue and cry about pollution as a plot to hamper the industrialization of the South, founded a new national environmental agency shortly after the Stockholm Conference adjourned. Scores of other developing countries have over the past decade created environmental ministries or agencies and passed laws to regulate pollution. And some now require analysis of the expected environmental impacts of major investments. Many in the Third World have learned through unpleasant experience that unconstrained pollution can have savage effects without lifting the poor into affluence. (Eckholm 1982, p. 7)

Eckholm discusses the "global underclass"—people throughout the world who live in poverty. He also talks about how poverty and overpopulation relate to health and environmental problems and reports on a variety of environmental issues, including ocean and air pollution, acid rain, species extinction, soil and forest management, and the economics of environmentalism. Calling his book "a survey of global environmental trends," he concludes that even though "appreciation of the material and spiritual importance of a healthy natural environment has spread" the earth still has many problems. (199) He advocates the establishment of an international environmental agency that would not only monitor environmental problems but also possess the authority to develop global solutions to those problems. He reports that this approach to environmentalism was suggested at the Stockholm Conference but never came to pass. (Eckholm 1982)

See also Air Pollution; Eckholm, Erik P.; Environmental Movement; Environmental Politics.

Downcanyon

Downcanyon: A Naturalist Explores the Colorado River Through the Grand Canyon is an excellent example of modern nature writing, combining personal narrative with information about natural history and environmental science. Published in 1995, the book won a prominent award for creative nonfiction; its author, Ann Haymond Zwinger, is one of the foremost nature writers in America today. *Downcanyon* relates Zwinger's observations as she rafts down the Colorado River once per month during an entire year. She says:

The year-round picture will, in the end, grant me a different perspective on the river than that of the summertime visitor

with only a week to shoot the rapids. The river is not folded up like a neoprene raft and stored away between summers, but is an ever-flowing, energetic, whooping and hollering, galloping presence, whether there's ice along the edge or a flotilla of yellow willow leaves floating in a back-eddy or summer sunshine glinting off a cross chop. Against the seeming immutability of the canyon walls pass a parade of seasonal delights: bald eagles fishing in Nankoweap Creek in February, redbuds blossoming in April in Saddle Canyon, the summer's hatch of cicada shells dangling from bushes beside Crystal Creek in July, magenta windmills blooming in a rich slice of autumn at Tanner Creek, snowflakes inhaled by the river in December, adding up to this observer's four-dimensional snapshot of "what's down there." (Zwinger 1995, 6)

Although Zwinger does concentrate on providing a snapshot of the area, so to speak, she also discusses river-related environmental issues. Yet unlike environmental authors who use their work to promote political activism, she approaches her subjects as a naturalist simply reporting the facts. This is the way she explains how the Glen Canyon Dam has altered its surrounding habitat:

When Glen Canyon Dam closed in 1964, the changes in the river below were instant and dramatic. Instead of a silt-laden, seasonally fluctuating river with varying seasonal temperatures, water now came from two hundred feet below the surface of Lake Powell at a constant, very cold, average 46F all year long, essentially sediment-free. The big yearly shifts in flow—rising, often flooding in the spring, falling in late summer—were replaced by daily fluctuations, sometimes rapid, tied to the flow of water through the generators in response to demands for electric power in the Western Area Power Administration grid. An average of 380,000 tons of silt a year used to grind past the gauging station at Bright

Angel Creek ninety miles downstream. . . . Now upper tributary streams enter Lake Powell and so almost no silt enters the river from upstream. . . . The dam also holds back the phosphorus that enhances plant productivity . . . After the dam closed, the river and some tributaries were heavily stocked [with game fish], and trout began to spawn up Bright Angel, Tapeats, and Clear Creeks. Now they are the most prevalent fish in the river, their large population a detriment to endemic fish like humpback chub already under pressure from the drastic habitat changes engendered by the dam. (13–14)

In contrast, environmentalist Edward Abbey's writings about Glen Canyon Dam harshly criticize the people who built it, and he called for its destruction in a public protest. Zwinger promotes environmentalism in a different way, sharing her experiences and encouraging people to become more connected with nature. She talks about this connection within herself as she describes her feelings upon leaving the river:

As I gained the asphalt walk at the top of the trail, the number of people dismayed me. After an idyllic two weeks spent at only two campsites, with time to wander far and alone every day, I felt as bewildered as Rip van Winkle must have: the world had gone on and left me behind. Maybe I didn't know how things like light switches and faucets and computers worked anymore. My head, my heart, my psyche lagged a dozen miles down in the canyon. I remembered John Burroughs quoting a lady tourist's comment that the canyon had been built a little too near to the lodge.

Out of one of the clusters of people stepped a nice-looking, neatly dressed, middle-aged woman, a question obvious in her face. I paused, uncomfortably conscious of how derelict I must appear. "Excuse me," she began, "is there anything down there?" (237)

Downcanyon is Zwinger's answer to that question. (Zwinger 1995)

See also Abbey, Edward; Burroughs, John; Nature Writing; Zwinger, Ann.

Doyle, Arthur Conan

English novelist Sir Arthur Conan Doyle is best known for creating the Sherlock Holmes character. But Doyle also authored one of the first fictional works that addressed evolutionary theory, the 1912 novel *The Lost World*.

Doyle was born in Edinburgh, Scotland, on May 22, 1859. He received a medical degree from Edinburgh University and practiced in Southsea, England, until 1891, when he abandoned medicine for writing. By this time he had already published his first Sherlock Holmes story ("A Study in Scarlet," 1887) and a sequel ("The Sign of Four," 1890). They were very popular, and in 1891 he started a series called "The Adventures of Sherlock Holmes," which was published in *Strand Magazine*. Two years later Doyle had grown tired of Holmes. He wrote the character's death scene, but the public became so irate that he resurrected Holmes in a subsequent story.

During the Boer War (1899–1902), Doyle served as a doctor in a field hospital and wrote a pamphlet supporting the English cause. These contributions to the war effort earned him knighthood in 1902. In his later years, he devoted himself to the study of spiritualism. He first became interested in the subject after his son died in World War I, and he continued to hope he might be able to contact his son's spirit. Doyle died on July 7, 1930. (Wood 1965)

See also Evolution; *Lost World, The*.

E

Earth in the Balance

Earth in the Balance: Ecology and the Human Spirit is important primarily because of its author's political power. The book was written in 1992 by U.S. Senator Al Gore, who was elected vice president in November of that year.

Gore contends that the earth is in the midst of a major global ecological crisis and calls for drastic changes in attitude, behavior, and government policies to avert disaster. Gore describes a variety of global environmental problems, including global warming, rain forest destruction, soil erosion, and waste disposal, from a historical perspective and addresses environmentalism in terms of attitudes, ethics, and morals, both in individuals and governments.

Gore believes that the greatest obstacle to solving environmental problems is U.S. economics. He discusses the relationship between economics and environmentalism at length and suggests that our current system is flawed because it "arbitrarily draws a circle of value around those things in our civilization we have decided to keep track of and measure" and then "artificially increase[s] the value of things inside the circle . . . at the expense of those things left outside the circle." As a result "a direct and perverse ratio emerges: the more pollution dumped into the river, the higher the short-term profits for the polluter and his shareholders; the faster the rain forest is burned, the quicker more pasture becomes available for cattle and the faster they can be turned into hamburgers. Our failure to measure environmental externalities is a kind of economic blindness, and its consequences can be staggering." (Gore 1992, 189)

Gore believes that this economic blindness is just one part of America's "dysfunctional civilization." He also criticizes radical environmentalists like Dave Foreman and deep ecologists like Arne Naess for promoting the view that human beings are "an alien presence on the earth" and are "inherently and contagiously destructive." (217) Gore argues that this view does not promote environmentalism, because it alienates people from nature.

Gore offers his own plan for addressing environmental problems, outlining an approach to environmentalism similar to the Marshall Plan developed to help Europe recover from World War II. Gore's "Global Marshall Plan" would "focus on strategic goals and emphasize actions and programs that are likely to remove the bottlenecks presently inhibiting the healthy functioning of the global economy." (297) Gore believes that countries must work together to create a global civilization in which everyone prospers.

Vice President Al Gore (right) tours Everglades National Park, Florida, December 1997 (AP Photo/Gregory Smith)

When it was published, *Earth in the Balance* received much attention, particularly from antienvironmentalists. For example, Wallace Kaufman, in his 1994 book, *No Turning Back: Dismantling the Fantasies of Environmental Thinking*, called *Earth in the Balance* utopian and suggested that Gore was exaggerating the seriousness of environmental problems. Similarly, in their book *Environmental Overkill: Whatever Happened to Common Sense?*, Dixy Lee Ray and Lou Guzzo accused Gore of being "an extremist on environmental issues" who "has completely ignored scientific impartiality" in favor of an emotional response to environmentalism. *Earth in the Balance* received renewed attention when Gore announced his intention to run for president of the United States in 2000, because it offered insights into how he might govern the country. (Ray and Guzzo 1993, 188)

(Gore 1992; Kaufman 1994; Ray and Guzzo 1993)

See also Deep Ecology Movement; *Environmental Overkill;* Foreman, Dave; Gore Jr., Albert; Guzzo, Lou; Kaufman, Wallace; Naess, Arne; *No Turning Back;* Ray, Dixy Lee.

Easterbrook, Gregg

Gregg Easterbrook is the author of *A Moment on the Earth: The Coming Age of Environmental Optimism* (1995). It represents a trend in environmentalism that developed during the 1990s, in which environmentalists began to question the validity of their approach to environmental issues. In its introduction Easterbrook calls himself a political liberal who nonetheless refuses to accept the pessimistic viewpoint of most environmentalists: "I have trouble fathoming why guarded optimism about the environment is politically incorrect." (Easterbrook 1995, xix) Easterbrook, who lives in Arlington, Virginia, has been an environmental reporter for several years, writing articles for *Newsweek* and *The New York Times Magazine.* (Easterbrook 1995)

See also Environmental Politics; *Moment on the Earth, A.*

Eckholm, Erik P.

Environmentalist Erik P. Eckholm is the author of the 1982 book, *Down to Earth: Environment and Human Needs,* which he calls "a survey of global environmental trends." (Eckholm 1982, p. 199) While writing the book, Eckholm was a visiting fellow at the International Institute for Environment and Development, and *Down to Earth* was written at the request of the United Nations Environment Programme, which funded the project. It commemorates the 10th anniversary of the 1972 United Nations Conference on the Human Environment, the so-called Stockholm Conference, the first major international meeting on global environmental issues.

In addition to *Down to Earth,* Eckholm has written many articles on environmental, development, and energy issues, as well as several books, including *Losing Ground: Environmental Stress and World Food Prospects* (1976), *The Picture of Health: Environmental Sources of Disease* (1977), *Planting for the Future: Forestry for Human Needs* (1979), and *Fuelwood: The Energy Crisis That Won't Go Away* (1984). He has worked as a researcher for the environmental group Worldwatch Institute and as a member of the U.S. State Department's Policy Planning Staff. (Eckholm 1982)

See also *Down to Earth;* Environmental Politics.

Ecology, Community, and Lifestyle

This 1976 book was first published in Norway and then translated into English by David Rothenberg during the 1980s. Its author, Norwegian philosopher Arne Naess, decided to dedicate himself to solving environmental problems. In thinking about the subject, he created the philosophy of deep ecology, which subsequently inspired the deep ecology movement.

Ecology, Community, and Lifestyle explains this philosophy in great detail. Naess supports the view that humans are connected to nature rather than separate from it. Therefore humans are no more important than the rest of earth's components. Based on this belief, he and fellow deep ecologist George Sessions developed a deep ecology platform comprising eight points. (Naess 1989, 28) They are:

1. The flourishing of human and non-human life on Earth has intrinsic value. The value of non-human life forms is independent of the usefulness these may have for narrow human purposes.
2. Richness and diversity of life forms are values in themselves and contribute to the flourishing of human and non-human life on Earth.
3. Humans have no right to reduce this richness and diversity except to satisfy vital needs.
4. Present human interference with the non-human world is excessive, and the situation is rapidly worsening.
5. The flourishing of human life and cultures is compatible with a substantial decrease of the human population. The flourishing of non-human life requires such a decrease.
6. Significant change of life conditions for the better requires change in policies. These affect basic economic, technological, and ideological structures.
7. The ideological change is mainly that of appreciating *life quality* (dwelling in situations of intrinsic value) rather than adhering to a high standard of living. There will be a profound awareness of the difference between big and great.
8. Those who subscribe to the foregoing points have an obligation directly or

indirectly to participate in the attempt to implement the necessary changes. (29)

To this end, Naess suggests that each individual free himself or herself "from the profit and consumption consciousness, in spite of the non-stop pressure from the mode of production which depends upon such mentality." (90) He advocates many changes in lifestyle based on a change in consciousness:

> Without a change in consciousness, the ecological movement is experienced as a never-ending list of reminders: "shame, you mustn't do that" and "remember, you're not allowed to. . . ." With a change in mentality we can say "think how wonderful it will be, if and when . . .," "look there! what a pity that we haven't enjoyed that before . . . ." If we can clean up a little internally as well as externally, we can hope that *the ecological movement will be more of a renewing and joy-creating movement.* (91)

He adds that "the necessity of efforts to change mentality is closely associated with the necessity of organised efforts for profound changes in the structure of society." (91–92) As an example of these social changes, he says:

> Let us imagine that just one of the lifestyle and consciousness changes . . . took place: if waste was reduced by 50 percent, hundreds of firms would immediately have sales problems. Within a year, unemployment would perhaps double. This and other unfortunate consequences can only be avoided if these changes are combined with other changes. The most important in this case is revamping production to dispel the spectre of unemployment. To avoid undesirable consequences, it is useful to consider the personal reduction in consumption as part of a total pattern of life which also includes political engagement. (92)

Naess discusses environmental politics at length, offering advice for ways to encourage changes within society. For example, he says:

In politics tactics are important. Even if this goes against the grain in many deep ecology people, it is important at least that they do not turn against those few supporters who are tactically minded. If we work within existing parties, we must use a terminology that encourages the voters to listen. For instance, it is not good to write and talk as if one is against industry in general. Our point of view should be that we should support 'industry,' and then point out that 'industry' has historically been something very different from what is going on at the moment—*big* industry. Similarly, we should not have general slogans against technology or belittle its importance. The diversity of human cultures through history shows a tremendous diversity of technologies, and without this diversity we would not have deep cultural diversity.

Naess also explains that it might not be in the planet's best interest to encourage the public to abandon cities for the rural lifestyle. He says: "Furthermore, derogatory talk about big cities and city lifestyles may be counterproductive. For centuries human population is likely to be colossal (if there are no major nuclear wars) and big concentrations within small areas are necessary to minimise devastating effects upon other kinds of life than the human, and upon the landscapes of the planet in general. More effort is needed to improve life quality in the areas of concentration, not more effort to spread the population all over the globe." (155)

In a 1989 edition of *Ecology, Community, and Lifestyle,* Naess concludes with a discussion of the future of the deep ecology movement, in which he discusses the changes that have occurred since the mid-1970s, when his work was first published. He feels hopeful because there is "increasing public awareness of the difference between standard of living and quality of life" (210) and is pleased that "the deep ecology demand for the establishment of large territories free from human development has recently gained in acceptance." (212)

However, he also believes that "significant deterioration of ecological conditions may well colour the next years in spite of the deepening of ecological consciousness. The situation has to get worse before it gets better." (211) Accordingly, he argues that the deep ecology movement needs to become better organized and more outspoken regarding the need for social change. (Dobson 1991; Naess 1989; Rothenberg 1993)

See also Deep Ecology Movement; Naess, Arne.

Eco-Scam

Ronald Bailey's 1993 book, *Eco-Scam: The False Prophets of Ecological Apocalypse,* is highly critical of the modern American environmental movement and is often cited by those who oppose environmental activism. Bailey contends that environmentalists are misleading the public about the health of the earth by promoting a "doomsday philosophy" that exaggerates environmental problems.

In discussing what he calls "the imagination of disaster," Bailey argues that many environmentalists are false prophets who incorrectly predict ecological disasters. For example, he attacks population expert Paul Ehrlich, who has predicted that overpopulation will deplete natural resources, saying:

Ehrlich is a master of sketching out imaginative doom-fraught future scenarios. His role as a population doomster has brought him considerable renown and financial security. . . . All this recognition notwithstanding, the fact is that not one of Ehrlich's many frightful predictions has ever come true. . . . He makes a prediction, and when refuted by scientific evidence or events, he simply makes another assertion incorporating the latest apocalyptic fads. Being proved wrong apparently never bothers him, and he has great faith that his population predictions must eventually come true. (R. Bailey 1993; 41–42)

Bailey discusses several environmental problems that he calls "myths," including global warming and the hole in the ozone layer, and offers reasons why environmentalists might be misleading the public regarding these problems. He believes that they have a motive to lie, because without the fear of environmental problems people would not donate money to environmental causes and groups. In his final chapter, entitled "The Media and the Messiahs," he advocates that people be more skeptical about environmental information that comes from biased sources, saying: "Don't let yourself get co-opted by your sources. It is especially difficult to resist the temptation to be on the side of those claiming to save the earth. After all, who wants to stand for the destruction of our home?" (176) He provides a list of tips "on how the public and reporters can tell that they may be dealing with a false prophet of doom," which includes:

Beware of moral fervor and high levels of righteous indignation. Just because people are willing to put their lives on the line for their beliefs . . . doesn't mean that they are right. After all there were hundreds of thousands of convinced Nazis and communists who died for their causes. . . .

Talk with scientists—other than those who are pushing the alleged crisis. Be aware, however, that scientists are often reluctant to criticize their fellow scientists and may even fear that their criticisms might endanger the funding of their own work if they speak up in opposition. No one wants to sound like they *favor* nuclear war or destroying the ozone layer. (178)

Throughout *Eco-Scam,* Bailey emphasized the need for the public to remain objective while considering emotionally charged issues, even though such objectivity is difficult to maintain. (R. Bailey 1993)

See also Antienvironmentalism; Climate Changes; Ehrlich, Paul and Anne; Environmental Apocalypse; Environmental Politics; Human Ecology; Nuclear Energy.

Ecotactics

Edited by John G. Mitchell with Constance Stallings, *Ecotactics: The Sierra Club Handbook for Environmental Activists* is a collection of articles about environmental activism. The book was published in 1970 under the direction of the Sierra Club, a large national environmental group, and therefore reflects the concerns of the early environmental movement. It was also extremely popular, and many of today's environmentalists credit the book with first interesting them in environmental activism.

The definition of *ecotactics* is "the science of arranging and maneuvering all available forces in action against enemies of the earth" (Mitchell 1970, 5); in the introduction, activist Ralph Nader argues that environmental destruction is one of the greatest threats to humanity. He says: "Pollution is violence and environmental pollution is environmental violence. It is a violence that has different impacts, styles and time factors than the more primitive kind of violence such as crime in the streets. Yet in the size of the population exposed and the seriousness of the harm done, environmental violence far exceeds that of street crime." (13–14)

Ecotactics advocates that people fight such violence through a variety of tactics. In the foreword, Michael McCloskey, executive director of the Sierra Club when *Ecotactics* was published, calls for an environmental "revolution" in this regard and explains:

A meaningful revolution must be engaged in at all levels. First, we shall need grand statements. The dialectics must include declarations of *environmental* rights, new statements of national policy and priority and redefinitions of public goals. We shall need political action: new laws and institutions must be created, old ones disbanded and thrown out; and direct mass action: rallies, marches, teach-ins. Perhaps more than anything else, we shall need individual action. Each person must become ecologically responsible—not only as a consumer of the planet's resources, but as

a procreator of its most prolific species. (11–12)

In the articles that follow, *Ecotactics* offers examples of environmental activism and gives tips on how to spread environmentalism throughout America. It also discusses the work of prominent environmentalists such as Rachel Carson and Aldo Leopold. But many people believe that the book's greatest significance is its emphasis on how to use the media to promote environmentalism. In *No Turning Back: Dismantling the Fantasies of Environmental Thinking,* Wallace Kaufman explains: "*Ecotactics* laid down the guidelines for the [environmental] movement's domination of the media. It was called 'advocacy journalism' and its intent was to 'destroy the dangerous anonymity afforded by objectivity or balance. . . .' Advocacy journalism on environmental issues has since spread to most major television and print outlets." (Kaufman 1994, 75) (Kaufman 1994; Mitchell 1970)

See also Carson, Rachel Louise; Environmental Activism; Environmental Groups; Environmental Politics; Kaufman, Wallace; Leopold, Aldo; Mitchell, John G.; *No Turning Back.*

Ehrlich, Gretel

Nature writer Gretel Ehrlich primarily writes about Wyoming and Colorado. Born in 1946, she was raised in Santa Barbara, California. After graduating from Bennington College she attended film school, and in 1976 she went to Wyoming to make a movie about sheep ranching. She decided to stay there and take up ranching herself. Her best known book, a collection of essays entitled *The Solace of Open Spaces* (1985), describes her experiences living among the sheep ranchers and learning their trade.

Ehrlich continues to live in Wyoming, where she and her husband now own their own ranch. Ehrlich's other works include *Drinking Dry Clouds: Stories from Wyoming* (1991), *Arctic Heart: A Poem Cycle* (1992), the novel *Heart Mountain* (1988), and a story collection, *City Tales, Wyoming Stories* (1986), which she coauthored with Edward Hoagland. She has also edited a collection of Western writings entitled *Life in the Saddle* (1995) and written a book for children, *A Blizzard Year* (1999).

See also Hoagland, Edward; *Solace of Open Spaces, The.*

Ehrlich, Paul and Anne

Paul and Anne Ehrlich have coauthored several nonfiction books related to human ecology. Paul Ehrlich's 1968 book, *The Population Bomb,* first brought public attention to the negative environmental impacts of overpopulation. In 1990 he and Anne published its sequel, *The Population Explosion,* and in 1995 they wrote *The Stork and the Plow,* which discusses the relationship between population and food supply. They also talked about endangered species in the book *Extinction: The Causes and Consequences of the Disappearance of Species* (1981). In addition, Paul Ehrlich was the sole author of the 1986 book, *The Machinery of Nature,* which defines and discusses ecology.

In addition to their popular works, the Ehrlichs have written hundreds of scientific articles. Born in 1933, Paul Ehrlich studied biology at the University of Pennsylvania, then went on to receive his doctorate in the subject at the University of Kansas. Shortly thereafter he joined the faculty of Stanford University, first as a professor of biology and later as a professor of both population studies and biological sciences. He is a member of the U.S. National Academy of Sciences and has won numerous awards, including the 1989 Science in the Service of Humankind prize from the American Association for the Advancement of Science, the 1993 World Ecology Medal, and a MacArthur Prize Fellowship (1990–1995). In 1994 he and Anne were jointly awarded the Sasakawa United Nations Environment Prize and the Heinz Foundation Prize for Environmental Achievement.

Anne Ehrlich is a research scientist at Stanford University and has chaired the Sierra Club's Committee on the Environmental Impacts of Warfare. She too has won numerous scientific awards and is a fellow of the American Academy of Arts and Sciences. The couple has one daughter. (Cox 1971; Ehrlich and Ehrlich 1981, 1990, and 1995; Shabecoff 1993)

See also *Extinction;* Human Ecology; *Machinery of Nature, The; Population Explosion, The; Stork and the Plow, The;* Wildlife Conservation.

Eight Little Piggies

Eight Little Piggies: Reflections in Natural History is a collection of essays on evolutionary science by anthropologist Stephen Jay Gould, whose work is extremely popular and has increased public awareness of the natural sciences. Published in 1993, the book addresses evolutionary theory, history, and biology, discussing individual animal species and earth's geology as well as the work of such scientists as Charles Darwin and Jean-Baptiste Lamarck.

Eight Little Piggies is divided into eight sections: "The Scale of Extinction," "Odd Bits of Vertebrate Anatomy," "Vox Populi," "Musings," "Human Nature," "Grand Patterns of Evolution," "Revising and Extending Darwin," and "Reversals—Fragments of a Book Not Written." Of these, Gould considers the seventh (on Darwin) to be the most challenging. (Gould 1993, 16) He says:

> This subject, too often ignored in popular presentations, cannot be bypassed by anyone who wishes to grasp the depth of evolutionary theory. . . . This section treats principles additional to . . . natural selection—internal constraints and historical legacies . . . and randomness as a force for change, not merely as a source of raw material for natural selection. . . . Evolution is much more than a story of matching form to local environments, with increments of general progress slowly accumulating through time—the usual view of pure Darwinian functionalism. Any genealogy is a complex tale of interplay between these Darwinian themes and a set of forces, based on the internal genetic and developmental architecture of organisms, that produce different historical patterns and conceptual meanings. . . . I have tried to approach this vital subject by concrete

example: the coloration of pigeons, fish tails and frog calls, . . . and the eye tissue of completely blind mole rats. (16)

The thirty-one essays in *Eight Little Piggies* were first published in Gould's monthly column, "This View of Life," for *Natural History* magazine. (Gould 1993)

See also Darwin, Charles Robert; Evolution; Lamarck, Jean-Baptiste.

Eiseley, Loren

Loren Eiseley was an anthropologist whose writings made the subject of evolution accessible to the general public. As Kenneth Heuer explains in *The Lost Notebooks of Loren Eiseley,* the scientist was one of the first "to use scientific material in a different way, trying to arouse the interest of the general reader in subjects that fascinated him. The problem was to make the knowledge upon which the article was based accessible and significant. Personal observations and speculations might lure the reader into a field of interest not inspected before and illuminate the material for him, while in no way replacing or obscuring facts." (Heuer 1987, 19)

Eiseley's style was simple yet poetic; Heuer calls him a "literary naturalist." (14) However, Eiseley's writings don't just describe his observations of nature and its fossils. They also offer his thoughts regarding the connection between prehistoric human evolution and modern human behavior. In this respect his work is similar to that of Stephen Jay Gould.

Eiseley was born in Lincoln, Nebraska, on September 3, 1907. He attended the University of Nebraska, graduating in 1933. Four years later he received a Ph.D. from the University of Pennsylvania, whereupon he joined the faculty of the University of Kansas. He remained there until 1944, when he took a position at Oberlin College.

In 1947 Eiseley became a professor of anthropology at the University of Pennsylvania and a curator at its museum. He remained in those positions until 1977. He was also provost of the university from 1959 to 1961, and from 1966 to 1967 he hosted a television show called *Animal Secrets.* By this time he was a popular author. His works include *The Immense Journey* (1957), *Darwin's Century* (1958), *The Firmament of Time* (1960), *The Mind as Nature* (1962), *The Invisible Pyramid* (1970), and *Night Country* (1971), as well as an autobiography and two collections of poetry. Eiseley died on July 9, 1977.

See also Evolution; *Night Country, The.*

Emerson, Ralph Waldo

Nineteenth-century American essayist Ralph Waldo Emerson wrote about nature in terms of spirituality. His works were widely read and helped increase public interest in naturalism and wilderness pursuits.

Born on May 25, 1803, in Boston, Massachusetts, Ralph was the son of a clergyman who died when Ralph was eight. He attended Harvard College and studied divinity, and in 1829 he was ordained as a Unitarian minister. He married, but when his wife died of an illness two years later he experienced a crisis of faith. In 1832 he left the ministry altogether. He traveled extensively abroad for a year before returning to the United States, where he settled in Concord, Massachusetts. There he wrote, lectured, and preached, arguing that man could transcend the physical world by exploring both the natural world and his own soul. That philosophy became known as "transcendentalism." It suggested that spirituality could better be found in the self and in nature than in a church, and it encouraged people to live simply off the land.

In 1836 Emerson anonymously published a small book entitled *Nature* to express his views, and transcendentalism quickly gained many followers. One of them, Henry David Thoreau, wrote his own work on simple living—*Walden.* In 1840, he and Emerson, along with other Transcendentalists, created a magazine, *The Dial,* to spread their philosophy. Emerson wrote many essays on the subject under his own name, and in 1841 and 1844 he published a two-volume collection entitled *Essays* that made him famous in the United States and Europe. He also wrote poems, publishing a collection entitled *Poems*

Ralph Waldo Emerson (Archive Photos)

(1846) and another entitled *May-Day* (1867). He continued to write and lecture until his death on April 27, 1882.

See also *Nature;* Thoreau, Henry David; *Walden.*

End of Nature, The

Published in 1989, *The End of Nature* by Bill McKibben argues that the current state of the environment is poor and predicts a future of more serious environmental problems if human beings do not change their antienvironmental behavior. It is therefore representative of the apocalyptic environmental literature of the 1980s, which warns of global disasters due to environmental destruction.

The book is divided into two parts, "The Present" and "The Near Future." In "The Present," McKibben discusses global warming, which he believes is one of the greatest threats to the environment. He says "we just happen to be living at the moment when the carbon dioxide has increased to an intolerable level" (McKibben 1989, 194) and explains:

In the past, we spoiled and polluted parts of nature, inflicted environmental "dam-

age." But that was like stabbing a man with toothpicks: though it hurt, annoyed, degraded, it did not touch vital organs. . . . We never thought that we had wrecked nature. Deep down, we never really thought we could. . . . But, quite by accident, it turned out that the carbon dioxide and other gases we were producing . . . *could* alter the power of the sun, could increase its heat. And that increase *could* change the patterns of moisture and dryness, breed deserts. Those things may or may not have yet begun to happen, but it is too late to altogether prevent them from happening. We have produced the carbon dioxide—we are ending nature. (48)

McKibben offers statistics, facts, and theories about the serious consequences of global warming and argues that it is vital for people to reduce their dependence on fossil fuels. But in warning that global warming is a dangerous threat to human and environmental health, he refrains from catastrophizing the problem, saying that such an attitude would make it "easier for people to ignore global threats." He explains:

In the late 1960s and early 1970s, a spate of horror books came out—books filled with the direst of predictions. . . . The greenhouse effect, [Paul Ehrlich] wrote, might raise ocean levels two hundred and fifty feet. . . . But that didn't happen. . . . The greenhouse effect could realistically raise the sea level ten feet, which is plenty bad enough but sounds like nothing next to two hundred and fifty. With every unfulfilled apocalyptic projection, our confidence in the environmentalists has waned, our belief that we'll muddle through been bolstered. (196–197)

McKibben believes that his own predictions of environmental problems are realistic and cannot be ignored. (McKibben 1989)

See also Climate Changes; Ehrlich, Paul and Anne; Environmental Apocalypse; McKibben, Bill.

The Stockmann family is startled when a crowd storms their home in the 1950 stage production of Henrik Ibsen's An Enemy of the People *(Photofest)*

Endangered Species
See Wildlife Conservation.

Enemy of the People, An

First published as *En folkefiende* in 1882 and performed in 1883, the play *An Enemy of the People* by Norwegian playwright Henrik Ibsen is one of the earliest calls for environmental activism expressed through fiction. Its story concerns a town unwilling to accept that it might be polluted. The town derives much of its income from its public baths, which are noted for their health benefits. But after several months of research, Dr. Thomas Stockmann, the baths' medical officer, has discovered that the water contains potentially deadly bacteria, probably as a result of a nearby tanning factory. He notifies town officials that a new drainage system will be necessary to purify the water. However, this system would be expensive, and the baths would have to be closed for two years during construction. The officials deny that the water is contaminated.

Incensed that the problem is being ignored,

Dr. Stockmann approaches the local newspaper, but its editors refuse to print his article on the subject. He calls a public meeting to air his concerns. His opponents cleverly take over the meeting and convince the crowd that the doctor is lying about the pollution in order to destroy the town. Consequently, the townspeople label Stockmann "an enemy of the people" and attempt to drive him out of town, throwing rocks at his windows and threatening his friends and family. Stockmann refuses to move away and decides to become a doctor to the poor, among whom he will start a revolution against such ignorance. (Ibsen 1978)

See also Environmental Activism; Environmental Fiction; Environmental Politics; Ibsen, Henrik; Water Pollution.

Environmental Activism

Activism is defined as the taking of direct action to achieve a goal, especially a political or social one. To that end, environmental activists often write books and articles to promote changes in environmental laws, policies, and practices. For example, in 1962 Rachel Carson published *Silent Spring* to convince the U.S. government to restrict pesticide use; Murray Bookchin did the same that year with *Our Synthetic Environment*. Similarly, the works of Dave Foreman and Christopher Manes were written to defend and promote radical environmentalism, which argues that defending the earth is more important than obeying property laws.

Radical environmentalism was also the subject of the most famous fictional portrayal of environmental activists, the 1975 novel *The Monkey Wrench Gang* by Edward Abbey. The book depicts a group of people attempting to stop development in the American West. Another important work featuring an environmental activist is Henrik Ibsen's 1882 play, *An Enemy of the People*, which shows the struggle of one man trying to convince people that their town has polluted water.

See also Abbey, Edward; Bookchin, Murray; Carson, Rachel Louise; *Enemy of the People, An;* Environmental Politics; Foreman, Dave; Ibsen, Henrik; Manes, Christopher; *Monkey Wrench Gang, The; Our Synthetic Environment; Silent Spring.*

Environmental Apocalypse

An *apocalypse* is a vision of cataclysmic end for the earth; *environmental apocalypse* is one caused by environmental disaster and destruction. Those who believe that environmental problems are extremely severe and possibly irreparable often write apocalyptic literature to express their views. There have been many nonfiction works of this type during modern times, including *The Stork and the Plow* and *Extinction* by Paul and Anne Ehrlich, *Our Plundered Planet* by Fairfield Osborn, *Our Angry Earth* by Isaac Asimov and Frederik Pohl, and *The End of Nature* by Bill McKibben. There have been many fiction works on environmental apocalypse as well, including Kurt Vonnegut's *Cat's Cradle* and Ursula LeGuin's *The Lathe of Heaven.* Suggestions of an incipient environmental apocalypse increase the public's fears regarding environmental problems and can be an effective tool for influencing environmental practices and policies. For this reason, this literature has been heavily criticized by antienvironmentalists, who address and refute apocalyptic theories in a series of books and articles.

See also Antienvironmentalism; Asimov, Isaac; *Cat's Cradle;* Ehrlich, Paul and Anne; *End of Nature, The;* Environmental Fiction; *Extinction; Lathe of Heaven, The;* LeGuin, Ursula; McKibben, Bill; *Our Angry Earth; Our Plundered Planet;* Pohl, Frederik; *Stork and the Plow, The;* Vonnegut, Kurt.

Environmental Ethics

Environmental Ethics: Choices for Concerned Citizens (1980) was written by the Science Action Committee with Albert J. Fritsch, Ph.D. It represents a period when environmental task forces and committees sought new approaches to environmental problems. In this regard, *Environmental Ethics* states: "This book is not intended as an effort to heighten environmental consciousness, or to pinpoint blame. Much has been written about the causes, symptoms, and detection of environmental deterioration. . . . Instead, we are attempting to explore the values that underlie this environmental degradation and the sets of principles that citizens must apply to remedy the situation." (Fritsch 1980, 1)

Environmental Ethics discusses a variety of environmental issues, such as pesticide use, nuclear waste, and fossil fuel emissions, in terms of ethics and morals. For example, on chemical use:

> The public has a right to be protected from the unreasonable risk of working or using untested chemicals. Chemical producers have the responsibility to do or have these tests performed, and the government should see that they are properly executed. These duties follow from the individual's right to . . . [a] clean and healthy environment, safe working conditions, and safe consumer products. . . . Consumers have the responsibility: to preserve their own health and safety and those of their neighbor; to protect the environment by proper use of resources and by disposing of waste materials properly; to educate themselves and others about the risks involved in hazardous chemicals; and to use existing judiciary systems to further the reduction of chemical insult on human beings and the environment. (156–157)

In addition, *Environmental Ethics* suggests that "our lifestyles are the outward manifestation of exactly how much we have interiorized the . . . [environmental] ethic": "When we are immersed in our consumer culture and uncritically accept materialistic goals, we find that our cars, clothes, food, and recreation reflect those values. When wasteful practices do not prick our consciences, then we accept energy inefficiency and ultimately environmental degradation—no matter what we say about ecology and sharing with the world's poor." (201) The book advocates a simple lifestyle and argues that if people refuse to change their behavior voluntarily, then governments must mandate them to do so. It states:

Societies must set the groundwork for a more just distribution of resources needed for lifestyle expression and foster creativity for the greater number. A truly human and environmental ethics should encourage concerned citizens to initiate actions—whether political, legal, economic, or even physical—that place roadblocks in front of excessive lifestyle. Society may restrict the use of fuel for recreational vehicles, challenge the manufacture of gas guzzlers or inefficient electric appliances, or demonstrate against a nuclear power plant. To restrict institutional and individual excess is to expand the lifestyle choices of the entire human community. (223)

Environmental Ethics also discusses the relationship between environmentalism and theology, offering several quotes from the Bible. It concludes with a list of "action criteria" (258) for activists to follow in attempting to change environmental attitudes, practices, and policies. (Fritsch 1981)

See also Environmental Activism.

Environmental Fiction

Environmental fiction is a genre in which some aspect of environmentalism or the environmental sciences plays an important role. Many works of environmental fiction can be classified as part of the broader genre of science fiction.

Environmental fiction falls into three basic categories: works that portray the environmental movement and/or environmental activism; works that depict a conflict over an environmental issue and express the author's beliefs regarding that issue; and works that feature an environmental apocalypse. Examples from the first category are Henrik Ibsen's 1882 play, *An Enemy of the People* (which concerns an environmental activist's unsuccessful struggle to convince townspeople that their water is polluted), and Edward Abbey's 1975 novel, *The Monkey Wrench Gang* (about a band of environmental activists using illegal tactics to fight development in the American Southwest). Examples from the second category are Frederik Pohl's 1987 novel, *Chernobyl* (on nuclear power), and Harry Harrison's 1966 novel, *Make Room! Make Room!* (overpopulation). The third category includes Kurt Vonnegut's 1963 novel, *Cat's Cradle* (which involves a scientific discovery that accidentally solidifies all of earth's water), and Ursula LeGuin's 1971 novel, *The Lathe of Heaven* (featuring a character whose dreams destroy earth, which has become severely polluted and overpopulated).

All works of environmental fiction have one element in common: the author's desire to promote environmentalism among the general public. The author might or might not discuss environmental science, but some focus exclusively on science without promoting environmentalism (evolution being the most common theme).

The earliest novels to discuss evolution appeared during the 19th century, when the concept was first developed. In 1872 Samuel Butler wrote *Erewhon* specifically to dispute the work of evolutionary theorist Charles Darwin, who published *The Descent of Man* the preceding year. Many more novels related to evolution appeared during the late 1800s and early 1900s, after scientists made important fossil discoveries and popular authors became fascinated with the idea of encounters between dinosaurs and humans. Jules Verne's 1864 novel, *A Journey to the Center of the Earth*, Sir Arthur Conan Doyle's 1912 novel, *The Lost World*, and Edgar Rice Burroughs's 1918 novel, *The Land That Time Forgot*, are among the best-known examples. Although these books provide information about environmental science, they are primarily adventure stories.

During the modern era, the focus of such novels has changed. Although they continue to include adventure, a message is typically offered: Human beings evolved to become the dominant species on earth; so too could another creature evolve to take their place. This concept of threatened human superiority first appeared during the early environmental movement, when people began to fear the consequences of pollution, nuclear war, and other forms of environmental destruction. The foremost example of environmental fiction from this period is Pierre Boulle's 1963 novel, *Planet of the Apes*, which depicts a world in which human beings have become ignorant, speechless beasts, whereas apes have evolved into intelligent, humanlike beings. (In the 1968 movie version of this novel, the story was given an apocalyptic twist: The main character discovers that the evolutionary reversal was the result of nuclear war.) In more recent years, the replacement of humans as the dominant species has been suggested in Michael Crichton's 1990 novel, *Jurassic Park*, in which scientists genetically create living dinosaurs that view human beings as prey.

See also Abbey, Edward; Boulle, Pierre; Burroughs, Edgar Rice; Butler, Samuel; *Chernobyl;* Crichton, Michael; Darwin, Charles Robert; *Descent of Man, The;* Doyle, Arthur Conan; *Enemy of the People, An;* Environmental Activism; Environmental Apocalypse; Environmental Movement; *Erewhon;* Evolution; Harrison, Harry; Ibsen, Henrik; *Jurassic Park; Land That Time Forgot, The; Lathe of Heaven, The;* LeGuin, Ursula; *Lost World, The; Make Room! Make Room!; Monkey Wrench Gang, The; Planet of the Apes;* Pohl, Frederik; Verne, Jules; Vonnegut, Kurt.

Environmental Groups

Environmental groups organize to address environmental problems on the local, national, and international levels: human ecology; air and water pollution; animal ecology; endangered species and habitats. They use a variety of tactics to achieve their goals, but in all cases they are dedicated to activism. In this respect they are different from the conservation groups of an earlier time. Conservation groups began to form in the United States during the late 1800s to support the enjoyment of the outdoors through bird-watching, hiking, camping, and similar activities. Although they did address environmental issues—particularly forestry management and wildlife conservation—environmental activism was not their primary focus.

Many conservation groups evolved into environmental groups during the 1960s, as the

Earth First! activist occupying a tree so that it cannot be logged (Corbis)

environmental movement gained strength. Books like Rachel Carson's *Silent Spring* (1962) began warning of environmental apocalypse, and many environmental groups organized to address environmental problems. Conservation groups responded to the emotional climate by moving from conservationism toward environmentalism. For example, the Sierra Club was founded in 1892 by conservationist John Muir to promote wilderness enjoyment, but today it is dedicated to protecting wilderness areas through environmental politics and activism.

The Sierra Club is one of many mainstream environmental groups, which work within existing political and social systems to promote environmentalism. Such groups are typically large and well funded (the Sierra Club has more than 550,000 members and an annual income of approximately $40 million). One of the wealthiest mainstream groups is The Nature Conservancy, which was formed by a group of scientists in 1946. It has more than 797,000 members and an annual budget of approximately $278.49 million. With such resources, mainstream environmental groups are able to maintain their own publishing companies. Both the Sierra Club and The Nature Conservancy, for example, publish books, magazines, calendars, and even greeting cards. Mainstream groups also support scientific research projects; many of the books are based on these projects, offering in-depth discussions of environmental issues.

In contrast, radical environmental groups are counterculture organizations; their members sometimes run afoul of the law to advance environmental goals. Earth First!, for example, sometimes sabotages building sites to stop development. Consequently, radical environmental groups do not have the wealth or social support of mainstream groups and have difficulty publishing and distributing their ideas. More often than not, radical groups have little interest in raising money through sales of books and cards. Instead, they seek to promote beliefs about environmentalism and convert more people to the cause. For this reason, most of the radical literature contains personal expressions and defenses of ideology rather than a scientific discussion of environmental issues. The works of Earth First! members Dave Foreman and Christopher Manes are foremost examples of this.

Grass-roots organizations, a third variant, are usually small entities formed to address local environmental problems, such as air and water pollution and waste management. Grass-roots groups typically do not publish, except perhaps for pamphlets, fact sheets, meeting notices, and the like. Even so, grass-roots activities are sometimes highlighted in others' works (Robert Gottlieb has written on environmental history, environmental politics, and water pollution issues; and Mark Dowie's *Losing Ground* offers a thorough discussion of all forms of environmentalism). Critics of modern environmentalism, or antienvironmentalists, have examined grass-roots, mainstream, and radical groups. (Netzley 1998)

See also Animal Ecology; Audubon, John James; Dowie, Mark; Easterbrook, Gregg; *Fierce Green Fire, A;* Foreman, Dave; Gottlieb, Robert; Human Ecology; *Losing Ground;* Manes, Christopher; *Moment on the Earth, A;* Muir, John; *Nature Conservancy Magazine, The;* Shabecoff, Philip; *Sierra.*

Environmental History
See Environmental Movement; Environmental Politics

Environmental Movement
The environmental movement in the United States and Europe began during the late 1950s. It grew out of the conservationism of the 19th and early 20th centuries, when modern nations became concerned over the depletion of natural resources. Conservationists wanted to preserve natural resources for the use and enjoyment of future generations. In contrast, early environmentalists sought to preserve natural resources in order to protect human health and well-being.

This shift in attitude stemmed from the state of the environment and modern technology during the 1940s and 1950s. Initially, the environmental movement was a response to fears regarding the development of nuclear weapons and an increase in pollution and pesticide use. As the planet's air, land, and water grew more toxic, scientists began to note that environmental damage could cause serious health problems, and authors began to express their fears that the earth would one day become uninhabitable. For example, in *Our Plundered Planet* (1948), Fairfield Osborn writes that people have "lost sight of the fact that the living resources of his life are derived from his earth-home and not from his mind-power. With one hand he harnesses greater waters, with the other he dries up the water sources. He must change with changing conditions or perish." (Osborn 1948, 30) However, such warnings had little impact on the public until 1962, when Rachel Carson published *Silent Spring*, an eloquent plea to restrict pesticide use. The work was extremely popular and is often credited with triggering the modern environmental movement.

This movement gained strength throughout the 1960s, 1970s, and 1980s. However, it did split into factions, as people disagreed over how to practice environmentalism and solve the earth's problems. Some participated in a back-to-nature movement—living simply off the land while condemning materialism; some practiced deep ecology or advocated social ecology. Some environmentalists formed mainstream groups devoted to environmental politics; others chose more radical forms of environmental activism. In any event, this lack of cohesiveness produced a huge range of environmental literature, as various authors sought to defend specific approaches to environmentalism. For example, Arne Naess, David Rothenberg, and George Sessions promoted deep ecology, whereas Barry Commoner and Murray Bookchin supported social ecology and Edward Abbey, Dave Foreman, and Christopher Manes argued for radical environmentalism. Meanwhile, scientists continued to write on specific environmental issues; for their part, opponents of the environmental movement published works that criticized both environmentalists and sci-entists. By the 1990s environmentalism was coming under scrutiny by environmentalists themselves, and some wrote books discussing the flaws of environmental groups and their factions. For example, Mark Dowie analyzes the successes and failures of environmentalism in *Losing Ground* (1995), and Gregg Easterbrook criticizes environmentalists' pessimistic attitudes in *A Moment on the Earth* (1995). (Netzley 1998)

See also Abbey, Edward; Bookchin, Murray; Carson, Rachel Louise; Commoner, Barry; Conservationism; Deep Ecology Movement; Dowie, Mark; Easterbrook, Gregg; Environmental Activism; Environmental Politics; Foreman, Dave; *Losing Ground;* Manes, Christopher; *Moment on the Earth, A;* Naess, Arne; Nuclear Energy; *Our Plundered Planet;* Pesticides and Chemicals; Rothenberg, David; Sessions, George; *Silent Spring;* Social Ecology.

Environmental Overkill

Environmental Overkill: Whatever Happened to Common Sense? (1993), by Dixy Lee Ray with Lou Guzzo, criticizes U.S. environmental policy and is one of the most frequently cited of all antienvironmental books. Ray was a politician, able to influence environmental policymaking, and consequently her opinions garnered more attention that most other opponents of modern environmentalism.

Ray and Guzzo argue that environmentalists "exaggerate the seriousness of environmental issues" and "downplay the remarkable resilience and recovery powers of nature." (Ray and Guzzo 1993, ix) Moreover, they say that government leaders often fail to base environmental policy decisions on scientific facts. To prove their point, the authors discuss environmental issues in detail. In the first part of the book, "The Air Above Us," they examine atmosphere-related environmental problems and suggest that many of them, such as global warming and ozone depletion, are not really problems at all: "Japanese scientists have described and discussed the annual Antarctic ozone 'hole' as a natural phenomenon. . . . But as far as the news media are concerned, what makes a better story: 'Man-Made

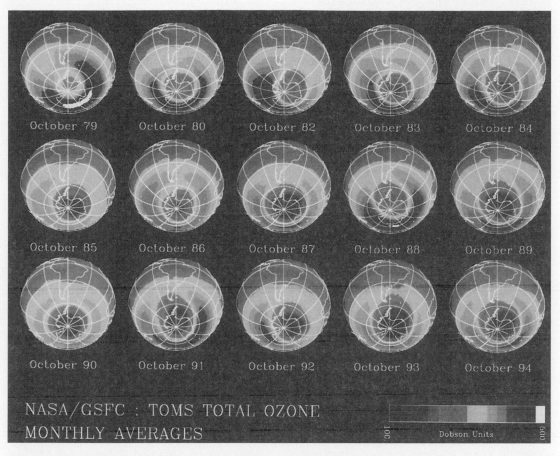

October 79 | October 80 | October 82 | October 83 | October 84

October 85 | October 86 | October 87 | October 88 | October 89

October 90 | October 91 | October 92 | October 93 | October 94

NASA/GSFC : TOMS TOTAL OZONE
MONTHLY AVERAGES

Dobson Units

This composite image shows a timeline of fifteen October monthly average images; the growth of the Antarctic ozone hole since 1979 is clearly visible (NASA)

Chemicals Punch Deadly Hole in the Sky' or 'Sun Spots Lead to Natural Fluctuation of the Ozone in the Stratosphere'? It all began with Chicken Little." (38)

Throughout *Environmental Overkill,* Ray and Guzzo blame the media for disseminating false information about environmental issues. They say that television, for example, "has manipulated programs to suit the political and social beliefs of producers, editors, writers, and staff":

> With the news media stacking the deck against common sense and scientific honesty in environmental affairs, it's little wonder, then, that polls indicate so many Americans believe "something must be done to protect the environment, no matter what the cost. . . ." How can the elec-

torate be expected to make truly intelligent decisions if the news media do not provide them with all the information on the environment, except what supports the most radical and outlandish environmental positions? (180–181)

In the second part of the book "About Food, People, and Animals," Ray and Guzzo attack several of those positions. They criticize environmentalist Paul Ehrlich, for example, for promoting the idea that overpopulation is a serious environmental threat. They also argue, contrary to environmentalists' claims, that many pesticides are safe and many "listed" endangered species are not endangered at all. In the third part, "This Land Is Our Land," they examine the issue of endangered species more deeply, examining various economic issues related to habitat protection. For example, they criticize government methods to define wetlands. They also defend modern logging practices:

> Even the much maligned practice of "clear-cutting," contrary to popular notion, does not leave the ground scraped bare. It is generally conducted on a checkerboard pattern, which leaves large nearby parcels of forest untouched until a future cycle of cutting. . . . The devastated appearance of a recently clear-cut area raises strong emotions. But the condition is temporary. As pointed out in a recent Report of the President's Advisory Panel on Timber and Environment: "If properly applied, clear-cutting does not lead to soil erosion, nutrient depletion, wildlife habitat damage, or stream sedimentation." And, according to the U.S. Forest Service: "Drastic as it may seem, clear-cutting plays a legitimate and prominent role in scientific forestry. Properly done, it paves the way for a new, unencumbered and hence, vigorously growing, forest." (114)

Ray and Guzzo complain about environmentalists and government officials who want to interfere with such practices. In addition, they criticize the current trend toward ignoring property rights, stating:

> Despite . . . constitutional guarantee, agencies of the government are taking control of private property at an accelerating rate, often with neither due process nor compensation. In the name of "protecting the environment," Congress has enacted laws that allow government regulators to confiscate private property, to prevent an owner from using his land, to levy fines for noncompliance . . . and to jail the landowner who may try to use his land for any purpose other than that prescribed by government—even if the citizen was unaware of the restrictions. (117)

In the part entitled "Rules and More Rules" they protest the rise in government regula-

tion, saying that much of it is unwarranted and/or overly expensive. They believe that "billions of dollars have been wasted on precipitous actions that weren't necessary, instances where political action moved faster than scientific research justified, and where government bureaucrats and the public just plain overreacted." (137) In "Communication, Education, and Politics," they suggest several reasons for the tendency to overreact to environmental problems. For example, they say that many environmentalists are alarmists and call Rachel Carson's book *Silent Spring* "an emotional, lyrical, and grossly unscientific and inaccurate book," adding that "Carson . . . exaggerated the danger of pesticides. It was the abuse, not the use, of pesticides that was the problem." (188–189) They also criticize Vice President Al Gore's book *Earth in the Balance,* writing that it shows "he is an extremist on environmental issues" who "has completely ignored scientific impartiality" in favor of an emotional response to environmentalism. (188)

In conclusion they call for a return to reason and common sense. They say that "the environmental movement is not about facts or logic" (205) but rather politics and power; they offer the hope that someday this will change. (Helvarg 1994; Ray and Guzzo 1993)

See also Antienvironmentalism; Carson, Rachel Louise; *Earth in the Balance;* Ehrlich, Paul and Anne; Environmental Politics; Gore Jr., Albert; Guzzo, Lou; Ray, Dixy Lee; *Silent Spring.*

Environmental Politics

Politics is an important aspect of modern environmentalism, because attempts to solve environmental problems often depend upon government support. Yet governments and environmentalists often have quite different priorities, which leads to clashes over how best to approach environmental issues. This conflict is a common subject in modern environmental literature.

In fiction, the topic appeared as early as the 19th century, most notably in Henrik Ibsen's 1882 play, *An Enemy of the People.* This drama depicts one man's unsuccessful struggle to convince town leaders that the water in their lucrative public baths is polluted. More recent examples are Edward Abbey's 1975 novel, *The Monkey Wrench Gang,* which features a band of environmental activists, and Frederik Pohl's 1987 novel, *Chernobyl,* which concerns the politics of Russia during an environmental disaster caused by nuclear energy.

Yet the subject of environmental politics is most often analyzed in nonfictional works, where authors present interpretations of environmental issues, either criticizing or applauding (and sometimes both) the government position. For example, John Muir discusses government wilderness policies in *Our National Parks,* as does Alston Chase in *Playing God in Yellowstone.* Robert Gottlieb and Marc Reisner examine the politics of water conservation in *A Life of Its Own* and *Cadillac Desert.* Ralph Nader talks about the political aspects of corporate pollution in *Who's Poisoning America,* and Carl Sagan addressed the politics of nuclear energy in *A Path Where No Man Thought.*

Some nonfiction authors avoid the politics of a particular issue and instead examine the overall politics of environmentalism. For example, Mark Dowie's *Losing Ground* analyzes the successes and failures of environmental groups, and David Helvarg's *The War Against the Greens* looks at the opponents of such groups. Michael Fumento's *Science Under Siege,* Ronald Bailey's *Eco-Scam,* Wallace Kaufman's *No Turning Back,* and Dixy Lee Ray and Lou Guzzo's *Environmental Overkill* focus on environmental laws, policies, and attitudes, arguing that the government has gone too far in its support of environmentalism. Meanwhile, Dave Foreman's *Confessions of an Eco-Warrior* and Christopher Manes's *Green Rage* argue that the government has not gone far enough. Works on environmental history also discuss environmental politics; examples of such literature are Philip Shabecoff's *A Fierce Green Fire,* Robert Gottlieb's *Forcing the Spring,* Roderick Nash's *The Rights of Nature,* Charles Reich's *The Greening of America,* and Charles Ponting's *A Green History of the World.* (Netzley 1998)

See also Abbey, Edward; Bailey, Ronald; *Cadillac Desert;* Chase, Alston; *Chernobyl; Confessions of an Eco-Warrior;* Dowie, Mark; *Eco-Scam; Enemy of the People, An;* Environmental Activism; *Environmental Overkill; Fierce Green Fire, A; Forcing the Spring;* Foreman, Dave; Fumento, Michael; Gottlieb, Robert; *Green History of the World, A; Green Rage; Greening of America, The;* Guzzo, Lou; Helvarg, David; Ibsen, Henrik; Kaufman, Wallace; *Life of Its Own, A; Losing Ground;* Manes, Christopher; *Monkey Wrench Gang, The;* Muir, John; Nader, Ralph; Nash, Roderick Frazier; *No Turning Back;* Nuclear Energy; *Our National Parks; Path Where No Man Thought, A; Playing God in Yellowstone;* Pohl, Frederik; Ray, Dixy Lee; Reisner, Marc; *Rights of Nature, The;* Sagan, Carl; *Science Under Siege;* Shabecoff, Philip; *War Against the Greens, The; Who's Poisoning America.*

Epitaph for a Peach

Published in 1995, *Epitaph for a Peach: Four Seasons on My Family Farm* by David Mas Masumoto is a memoir of the author's experiences on his family's peach farm in Del Ray, California. Masumoto is of Japanese descent and a third-generation California fruit grower.

The prologue, entitled "Epitaph for a Peach," was originally published in the *Los Angeles Times* on August 16, 1987. This essay explains that the author's orchard of Sun Crest peaches will be bulldozed because markets no longer want "one of the last remaining truly juicy peaches" because "when ripe, they turn an amber gold rather than the lipstick red that seduces the public." (Masumoto 1995, x)

After the essay appeared, people began writing to Masumoto, encouraging him to keep his Sun Crests, which he decided to do for one more harvest. His book documents his experiences the following year, and in the end he decides to keep the peaches for yet another season.

Epitaph for a Peach provides details on life as a fruit grower, as well as Masumoto's comments about his relationship with nature. For example, he writes:

Farmers fool themselves when they talk about taking land from the wild. Some believe they can outwit nature and grow a lush vineyard in poor soils and on land where vines don't belong. But I sense that farming is only a temporary claim on a piece of earth, not a right; farmers borrow the land from nature to squeeze out a living.

With each generation we may be losing that sense of "claiming the land." Armed with our machinery and with youthful confidence, we've never felt nature beat us. In the end, though, nature has a way of keeping us in our place by a thunderstorm on our table grapes, a heat wave that burns the peaches, or showers that fall on unprotected grapes trying to dry into raisins. We are humbled. (111)

Ultimately, Masumoto's connection to the land is also a connection to his birthright. (Masumoto 1995)

Erewhon

Samuel Butler's *Erewhon* (1872) is a satirical novel that criticizes aspects of British society. However, it also reflects Butler's opinions of Charles Darwin's theory of evolution and was the first major work of fiction to address the subject. When Darwin published *Origin of Species* in 1859, Butler initially supported the idea that man evolved through a fairly mechanical process. But within a few years he rejected Darwinism, believing it ignored the existence of God.

Butler wrote two articles relating this view, "Darwin Among the Machines" (1863) and "Lucubratio Ebria" (1865). In the first he speculates on the possibility of machines evolving into sentient beings; in the second he explores the idea that a man can evolve into a more superior being by attaching himself to machines. Published in the New Zealand *Press,* these articles inspired several sections of *Erewhon.*

The novel describes one man's adventures in a strange country called Erewhon (a letter scramble of the word "nowhere"). The first-person narrator stumbles upon Erewhon accidentally while searching for gold and grazing land in an unexplored mountain region. Its people treat him well but do not allow him to leave. Instead, they expect him to join their society and adhere to its philosophies.

The Erewhons believe that physically healthy people are superior to sickly ones. They sentence the chronically ill to life in prison and arrange marriages on the basis of physical attributes. Accordingly, their society is filled with people of unusual strength and beauty. Yet they have no modern technology. They had banned machines years earlier, when someone theorized that mechanized objects could eventually evolve into sentient beings. The narrator translates one of their books, "The Book of Machines," and finds an explanation of this theory of machine consciousness. In part it says:

There was a time when the earth was to all appearance utterly destitute both of animal and vegetable life, and when according to the opinion of our best philosophers it was simply a hot round ball with a crust gradually cooling. Now if a human being had existed while the earth was in this state and had been allowed to see it as though it were some other world with which he had no concern, and if at the same time he were entirely ignorant of all physical science, would he not have pronounced it impossible that creatures possessed of anything like consciousness should be evolved from the seeming cinder which he was beholding? Would he not have denied that it contained any potentiality of consciousness? Yet in the course of time, consciousness came. Is it not possible then that there may be even yet new channels dug out for consciousness, though we can detect no signs of them at present? (Butler 1923, 175)

Many of Butler's contemporaries believed that "The Book of Machines" was an attempt to ridicule Charles Darwin. However, Butler said that ridicule was not his intent. In 1872 he wrote:

I regret that reviewers have in some cases been inclined to treat the chapters on Machines as an attempt to reduce Mr. Darwin's theory to an absurdity. Nothing could be further from my intention, and few things would be more distasteful to me than any attempt to laugh at Mr. Darwin; but I must own that I have myself to thank for the conception, for I felt sure that my intention would be missed, but preferred not to weaken the chapters by explanation, and knew very well that Mr. Darwin's theory would take no harm. The only question in my mind was how far I could afford to be misrepresented as laughing at that for which I have the most profound admiration. (xix–xx)

Although Butler admired Darwin, he did not agree with him. Similarly, the narrator of *Erewhon* professes admiration for his hosts but is morally opposed to their beliefs. He also bemoans their tendency to follow false prophets who present "absurd views of life." (222) One such prophet argued that animals have rights and should not be eaten; the Erewhons accepted this philosophy until the argument was extended to vegetables. Like "The Book of Machines," the discussion of animal and vegetable rights is a veiled criticism of Darwin, who often spoke of "sympathy beyond the confines of man" and "humanity to the lower animals." (Callicott 1987, 6)

In the end, the narrator believes that the solution to such misguided thinking is Christianity. He builds a hot-air balloon, escapes the country with his Erewhonian fiancée, travels to Europe, and tries to assemble a group of missionaries who will bring true religion to the people of Erewhon. (Butler 1923; Callicott 1987)

See also Butler, Samuel; Darwin, Charles Robert; Environmental Fiction; *Origin of Species, The.*

Essay on the Principle of Population, An

Formally titled *An Essay on the Principle of Population, as It Affects the Future Improvement of Society, with Remarks on the Speculations of Mr. Godwin, M. Condorcet, and Other Writers,* this work, by the Reverend Thomas Robert Malthus, was published anonymously in 1798. It was one of the earliest works to address the problem of overpopulation. It was intended as an argument against the optimism of radical William Godwin and similar social reformers of the time, who believed that people would eventually prosper if left unrestrained by government or social institutions. Malthus countered that the future of human beings would remain bleak despite any reforms, because as people prosper they inevitably increase in number and eventually exhaust the earth's food supply. That, in turn, causes famine, disease, war, and death.

Malthus's theory immediately generated great controversy. Some used it to argue against social reform, whereas others took it as a call to change welfare practices that seemed to encourage the poor to have large families. The theory also engendered discussions about ways to control population. In a revised second edition of the essay, published in 1803, Malthus suggested that late marriage and abstinence were two ways to lower the birth rate. He later expanded on this discussion, publishing six increasingly larger versions of his work, the final one appearing in 1826.

However, according to Clive Ponting in *A Green History of the World,* Malthus's work had no lasting effect on people's optimism toward the future of humanity. He explains:

Essay on the Principle of Population . . . argued that there was a permanent cycle in history in which human numbers increased until they were too high for the available food supply, at which point famine and disease would reduce the population until it was again in balance with the amount of food that could be produced. Malthus could see no way out of this terrible cycle. During the nineteenth century this Malthusian view of history was largely ignored and the idea of progress became almost universally accepted as the natural, unspoken assumption. Such optimism was felt to be justified by the huge material progress made by Europe in the nineteenth century: its ability to feed an ever larger population, the growth of cities, new inventions and the development of industry. . . . By the end of the late nineteenth century the idea of progress had become a part of popular culture . . . almost any change could be automatically equated with progress. Although battered by some of the events of the twentieth century, it remains a widely accepted assumption about the nature of human history. (Ponting 1991, p. 151)

Nonetheless, *An Essay on the Principle of Population* has inspired efforts to control population growth. From 1877 to 1927 the Malthusian League, a social-reform group named after Malthus, worked to encourage birth control among the poor, and experts continue to analyze the relationship between overpopulation and social and environmental problems. (Malthus 1976; Ponting 1991)

See also Human Ecology; Malthus, Thomas Robert.

Evelyn, John

John Evelyn is best known for his 1664 work on forest conservation: *Sylva: A Discourse of Forest-trees and the Propagation of Timber,* which he completed on commission for England's Royal Navy. It was the first major work on the subject.

Born on October 31, 1620, in Wotton, Surrey, England, Evelyn was a member of the wealthy landowning class. As such he was well educated and well traveled. He attended Balliol College in Oxford, and from 1643 to 1652 he lived abroad, where he met and married the daughter of an English diplomat. He returned to Deptford, England, to run her father's estate. He also began writing political pamphlets. This led to appointments on several royal commissions devoted to public improvement, including a 1662 project on London street repairs, as well as a commission devoted to addressing the concerns of sick and injured seamen.

In 1662 Evelyn was appointed to the Royal Society, for which he began a study of England's forestry practices. *Sylva* was the result of this work. From 1671 to 1674 he focused his attention on colonial affairs. However, he continued to write on forestry issues. He also wrote books and articles on other subjects, particularly religion. In fact *Sylva* contains Evelyn's religious views as they relate to the balance of nature.

At age 11 Evelyn started a diary, which he kept throughout his life; he died on February 27, 1706. His diary writings, published posthumously in 1818, detailed more than 50 years of English history and society.

See also Forest Management; *Sylva.*

Evolution

Evolution is the process whereby species develop variations over time. One species might be said to evolve from another, and animals with similar anatomical structures often have a common ancestor.

The idea that species evolve did not develop until the early 19th century, when Jean-Baptiste Lamarck suggested that creatures change in response to their environment and pass on those changes to the next generation. Although this theory was later proved wrong, it paved the way for later evolutionary theorists, most notably Charles Darwin. Darwin's book *On the Origin of Species by Means of Natural Selection* (1859) introduced modern evolutionary theory to the public, and his *The Descent of Man and Selection in Relation to Sex* (1871) suggested that humans and apes have a common ancestor. Darwin's work was thus a matter of controversy, as many people refused to consider humans as anything but superior to animals. They also insisted that God, and not a natural process, was responsible for the similarities among and variations within species.

Today there are people who still believe this. However, modern technology—particularly genetic testing—has supported the idea that one species can evolve from another, although the process now appears to be more complex than Darwin proposed. Fossil discoveries have also supported the theory of evolution. In regard to human fossils, the works of anthropologists Louis and Mary Leakey have been especially significant, and recently their son, Richard Leakey, has suggested that evolution must be considered in tandem with extinction, which is an integral part of the way species change.

See also Darwin, Charles Robert; *Descent of Man, The;* Lamarck, Jean-Baptiste; Leakey, Louis; Leakey, Richard; *Origin of Species, The.*

Experiments and Observations on Different Kinds of Air

The six-volume work *Experiments and Observations on Different Kinds of Air* by Joseph Priestley was published from 1774 to 1786. Its author studied the atmosphere and discovered many of its components, including oxygen. He also realized that animals depleted oxygen by breathing and that somehow nature was restoring this depleted oxygen. He wrote:

Joseph Priestley (Library of Congress)

That candles will burn only a certain time in a given quantity of air is a fact not better known than it is that animals can live only a certain time in it; but the cause of the death of the animal is not better known than that of the extinction of flame in the same circumstances; and when once any quantity of air has been rendered noxious by animals breathing in it as long as they could, I do not know that any methods have been discovered of rendering it fit for breathing again. It is evident, however, that there must be some provision in nature for this purpose, as well as for that of rendering the air fit for sustaining flame; for without it the whole mass of the atmosphere would, in time, become unfit for the purpose of animal life; and yet there is no reason to think that it is, at present, at all less fit for respiration than it has ever been. (Boynton 1948, 443)

Priestley's work eventually led a Dutch physician, Jan Ingenhousz, to discover the process of photosynthesis, by which plants re-

plenish the earth's oxygen. (Boynton 1948; Spangenburg and Moser 1993)

See also Animal Ecology; Priestley, Joseph.

Experiments Upon Vegetables

This work by Jan Ingenhousz, formally titled *Experiments Upon Vegetables, Discovering Their Great Power of Purifying the Common Air in the Sun-Shine, and of Injuring It in the Shade at Night,* was published in 1779. It reports the author's discovery that plants take in carbon dioxide and give off oxygen. Ingenhousz correctly recognized that this process—photosynthesis—requires light:

I observed, that plants not only have a faculty to correct bad air in six or ten days, by growing in it . . . but that . . . this wonderful operation is by no means owing to the vegetation of the plant, but to the influence of the light of the sun upon the plant. . . . This operation is far from being carried on constantly, but begins only after the sun has for some time made his appearance above the horizon and has, by his influence, prepared the plants to begin anew their beneficial operation upon the air, and thus upon the animal creation, which was stopt during the darkness of the night. (Boynton 1948, 452–453)

Ingenhousz's work was consequently a major contribution to science. (Boynton 1948, Spangenburg and Moser 1993)

See also Ingenhousz, Jan.

Extinction

Extinction: The Causes and Consequences of the Disappearance of Species was written by Paul and Anne Ehrlich, noted for their controversial apocalyptic writings on human ecology and overpopulation. Published in 1981, the book takes a similar apocalyptic stance on the problem of endangered species, warning of the dire consequences of species extinction.

Extinction is divided into four parts. The introduction begins with a description of Jane Goodall's research into wild African chimpanzees. The natural habitat of these animals was being threatened by builders and farmers, and the Ehrlichs speculate that as human populations rise in the region Goodall's chimpanzees will become extinct. Of this event, the authors say: "Most sensitive human beings will care, will mourn the loss. But only a relative few will realize that the coming disappearance of this prominent endangered species is not just a single tragedy but symptomatic of a planetary catastrophe that is bearing down upon all of us. For along with the chimp will go the other living elements of the chimp's ecosystem—components of all Earth's crucial life-support systems." (Ehrlich and Ehrlich 1981, 6) The Ehrlichs believe that all species "are living components of vital ecological systems (ecosystems) which provide humanity with indispensable free services—services whose substantial disruption would lead inevitably to a collapse of civilization. By deliberately or unknowingly forcing species to extinction, *Homo sapiens* is attacking *itself;* it is certainly endangering society and possibly even threatening our own species with extermination." (6)

The Ehrlichs acknowledge that species have become extinct naturally, through evolution or environmental changes such as those that caused the dinosaurs to disappear. However, they believe that because such disappearances were caused by nature they occurred when nature was ready to deal with them: "The crucial point is that the dinosaurs became extinct at a time when evolutionary processes were capable of replacing them with the mammals." (9) They discuss evolution at length and argue that humans are causing species to become extinct at an unnatural rate: "The rate of extinction of bird and mammal species between 1600 and 1975 has been estimated to be between five and fifty times higher than it was through most of the eons of our evolutionary past. Furthermore, in the last decades of the twentieth century, that rate is projected to rise to some forty to four hundred times 'normal.'" (8)

The second part of *Extinction,* "Why Should We Care?," explains why people should be concerned over the abnormal rate of extinction. It focuses on the moral and ethical aspects of saving endangered species, mentioning conservationist Aldo Leopold's work in that regard, and discusses the economic benefits of preserving plants and animals. The Ehrlichs explain that many helpful products and medicines have come from endangered species, contending that biological diversity is necessary to maintain the health of the planet's soil, water, air, and climate. They add that ecosystems are delicate; when one species disappears, the loss can cause serious repercussions. For example, "when a predatory starfish was removed from an intertidal community . . . the community collapsed from fifteen to eight species in less than two years. The mussels that were the preferred prey of the starfish increased in its absence and outcompeted other species, forcing them to local extinction." (97)

In the third part, "How Are Species Endangered by Humanity?," the authors offer many other examples of how human interference has endangered various plants and animals. They talk about "direct endangering," which occurs through such practices as hunting, the fur trade, and predator control; and "indirect endangering," caused by various types of habitat destruction, such as urbanization, agriculture, logging, overgrazing, pesticide spraying, and wilderness recreation.

In the fourth part, "What Are We Doing and What Can We Do?," the Ehrlichs discuss environmental politics, the Endangered Species Act and other U.S. laws and policies, zoo and game preserve management, and conservation strategies in rich and poor countries. They argue that the best way to protect endangered species would be to "put the brakes on material growth of the economy, and put them on hard. No more land paved over; if new housing is needed, redevelop slums. No more land plowed under or grazed. . . . Open no more mines; recycle everything. . . . Make durability, not disposability, the goal of production." (245–246) However, because "to put the brakes on material economic growth now would be to condemn the majority of the world's populations to lives of misery," they recommend that global wealth be redistributed, so that rich countries are helping to support poor ones. (246) They conclude that "aid to the poor is the best investment rich countries could ever make; there is considerable question whether the rich will realize it in time. But overhaul of the international economic system is long overdue, and perhaps the intertwined issues of resource shortages and extinctions will at last trigger it." (248)

Extinction concludes with a call to action, which suggests that "just as President Kennedy put the United States on the road to space, another president could put the nation—and, one would hope, the world—on the road to treating Earth as a spaceship. Someone had better get on with the job, for *Homo sapiens* is no more immune to the effects of habitat destruction than the Chimpanzee, Bengal Tiger, Bald Eagle, Snail Darter, or Golden Gladiolus." (25) In an appendix, the Ehrlichs provide a guide for understanding the scientific classifications of such species. (Ehrlich and Ehrlich 1981; Shabecoff 1993)

See also Agriculture; Biodiversity; Ehrlich, Paul and Anne; Environmental Apocalypse; Goodall, Jane; Habitat Protection; Wildlife Conservation.

F

Fabre, Jean-Henri

Born on December 22, 1823, in Saint-Leons, France, Jean-Henri Fabre was a largely self-educated entomologist who studied insect anatomy and behavior. He was the first person to suspect that insects communicated through smell. He also wrote several books that popularized science. His most famous work, *Souvenirs Entomologiques,* is a ten-volume collection of nature writings published in 1879. Some of these writings were republished as *The Passionate Observer: Writings from the World of Nature* (1998). Fabre also taught at various French lycées. He died on October 11, 1915.

Face of the Earth, The

Published between 1883 and 1904, *The Face of the Earth* presented new theories regarding the creation of mountains and other geological events. Its author, geologist Eduard Suess, was the first to propose that the earth's continents were once a single landmass. His book explains the forces that broke apart this single continent, which he called Gondwanaland, to create new oceans. (Bowler 1993)

See also Geological Research; Suess, Eduard.

Fierce Green Fire, A

Philip Shabecoff's *A Fierce Green Fire: The American Environmental Movement* (1993) is often cited by environmentalists as one of the most comprehensive histories of American environmentalism ever published. The work discusses the conservation and environmental movements in the United States and offers biographical information about most of the country's important conservationists and environmentalists.

However, Shabecoff states that the book "is not a work of historical scholarship," adding: "I am a journalist, not a historian. . . . My task is to present the news—the news of a great emerging social force and how it is likely to affect our time and the future." (Shabecoff 1993, xiv–xv) To this end, he examines "how an unspoiled land of great beauty and wonder began to change when Europeans came here five hundred years ago" and shows "how our land was settled and tamed by westward expansion, how much of its resources were squandered, how large areas were sullied, disfigured, and degraded, and how our negligent use of the Promethean forces of science and technology has brought us to the verge of disaster." (xiii)

Shabecoff also discusses "the intellectual and institutional foundations of the environmental movement and how knowledge, ethics, aesthetics, fear, anger, communications, and politics have transformed the movement into a mass crusade" and talks about "how the environmental impulse has penetrated our legal system, our economy, our politics, our educational system, our science, our agriculture, our recreation, our mass media, our aesthetics, our religion, and our values." (xv) But the author is not without his biases. He admits that he believes "that environmentalism, despite its limited successes, offers the best hope that we will be able to save ourselves from the grave dangers we have created by our destructive use of the natural world." He continues:

What this book is chiefly about . . . is how we have at last come fully to recognize the danger and how we are trying to pull ourselves back from the edge of the precipice. We have only slowly accepted individual and collective responsibility for protecting and preserving the natural world and ourselves. It is that hard-earned knowledge and the realization that we must act upon it that forms the basis of the environmental movement. (xiii)

To this end, Shabecoff includes his own opinions and suggestions regarding modern environmentalism, particularly in the final chapter, "Rebuilding the House." For example: "Progress [in protecting the environment] cannot be made with regulatory Band-Aids . . . or other facile remedies. There must be changes in our institutions, in our economic systems, in technology, and in social relationships in ways that reflect our hard-won understanding of the changing balance between human beings and nature. It is, in short, time for society to catch up to the accelerated pace of evolution in the physical world created by human numbers and human power." (277) In addition, he argues:

If environmentalism is to gain genuine power, it will have to do it the old-fashioned way—by building coalitions brawny enough to compel the political system, including the two major parties, to adopt its agenda. . . . [Moreover,] ways must be found to close the gap between the large national environmental organizations and the grass-roots groups whose members comprise an army of millions ready to be mobilized in the war for political power. . . . The national organizations have the knowledge, professionalism, and experience in the niceties and not-so-niceties of national, regional, and statewide politics. They can reinforce the grass-roots activists with an array of skills that can be used where direct political confrontation would be unproductive overkill. They bring their own substantial and relatively affluent membership into the political arena. . . . When the national and grass-roots environmentalists forge themselves into a unified force—if they ever do—they would constitute a formidable new presence on the national political stage. (280–281)

Shabecoff concludes that although the modern environmental movement has great potential, it "has yet to exercise its strength decisively" and "may never do so." Nonetheless, he expresses the hope that it will succeed because "the history of this country is a history of regeneration, of continual social restoration." (294) He adds: "Today, the frontier, the new beginning, is the challenge of restoring and safeguarding our environment." (294)

See also Agriculture; Conservationism; Environmental History; Environmental Movement; Shabecoff, Philip.

Fight for Conservation, The

Published in 1910, *The Fight for Conservation* was written by Gifford Pinchot, one of the most important conservationists of the early 20th century. The book was his attempt to gain public support for conservationism. He did so by trying to make people see the direct and immediate benefits of preserving natural resources. For example, he wrote:

The first great fact about conservation is that it stands for development. There has been a fundamental misconception that

Construction of the Wheeler hydroelectric dam project, Tennessee (Tennessee Valley Authority)

conservation means nothing but the husbanding of resources for future generations. There could be no more serious mistake. Conservation does mean provision for the future, but it means also and first of all the recognition of the right of the present generation to the fullest necessary use of all resources with which this country is so abundantly blessed. Conservation demands the welfare of this generation first, and afterward the welfare of the generations to follow. (Pinchot 1910, 42–43)

To this end, Pinchot recommends the development of natural resources such as coal and water power through mining and the building of dams. His form of conservationism advocates the reduction of waste in regard to natural resources rather than their complete protection. He argues that "conservation means the greatest good to the greatest num-

ber for the longest time" and says that "the outgrowth of conservation, the inevitable result, is national efficiency." (49–50) *The Fight for Conservation* therefore illustrates one of the most important differences between early conservationism, which allowed for controlled exploitation of the environment, and environmentalism, which called for an end to such exploitation. (Pinchot 1910)

See also Conservationism; Environmental Movement; Pinchot, Gifford.

Finch, Robert

Nature writer Robert Finch is the author of three essay collections focusing on the Cape Cod region of Massachusetts: *Common Ground: A Naturalist's Cape Cod* (1981), *The Primal Place* (1983), and *Outlands: Journeys to the Outer Edges of Cape Cod* (1986). He also coedited with John Elder *The Norton Anthology of Nature Writing* (1990).

Born in 1943 in New Jersey, Finch spent his adolescence in West Virginia. While attending college he worked at a summer sailing camp in Cape Cod, settling there permanently in 1971. Prior to that, he taught English at Oregon State University. He currently leads writing workshops in the Cape Cod area.

Flavin, Christopher

Christopher Flavin is the author of several books related to energy resources and policies, including *Energy and Architecture: Conservation Potential* (1980), *Wind Power: A Turning Point* (1981), *Electricity from Sunlight: The Future of Photovoltaics* (1982), and *World Oil: Coping with the Dangers of Success* (1985). He is currently senior vice president and director of research for Worldwatch Institute, a nonprofit organization that studies global environmental issues.

Forcing the Spring

Forcing the Spring: The Transformation of the American Environmental Movement (1993) was written by Robert Gottlieb, an expert in environmental policy and analysis. This book offers a comprehensive history of American environmentalism and discusses ideological differences among environmentalists and environmental groups. But it is perhaps most noted for its discussion of the future of environmental activism, in which it addresses the issues of racism, classism, and sexism within the modern environmental movement. Gottlieb was the first to address these problems in depth.

In the first part of the book, "Complex Movements, Diverse Roots," the author discusses early conservationists, like John Muir, as well as early activists in environmental health issues, such as Alice Hamilton. He then discusses the environmental movement of the 1960s, offering information on Rachel Carson, Murray Bookchin, and other environmentalists prominent at that time. The second part, "Contemporary Movements," focuses on more recent developments in environmentalism, particularly the schism between large national environmental groups and small grass-roots ones; he advocates new

approaches to environmentalism: "The conflicts and uncertain relationships among the different segments of the [environmental] movement remain the most difficult, unresolved questions facing environmentalism in the years to come." (Gottlieb 1993, 204) In the third part, "Issues of Gender, Ethnicity, and Class," he explores social justice issues within the environmental movement and argues that labor leaders should be more involved in environmentalism. He highlights the economic impact of environmentalism:

Labor activists have reason for their common perception that environmentalists overlook the job circumstances of working people. At the same time, labor unions, often set into old forms of dispute concerning wages and work rules, have not taken up the opportunity for developing a constructive coalition with environmental groups. [Steelworker and activist] Larry Davis's insight that "if you have a modern facility that produces less pollution, you certainly have a more secure job and you have a cleaner community to live in," has not yet become a substantial component of either union or mainstream environmental agendas or strategies. (306)

Forcing the Spring concludes with a summary of the changes that have occurred in the environmental movement and the challenges it will face in the future. It asks several questions: "Who . . . will speak for environmentalism in the 1990s and beyond? Will it be the mainstream [national] groups with their big budgets, large staff, and interest group identity? Can alternative groups, many of whom reject the label 'environmentalist,' lay claim to a tradition that has yet to be considered environmental? . . . Can mainstream and alternative groups find a common language, a shared history, a common conceptual and organizational home?" (319) Gottlieb answers these questions himself:

The figures of Alice Hamilton and Rachel Carson provide a clue. These compassionate, methodical, bitterly criticized women, accused of being sentimentalists, biased researchers, and pseudoscientists, opened up new ways of understanding what it meant to be concerned about human and natural environments. They were figures who transcended the narrow, limiting discourse of their eras, forcing their contemporaries to realize that much more was at stake than one industrial poison or one dying bird. Their language was transformative, their environmentalism expressed in both daily life and ecological dimensions. . . . To learn the lessons of Rachel Carson and Alice Hamilton and how they are linked in their concern for the world we live in helps begin that process of redefining and reconstituting environmentalism in . . . broader terms. . . . It involves a redefinition that leads toward an environmentalism that is democratic and inclusive, an environmentalism of equity and social justice, an environmentalism of linked natural and human environments, and environmentalism of transformation. The complex and continuing history of this movement points the way toward these new possibilities for change. (319–320)

Gottlieb believes not only that the environmental movement is capable of change but that such change is likely. (Gottlieb 1993)

> See also Bookchin, Murray; Carson, Rachel Louise; Environmental History; Environmental Movement; Environmental Politics; Gottlieb, Robert; Hamilton, Alice; Muir, John.

Foreman, Dave

Born in 1946, Dave Foreman is one of the best-known environmental activists in America today. He originally intended to become a politician but changed plans after receiving a dishonorable discharge from the U.S. Marines during the Vietnam War. Shortly thereafter, Foreman joined the Black Mesa Defense Fund, a New Mexico group dedicated to stopping construction of a coal mine on Navaho and Hopi lands. In 1971 Foreman formed River Defense, an offshoot of Black Mesa. He also enrolled in undergraduate science classes at the University of New Mexico, intending to become a biologist; he was also involved with a campaign to protect Gila National Forest. This work brought him to the attention of the Wilderness Society, a national environmental group.

In 1970 the Wilderness Society hired Foreman as a New Mexico field consultant. He continued working for the group for many years, and in 1978 he moved to Washington, D.C., to work with its political lobbyists. Later he became a lobbyist himself. This experience led him to question the effectiveness of promoting environmentalism through politics, and gradually he decided that a different approach was needed. In 1980 he and some friends formed Earth First!, a radical environmental group that uses illegal methods, such as destroying bulldozers and sabotaging logging equipment to stop wilderness destruction. Foreman based his group on a fictional band of ecoterrorists described in environmentalist Edward Abbey's 1975 novel, *The Monkey Wrench Gang;* its tactics were called "monkeywrenching" (also known as "ecotage").

In 1987 the FBI began an investigation of Earth First!, and in May 1989 the government arrested Foreman for conspiring to destroy three nuclear power plants. Released on bail, Foreman continued to promote environmental activism. However, as part of a plea bargain in 1991 he agreed to stop advocating monkeywrenching. He disassociated himself from Earth First! and formed a new environmental group, The Wildlands Project, which uses more conservative tactics to promote environmental change.

Foreman talks about his experiences in environmental activism in his 1991 book, *Confessions of an Eco-Warrior.* He is also the coauthor of a guide to roadless areas, entitled *The Big Outside* (1989), as well as an earlier book on Earth First! tactics entitled *Ecodefense: A Field Guide to Monkeywrenching* (1985). (Foreman 1991; Zakin 1993)

> See also Abbey, Edward; *Confessions of an Eco-Warrior; Coyotes and Town Dogs;* Environmental Activism; Environmental Groups; Environmental Politics; *Monkey Wrench Gang, The;* Zakin, Susan.

Controlling a forest fire (USDA Forest Service, Washington, DC)

Forest Management

The health of forests has been the subject of environmental literature since ancient times. Sometime around 350 B.C., for example, the Greek philosopher Plato wrote of his concerns regarding deforestation, pointing out that it was causing severe soil erosion. Others continued to expound on this theme, particularly as exploration and settlement of new regions encroached upon forests throughout the world.

Europeans became aware of forestry issues during the Middle Ages. In England during the 1600s John Evelyn undertook a study of forest depletion for the government, which was eventually published as *Sylva: A Discourse of Forest-Trees and the Propagation of Timber in His Majesty's Dominions* (1662). It advocated a more careful approach to logging and a more aggressive program of replanting. Similar arguments were raised in the United States during the late 1800s, when Americans began to realize the extent of their own forest destruction.

One of the most important books on the subject during this period was *Man and Nature* by George Perkins Marsh, considered by many to be the first American conservationist. His work was published in 1863 and influenced subsequent conservationists such as Gifford Pinchot, who founded the Yale School of Forestry in 1903, and John Muir, who helped establish America's National Park System and founded the Sierra Club, which today is one of the largest environmental groups in the United States. Muir's writings on forestry issues would become instrumental in inspiring America's conservation movement.

Forestry issues remained a matter of concern long after the conservation movement became the environmental movement and people began studying the impact of environmental problems on human health and well-being. Forest-related literature from this period focuses on the human need to experience forested wilderness areas rather than the details of balancing logging and planting.

One of the authors who helped change the focus was Aldo Leopold, whose 1949 book, *A*

Sand County Almanac, questioned whether forests should be logged at all. An acknowledged expert in forest management, he suggested that some wilderness areas should remain untouched, not only by loggers but by tourists. This idea was furthered by later environmentalists who argued in favor of ending all exploitation of forest lands.

For example, in his 1990 book, *The Practice of the Wild,* Gary Snyder wrote: "There should be *absolutely no more logging* in the remaining ancient forests. In addition we need the establishment of habitat corridors to keep the old-growth stands from becoming impoverished biological islands." (Snyder 1990, 134) Similarly, Catherine Caufield's 1981 book, *In the Rainforest,* discusses the need to protect rainforests from human destruction in order to preserve endangered species.

Forests are often mentioned in literature related to habitat protection and species extinction, because they provide a home for so many of earth's living organisms. They are also mentioned frequently in works related to air pollution, because trees release oxygen into the atmosphere. In fact some scientists believe that deforestation is a contributing cause to global warming, a phenomenon that threatens to change the earth's climate.

> See also Agriculture; Air Pollution; Caufield, Catherine; Climate Changes; Evelyn, John; Global Warming; *In the Rainforest;* Leopold, Aldo; *Man and Nature;* Marsh, George Perkins; Muir, John; Pinchot, Gifford; Plato; *Practice of the Wild, The; Sand County Almanac, A;* Snyder, Gary; *Sylva.*

Forests: The Shadow of Civilization

Published in 1992, *Forests: The Shadow of Civilization* by Robert Pogue Harrison discusses the importance of forests in the development of Western civilization as well as the place the forests hold in the human imagination. The book talks about the way that forests have been presented in literature, from ancient times to the present, and examines forest-related ecological problems and government responses to them.

Forever Free

Published in 1962, *Forever Free* is the sequel to author Joy Adamson's two previous nonfiction books, *Born Free* and *Living Free.* All three books are first-person accounts of Adamson's experiences with an African lioness named Elsa; they include many black-and-white photographs by the author. Immensely popular, these books called attention to the plight of African lions during the 1960s, when poachers regularly killed these animals and many others.

In *Born Free,* Adamson raises a lion cub named Elsa and teaches her to live in the wild. In *Living Free,* she watches Elsa bear and begin to raise three cubs. In *Forever Free,* she witnesses Elsa's death and becomes responsible for the cubs' safety.

Orphaned at only one year, the cubs become wild and disappear. However, their experience with the Adamsons makes them unafraid of human enclosures, and they begin killing the goats of local tribesmen. As Adamson explains: "They were too young to know how to hunt wild animals successfully and they must have gone through a ghastly period of starvation before they came upon the goats, which they would regard as their natural food." (Adamson 1962, p. 59) The tribesmen threaten to kill the lions, and it is more necessary than ever for the Adamsons to relocate the animals farther away from human settlement.

Adamson details the events surrounding the capture of the cubs, which are trucked almost 700 miles to Serengeti National Game Park in Tanganyika, Africa, and released near an animal migration path. The area has many wildebeests, zebras, and other prey, but it also has several prides of lions, who resent the cubs' intrusion into their territory. The cubs quickly leave to find their own territory. *Forever Free* includes hand-drawn maps of the area that chart the Adamsons' attempts to follow the cubs' tracks. When they find the lions, the Adamsons feed them, but government officials forbid doing so again; according to Adamson, the policy of the national parks is "to let nature take its course." (116) Adamson can only observe the cubs from a distance

Zoologist Dian Fossey with mountain gorillas (Dian Fossey Gorilla Fund)

from now on. She quickly loses track of them and fears that poachers may have killed them.

Forever Free offers a discussion of poaching and explains how it is decimating the African wildlife population. Adamson then discovers that the cubs have not been killed, although one of them has a seriously infected wound where an arrow has pierced his hip. Adamson tries to convince government officials to allow him to be operated upon, but they refuse. For nine months she argues the issue, but the government remains firm. Meanwhile, the cubs disappear again, and they are never found. (Adamson 1962)

> **See also** Adamson, Joy; Animal Behavior; *Born Free; Living Free;* Wildlife Conservation.

Forster, Johann Reingold

German naturalist Johann Reingold Forster added a great deal of new information to 18th-century knowledge of plant and animal species. He lived from 1729 to 1798, settling in England in 1766 as John Forster. He became a fellow in the Royal Society of London, which was dedicated to advancing the natural sciences, and in 1772 he was appointed the

official naturalist for British explorer Captain James Cook's second voyage around the globe. Forster kept extensive journals of his trip, which the society published in 1777 as *Observations Made During a Voyage Round the World.* (Bowler 1993; Forster 1778)

> **See also** Geological Research; *Observations Made During a Voyage Round the World;* Species Identification and Classification.

Fossey, Dian

Dian Fossey is best known for her research on rare mountain gorillas. To study the animals she established the Karisoke Research Center in Rwanda, Africa. Her 1983 book, *Gorillas in the Mist,* describes her experiences there and calls for stricter laws to protect endangered species.

Born in San Francisco on January 16, 1932, Fossey received a degree in occupational therapy in 1954 and began working with disabled children. However, in 1963, after reading about the gorilla research of American zoologist George Schaller, she decided to travel to Africa, where she met British anthropologist Louis Leakey. In 1966 Leakey hired

Fossey to undertake her own study of the gorillas. She set up the Karisoke research site the following year.

Awarded a Ph.D. in zoology from Cambridge University in 1974, Fossey provided a great deal of new information about gorilla behavior. After gaining the gorillas' trust, she came into close contact with them; however, some scientists have criticized Fossey for familiarizing the gorillas with human interaction, thereby making them more vulnerable to poachers. Several of the gorillas in Fossey's group were killed by poachers during her 22-year study. In 1985 Fossey herself was murdered, probably by poachers. By that time her efforts had led to an increase in antipoaching laws and enforcement practices. Today an environmental group called the Dian Fossey Gorilla Fund continues to work on gorilla conservation issues. (Fossey 1983; Mowat 1987)

See also *Gorillas in the Mist;* Habitat Protection; Wildlife Conservation.

Foster, John Bellamy

Environmental historian John Bellamy Foster is the author of *The Vulnerable Planet: A Short Economic History of the Environment* (1994), which discusses environmental degradation and public policy. His other works include *The Faltering Economy: The Problem of Accumulation Under Monopoly Capitalism* (1984), *The Theory of Monopoly Capitalism: An Elaboration of Marxism Political Economy* (1986), and *In Defense of History: Marxism and the Postmodern Agenda* (1997).

Fouts, Roger

Roger Fouts is the author of *Next of Kin: What Chimpanzees Have Taught Me About Who We Are* (1997), in which he describes his work teaching sign language to a chimpanzee named Washoe. The book relates primate development to human development and comments on evolutionary theory. Fouts is a professor of psychology at Central Washington University and codirector of the Chimpanzee and Human Communication Institute in Ellensburg, Washington. He is also an active environmentalist.

Friendship of Nature, The

Published in 1894, *The Friendship of Nature: A New England Chronicle of Birds and Flowers* is one of the first books on bird species written by an American woman. Its author, Mabel Osgood Wright, was the editor of a bird magazine and a founder of the Connecticut chapter of the Audubon Society. Her book describes the birds and plants of New England. However, it is not a mere chronicle of facts. Instead, it shares Wright's experiences as an amateur ornithologist, encourages others to enjoy bird-watching, and advocates bird conservation. For example, Wright says:

Go from the garden down through the lane to the meadow. What a burst of bird music greets you, solo, quartet, and chorus, led by the vivacious accentor, the golden-crowned thrush, with his crescendo of "Teacher—teacher—teacher!" This is the time and season to study the birds, while their plumage is fresh and typical, and they never sing so freely as in the first notes of their love song. The most puzzling part of the task is their modification of plumage; for not only in many species are males and females totally different, but the male also changes his coat after the breeding season, and the nestlings wear a hybrid dress, half father, half mother. Does the gunner know that the bobolink, the jaunty Robert of Lincoln, whose glossy black coat, patched with white and buff, is so conspicuous in the lowlands when in May and June he rings out his delicious incoherent song, but who becomes silent in August and changed to a sober brown, is the reedbird that he slaughters? (Knowles 1992, 30)

Wright continued to promote bird-watching throughout her life. (Knowles 1992)

See also Audubon, John James; Nature Writing; Species Identification and Classification.

Fritsch, Albert J.

Albert J. Fritsch, Ph.D., is an organic chemist who writes and edits books on environmental

R. Buckminster Fuller stands in front of his geodesic dome (Archive Photos)

issues. His best-known work is *Environmental Ethics* (1980), which he created for the Science Action Coalition (SAC) while serving as its director. SAC is a nonprofit research organization involved in environmentalism, consumer safety, and other health-related issues. Fritsch has also served as codirector of the Center for Science in the Public Interest; he created *The Household Pollutants Guide* for that organization in 1978. (Fritsch 1980)

> **See also** Environmental Activism; *Environmental Ethics;* Environmental Groups; Environmental Politics.

Fuller, R. Buckminster

R. (Richard) Buckminster Fuller was an inventor and philosopher who believed that expanding technological knowledge would eventually solve many environmental problems. He also argued that inventors should work toward decreasing the amount of materials needed to make common items, thereby helping to preserve the earth's limited natural resources. Born in Milton, Massachusetts, on July 12, 1895,

Fuller came from a family of nonconformists and was expelled from Harvard University for his untraditional views. He served in the U.S. Navy during World War I and was commended for inventing new lifesaving equipment. In 1917 he married the daughter of architect James Monroe Hewlett, and the two men formed a construction company.

Fuller became interested in ecology after his four-year-old daughter, Alexandra, died from a series of communicable diseases in 1922. Fuller believed that an unhealthy environment had partially contributed to her illness, and he began thinking of ways to improve the earth. Shortly thereafter, his construction company ran into financial difficulty, and the stockholders forced him out. He decided to devote himself to inventing ecologically beneficial products.

In 1927 Fuller created the Dymaxion, a streamlined, energy-efficient vehicle; a 1943 version of the Dymaxion averaged 40–50 miles per gallon of gasoline and did not pollute the air as much as conventional autos.

However, the automobile industry refused to sell the car, believing it would not be popular with the public. Fuller also invented the geodesic dome, a revolutionary form of housing, and proposed the creation of underwater, geodesic-domed farms. He created the U.S. Pavilion at the World's Fair in Montreal in 1967.

Eventually Fuller held more than 2,000 patents for various inventions. He became a professor at Southern Illinois University in 1959 and received many prestigious awards. He also wrote more than 25 books, including *Utopia or Oblivion: The Prospects for Humanity* (1969), which presented his views on environmental issues. Fuller died on July 1, 1983. (Fuller 1969; Hatch 1974)

See also Human Ecology; *Utopia or Oblivion.*

Fumento, Michael

Journalist Michael Fumento writes books and magazines and newspaper columns on health and science issues such as AIDS, obesity, air pollution, and environmentalism. His best-known book is *Science Under Siege: How the Environmental Misinformation Campaign Is Affecting Our Laws, Taxes, and Our Daily Life,* published in 1993. It is an indictment of the way environmentalists present environmental problems to the American public. (Fumento 1993)

See also Air Pollution; Antienvironmentalism; Environmental Politics; *Science Under Siege.*

G

Gaia

Published in 1979, *Gaia: A New Look at Life on Earth* advances author James Lovelock's revolutionary view that the earth is a living entity that seeks to survive and protect itself. Gaia was the name of an earth goddess worshipped in ancient Greece.

Lovelock first developed his Gaia hypothesis while studying the Martian atmosphere for the National Aeronautics and Space Administration (NASA). In comparing Mars to the earth, the scientist realized that this planet's atmosphere is an "improbable mixture" of gases that must be "manipulated on a day-to-day basis" in order to continue to support life. (Dobson 1991, 264) But who was doing the manipulating? In *Gaia,* Lovelock writes: "The climate and chemical properties of the earth now and throughout history seem always to have been optimal for life. For this to have happened by chance is as unlikely as to survive unscathed a drive blindfolded through rush-hour traffic." (266)

Lovelock proposes that the earth is actually "a planet-sized entity . . . with properties which could not be predicted from the sum of its parts . . . a complex entity involving the earth's biosphere, atmosphere, oceans, and soil; the totality constituting a feedback or cybernetic system which seeks an optimal phys-

Visions of the Earth's wholeness inspire the Gaia hypothesis (NASA)

ical and chemical environment for life on this planet." (267) He also says:

> If the earth were simply a solid inanimate object, its surface temperature would follow the variations in solar output. No amount of insulating clothing will indefinitely protect a stone statue from winter cold or summer heat. Yet somehow, through three and a half aeons, the surface temperature has remained constant and

105

favourable for life, much as our body temperatures remain constant whether it is summer or winter and whether we find ourselves in a polar or tropical environment. (267)

Lovelock's work has been embraced by many American environmentalists, particularly those who view environmentalism as a way to express spirituality. For them, Lovelock's earth goddess is a powerful image. However, environmentalist Michael Allaby, who once worked with Lovelock, contends that one can accept the idea of the earth as a complex living entity without embracing the Gaia hypothesis as a form of religion. In *A Guide to Gaia* he says: "Gaia . . . is wholly self-absorbed, a system whose only function is to continue functioning. The Gaian concept has no moral dimension unless you make the false assumption that Gaia is an intelligence, and in that case it is far from benign." He continues: "This Gaia has no concern for human welfare, moral or even physical. . . . Worship this 'god,' therefore, and you worship something that is close to being the antithesis of what most people understand by the word 'God.' It leads to a pseudoreligion of despair, and that is harmful. . . . Gaia is not an intelligent being, not a god, not anything you can talk to, pray to, or hope to influence by persuasion or ritual." (Allaby 112–114) (Allaby 1989; Dobson 1991)

See also Gaia Hypothesis; *Guide to Gaia, A;* Lovelock, James.

Gaia Hypothesis

The Gaia hypothesis was developed by scientist James Lovelock during the early 1970s. It proposes that the earth is a single, complex entity that regulates itself, keeping all of its parts—both living and nonliving—in an optimal condition to further its own existence. In other words, Lovelock believes that earth has a life force, which is why he chose the word "Gaia" for his hypothesis. Gaia was an earth goddess worshiped by ancient Greeks.

The Gaia hypothesis has many supporters. However, not all of them interpret Lovelock's

work in the same way. Some consider it an expression of spirituality, taking its reference to an earth goddess literally. Others argue that Lovelock's earth entity has no intelligence and should not be viewed as a goddess, but rather as merely a large ecological system. For example, Lovelock associate Michael Allaby, in *A Guide to Gaia,* says: "You can say Gaia, or the living Earth, exists; perhaps you can say something about the way it works; but that is all you can say. . . . [Because] there is no consciousness at work, no planning, and there are no goals to be attained." (Allaby 1989, 13)

Whether or not they believe Earth to possess a consciousness, most Gaia supporters agree that the hypothesis has grave implications for the future of human beings. If the earth is a self-regulating mechanism, then any species that threatens its survival risks being destroyed—including human beings. Accordingly, much of the environmental literature on extinction and evolution also mentions the Gaia hypothesis. (Allaby 1989)

See also Evolution; *Gaia; Guide to Gaia, A;* Lovelock, James.

Garden Cities of Tomorrow

Originally published in 1898 as *Tomorrow: A Peaceful Path to Social Reform,* the book *Garden Cities of Tomorrow* by Ebenezer Howard was the first to propose the garden city concept, a form of urban planning that became popular during the 1920s and 1930s. Garden cities were conceived as ecologically balanced communities surrounded by and connected to one another by a series of greenbelts and parkways. Howard envisioned an entirely new civilization, a new way of living, brought about by restructuring urban areas and redistributing population. In 1903 he established the first garden city: Letchworth, Hertfordshire, England. His work foreshadowed many aspects of the modern environmental movement, particularly its suggestion that cities of concrete are undesirable places to live. Greenbelts are being incorporated into planned communities even today. (Gottlieb 1993)

See also Howard, Ebenezer; Human Ecology; Social Ecology.

Geographical Research

Most ancient scholars studied the environment with an eye toward practical matters. They wanted to understand and map the known world to provide information on geography to conquerors, explorers, and merchants. One of the earliest works to do this was Ptolemy's *Guide to Geography,* written sometime before 145 A.D. It remained an important reference tool for map makers until the 1700s.

Many other works on geography subsequently appeared; perhaps the most significant of these was *The Physical Geography of the Sea* by Matthew Fontaine Maury. Published in 1855, it is significant because it is the first textbook to deal with ocean geography. Maury developed new techniques for charting the ocean floor and is considered to be one of world's first oceanographers.

See also *Guide to Geography;* Maury, Matthew Fontaine; *Physical Geography of the Sea;* Ptolemy.

Geological Research

One of the primary methods to learn about the environment is geological research. Studies of rocks, minerals, and geological formations and phenomena have provided information not only about the composition of the earth but about prehistoric time and the evolution of the planet's life-forms. Consequently, ancient scholars like Aristotle interested themselves in geology, as did later ones like Albertus Magnus in the 13th century, Georgius Agricola in the 16th century, and Niels Steensen and Gottfried Wilhelm Leibnitz in the 17th century. But as scholar Holmes Boynton points out, "The science of geology was . . . one of the latest to reach maturity," probably because "the study of the earth presented problems whose solution had to await the development of complex instruments and techniques." (Boynton 1948, 337)

Consequently, the most extensive writings on geology occurred during the 19th century, which modern scholar Peter J. Bowler calls the "heroic age" of geology because it was a time of such great geologic exploration. (Bowler 1993, 129) Many discoveries and theories related to the field were advanced during the 1800s. For example, in his 1837 book, *Studies on Glaciers,* Louis Agassiz theorized that the earth once experienced an ice age, when glaciers covered its surface; and in his 1831 book, *The Face of the Earth,* Eduard Suess theorized that the earth's many continents were once a single landmass.

Also during the 1830s, geologist Charles Lyell published the three-volume work *Principles of Geology,* which proposed that earth's geological features formed over an extremely slow period. This concept influenced the work of others studying how the environment influenced the evolution of species, most notably Charles Darwin.

See also Agassiz, (Jean) Louis (Rodolphe); Albertus Magnus, Saint; Aristotle; Darwin, Charles Robert; Leibnitz, Gottfried Wilhelm; Lyell, Charles; *Principles of Geology;* Steensen, Niels; *Studies on Glaciers.*

Gesner, Conrad

Conrad Gesner was a 16th-century physician who compiled detailed information on plants and animals. His multivolumed work *Historiae animalium,* published from 1551 to 1587, greatly furthered his contemporaries' knowledge of the natural world.

Gesner was born in Zurich, Switzerland, on March 26, 1516. A few years later his father, a furrier, sent him to live with his uncle, an expert in medicinal herbs, in order to attend a nearby school. Gesner learned about plants in addition and become proficient in Latin and Greek. During this period, he grew close to several of his teachers, who helped him attain a university scholarship.

Gesner studied at Bourges and Paris before becoming a medical student in Basel. During his spare time he wrote a Latin-Greek dictionary, which was published in 1537, and taught Greek, struggling to support a wife he married when he was 19. In 1541 he was finally qualified to practice medicine, and he became a doctor in Zurich.

Gesner subsequently wrote and edited many books, including medical texts, an encyclopedia of general knowledge, a reference book on all known languages, and a bibliographical work that offered information on hundreds of authors and their works. In addition, he compiled information on animals, plants, flowers, and seeds. His writings on botany included detailed illustrations. He also detailed his practices as a naturalist, thereby modeling objective methodology for future scientists. Gesner died on December 13, 1565, in Zurich.

See also *Historia Anamalium; Historiae animalium;* Species Identification and Classification.

Global Warming
See Climate Changes.

Global Warming
Written by climatologist Stephen H. Schneider, *Global Warming: Are We Entering the Greenhouse Century?* was published in 1989 by the Sierra Club, an environmental group. The book is representative of environmentalist works that focus on a single issue—global warming, a prominent, controversial topic of modern science.

Global Warming discusses the impact of pollution on climate and argues that the earth is currently experiencing a greenhouse effect, whereby atmospheric changes are causing global temperatures to reach extreme highs and lows. According to Schneider, if the greenhouse effect is not checked, the planet's future will be bleak. In his first chapter, "Shadows of the Climate Future," he predicts a time of extreme heat waves, massive droughts and floods, and other strange weather phenomena. Throughout the six chapters that follow, he explains the scientific factual basis for and clarifies his climate predictions. For example:

In today's concern over a general global warming trend, there does not appear to be any serious concern about a radical breakdown in climate stability, such as would result in an ice-covered earth or a runaway greenhouse effect (in which most of the carbon in the carbonate rocks would end up in the atmosphere and the planet's surface would become a Venus-like oven). No one I know has demonstrated even the remotest possibility that any disturbance from human events over the next hundreds of years (or even known extraterrestrial events over millions of years) could create that level of instability. But before we take too much comfort in that very optimistic view of our planet's habitability for some forms of life, we must remind ourselves that an ice age is only 5° C (9° F) or so colder than present, and change of that magnitude would be an immense stress for us and many other living things. (Schneider 1989; 37–38)

In his final chapter, "Coping with the Greenhouse Century," Schneider discusses how the greenhouse effect might be reversed or stabilized. He also suggests ways that people can prepare for and adapt to extreme climates and a damaged atmosphere. For example, he recommends "accelerated development and testing of crop strains and agricultural practices for more efficient adaptation to higher CO_2 levels" (257) and says that governments should "maintain a diversity of international economic ties. Trade is a principal means of adapting to regional imbalances [in food] caused by climactic anomalies." (256) He explains that even though "the prospects for alleviating most foreseeable atmospheric problems are good" he doubts that "anything much more aggressive than research funding will be instituted on a large enough scale before the atmosphere has itself performed its own experiments, now under way, with all of life on earth inside this unique laboratory—unless, of course, enough people demand otherwise." (285) (Kaufman 1994; Schneider 1989; Shabecoff 1993)

See also Climate Changes; Schneider, Stephen H.

Goodall, Jane
Jane Goodall is famous for her research studies, books, and articles concerning the be-

Jane Goodall with the African baboons of Gombe, September 27, 1974 (Fotos International/Archive Photos)

havior of wild chimpanzees. Born in London on April 3, 1934, she left school at age 18 to work as a secretary, first in England and then in Africa. In 1957 she became an assistant secretary to the famous anthropologist Louis Leakey, who was also the curator of the National Museum in Nairobi, Kenya. Goodall accompanied Dr. Leakey and his wife, Mary, on their archaeological expeditions. Eventually he asked her to undertake a study of chimpanzees in the wild, explaining that the only previous study had been too brief. Of her reaction to his offer, Goodall says:

> I could hardly believe that he spoke seriously when, after a pause, he asked me if I would be willing to tackle the job. Although it was the sort of thing I most wanted to do, I was not qualified to undertake a scientific study of animal behavior. Louis, however, knew exactly what he was doing. Not only did he feel that a university training was unnecessary, but even that in some ways it might have been disadvantageous. He wanted someone with a mind uncluttered and unbiased by theory who would make the study for no other reason than a real desire for knowledge; and, in addition, someone with a sympathetic understanding of animals. (Goodall 1971, pp. 27–28)

Goodall began her research in 1960, observing chimpanzees at Gombe Stream Chimpanzee Reserve beside Lake Tanganyika in Tanzania, Africa. She was accompanied there by her mother, Vanne Goodall, because the African authorities would not allow a young unmarried woman to live without a female companion; however, five months later they allowed Vanne to return to England. In 1961 Goodall also went to London, where Leakey had arranged for her to attend Cambridge University. She returned to Gombe each summer.

Goodall received her Ph.D. in ethology, the study of animal behavior, in 1965. That same year she married wildlife photographer Hugo van Lawick. Goodall had met him four years earlier, when he was filming her chimpanzees for a National Geographic documentary. Goodall's book *In the Shadow of Man* (1971), which documents the first 10 years of her research at Gombe, includes some of van Lawick's photographs.

Goodall remains active in chimpanzee research and conservation today and lectures on environmental issues. In 1977 she founded the Jane Goodall Institute, which is dedicated to the preservation of wild chimpanzees. She also continues to write about her experiences in Africa; her works include *The Chimpanzees of Gombe: Patterns of Behavior* (1986) and *Through a Window: My Thirty Years with the Chimpanzees of Gombe* (1990). (Goodall 1971)

See also Animal Behavior; Fossey, Dian; *In the Shadow of Man;* Wildlife Conservation.

Goodbye to a River

Published in 1959, *Goodbye to a River* by John Graves recounts the author's experiences paddling down Brazos River through part of Texas to the Gulf of Mexico. Graves took the voyage because he wanted to document the landscape before the completion of a dam that would destroy the river. His first-person account is one of the last records of the area's terrain and wildlife. In addition, the work comments on the relationship between humans and nature:

> The terms of today's human beings are air conditioners and suburbs and water impoundments overlaying whole countrysides, and the hell with nature except maybe in a cross-sectional park here and there. In our time quietness and sun and leaves and bird song and all the multitudinous lore of the natural world have to come second or third, because whether we wanted to be born there or not, we were all born into the prickly machine-humming place that man has hung for himself above that natural world. (Finch and Elder 1990, 611–612)

Gore Jr., Albert

Born in Washington, D.C., on March 31, 1948, Al Gore was elected U.S. vice president in 1992. He graduated from Harvard University with a degree in government in 1969, then volunteered to serve in the army in Vietnam. After his service in the Vietnam War, he became an investigative reporter for *The Tennessean,* a Nashville newspaper. In 1976 he was elected to the U.S. House of Representatives, where he served from 1977 to 1985, and in 1984 he was elected to the U.S. Senate, where he served from 1985 to 1993. In addition to his career in politics, Gore is a prominent environmentalist and the author of a best-selling book on the subject, *Earth in the Balance: Ecology and the Human Spirit* (1992). (Gore 1992)

See also *Earth in the Balance;* Environmental Politics.

Gorillas in the Mist

Published in 1983, *Gorillas in the Mist* is Dian Fossey's first-person account of her attempts to study and protect mountain gorillas in Africa. It is famous not only because of Fossey's research but also because of her much-publicized fight against wildlife poachers, which eventually contributed to her untimely death.

Fossey first became involved with gorillas in 1966, when noted British anthropologist Louis Leakey asked her to begin a research project that would be supported largely by the philanthropist Leighton Wilkie, who also financed the research of Dr. Jane Goodall, and the National Geographic Society. In the introduction to her book, Fossey writes that it was Dr. Leakey's hope "that the mountain gorilla research project would be as successful as Dr. Jane Goodall's great study of free-living chimpanzees." (Fossey 1983, p. vii)

Gorillas in the Mist describes 13 years of Fossey research, which at the time of publication was ongoing. In the preface, Fossey explains that mountain gorillas exist only in Africa's Virunga Mountains within a region only 25 miles long and 6–12 miles wide. Part of that region lies in the country of Zaire (then the Democratic Republic of Congo), part in Rwanda, and part in Uganda. She reports that there are fewer than 250 mountain gorillas in the wild, and none in captivity. Of

Sigourney Weaver holds a baby gorilla in her arms during the filming of Gorillas in the Mist *(Archive/Fotos International)*

the proposal that zoos capture mountain gorillas, she says:

> Because of the strong kinship bonds of gorilla families, the capture of one young gorilla may involve the slaying of many of its familial group, and certainly not every animal collected from the wild reaches its destination alive. . . . I cannot concur with those who advocate saving gorillas from extinction by killing and capturing more free-living individuals only to exhibit them in confinement. (xvii)

Instead, Fossey advocates more protection in the wild, stating: "Conservation of any endangered species must begin with stringent efforts to protect its natural habitat by enforcement of rigid legislation against human encroachment into parks and other game sanctuaries." (xvii) This encroachment affected Fossey's studies. She explains that at the time her research began, "40 percent of the mountain gorillas' protected habitat was in the process of being appropriated for cultiva-

tion purposes. The human encroachment pressure on the Virunga parks subjects gorilla groups to increased overlapping of their home ranges, and causes higher frequencies of aggression between groups." (xviii)

In *Gorillas in the Mist,* Fossey discusses the gorillas' rain forest habitat in great detail, describing its vegetation and the balanced ecosystem that enables the animals to thrive. Her studies take place at two locations within the forest: first at the Kabara Meadow in Zaire and then at the Karisoke Research Center in Rwanda, which she established in 1967. The bulk of her book takes place in the area around Karisoke, where Fossey makes contact with several social groups of mountain gorillas, learning their behaviors and gaining their confidence.

Eventually she becomes attached to individual group members and names them. Two of her favorites are Digit and Uncle Bert. When Digit is brutally killed by poachers while defending his family, Fossey is grief-stricken. In honor of his memory, she creates the Digit Fund to support active conservation of gorillas and expand antipoacher foot patrols within the park. Nonetheless, Uncle Bert is soon killed as well.

Fossey believed that the Rwandan Conservator of the Parc des Volcans was responsible for the second death. Because of the Digit Fund, the Park des Volcans has been receiving many direct donations from the public, and Fossey concludes that the Conservator believed he could bring in even more money by killing another gorilla. At the same time, he made sure that the attack took place just outside the border of Rwanda, so that the neighboring country of Zaire would get any blame for the incident.

Zaire's response to Uncle Burt's well-publicized death was to increase efforts to capture poachers. However, the Rwandans do not follow suit, and Fossey continues to find her gorilla study groups threatened by poaching. At the conclusion of *Gorillas in the Mist,* she calls for "an internationally coordinated policy of stringent law enforcement against any type of human encroacher." (240)

Fossey was murdered at Karisoke on December 27, 1985; her killers have never been found but are believed to have been poachers. Three years after her death, *Gorillas in the Mist* was released as a major motion picture, and today an environmental group called the Dian Fossey Gorilla Fund continues to support gorilla conservation efforts. (Fossey 1983; Mowat 1987)

See also Animal Behavior; Fossey, Dian; Goodall, Jane; Habitat Protection; Wildlife Conservation.

Gottlieb, Robert

Environmentalist and social-justice activist Robert Gottlieb writes books and articles on environmental policy and history. They include *Empires in the Sun: The Rise of the American West* (1982), *War on Waste: Can America Win the Battle with Garbage?* (1989), *A Life of Its Own: The Politics and Power of Water* (1991), and *Forcing the Spring: The Transformation of the American Environmental Movement* (1993). In addition, he edited *Reducing Toxics: A New Approach to Policy and Industrial Decision-Making* (1995) and teaches classes in environmental policy at Occidental College in Los Angeles, California. Gottlieb also conducts research on urban, industrial, and environmental issues. (Gottlieb 1988; Gottlieb 1993)

See also *Forcing the Spring; Life of Its Own, A.*

Gould, Stephen Jay

American paleontologist and geology professor Stephen Jay Gould is the author of more than a dozen books and essay collections on natural history and other science-related subjects. Many of the essay collections are part of an ongoing series related to evolutionary theory; subtitled *Reflections in Natural History,* they include *Ever Since Darwin* (1977), *The Panda's Thumb* (1980), *Eight Little Piggies* (1993), and *Dinosaur in a Haystack* (1996). Gould is best known for his criticism of Charles Darwin's theory of evolution. He disagrees with Darwin's belief that evolution takes place at a steady pace, arguing instead that changes in species occur only during sudden bursts of evolutionary progress.

Gould was born on September 10, 1941, in New York City. He received his Ph.D. from Columbia University in 1967 and has taught at Harvard University. He also writes magazine articles and was the editor of a 20-volume series, *The History of Paleontology.* (Bowler 1993; Gould 1980; Gould 1993)

See also Darwin, Charles Robert; *Eight Little Piggies;* Evolution; *Panda's Thumb, The.*

Green Fires

A self-styled "novel of the Ecuadorian rain forest," *Green Fires: Assault on Eden* (1994) by Marnie Mueller has been called an ecological thriller. The story concerns a former Peace Corps volunteer, Annie Saunders, who becomes embroiled in a conflict between American oil companies and the native people of the rain forest. Years earlier, Saunders had tried to help these same people by encouraging them to engage in political protest, and they were tortured for it. Saunders left the country feeling that she had failed. Now she has returned on a vacation, and she soon finds herself coming to terms with her past while fighting to preserve the future of the forest.

Green History of the World, A

Written by historian Clive Ponting and published in 1991, *A Green History of the World: The Environment and the Collapse of Great Civilizations* considers environmental destruction from a historical perspective and is frequently cited in other works of environmental history. However, the book not only offers historical facts but also comments on environmental ideology.

In the introduction, Ponting writes: "I am convinced, after nearly twenty years of supporting 'environmental' causes, that 'green' issues are not simply about the state of the natural world but have to include central problems such as the use of resources and energy, the distribution of poverty and wealth, how people treat other people, and the way people think about the world they inhabit." (Ponting 1991, p. xiv)

A Green History of the World discusses various forms of environmental exploitation from ancient times to the present, including agriculture, hunting, forestry, and mining, and argues that many ancient civilizations collapsed after exhausting their natural resources. Ponting warns that modern civilizations might suffer the same fate:

> Many societies in the past believed that they had a sustainable way of life only to find some time later that it was not so and that they were unable to make the social, economic and political changes necessary for survival. The problem for all human societies has been to find a means of extracting from the environment their food, clothing, shelter and other goods in a way that does not render it incapable of supporting them. Some damage is clearly inevitable. Some depredation is tolerable. The challenge has been to anticipate or recognise at what point the environment is being badly degraded by the demands placed upon it and to find the political, economic and social means to respond accordingly. Some societies have succeeded in finding the right balance, some have failed. (407)

Ponting says that modern people must guard earth's natural resources, being careful not to disrupt delicate ecosystems, and keep human populations to sustainable levels. (Ponting 1991)

See also Environmental History; Environmental Movement; Environmental Politics.

Green Rage

Published in 1990, *Green Rage: Radical Environmentalism and the Unmaking of History* defends the beliefs and practices of radical environmental groups like Earth First! Along with *Confessions of an Eco-Warrior*, which was written by Earth First! cofounder Dave Foreman, it is the most frequently cited book of environmental radicalism.

The book's author, Christopher Manes, is a longtime member of Earth First! He therefore begins his book with a preface explaining that *Green Rage* "does not pretend to be objective or dispassionate about the radical environmental movement and its controversial efforts to stop the culture of technology from unraveling the fragile, resplendent web of life on this planet." (Manes 1990, p. xi) Manes explains that radical environmentalism advocates civil disobedience, which includes "ecotage, ecologically motivated sabotage, against bulldozers and the other tools of industry that are pushing back the wild." (xi) He personally supports the practice of ecotage, which was first promoted by environmental activist Edward Abbey in the 1975 novel *The Monkey Wrench Gang.*

Green Rage discusses Abbey and the history of radical environmentalism, as well as the activities of Earth First! Manes explains the motivation for the group's ecotage practices, quoting from radical environmentalists who compare their movement to the civil rights movement. On that point, he writes:

> The American people, not to mention humankind in general, are not accustomed to thinking of such nonhuman entities as mountain lions, forests, and rivers as exploited groups whose rights can be violated. From the perspective of the . . . civil rights movement, this state of affairs is exactly the problem. In the antebellum South, people were not accustomed to thinking of slaves as human beings who had any claim to the protection of the law. We now find this position both repugnant and ridiculous. In the future, so goes the . . . argument [of some radical environmentalists], we will feel the same toward contemporary society's refusal to extend legal and ethical standing to the "deer people" and "tree people." (167)

Manes also discusses deep ecology, the philosophy behind radical environmentalism, and criticizes industry and technology. He argues that overpopulation is one of the biggest threats to the environment, citing the work of population expert Paul Ehrlich to support this view:

> Paul Ehrlich's *Population Bomb* has inspired almost universal condemnation

from technocrats and humanists alike for predicting a disaster that has not yet happened. But with the population doubling every half century in a world already undergoing biological meltdown, it is difficult to conceive how human population can draw down in a sensible manner without the catastrophe Ehrlich foresaw. (233)

Manes believes that to solve such problems people must reject technology and learn how to live in a more primitive society. In the concluding chapter of *Green Rage* he says:

A future primitive society based on hunting-gathering . . . may sound unrealistic, and given the present population of the planet it is. But the concept does provide a sense of direction, of context, for an environmental sensibility beyond technocracy. . . . It is a starting place for learning to reinhabit the world. George Sessions and Bill Devall write, "As deep ecologists reevaluate primal peoples, including the diverse nations and tribes of Native Americans, they seek not a revival of the Romantic version of primal peoples as 'noble savages,' but a basis for philosophy, religion, cosmology, and conservation practices that can be applied to our own society."

He expands on this idea in the book's epilogue, in which he lauds those who have suggested a simpler lifestyle and suggests that "the time to make the choice between the natural and cultural world has come." (248) (Manes 1990)

See also Abbey, Edward; Deep Ecology Movement; Devall, Bill; Ehrlich, Paul and Anne; Environmental Activism; Environmental Groups; Environmental Movement; Environmental Politics; Manes, Christopher; *Monkey Wrench Gang, The;* Naess, Arne; *Population Explosion, The;* Sessions, George.

Greening of America, The

The Greening of America: How the Youth Revolution Is Trying to Make America Livable (1970) was written by Charles Reich, a law professor who correctly predicted that the new environmental movement of the late 1960s would permanently change many aspects of American society. His book examines the early environmental movement in terms of history, law, economics, philosophy, sociology, psychology, and ideology. It offers a glimpse into the attitudes of the period. In comparing the environmental movement to other revolutions in American history, Reich says:

This is the revolution of the new generation. Their protest and rebellion, their culture, clothes, music, drugs, ways of thought, and liberated life-style are not a passing fad or a form of dissent and refusal, nor are they in any sense irrational. The whole emerging pattern, from ideals to campus demonstrations to beads and bell bottoms to the Woodstock Festival, makes sense and is part of a consistent philosophy. . . . The logic and necessity of the new generation—and what they are so furiously opposed to—must be seen against a background of what has gone wrong in America. It must be understood in light of the betrayal and loss of the American dream, the rise of the Corporate State of the 1960s, and the way in which that State dominates, exploits, and ultimately destroys both nature and man. (Reich 1970, 14)

Reich, a law professor at Harvard University, applauds the new environmental activism and concludes that it will soon spread beyond the country's youth. He believes that it will create a "change of consciousness" (297) in American society and offers a utopian vision of what the world will be like when people choose "a new set of values." (303) In fact he says, "we are only beginning to realize the incredible vastness of the changes that are coming. Most views of what is happening are woefully inadequate. . . . But if we think of all that is now challenged—the . . . nature and purposes of work, the course of man's dealing with the environment, the relationship of self to technology and society—we can see that the present transformation goes beyond any-thing in modern history. . . . What is coming is nothing less than a new way of life and a new man—a man with renewed energies and imagination—a man who is part of the living world." (305–306) (Reich 1970)

See also Environmental History; Environmental Movement; Environmental Politics.

Grew, Nehemiah

Seventeenth-century English physician Nehemiah Grew is one of the founders of plant anatomy. His first book on the subject, *The Anatomy of Vegetables Begun,* appeared in 1672; his most important work, *The Anatomy of Plants,* was published in 1682. Grew was born in Warwickshire, England, in 1641. He became a physician in 1671 after studying medicine in the Netherlands. He then established a practice in London and remained there until his death on March 25, 1712. (Boynton 1948)

See also *Anatomy of Plants, The;* Species Identification and Classification.

Guide to Gaia, A

A Guide to Gaia: A Survey of the New Science of Our Living Earth by Michael Allaby is one of the most comprehensive discussions of the Gaia hypothesis ever published. The book's author worked with the developer of the hypothesis, James Lovelock, and made his own mark on the Gaia branch of modern environmentalism.

A Guide to Gaia first appeared in print in 1989. In the preface, Allaby calls Gaia a revolutionary new idea that "redefines the word 'Earth,'" explaining that the hypothesis "states that for most practical purposes our planet is a single living organism and its inhabitants, the countless species of plants and animals we see around us, may be likened to the organs of a body. The implications reach far and to many levels of understanding." (Allaby, vii) The author then places the concept of a living earth—Mother Earth—in historical context. For example, in discussing James Lovelock's work on the hypothesis, he states:

Lovelock is not the first scientist to think of the Earth as being alive, though he has taken the idea much further than any of his predecessors. James Hutton, the 18th-century Scottish geologist, often described as the father of geology, took a similar view. . . . He once said, in 1785 in a lecture to the Royal Society of Edinburgh, that the Earth should be regarded as a 'superorganism' and it should be studied by the science of physiology. His reasons have a distinctly modern ring, for he likened the movement of nutrients through the soil into plants and animals then back into the soil, and the movement of water from the oceans to the land and back to the oceans again, to the circulation of the blood. (Allaby 10–11)

Nonetheless, Allaby says that "the new Gaia differs from her old manifestation subtly but profoundly" in that "our ancestors believed literally that Gaia had an intelligence. The new Gaia does not. . . . Gaia is not an intelligence, not some kind of superhuman being. We cannot talk to her, reason with her, even pray to her, and expect to be heard, for there is nothing there to hear us. . . . You can say Gaia, or the living Earth, exists; perhaps you can say something about the way it works; but that is all you can say. . . . [Because] there is no consciousness at work, no planning, and there are no goals to be attained." (12–13)

Allaby goes on to discuss the nature of the planet organism, talking about its chemical and living components and the way they remain optimally balanced to support what he refers to as "a system, complicated, beautiful, but nothing more than a system" rather than a being with a "full consciousness of self." (146) In addition, he examines the relationship between humans and animals and between animals of different species. In this regard, he considers Charles Darwin's theory of evolution in terms of the Gaia hypothesis, saying:

Darwinism and the more modern neo-Darwinism, which extends Darwin's work to embrace genetics and most aspects of ecology (the study of relationships among communities of organisms and between communities and their inanimate environment) are concerned with the evolution of species. The concept of Gaia, of the totality of all species acting together like a single organism, does not conflict with this accepted view. (89–90)

However, Allaby disagrees with Darwin's view that only the most fit members of a species survive. Instead, he believes that cooperation and other social skills are the most beneficial traits for individual animals, saying: "'Survival of the socially cohesive' lacks the ring of 'survival of the fittest,' but it may be more accurate." (102)

After explaining this and other aspects of the Gaia hypothesis in depth, Allaby addresses Earth's mortality. He argues that "there are ways in which our behaviour may cause severe damage, subtly, by disturbing the Earth's regulatory mechanisms and in particular by interfering with the climate" and then examines various destructive practices, including pollution and the greenhouse effect. (135) For example, he says: "Pollutants are poisons so far as the natural environment is concerned, so we can regard pollution in the same way that we regard the poisoning of humans or other animals." (162) However, he adds:

There really is no way humans could blast, burn, irradiate or even poison a large enough proportion of living things to make recovery impossible once the abuses ceased. . . . [This position] does not mean the Gaia idea implies absolute freedom for people to do as they like with impunity, for there are other values to be considered. Jim Lovelock and I both love the countryside and its wildlife and are deeply offended when large tracts are converted

into tedious agricultural or afforested monocultures. We object strongly to the pollution of rivers and the persecution of species, even those designated "pests." Such insults will not destroy the planet, but this does not make them acceptable or harmless. An assault does not have to be fatal before we condemn it. (134–135)

Moreover, Allaby believes that the Gaia hypothesis can be used to gain new insights into environmental problems and priorities, because it "allows us to examine each issue in the light of its possible effects on the operation of the system that is the planet. . . . An approach along these lines can lead to a system of classification for environmental problems. We can say, for example, that the hunting and killing of whales is unlikely to have any serious effect on the planet as a whole. Whales have always been too few in number to have much influence. The Gaian consequences of whaling are trivial." (159) Allaby stresses that this does not mean he supports whaling but that in deciding which environmental problems deserve the most resources whaling should not be considered as important as global warming. The author suggests that the Gaia hypothesis be used to identify the most important environmental issues. (Allaby 1989)

See also Gaia Hypothesis; Lovelock, James.

Guzzo, Lou

Reporter Lou Guzzo is the coauthor of the 1995 book, *Environmental Overkill: Whatever Happened to Common Sense?* He has written articles for the *Cleveland Plain Dealer* and the *Seattle Times* and was once managing editor of the *Seattle Post-Intelligencer.* He has done TV and radio commentaries in Seattle. (Ray and Guzzo 1993)

See also *Environmental Overkill.*

H

Habitat Protection

In simple terms, a habitat is an organism's natural home. It can be land or water, large or small, depending on an organism's needs; regardless of type and size, if a habitat is destroyed then the creatures that depend on it will perish. For this reason, habitat protection is vital to maintain the diversity of plant and animal species on earth and is a matter of concern to people interested in animal ecology, wildlife conservation, and biodiversity.

Habitat protection is therefore an important topic in environmental literature. For example, Catherine Caufield's book *In the Rainforest* and Diane Ackerman's *The Rarest of the Rare* discuss species extinction in terms of habitat endangerment, as do Edward O. Wilson's *The Diversity of Life* and John McPhee's *The Control of Nature*. Many other works connect not only the subject of extinction but also evolution to the issue of habitat protection. These include Paul and Anne Ehrlich's *Extinction* and Richard Leakey and Roger Levin's *The Sixth Extinction*.

See also Ackerman, Diane; Caufield, Catherine; *Control of Nature, The; Diversity of Life, The;* Ehrlich, Paul and Anne; Evolution; *Extinction; In the Rainforest;* Leakey, Richard; McPhee, John; *Rarest of the Rare, The; Sixth Extinction, The;* Wilson, Edward O.

Haeckel, Ernst

German zoologist Ernst Haeckel wrote about evolution and was a major supporter of contemporary Charles Darwin. Perhaps more importantly, in one of his works on evolution, *Generelle morphologie der organismen* (General Morphology of Organisms, 1886), Haeckel used the Greek word *oikos,* or "household," to

Ernst Haeckel, 1880 (Corbis/Hulton-Deutsch Collection)

invent the term *oecologie,* or "ecology," to refer to the relationship between living things and their surroundings.

Haeckel was born on February 16, 1834, in Potsdam, Prussia. In 1857 he received a medical degree from the University of Berlin, but eventually he abandoned the practice of medicine to become a zoologist. He began teaching the subject in 1862 in Jena, Germany. He also lectured on Darwinism. In later years he studied and wrote about heredity and biology. Haeckel died in Jena on August 9, 1919. (Bolsche 1906)

See also Darwin, Charles Robert; Evolution.

Haines, John

Born in 1924, John Haines has written numerous poems and nature essays related to his experiences as a homesteader and trapper in Alaska between 1954 and 1969. His poetry collections include *Winter News* (1966), *The Stone Harp* (1971), and *News from the Glacier* (1982); his essay collections include *Living Off the Country: Essays on Poetry and Place* (1981) and *The Stars, The Snow, The Fire: Twenty-five Years in the Northern Wilderness* (1989).

See also *Living Off the Country.*

Hales, Stephen

A clergyman and a botanist, Stephen Hales changed scientists' approach to plant studies during the 18th century. He was the first to measure water before giving it to a plant and then weigh the plant later to determine its intake and water retention. He also concluded that sap flows upward from a plant's roots, measured plants' rate of growth, and suggested that plant systems could be compared to animal systems. Much of Hales's work on plants was published in 1727 as *Vegetable Staticks,* which later became the first volume of *Statical Essay;* the second volume of this 1733 work concerns blood circulation and blood pressure. He was born in 1677 in Bekesbourne, Kent, England, and became a minister in 1703, devoting almost all of his spare time to science. He died on January 4, 1761, near London.

See also *Vegetable Staticks.*

Hamilton, Alice

An American physician, Alice Hamilton was active in social reform, trying to improve working conditions in factories. Her research into health hazards associated with industry ultimately benefited not only workers but also the environment. In 1925 she published her most important work, *Industrial Poisons in the United States,* which she followed with *Industrial Toxicology* (1934, revised in 1949) and an autobiography entitled *Exploring the Dangerous Trades* (1943).

Hamilton was born in 1869 in New York City. Raised in Indiana, she received her medical degree from the University of Michigan in 1893 and furthered her studies at hospitals in Minneapolis and Boston. In 1897 she began teaching pathology at Northwestern University in Chicago. While there she also volunteered her medical services at a clinic for poor people, where she saw many industrial plant workers suffering from job-related illnesses.

In 1908 Hamilton became a member of the Illinois Commission on Occupational Diseases and began studying work-related health hazards. A report of her findings was published in *Survey of Occupational Diseases* in 1910. The following year she began similar studies for the federal government. Her work is credited with prompting new state labor laws related to worker safety.

In 1919 Hamilton became the first woman faculty member at Harvard University, where she taught industrial medicine and wrote her landmark books on the subject. She retired from Harvard in 1935 but continued her efforts as an advocate for workplace safety until her death in 1970. (Gottlieb 1993)

See also Human Ecology; *Industrial Poisons in the United States;* Pesticides and Chemicals.

Handbook of Nature Study

Published in 1911, *Handbook of Nature Study* by Anna Botsford Comstock was the result of a trend that Polly Welts Kaufman, in *National Parks and the Woman's Voice,* calls the "nature study movement," which "first offered wide-scale employment to women naturalists as nature study teachers in public schools." (Kaufman 1996, 68) Kaufman explains the significance of the work:

> The publication of Anna Botsford Comstock's *Handbook of Nature Study* in 1911 made Comstock the most widely-recognized leader of the nature study movement. Her massive compendium, including sections on birds, mammals, fishes, insects, amphibians, rocks, plants, climate, weather, and stars, went through twenty-four editions between 1911 and 1939. It began as leaflets, many written by women, published as a correspondence course for nature study teachers and as articles published in the *Nature Study Review,* founded in 1906. That her influence was nationwide was demonstrated by a poll conducted by the League of Women Voters in 1923 that selected her as one of America's twelve greatest living women. (68)

Kaufman also explains that Comstock's writings did not just describe nature but encouraged a new approach to it. She reports:

> The nature study movement coincided with the professionalization of the natural sciences, a trend that soon separated amateurs from professionals—the professionals valuing experimentation over observation and the study of physiology over building a taxonomy. Although the nature study movement encouraged "investigation" and used simple scientific equipment, it also ascribed a moral value to nature study. Beginning as a way of interesting farm children in nature as a step toward improving agriculture, it soon spread to being perceived as a cure for urban problems. (68)

Comstock not only wrote *Handbook of Nature Study* to support the nature study movement but also actively participated in nature study education. In 1895 she developed a nature study course in New York and began working with the American Nature Study Society and the American Nature Association to promote school nature study programs. (Kaufman 1996)

See also Comstock, Anna Botsford.

Hardin, Garrett

Garrett Hardin is best known for his essay "The Tragedy of the Commons," in which he argues that social intervention is necessary to limit population growth and the use of common resources. It was first published in *Bioscience* magazine and appears in *Managing the Commons (1977),* a collection of essays that Hardin coedited with John Baden.

Hardin has also written several books on environmental issues, including *Exploring New Ethics for Survival* (1968), *Stalking the Wild Taboo* (1978), *Filters Against Folly* (1985), *Living Within Limits: Ecology, Economics, and Population Taboos* (1993), and *The Immigration Dilemma: Avoiding the Tragedy of the Commons* (1995). He is currently a professor at the University of California–Santa Barbara.

See also *Managing the Commons.*

Harr, Jonathan

Jonathan Harr is the author of *A Civil Action* (1995), a nonfiction book about a 1981 environmental pollution lawsuit brought by eight families whose children had died of cancer. The families blamed Beatrice Foods and W. R. Grace Co. for polluting the drinking water in their city of Woburn, Massachusetts. Harr carefully chronicled the case, which resulted in a settlement of $375,000 for each family, and reported on the professional and personal difficulties faced by the attorney representing the plaintiffs, Jan Schlichtmann.

Harrison, Harry

Science fiction author Harry Harrison has written more than a dozen novels, several of which address environmental issues. His novel *West of Eden* (1984) and its sequels, *Winter in Eden* (1986) and *Return to Eden* (1988), depict an alternate scenario of evolution, in which dinosaurs develop intelligence and do not become extinct. These books foreshadowed Michael Crichton's 1990 novel, *Jurassic*

Park, and its sequel, *The Lost World,* which also put humans in conflict with dinosaurs.

Harrison's most significant work of environmental fiction is his 1966 novel, *Make Room! Make Room! A Realistic Novel of Life in 1999.* This book presents a future of extreme overpopulation and was based on scientific research. It includes a bibliography of nonfiction resources, and later editions include an introduction by overpopulation expert Paul Ehrlich.

Born in Stamford, Connecticut, Harrison began his career as an artist and then worked as an art director. Eventually he became an editor, which led him to writing. He continues to work on science fiction novels and anthologies today.

See also Crichton, Michael; Ehrlich, Paul and Anne; Environmental Fiction; Evolution; Human Ecology; *Jurassic Park; Make Room! Make Room!*

Hasselstrom, Linda

Linda Hasselstrom writes poetry and books about her experiences as a woman rancher in the American West. Her poetry collections include *Caught by One Wing: Poems* (1984) and *Roadkill* (1987); her books include *Windbreak: A Woman Rancher on the Northern Plains* (1987), *Going Over East: Reflections of a Woman Rancher* (1987), and *Land Circle: Writings Collected from the Land* (1991). She also edited a collection entitled *Leaning into the Wind: Women Write from the Heart of the West* (1997).

Born in 1943, Hasselstrom grew up on a ranch in South Dakota, and after living elsewhere she settled there in 1971. She established her own publishing company, Lame Johnny Press, and edited a journal entitled *Sunday Clothes,* which featured the works of writers and artists. During the late 1980s Hasselstrom left her ranch and moved to Cheyenne, Wyoming, to care for her aging parents while continuing to write.

Hawken, Paul

Paul Hawken has written several books on business practices as they relate to environmental issues, including *The Next Economy* (1983), *Growing a Business* (1987), and *The Ecology of Commerce* (1993), which outlines an ecological economic system. He is the founder of Erewhon Trading Company, a natural foods distributor and retailer, and Smith and Hawken, a mail-order gardening catalog. Hawken serves on the Board of Directors of the environmental group Friends of the Earth. He also lectures to corporations regarding sound ecological business practices.

See also *Erewhon.*

Hawkes, Jacquetta

Born in 1910, Jacquetta Hawkes is an archaeologist who writes about archaeology, geology, and natural history, particularly as they relate to Great Britain. In an introduction to one of Hawkes's most popular books, *A Land* (1951), naturalist Robert Finch reports:

As a writer, Jacquetta Hawkes represents the best of the English intellectual tradition. Her ability to combine not only geology and archaeology but sociology, cognitive psychology, architecture, art history, and mythology with unassuming ease is impressive. Her style is disciplined and clear, yet dynamic and richly colored, an intriguing mix of poise and passion, the scientific and the sympathetic, the personal and the objective. (Hawkes 1991, xii)

Finch compares *A Land* to the works of Aldo Leopold, Rachel Carson, and Loren Eiseley, all of whom helped popularize naturalism by imparting scientific facts through personal narrative. Her other works include *Prehistory and the Beginnings of Civilization* (1963), *Dawn of the Gods* (1968), and *The First Great Civilizations* (1973). (Hawkes 1991)

See also Carson, Rachel Louise; Eiseley, Loren; *Land, A;* Leopold, Aldo; Nature Writing.

Hay, John

John Hay writes books about natural history and his experiences as a naturalist on Cape Cod, Massachusetts. His works include *The Run* (1959; reissued in 1999), *The Great Beach* (1963), *In Defense of Nature* (1970),

The Undiscovered Country (1982), *A Beginner's Faith in Things Unseen* (1995), and *In the Company of Light* (1998).

Born in Ipswich, Massachusetts, in 1915, he served in World War II before attending Harvard University. In 1947 he published his first book, which was a collection of poems, and from 1972 to 1987 he taught nature writing at Dartmouth College. He has also been politically active to prevent overdevelopment in the Cape Cod area.

See also *In Defense of Nature;* Nature Writing; *Undiscovered Country, The.*

Health Problems
See Human Ecology.

Hearne, Vicki

Born in 1952, Vicki Hearne is an animal trainer and a professor of English who writes about the relationship between humans and animals. Her poetry collections include *Nervous Horses* (1980), *In the Absence of Horses* (1984), and *The Parts of Light: Poems* (1994); her books include *Adam's Task: Calling Animals by Name* (1989), a narrative related to animal domestication, *Bandit: Dossier of a Dangerous Dog* (1991), and *Animal Happiness* (1994). She also wrote *The White German Shepherd: A Novel* (1988).

Helvarg, David

David Helvarg is a journalist and private investigator whose book *The War Against the Greens* (1994) offers an in-depth discussion of antienvironmental groups in contemporary America. He has also written television documentaries as well as newspaper and magazine articles on a variety of subjects. For example, he has criticized the U.S. Central Intelligence Agency (CIA) and written about government corruption in El Salvador. (Helvarg 1994)

See also Antienvironmentalism; *War Against the Greens, The.*

Histoire naturelle

Histoire naturelle, or *A Natural History of the Globe, of Man, of Beasts, Birds, Fishes, Reptiles, Insects, and Plants,* was intended as the most detailed natural history of the earth and its inhabitants ever written. Its author, French naturalist and zoologist Comte de Georges Louis Leclerc Buffon, planned to write 50 volumes. He published thirty-six before his death in 1788; an additional eight were published posthumously.

The first 15 volumes (1749–1767) introduced Buffon's theories on the formation of the planet, its surface features, and its geological processes. Some of these theories angered those who believed in the biblical creation; the Catholic Church even banned the early volumes of *Histoire naturelle.*

Subsequent volumes were less controversial. Nine volumes published between 1770 and 1783 offered detailed descriptions of birds. Five volumes published between 1783 and 1788 described minerals. Another eight volumes, published posthumously, discussed reptiles, fish, and sea mammals. In total, these works provided a thorough catalog of information about the earth's creatures.

However, many of Buffon's theories regarding earth's creation and other prehistoric events were incorrect. For example, he speculated that the earth was formed from a piece of the sun, broken off by a colliding comet, and theorized that the planet began as a boiling-hot world that took thousands of years to cool. In his mind, fossils of extinct sea creatures represented species who thrived in boiling water and died off as temperatures decreased. Although he was wrong on that score, he was one of the first authors to accept and try to explain the idea of species extinction. He was also one of the first to support the belief that the earth's surface was formed as part of a long, gradual process with several stages. (Buffon 1831; Fellows and Milliken 1972)

See also Buffon, Georges Louis Leclerc, Comte de; Evolution.

Historia Anamalium

Historia Anamalium was written by the Greek philosopher Aristotle (ca. 384–322 B.C.). Based on Aristotle's own research and observations, it provided new information on more than 500 species of animals, fish, and insects classified according to certain common characteristics. For this reason, Aristotle is sometimes called the founder of biological taxonomy. (Bowler 1993)

See also Aristotle; Species Identification and Classification.

Historia Plantarum

Historia Plantarum was written by Greek scholar Theophrastus, who succeeded the philosopher Aristotle as the head of the Lyceum in 323 B.C. The work offers several volumes of information on plant species, including explanations of their growth habits and usefulness to mankind. Theophrastus wrote extensively in the natural sciences, but few of his works survive today. (Bowler 1993)

See also Theophrastus.

Historiae animalium

Published during the Renaissance, *Historiae animalium* by Conrad Gesner significantly advanced 16th-century knowledge regarding animal species and the natural world. It is a large work, five volumes in all, each devoted to a particular type of creature. The first volume appeared in 1551, offering 1,100 pages of detailed descriptions of animals that bear live offspring; the second (1554) details animals that lay eggs; the third (1555) studies birds; the fourth (1556) focuses on aquatic creatures, particularly fish; the fifth, unfinished upon Gesner's death in 1565, provides facts about reptiles and was published posthumously in 1587.

Taken in its entirety, *Historiae animalium* not only summarized known facts but provided new information to Renaissance scholars. Gesner gathered and presented his material very carefully. In addition to providing physical descriptions, his work offers observations on animals' behavioral characteristics, habitats, and usefulness to humans. It also explains how certain creatures were named.

Gesner was once a professor of Greek and retained a life-long interest in Classic literature. Consequently, *Historiae animalium* includes discussions of ancient works on animals—even mythological creatures. For this reason, some scholars have minimized the importance of Gesner's work in advancing scientific thought. Nontheless, *Historiae animalium* was widely read and brought the field of naturalist study to the attention of the non-scientific community.

See also Gesner, Conrad; Species Identification and Classification.

Hoagland, Edward

Born in New York City in 1932, Edward Hoagland is a prominent nature writer. His first essays were published in the 1971 collection *The Courage of Turtles*. Subsequent collections include *Walking the Dead Diamond River* (1973), *Red Wolves and Black Bears* (1976), and *The Tugman's Passage* (1982). One of the essays in *Walking the Dead Diamond River*, "Hailing the Elusory Mountain Lion," has been reprinted in two important nature writing anthologies, *Words from The Land* by Stephen Trimble and *This Incomperable Lande* by Thomas Lyon.

In writing about Hoagland's work, Lyon notes how the author realizes "that wilderness exists today only if human society wants it to exist" (Lyon 1989, 88) and then explains:

He hears the wilderness singing, but it is, in his words, a "swan song." He gravitates toward old-timers and field men who can perhaps convey what it was like to touch the former world. In *Notes from the Century Before: A Journal from British Columbia* (1969), Hoagland's most fully developed travel essay, he describes a journey into a realm of health and variety and interest which even now may be as remote as any fictional Shangri-La. . . . [While traveling through British Columbia] he moved swiftly from one discovery to the next, exhilarated both by the country and the people. An undertone of elegy was provided by the trembling fragility of some of the old-timers and by the always ominous presence of helicopters—there had been a copper strike nearby. But Hoagland didn't snag on nostalgia; he was busy making a record. (Lyon 89)

In addition to his nature essays, Hoagland writes novels. His first novel, *Cat Man*, was published in 1956; his last novel, *Seven Rivers West*, appeared in 1986. He is also the author of two travel books: *Notes from the Century Before: A Journal from British Columbia* (1969) and *African Calliope: A Journey to the Sudan* (1979). He currently lives in a farmhouse in Barton, Vermont.

See also Trimble, Stephen.

Hogan, Linda

Native American author Linda Hogan has written about nature in poems, stories, novels, and nonfiction books. She has a master's degree in English and Creative Writing from the University of Colorado and is now an associate professor at that university. She has also received several grants, including one from the National Endowment for the Arts. Hogan's works include two poetry collections entitled *Eclipse* (1983) and *Seeing Through the Sun* (1985), *Red Clay: Poems and Stories* (1991), the novel *Solar Storms* (1995), and the nonfiction books *Dwellings: A Spiritual History of the Living World* (1995) and *Intimate Nature: The Bond Between Woman and Animals* (1998), which she coedited with Deena Metzger and Brenda Peterson. The latter includes writings by women environmentalists and nature writers such as Jane Goodall, Ursula LeGuin, Diane Ackerman, Gretel Ehrlich, and Terry Tempest Williams.

See also Ackerman, Diane; Ehrlich, Gretel; Goodall, Jane; LeGuin, Ursula; Williams, Terry Tempest.

Holy Earth, The

Published in 1915, *The Holy Earth* by Liberty Hyde Bailey discusses human exploitation of the land and recommends ways to achieve sustainable use. It was considered a radical agrarian text for its time. In fact many scholars consider Bailey to be one of the first deep ecologists, comparing him to Wendell Berry, who discussed agricultural issues in a similar fashion.

In *The Holy Earth*, Bailey criticizes people for depleting the earth's resources:

We have been greatly engaged in digging up the stored resources, and in destroying vast products of the earth for some small kernel that we can apply to our necessities or add to our enjoyments. We excavate the best of the coal and cast away the remainder; blast the minerals and metals from underneath the crust, and leave the earth raw and sore; we box the pines for turpentine and abandon the growths of limitless years to fire and devastation; sweep the forests with the besom of destruction; pull the fish from the rivers and ponds without making any adequate provision for renewal; exterminate whole races of animals; choke the streams with refuse and dross; rob the land of its available stores, denuding the surface, exposing great areas to erosion. . . . How many and many are the years required to grow a forest and to fill the pockets of the rocks, and how satisfying are the landscapes, and yet how desperately soon may men reduce it all to ruin and to emptiness, and how slatternly may they violate the scenery! (Lyon 1989, 247–248)

Bailey suggests that people become more aware of the land's needs despite modern America's transition from an agricultural to an urban society. He argues that all people, not just farmers, should have a relationship with the earth. However, he insists that he is "not thinking of any back-to-the-farm movement" as a way to rekindle people's interest in the land. Instead, he advocates a change in attitude rather than location. Consequently, professor Thomas Lyon, in *This Incomperable Lande*, suggests that Bailey "was proposing the same ecological and ethical outlook as John Burroughs, for example, or Aldo Leopold . . . [who] acknowledged Bailey as an influence." (Lyon 87) (Lyon 1989)

See also Bailey, Liberty Hyde; Berry, Wendell; Burroughs, John; Deep Ecology Movement; Leopold, Aldo.

Hooke, Robert

English physicist Robert Hooke performed research on a variety of subjects, including

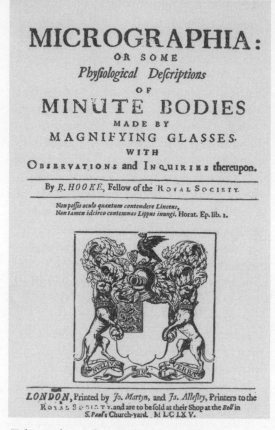

Title page from Robert Hooke's Micrographia, *first published in 1665 (Corbis/Bettmann)*

elasticity, astronomy, planetary motion, snowflakes, fossils, evolution, gravity, geometry, and microscopic life. He was the first scientist to use the word "cell" in its modern sense, and his 1705 book, *Discourse of Earthquakes,* offered new insights into geology. Born on July 18, 1635, he attended Oxford University and later became an assistant to scientist Robert Boyle. In 1662 he was appointed curator of experiments for the Royal Society of London, which he served for 15 years. In addition, he became a professor of geometry at Gresham College, London, in 1665. He died on March 3, 1703. (Bowler 1993)

> See also *Discourse of Earthquakes;* Evolution; Geological Research.

Howard, Ebenezer

Born in London on January 29, 1850, Ebenezer Howard founded the garden city

movement, a new approach to urban planning. He advocated the creation of privately owned communities, called "garden cities," that would be ringed with greenbelts of open land to control urban sprawl and provide city-dwellers access to nature. In 1898 Howard published a book on his proposals, entitled *Tomorrow: A Peaceful Path to Social Reform;* in 1902 it was revised as *Garden Cities of Tomorrow.* He subsequently convinced several businessmen to support his ideas, and in 1903 he established the first garden city: Letchworth, Hertfordshire, England. He established Welwyn Garden City, also in Hertfordshire, in 1920. Eventually the greenbelt principle spread to other countries, and in 1927 Howard was knighted for his efforts. He died on May 1, 1928, in Welwyn Garden City. (Ward 1992)

> See also *Garden Cities of Tomorrow;* Human Ecology.

Hubbell, Sue

A beekeeper in the Missouri Ozarks, Sue Hubbell's first and best-known book, *A Country Year: Living the Questions* (1986), recounts her observations of nature and rural life in the region. The book also points out the differences between her and her native Ozark neighbors, who do not share her belief that a bobcat, for example, should not be killed just because its pelt is worth a lot of money.

Hubbell was born in Kalamazoo, Michigan, in 1935. Her father was a botanist; her brother, Bill Gilbert, writes nature books, including *How Animals Communicate* (1966), *The Weasels* (1970), *Our Nature* (1986), and *Chulo: A Year Among the Coatimundis* (1984). Hubbell moved to the Ozarks in 1973 upon buying a 105-acre farm with her husband. Shortly thereafter the couple divorced, but Hubbell remained on the land. She later remarried, and today she splits her time between the Ozarks, where she maintains 300 beehives on her own and twenty other farms, and a second home in Washington, D.C. Her other works include *A Book of Bees . . . and How to Keep Them* (1988), *Far-Flung Hubbell: Essays from the American Road*

(1995), and *Waiting for Aphrodite* (1999), about invertebrates.

Hudson, William Henry

William Henry Hudson was a British author whose books on the English countryside helped inspire a naturalist movement in England during the 1920s and 1930s. Those works include *Afoot in England* (1909), *A Shepherd's Life* (1910), and *A Hind in Richmond Park* (1922). He also wrote novels, as well as several books on ornithology, including the popular *British Birds* (1895).

Hudson was born on August 4, 1841, in Argentina, where his New England parents had moved to take up sheep farming. After their death he traveled extensively before moving to England in 1869. He married in 1876 and lived primarily on his wife's income from investment property and inheritance while writing books. His first works were novels and short stories, which brought him the friendship of other fiction writers of the period, including George Gissing and Joseph Conrad. During the late 1880s Hudson began writing on birds. His last novel, *Green Mansions*, was published in 1904, three years after he became a naturalized British citizen. He subsequently turned his attention to nature writing, which occupied him until his death on August 18, 1922. (Frederick 1972)

See also Afoot in England.

Hughes, Ted

Once the Poet Laureate of England, Ted Hughes authored 16 volumes of poetry; much of his work deals with nature. His books include *The Hawk in the Rain* (1968), *Crow: From the Life and Songs of the Crow* (1971), *Spring, Summer, Autumn, Winter* (1973), *Season Songs* (1976), *A Solstice* (1978), *River* (1983), and *Winter Pollen: Occasional Prose* (1994). Hughes was born on August 17, 1930, in Yorkshire, England. His first poems were published in 1946 in his school magazine. He entered Cambridge University in 1951. After graduation, he worked at a variety of jobs, including night watchman and zoo attendant. He also wrote poetry and children's books. In 1956 he married poet Sylvia Plath, who committed suicide in 1964. Hughes remarried in 1970. In his later years he bought a farm and bred sheep and cattle. He died in October 1998.

Human Ecology

Ecology is the study of how all the parts of an environment interact. *Animal ecology* is the study of how animals are affected by these interactions; *human ecology* is the study of how humans are affected by their environment.

It could be argued that any work of environmental literature addressing the risks to the planet is a work of human ecology, because any thing that affects the earth affects all of its creatures. However, human ecology generally refers to direct and immediate hazards to human health, such as the misuse of toxic pesticides and chemicals that may cause cancer. One of the most important authors to address this aspect of human ecology was Dr. Alice Hamilton, whose 1925 book, *Industrial Poisons in the United States,* discussed the plight of factory workers exposed to industrial chemicals.

Another issue of human ecology is overpopulation. Thomas Malthus wrote extensively on this problem in his 1798 work, *An Essay on the Principle of Population,* which argues that human overpopulation threatens to deplete the earth's resources. Modern environmentalists Paul and Anne Ehrlich have devoted much of their lives to this argument, publishing numerous books and articles during the 1980s and 1990s on the dangers of overpopulation, which include an increase in pollution and the depletion of soil due to overfarming.

Many other human ecologists have addressed these and similar problems; some suggest that the only solution is to restructure society. These people, called "social ecologists," argue that environmental issues cannot be separated from social issues. The first to develop this concept was Murray Bookchin, who founded a nonprofit institute to study environmental problems using social analyses.

See also Bookchin, Murray; Ehrlich, Paul and Anne; *Essay on the Principle of Population, An;* Hamilton, Alice; *Industrial Poisons in the United States;* Malthus, Thomas Robert; Social Ecology.

Humboldt, Alexander Von

A 19th-century Prussian baron, Friedrich Wilhelm Henrich Alexander von Humboldt was one of the first true ecologists. He studied the relationship between various life-forms and their environments, seeing how climate and aspects of geography affected their physical and behavioral characteristics. Moreover, he believed that human beings were an integral part of their environment and should live in harmony with the natural world rather than try to master it. This ran contrary to the prevailing view of the time.

Born in Berlin on September 14, 1769; his father, an army officer, died when Alexander was only 10. His widowed mother intended for him to become a public official and educated him accordingly. He studied politics, history, and economics, first with private tutors and later at the University of Frankfurt. Gradually, however, he became interested in botany and began collecting plant specimens.

Humboldt's interest soon extended to other sciences as well. In 1789 he attended the University of Gottingen, where he studied geology and mineralogy. In 1790 he left Gottingen for the School of Mines in Freiberg, Saxony, remaining there for two years to study mining. In 1792 he began working as a mining expert for the Prussian government. He held this position until 1797, when he decided to devote his life to scientific discovery.

After some additional study, Humboldt received permission from the Spanish government to explore their lands in South and Central America. By this time his mother had died, and he had inherited enough wealth to finance his own research expedition. From 1799 to 1804 he and French botanist Aime Bonpland traveled throughout the region under arduous conditions, investigating all aspects of the South American environment and collecting plant and animal specimens. They also made several important discoveries. For example, contrary to common belief, they learned that the Amazon River system was not isolated but was linked to the Orinoco River system by the Casiquiare River.

Humboldt and Bonpland also climbed several mountains in the Andes and learned that such mountaineering at high altitudes brought on a kind of sickness caused by the reduced oxygen. In addition to this discovery of altitude sickness, they were the first to note variations in vegetation related to changing altitude, temperature, and climate. The two men went as high as 19,280 feet above sea level while ascending Mount Chimborazo, and for almost 30 years that feat remained the highest mountain climb on record. Humboldt and Bonpland also studied ocean currents off South America and made important discoveries in that field as well.

When Humboldt returned to Europe, first to Paris and then to Berlin, he worked toward publishing the material he had gathered during his expedition. Between 1804 and 1827 thirty volumes of his work appeared. They included temperature recordings, climate information, descriptions of geology and volcanic activity, and a thorough discussion of plants and animals and their relationship to their environment. In addition, Humboldt published a narrative of his adventures entitled *Political Essay on the Kingdom of New Spain,* in which he discussed the land's people, politics, and economy as well as mining practices and physical features. Taken together, the publication of Humboldt's South American works nearly exhausted his fortune. Nonetheless, he offered financial assistance to promising young scientists such as Louis Agassiz.

In 1827 Humboldt accepted a position as tutor for the crown prince of Prussia. He also taught a geography course at the University of Berlin and organized a major scientific conference. During 1829 he went on another scientific expedition, this time through Central Asia as the invited guest of the tsar of Russia, who sought advice on mining practices. While on this trip Humboldt collected information about Asian geography and geology.

Back in Berlin, he began writing *Kosmos,* considered to be his greatest work. It not only presented facts about the earth and its creatures but also showed the connection between creatures and their environments. The first volume of *Kosmos* was published in 1845; Humboldt was working on the fifth volume when he died on May 6, 1859. *Kosmos* was extremely popular and was translated into several languages. (Botting 1973; De Terra 1979)

See also Animal Ecology; Geological Research; *Kosmos.*

Huxley, Thomas Henry

During the 19th century prominent English biologist and paleontologist Thomas Henry Huxley was a major supporter of Charles Darwin's theory of evolution, arguing in favor of his contemporary's work at scientific meetings. But Huxley also made his own contributions to evolutionary science. For example, in 1863 he published *Evidence as to Man's Place in Nature,* which compared the anatomies of humans and apes.

Huxley was born on May 4, 1825, in Ealing, Middlesex, England. He had almost no formal schooling, but after he taught himself many advanced subjects he received a scholarship to medical school. Unfortunately, the funds ran out before he was awarded his degree. Nonetheless, he was considered qualified enough to work as an assistant surgeon on a Royal Navy ship. During his voyages he collected marine specimens and wrote about them in articles that were quickly published in prestigious scientific journals.

When Huxley returned to England he was famous in scientific circles and elected to the Royal Society. He spent the next few years conducting research on his marine specimens, then took a teaching position at London's School of Mines, which later became the Royal College of Science. He remained at the college until 1885, continuing to study and write about various scientific subjects. In addition, he participated in many scientific societies and served on several committees and royal commissions; he was a popular lecturer.

Huxley died on June 29, 1895, in Eastbourne, Sussex. Forty-seven years later, his grandson, Sir Julian Huxley, continued the family tradition of studying evolution, publishing *Evolution: The Modern Synthesis* (1942), which discussed evolution in terms of human genetics and racial characteristics. (Bibby 1972)

See also Darwin, Charles Robert; Evolution.

I

Ibsen, Henrik

Norwegian playwright and social critic Henrik Ibsen is the author of *An Enemy of the People* (1882), which depicts a town eager to conceal the fact that its public baths are contaminated with disease-causing bacteria. Ibsen was born on March 20, 1828, in Skien, Norway. His father, once a prosperous merchant, went bankrupt in 1836. Seven years later, the 15-year-old Ibsen left home to become apprentice to an apothecary. In 1850 he entered university in Christiania (now Oslo) and became involved in theater. The following year he was appointed director and playwright for a theater in Bergen, Norway, and from 1857 to 1862 he took the same position at Christiania Theater. (Ibsen 1978)

See also *Enemy of the People, An;* Environmental Politics; Water Pollution.

Idea of Wilderness, The

Published in 1991, *The Idea of Wilderness* by Max Oelschlaeger is, according to its author, an attempt to construct "a universal history organized around one steadfast theme—namely, the idea of wilderness, the study of an ever-changing yet constant relationship between humankind and nature." (Oelschlaeger 1991, x) To this end, Oelschlaeger discusses the relationship between humans and the land during prehistoric and ancient times, the "transmutation of wilderness to nature" during modern times, and the coming of the "age of ecology." (68, 205) He also examines the writings of Henry David Thoreau, John Muir, Aldo Leopold, Robinson Jeffers, and Gary Snyder. (Oelschlaeger 1991)

See also Jeffers, (John) Robinson; Leopold, Aldo; Muir, John; Snyder, Gary; Thoreau, Henry David.

In Defense of Nature

In Defense of Nature is one of the best-known books by nature writer John Hay. Published in 1969, it is typical of nature works written during the early environmental movement, combining personal observations of nature with arguments in favor of environmentalism. In regard to the latter, Hay says:

> Conservationism, along with world poverty, ought to get all the support that is reserved for war and supersonic jets; but there are times when I wonder what the term means, or if its meaning has not been so dimmed by public usage that it has lost some of its efficacy in the process. . . . We have not been effectively persuaded that our livelihood, even our sanity, depends on a natural environment

which is allowed its own proper growth and functions. We have not been taught that our replacements of ecological systems have on the whole left the world much poorer than it used to be. Conservation should be against the impoverished and denuded world which man is threatening. Its name should stand out clearly in favor of an earthly society where men and nature do not simply coexist in uneasy terms but live together. Any politically involved movement is bound to compromise, but there is a point beyond which conservation cannot compromise and fulfill itself. It cannot backtrack from a fundamental stand against the careless and arbitrary dismissal of living species on this planet. The least we can do, whatever we think of ourselves as capable custodians of the earth environment, is to put our emphasis on caring whether these lives continue or not. (Hay 1969, 34–35)

In discussing extinct or endangered species, Hay focuses on the threat of pesticide use, saying that chemicals like DDT (dichloro-diphenyl-trichloroethane) are killing hawks and eagles. He reports: "A government survey . . . states that breeding populations of osprey and bald eagles once plentiful in the lakes of Ontario have begun to die out, because of the use of poison sprays. The peregrine falcon, the loon, and also fish, are included in the category of wildlife being killed off, or their reproductive capacity impaired, by the use of pesticides, especially 'hard' ones like DDT." (42) Hay's criticism of DDT is similar to that of Rachel Carson in her classic book *Silent Spring*.

Whereas Carson's work focuses almost entirely on pesticides, Hay's book also includes his observations on animals, wilderness areas, and the emotional satisfaction that he receives from the wild. For example, he states:

Just so long as there is a wildness to find I can stay alive. It is not that I want it for an escape, since that is impossible in this world, but to share. The exchange of life is what is important. Unless we can see the

"non-human" environment in terms of a whole that only acts, gives and receives fully when all its elements are in full play, then we will still be on the outside looking in. It may be that what we need more than anything else is to shake hands with the "insignificant." (65)

Hay believes that all people are drawn to nature, particularly the seashore. Of one beach, he says:

Almost daily, the year around, people drive down to the landing. . . . There they sit in their cars and just look out toward the horizon, watching for ships and birds, or nothing at all. . . . I wonder if we do not feel invited to this open landscape not only because it soothes us but because we need it. Is there still a residual earth man inside us that looks to a wilderness where all his reactions fit and where it is natural to meet existence directly, with no artificial aid, no go-betweens?

This environment not only invites us to sunbathing and gathering shells and pebbles on the beach; it is a junction of several worlds, a meeting place. It has something of the stable power of the land, something of the wide, procreant wash of the sea. (70–71)

Hay fears that humankind might one day destroy such places "with the random ferocity of bluefish attacking a school of herring." (208). He suggests that people not only protect the natural world but also become more connected to it, pointing out that "direct experience of the natural earth is becoming rare." (4) (Hay 1969)

See also Hay, John; Nature Writing.

In the Rainforest
Published in 1981, *In the Rainforest* by American journalist Catherine Caufield describes the delicate rain forest ecosystems in Africa, Central and South America, India, the Philippines, and Indonesia and discusses their destruction due to such practices as cattle ranch-

ing, logging, and intentional flooding to create hydroelectric dams. It was one of the first books to focus on the issue of rain forest conservation. Written in the first person, *In the Rainforest* combines hard facts about rain forest extinction with Caufield's personal experiences investigating these regions. It includes a map showing the location of rain forests throughout the world, as well as extensive notes and a bibliography for further reading. (Caufield 1989)

See also Balanced Ecosystems; Caufield, Catherine; Forest Management.

In the Shadow of Man

In the Shadow of Man (1971) is author Jane Goodall's first-person account of her experiences with African chimpanzees in the wild. Goodall is one of the foremost authorities on chimps, having led the first long-term field study of their behavior. Her book documents the first 10 years of that study, which began in 1960 at the request of noted British anthropologist Louis Leakey and was funded in part by the Wilkie Foundation and the National Geographic Society. Both of these groups later contributed to the mountain gorilla research of Dian Fossey, another Leakey protégé.

Goodall established her research site on the shores of Lake Tanganyika, at Gombe Stream Chimpanzee Reserve in Tanzania, Africa. Initially she maintains only a campsite, but later she presides over the construction of a permanent facility. Called the Gombe Stream Research Center, its construction was financed by the National Geographic Society.

Goodall lives at the facility with her husband, Hugo, whom she met at Gombe in 1961. A wildlife photographer, he had traveled there to film a documentary on chimpanzees for the National Geographic Society. Some of his photographs are included in *In the Shadow of Man*.

The book offers Goodall's detailed descriptions of chimpanzee behavior. For example, in discussing adolescents, she writes:

At this age the young female is, if anything, even more fascinated by infants

than she was as a juvenile. Not only does she frequently carry an infant short distances, play with and groom it, but she also shows concern for its welfare. When [a chimpanzee named] Pooch was about eight years old she once carried a six-month-old infant up a tree and began to groom him. It so happened that the tip of a palm frond, swaying gently in the breeze, occasionally brushed past Pooch's shoulders as she sat there. I noticed that the infant was watching this frond as though fascinated. All at once he grabbed hold of it, wriggling off Pooch's lap, and the frond swung with his weight back toward the trunk of the palm tree. For a moment Pooch stared after the infant as if she couldn't believe her eyes; her face contorted with a huge grin of fear. Frantically she climbed down her tree and rushed up another, from a branch of which she was just able to reach the frond as it swung like a pendulum back toward her. Then she seized the infant, who was not at all frightened and probably thoroughly enjoying the swing, and hugged him tight. The grin of fright only slowly left her face. (Goodall 1971, 175)

A major section of *In the Shadow of Man* contains such observations, yet it also offers commentary on chimpanzee conservation. For example, Goodall says:

The chimpanzee is only one of the many species threatened with extinction in the wild; but he is, after all, our closest living relative and it would be tragic if when our grandchildren are grown the chimpanzee exists only in the zoo and the laboratory—a frightening thought, since for the most part the chimpanzee in captivity is very different from the magnificent creature we know so well in the wild. (239)

Goodall further explains that a zoo chimpanzee "is a very different creature from the chimpanzee we know at the Gombe Stream. The zoo chimp has none of the calm dignity, the serenity of gaze, or the purposeful individuality of his wild counterpart." (240) She discusses zoo enclosures and ways that life can be improved for captive chimpanzees in both zoos and laboratories.

Goodall briefly explains the status of her research study in the wild. She says that because she and Hugo have had a child they can no longer spend as much time at Gombe, because "chimpanzees have been known to prey on small human children." (244) However, their work continues. According to Goodall:

> Despite the fact that I have been away from Gombe for months at a stretch there has, of course, been no break in the records—thanks to our students. It is never quite the same to hear about something as actually to witness it, but it remains exciting, and most people who work at the Gombe Stream share our enthusiasm for the chimpanzees as individuals, so their accounts are vivid as well as accurate. (243)

In the Shadow of Man concludes with several appendices summarizing Goodall's work. They provide a list of common behaviors, sketches of typical chimpanzee facial expressions, and an overview of chimpanzee tool use and diet. (Goodall 1971)

See also Animal Behavior; Fossey, Dian; Goodall, Jane; Wildlife Conservation.

Industrial Poisons in the United States

Published in 1925, *Industrial Poisons in the United States* was the first major work to address the relationship between occupational and environmental health. Author Alice Hamilton, a professor of industrial medicine at Harvard University, conducted studies on how industry affected the environment as related to health issues.

In discussing Hamilton's work in *Forcing the Spring*, Robert Gottlieb says that it was particularly unique because "she was concerned not only about the visible, acute problems of occupational hazards but also generational issues associated with 'race poisons,'

reproductive toxins such as lead whose 'effects are not confined to the men and women who are exposed to it in the course of their work, but are passed on to their offspring.'" (Gottlieb 51) Moreover, she addressed "issues of class, race, and gender in the workplace and the long-term hazards of the production system" and "was able to communicate effectively with industry and government figures because of her sincerity in the goals and substance of her research, while developing a sympathetic relationship with workers due to her compassion and her commitment to change." (51) (Gottlieb 1993)

See also Hamilton, Alice; Human Ecology.

Industrialization
See Human Ecology.

Ingenhousz, Jan
Jan Ingenhousz discovered photosynthesis, a process whereby plants take in carbon dioxide and give off oxygen. He published his work on this subject in 1799 as *Experiments Upon Vegetables, Discovering Their Great Power of Purifying the Common Air in the Sun-shine, and of Injuring It in the Shade at Night*. It made people more aware of the significance of plants in the natural world.

Ingenhousz was born on December 8, 1730, in Breda, The Netherlands. He practiced medicine there until 1765, when he became a physician in London. In 1768 he was named the court physician of the empress of Austria, a position he retained until 1779. Ingenhousz was interested in scientific study throughout his life. In addition to his work on plants, he experimented with electricity and heat. He died on September 7, 1799, in Bowood, Wiltshire, England. (Boynton 1948; Spangenburg and Moser 1993)

See also *Experiments Upon Vegetables*.

Inland Island, The
Published in 1969, *The Inland Island* by Josephine Winslow Johnson portrays one year spent on her Ohio land. The site of a former family farm, she allowed the acreage to go wild in a desire to create a private "na-

ture preserve," a term she says typically belongs "to vaster things such as the Serengeti Plain." (Johnson 1969, 10). Of this desire, Johnson writes: "I have had a love of the land all my life, and today when all life is a life against nature, against man's whole being, there is a sense of urgency, a need to record and cherish, and to share this love before it is too late. Time passes—mine and the land's." (8) Johnson's book is divided into 12 chapters, one for each month of the year, recording detailed observations about the wildlife on her land.

International Wildlife

International Wildlife is published by the National Wildlife Federation (NWF), an environmental group dedicated to wildlife conservation. The magazine covers international wildlife issues and is a companion to another NWF periodical, *National Wildlife,* which covers national wildlife issues. Another NWF magazine, *Ranger Rick,* covers wildlife conservation issues for children.

All three publications are popular in the United States and have done much to interest the American public in subjects such as endangered species and habitat protection. In addition, they function as fund-raising tools, because they not only make people aware of wildlife conservation problems but also call for monetary donations to help solve them.

See also Environmental Groups; *National Wildlife;* Wildlife Conservation.

Irving, Washington

American author Washington Irving is best known for his stories "Rip van Winkle" and "The Legend of Sleepy Hollow," which first appeared in a collection entitled *The Sketch Book of Geoffrey Crayon, Gent* (1819–1820). However, in terms of nature writing, his most significant work is *A Tour of the Prairies* (1835) and *Astoria* (1836), in which he describes his travels through frontier America during the early 1830s. For example, in *A Tour of the Prairies* he relates his experiences during a buffalo hunt and provides information about the terrain:

Undated engraving of American author Washington Irving (Corbis/Bettmann)

A gallop across the prairies in pursuit of game is by no means so smooth a career as those may imagine, who have only the idea of an open level plain. It is true, the prairies of the hunting ground are not so much entangled with flowering plants and long herbage as the lower prairies, and are principally covered with short buffalo grass; but they are diversified by hill and dale, and where most level, are apt to be cut up by deep rifts and ravines, made by torrents after rains; and which, yawning from an even surface, are almost like pitfalls in the way of the hunter, checking him suddenly, when in full career, or subjecting him to the risk of limb and life. The plains, too, are beset by burrowing holes of small animals, in which the horse is apt to sink to the fetlock, and throw both himself and his rider. (Finch and Elder 1990, 114–115)

Irving was born on April 3, 1783, in New York City. His first writings were for a newspaper, *The Morning Chronicle,* in 1802–1803. From 1804 to 1806 he traveled Europe; upon his return to the United States he became a lawyer. However, he continued to write and soon published a series of magazine essays followed by a humorous book entitled *History of New York . . . by Diedrich Knickerbocker* (1809).

In 1811 he began working as a political lobbyist in Washington, D.C., where he remained until 1815. At that time he went to England to manage a family business, but after meeting novelist Sir Walter Scott he decided to concentrate more on his writing. His most significant work, *The Sketch Book,* appeared shortly thereafter. Its success enabled Irving to travel Europe extensively, and in 1826 he began living in Spain, where he wrote *Columbus* (1828), *The Companions of Columbus* (1831), *Conquest of Granada* (1829), and *The Alhambra* (1832). In 1832 he returned to the United States to travel along the Ohio and Mississippi Rivers. In addition to *A Tour of the Prairies* and *Astoria,* his work from this period includes *The Adventures of Captain Bonneville* (1837). Irving died in New York on November 28, 1859.

Is It Painful to Think?

Is It Painful to Think? by David Rothenberg is a transcript of his conversations with Arne Naess, a Norwegian philosopher who developed the concept of deep ecology. Published in Norway in 1992 and in the United States in 1993, the book offers Naess's comments on his life and beliefs, as well as Rothenberg's explanations of Naess's ecological philosophy.

For example, Rothenberg defines deep ecology as "a philosophy of environmentalism that encourages us to ask basic questions about the place of our species in nature, in the hopes that deeper questioning will lead to more profound solutions to the growing environmental crisis faced today." (Rothenberg 1993, 126) He criticizes people for misusing the term:

> Deep ecology has become an attractive phrase for many people, who tend to bend the term to their needs without bothering to learn what it was originally meant to imply. There are those who use the term to label themselves the real, bold, and serious environmentalists, opposing their chosen few to the vast majority of weak reformist thinkers, who they deem to call "shallow." And there are others who use "deep" simply as a substitute for "radical," which leads their opponents to criticize them for being far "off the deep end" in respect to real problems and workable solutions. (126–127)

In his dialogue with Naess, Rothenberg questions the philosopher about many aspects of deep ecology, and the two explore many issues together. For example, in an exchange on the priorities of the movement, Naess says:

> There is a tendency in the deep ecology movement to say, "Earth first!" in the sense that we are more fond of nature than of people. Priorities should always have an ecological base before thinking only of their human value. . . . In the deep ecology movement, this kind of empathy for other living beings is a very deep-seated premise. I think we all agree that a father who has no options but to kill the last animal of this or that species, or to ruin the last patch of tropical forest, in order to feed a baby that otherwise will be ruined through hunger, just has to kill or burn. There's no question of that. But Americans and Norwegians are ruining what's left of our free nature without good reason, and that's a crime. (140–141)

Rothenberg points out that the title of his book, *Is It Painful to Think?*, reflects Naess's belief that people find it painful to question their existence but must do so nonetheless. To encourage a more thorough study of environmental issues, he concludes *Is It Painful to Think?* with a list of many of Naess's works. (Glotfelty and Fromm 1996; Rothenberg 1993)

See also Deep Ecology Movement; Environmental Movement; Naess, Arne; Rothenberg, David.

Ishimure, Michiko

Born in 1927, Japanese author Michiko Ishimure publicized a major environmental disaster in Japan through several articles and books, the latter of which include *Tsubaki no umi no ki* (Story of the Sea of Camellias, 1983*)* and *Kugai jōdo* (1988; published as *Paradise in the Sea of Sorrow: Our Minamata Disease* in 1990).

Ishimure's works focuses on a crisis in Japan's Minamata Bay, which was a dumping ground for organic mercury waste beginning in 1932. During the early 1950s doctors began to encounter people with strange neurological disorders, and they eventually discovered that the fish in Minamata Bay had become toxic. Chisson Chemical Company, which had dumped the mercury, disputed this fact, and the Japanese government tried to cover it up until 1968, when officials acknowledged the problem. Meanwhile, hundreds of people, especially unborn children, were crippled or died from mercury poisoning, or Minamata disease. In 1996 the government ordered the chemical company to pay the families of the victims $184 million in compensation; a fishing moratorium was imposed on Minamata Bay from 1972 to 1998.

J

Jefferies, (John) Richard

English naturalist Richard Jefferies is best known for his nature essays, which were published collectively as *The Life of the Fields* (1884), *The Open Air* (1885), and *Field and Hedgerow* (1889). However, he began his writing career as a reporter examining agricultural labor issues and the relationship between landowners and tenant farmers. Born on November 6, 1848, near Swindon, Wiltshire, England, Jefferies was the son of a farmer but was hired as a reporter for the local paper in 1866. By the early 1870s his articles were being published in London newspapers as well. In 1882 he produced a popular book for boys, *Bevis: The Story of a Boy;* the following year his autobiography, *The Story of My Heart,* appeared. He also wrote three novels: *Green Ferne Farm* (1880), *Dewy Morn* (1884), and *Amaryllis at the Fair* (1887). Jeffries died on August 14, 1887.

Jeffers, (John) Robinson

American poet Robinson Jeffers produced a large body of work. A great deal of it expresses the author's controversial views on religion and humanity, but much of it also celebrates the beauty of the Pacific coast near the town of Carmel, California, where Jeffers lived for 46 years. His poetry collections include *Tamar and Other Poems* (1924), *Cawdor* (1928), *Thurso's Landing* (1932), and *Be Angry at the Sun* (1941).

Born in Pittsburgh on January 10, 1887, Jeffers studied medicine and forestry before an inheritance allowed him to write full-time. He died in Carmel on January 20, 1962.

Jevons, William Stanley

William Stanley Jevons was an economist who applied mathematical logic to the problem of coal consumption in *The Coal Question* (1865). Born in Liverpool, England, on September 1, 1835, he studied natural sciences at the University College of London, but in 1854 he interrupted his studies to become an assayer at the New Sydney Mint in Australia. He lived there for five years, making systematic observations in the fields of botany, geology, and meteorology. He also experimented with photography. In 1859 he returned to England and became a political economist. He wrote books and papers on economics, mathematics, and science until his death on August 13, 1882, in Hastings, England. (Jevons 1906)

See also Air Pollution; *Coal Question, The.*

Journey to the Center of the Earth, A

A Journey to the Center of the Earth by Jules Verne is a classic science fiction novel featuring the environmental sciences. Published in 1864, it mentions research related to geology, mineralogy, and evolution, particularly the work of George Cuvier, thereby raising public awareness of the scientific issues of the day.

The plot concerns a German professor of geology and mineralogy, professor Von Hardwigg, who accidentally finds a note from a 12th-century Icelandic scientist. The note tells of a crater that leads down to the center of the earth, and Von Hardwigg decides to explore it. He takes along his nephew, Harry, who narrates the story, and a hired guide, Hans. Beneath the surface of the earth, the men find many wonders. For example, Harry says:

As we descended, successions of layers composing the primitive soil appeared with the utmost fidelity of detail. Geological science considers this primitive soil as the base of the mineral crust, and it has recognized that it is composed of three different strata or layers, all resting on the immovable rock known as granite.

No mineralogists had ever found themselves placed in such a marvellous position to study nature in all her real and naked beauty. Across the streak of the rocks, colored by beautiful green tints, wound metallic threads of copper, of manganese, with traces of platinum and gold. I could not help gazing at these riches buried in the entrails of Mother Earth . . . These treasures, mighty and inexhaustible, were buried in the morning of the earth's history, at such awful depths that no crowbar or pickaxe will ever drag them from their tomb. (Verne 1965, 128–129)

As they progress toward the center of the earth, the explorers have many adventures and learn several new scientific facts. They also encounter prehistoric plants and animals, including mastodons and a giant apeman, that have remained alive in this subterranean world. After sailing on an underground sea, however, they finally land, only to find their path blocked by a large boulder. They use dynamite to blast it apart while they wait on

their raft. Unfortunately, the explosion causes the sea to rush into the breach, carrying the raft along with it. It rises toward the earth's surface, and when the water is replaced with lava the men realize that they are part of a volcanic eruption. Shortly thereafter they are violently expelled from the volcano but manage to land safely. When they return home, they discover that the whole world knows of their expedition, and they are lauded as heroes. (Verne 1965)

See also Cuvier, Georges; Environmental Fiction; Evolution; Verne, Jules.

Jurassic Park

The 1990 novel *Jurassic Park* by Michael Crichton presents a contemporary spin on evolutionary theory. It also expresses an attitude toward environmentalism that developed during the modern environmental movement: the idea that human arrogance, through science, is destroying nature, and that people should consequently stop interfering with the natural world. One character, a mathematician named Malcolm, explains:

What we call "nature" is in fact a complex system of far greater subtlety than we are willing to accept. We make a simplified image of nature and then we botch it up. I'm no environmentalist, but you have to understand what you don't understand. How many times must the point be made? How many times must we see the evidence? We build the Aswan Dam and claim it is going to revitalize the country. Instead, it destroys the fertile Nile Delta, produces parasitic infestation, and wrecks the Egyptian economy. (Crichton 1990, 93)

Malcolm is part of a group of people inspecting Jurassic Park, an island tourist attraction featuring living dinosaurs. Geneticists have cloned the creatures from ancient DNA, and they believe they know how to control them. Malcolm disagrees:

When the hunter goes out in the rain forest to seek food for his family, does he expect to control nature? No. He imagines that nature is beyond him. Beyond his understanding. Beyond his control. Maybe he prays to nature, to the fertility of the forest that provides for him. He prays because he knows he doesn't control it. He's at the mercy of it.

But you decide you won't be at the mercy of nature. You decide you'll control nature, and from that moment on you're in deep trouble, because you can't do it. Yet you have made systems that require you to do it. And you can't do it—and you never have—and you never will. Don't confuse things. You can make a boat, but you can't make the ocean. You can make an airplane, but you can't make the air. Your powers are much less than your dreams of reason would have you believe. (349)

Throughout the novel, Malcolm expresses his disdain for uncontrolled science, which allows humans to destroy the natural order of the world. Meanwhile, another member of the inspection team, Alan Grant, is awed by the living dinosaurs. Unlike Malcolm, he possesses an appreciation for science, and he recognizes its potential for helping humankind.

Eventually, however, Grant realizes that the scientists at Jurassic Park do not really understand the creatures they have created and have made several mistakes in bringing them to life and recreating their primeval environment. More importantly, they have not anticipated the dinosaurs' behavioral traits and find themselves ill-equipped to handle some of the most dangerous species. Consequently, some of the dinosaurs escape confinement and kill several people, including Malcolm. Shortly before

dying, he suggests that humans will someday become extinct, but life itself will continue:

Let's say we had a bad [radiation accident], and all the plants and animals died, and the earth was clicking hot for a hundred thousand years. Life would survive somewhere—under the soil, or perhaps frozen in Arctic ice. And after all those years, when the planet was no longer inhospitable, life would again spread over the planet. The evolutionary process would begin again. It might take a few billion years for life to regain its present variety. And of course it would be very different from what it is now. But the earth would survive our folly. Life would survive our folly. (365–366)

Such statements make *Jurassic Park* as much an expression of modern environmental thinking as a story about dinosaurs. This is an important difference between recent environmental fiction and earlier novels. For example, Sir Arthur Conan Doyle's 1912 novel, *The Lost World,* also concerns dinosaurs, but it is an adventure tale without any messages regarding environmentalism. What the two works share, however, is the fact that both present the prevailing evolutionary theories of their times. Crichton offers a great deal of information about evolution, dinosaurs, and related scientific controversies, and he acknowledges the help of many modern paleontologists and geneticists in writing *Jurassic Park.* (Crichton 1990)

See also Crichton, Michael; Doyle, Arthur Conan; Environmental Fiction; Environmental Movement; Evolution; *Lost World, The.*

K

Kaufman, Wallace

A former professor of English, Wallace Kaufman was once active in the environmental movement, lobbying for the Wilderness Society and fighting to improve regulations related to nuclear power plants. He also worked as a book and video reviewer for a national environmental magazine, *American Forests*. However, he gradually became disillusioned with environmental groups and wrote a book critical of their approach to environmental issues. Entitled *No Turning Back: Dismantling the Fantasies of Environmental Thinking*, it was published in 1994. From 1993 to 1995 Kaufman lived in Kazakhstan, where he advised the government on policies related to housing and land issues. (Kaufman 1994)

> **See also** Antienvironmentalism; Environmental Politics; *No Turning Back*.

Kent, Rockwell

Rockwell Kent was a noted painter and illustrator who concentrated on depicting nature scenes. He also wrote books about his travels to Alaska, Greenland, Newfoundland, southern South America, and the Maine coastline. His works include *Wilderness: A Journal of Quiet Adventure in Alaska* (1920), *N by E* (1930), *Greenland Journal* (1962), and *Voyaging Southward from the Strait of Magellan*

Artist Rockwell Kent poses with his assistants while producing a mural at the 1939 World's Fair in New York (Corbis/Schenectady Museum; Electrical History Foundation)

(1968). Born on June 21, 1882, in Tarrytown Heights, New York, Kent studied architecture before turning to art. To supplement his income, he worked at various odd jobs, including one as a Maine lobsterman. Kent died on March 13, 1971.

Kosmos

Kosmos was one of the first works to emphasize the connection between earth's life-forms and their physical environment. Its author, 19th-century Prussian scientist Alexander von Humboldt, did not hold the prevailing view that man was a conqueror who should hold sway over nature. Instead, he believed that man should live in harmony with all other living things, because the environment is delicately balanced. For this reason, many people consider Humboldt to be the first true ecologist. He published the first volume of *Kosmos* in 1845, followed by volumes two through four; Humboldt was working on the fifth volume when he died in 1859 (it was published posthumously). In its entirety, the work was extremely popular, not only among scientists but also among the general public. This popularity was a direct result of Humboldt's writing style, which made science accessible to laypersons—rare for that time. Consequently, *Kosmos* was translated into several languages and remained successful for many years.

In addition to showing the relationship between life and the environment, the work provided observations about plants, animals, geology, and geography gathered during Humboldt's many travels throughout the world. Humboldt was also an explorer who endured many hardships to make his discoveries; these adventures made his work even more interesting to the public. (Botting 1973; De Terra 1979)

See also Balanced Ecosystems; Humboldt, Alexander von.

Krutch, Joseph Wood

Born on November 25, 1893, in Knoxville, Tennessee, Joseph Wood Krutch was a well-known drama critic from 1924 to 1952, teaching dramatic literature at Columbia University from 1943 to 1952. However, he was also an active conservationist who wrote books and essays about nature and ecology.

Krutch graduated from the University of Tennessee in 1915 and received a Ph.D. from Columbia University in 1923. He then became a schoolteacher and started writing magazine articles. In 1924 he became drama critic for a magazine, *The Nation;* he also began writing books. His first book, *The Modern Temper,* was published in 1929. In 1948 he wrote a biography of Henry David Thoreau,

an advocate of living simply in the wilderness, and his interest in nature grew.

As a result in 1952 he moved to Arizona and became a trustee of Tucson's Arizona–Sonora Desert Museum. He also began writing books on naturalism and conservation issues, including *The Desert Year, The Voice of the Desert, The Measure of Man* (1954), and *The Great Chain of Life* (1956). *The Measure of Man* warned of the dangers of overpopulation and won the National Book Award for nonfiction in 1955.

In discussing Krutch's significance as an author, biographer Donald Cox says:

He was definitely in the vanguard of other conservationists of his time who saw the interrelationships of all living things which he first expounded in his *Great Chain of Life* (1956). Many of the earlier conservationists did not see this relationship, often focusing their interests on a single aspect of nature such as trees or birds. Krutch, however, not only clearly saw this web of life phenomenon but was one of the first to warn us that the universe might one day "consist of man and the whirl of atoms and the stars. He alone will be in an otherwise dead world." (Cox 78–79)

Much of Krutch's work expressed anti-science sentiments, and in his later years he became increasingly pessimistic about the fate of the earth. In a newspaper article he wrote: "The Seventies may be the beginning of the end, or the beginning of a new civilization. If it becomes the latter, it will not be because we have walked on the moon and learned how to tinker with the genes of unborn children, but because we have come to realize that wealth, power and even knowledge are not good in themselves but only the instruments of good and evil." (79) He died on May 22, 1970, leaving behind an autobiography entitled *More Lives Than One* (1962). (Cox 1971)

See also Conservationism; Thoreau, Henry David.

L

Lamarck, Jean-Baptiste

Born on August 1, 1744, in Bazentin-le-Petit, Picardy, France, scientist Jean-Baptiste Lamarck suggested that an animal's behavior could influence the physical traits it passes on to its offspring. For example, Lamarck speculated that giraffes originally had short necks but lengthened their neck muscles by stretching to reach high leaves. These stretched muscles were then inherited by subsequent generations of giraffes. In other words, Lamarck believed that animals changed their appearance as a direct result of their actions and that such changes were passed on to future generations. This theory, which Lamarck promoted during the late 1700s and early 1800s, was in direct opposition to the subsequent work of Charles Darwin, who attributed evolution to natural selection. After Darwin's *Origin of Species* was published in 1859, interest in Lamarck's work was renewed, and Lamarckism and Darwinism became two prevailing—and opposing—views during the 19th century.

Interestingly, Lamarck did not originally set out to be a scientist. His father, a nobleman who served in the military, wanted his son to become a priest. Lamarck attended Jesuit school until his father's death, whereupon the young man enlisted in the infantry. He remained in the military until 1768.

Shortly thereafter, he began studying botany at the Jardin du Roi (the royal botanical gardens) in Paris. In 1778 he published a three-volume work on his botanical studies, entitled *Flore francaise* (French Flora). As a result he was appointed to the Academie des Sciences. He subsequently became a tutor for the son of naturalist Comte de Buffon, a position that gave Lamarck an opportunity to travel Europe and gather more botanical information.

Lamarck wrote an encyclopedia based on his work and collected samples of invertebrates during his travels. In 1793 he became curator of the invertebrate collection at the Museum National d'Histoire Naturelle, having already lectured extensively on museum display techniques. Lamarck is credited with bringing order to the way museum artifacts are displayed and to inspiring the modern museum cataloging system.

While associated with the museum, Lamarck continued to study the sciences and to write on a variety of scientific subjects. However, according to contemporaries, he proposed theories based on insufficient facts, and his writings were often ignored by the scientific community. Nonetheless, his *Natural History of Invertebrate Animals,* published between 1815 and 1822, was considered an important work. It was based on his earlier *System of Invertebrate Animals,* published in 1801, which reorganized the invertebrate classification system.

In creating these volumes, Lamarck relied extensively on the museum's invertebrate collection. He also used museum fossils to develop his theories on Lamarckism. In 1802 he coined the word "biology" to identify his studies of animal species, and he is considered a founder of the field. Despite such contributions to science, during his later years he fell into poverty. He died on December 18, 1829, in Paris. (Glass et al. 1959)

See also Darwin, Charles Robert; Evolution; *Philosophie zoologique;* Species Identification and Classification.

Land, A

A Land by British archaeologist Jacquette Hawkes is considered one of the classics of nature writing. Originally published in 1951, the book concerns the natural history of the British Isles and is significant because of its approach to the subject. As naturalist Robert Finch explains in a 1991 introduction to the work:

If *A Land* were no more than a popular account of British land formation and cultural history, however excellently told, it would by now have been relegated to that dust bin of useful, well-written natural history books since rendered obsolete by subsequent research and discovery. . . . *A Land* is, in essence, not so much popular science as a poetic meditation, rooted in geological and archaeological fact as best as we can know it, on the nature of consciousness, time, and human nature. It is a work primarily of imagination, and as such its scientific content, though still essentially sound, is no more its measure than Shakespeare's anachronisms. Its questions expand beyond matters of scientific and historic inquiry. They are the poet's questions, asked by an archaeologist: *Who are we? Where did we come from? Where are we going?* (Hawkes 1991, xi)

Finch sees the book as highly similar in style to other works published around the same time, particularly those of scientists seeking to write for laypersons. He says:

A Land was written in 1950, at a period when, for the first time since Darwin's era, recognized scientists were beginning to permit themselves the use of a personal voice and personal experience in order to talk about the larger concerns of their fields to a popular audience. In [the United States] Aldo Leopold had published his watershed book, *A Sand County Almanac,* in 1948; Rachel Carson was writing her series of lyrical tributes to the marine world; and Loren Eiseley was exploring the implications of paleontology and archaeology in brooding, personal essays that would appear a few years later in *The Immense Journey.* . . . With the other mid-century classics of nature writing, *A Land* can be considered a book of popular science. . . . As such it is a story brilliantly told, in its narrative sweep, in its sense of drama, and in Hawkes's unparalleled ability to humanize history and geology, and to relate the two. Her power to imagine the texture of everyday life in long past eras enables us to feel the continuity of human sensibility through time. (ix-x)

To this end, Hawkes not only discusses natural history, describing the British landscape and its creatures, but also talks about the relationship between humankind and nature. For example, she writes:

We have become very conscious of the individual being, apparently neatly enclosed by its covering of skin, recognizable as "me," a being to be disliked or desired but certainly a distinct and particular entity. It is the natural tendency of our mode of perception. Even a fire we contrive to see as a separate thing rather than as a chemical process affecting a wide area round the visible flames and smoke. A human being is hardly more cut off from its surround-

Typical British farm landscape with small enclosed fields and dry stone walls (British Tourist Authority)

ings than is a naked fire. It is continuously exuding gas and moisture and consuming other gas; a variety of waves can pass through a wall, through air and through a human body almost without interruption. It seems that the mind itself can issue waves, or something akin to them, that can penetrate and be received by other minds. Every being is united both inwardly and outwardly with the beginning of life in time and with the simplest forms of contemporary life. "Me" is a fiction, though a convenient fiction and one of significance to the consciousness of which I am the temporary home. (39–40)

Hawkes sees a change in this relationship, continuing:

I think that we are returning to an awareness of our unity with our surroundings, but an awareness of a much more exalted kind than anything that has existed before.

The primitive tribesman, to go no further back than the early days of our own species, was still so deeply sunk in nature that he hardly distinguished himself from his environment or from his fellows. This sense of oneness shows itself in totemism and in many forms of magic. . . . It is in this natural unity that the savage may truly be said to be happy. Certainly civilization must always destroy it. In urban, literate surroundings self-consciousness becomes a sharp knife cutting man away from his matrix. (39–40)

Hawkes discusses this separation of humans from nature, talking about how "town-dwellers, cut off from the soil and from food production, soon lost all those arts and skills which had always been the possession if not of every man, then of every small community." (199–200) She criticizes the arrival of the Industrial Revolution for encouraging a "new rapacious treatment of the land" that involves "an exploitation designed to satisfy man's vanity, his greed and possessiveness, his wish for domination." (202) Because of such comments, when *A Land* was published it became popular with not only amateur naturalists but also people involved in the environmental movement. (Hawkes 1991)

See also Carson, Rachel Louise; Eiseley, Loren; Environmental Movement; Hawkes, Jacquetta; Leopold, Aldo; Nature Writing; *Sand County Almanac, A.*

Land That Time Forgot, The

Published in 1918, *The Land That Time Forgot* by Edgar Rice Burroughs helped popularize the subject of evolution, offering detailed descriptions of dinosaurs and their primeval world based on early-20th-century theories. The book also mentions recent fossil discoveries, particularly in regard to early humans such as Neanderthals.

The narrator of the story is Bowen Tyler, an American submarine designer. While traveling to France during World War I, he and his shipmates are captured by a German submarine. Later the Americans overpower the Germans and try to head home but end up in uncharted seas, where they find a strange island. One of the men recalls reading about a continent named Caprona that was discovered and then lost again. The Americans believe they have accidentally stumbled upon this continent. They can find no place to land but realize that a river from Caprona's interior is flowing into the sea. Submerging the submarine, they pass under the rock walls that encircle the island; they travel up the inland river.

Within Caprona they discover a primeval world, where all stages of evolution exist together. In other words, dinosaurs inhabit the same world as tapirs, apemen with early humans. They also find pools of crude oil, which they refine for their submarine. When enough supplies are on board, the Germans overpower the Americans and leave in their vessel. After several adventures, Bowen and a woman, Lys, decide to live among the most advanced of the primitive humans. Hoping one day they'll be rescued, Bowen writes down his story, puts it in a bottle, and throws it off a cliff into the sea.

Burroughs wrote two sequels: *The People That Time Forgot* and *Out of Time's Abyss*, both published in 1918. In the first, Bowen's manuscript is found and given to his friend, Tom Billings, who organizes a rescue mission. After many adventures, Billings finds Bowen, who leaves Caprona with Lys; Billings stays behind to marry a native girl. In the second sequel, Billings and the girl leave the island with some of the Americans who were originally stranded with Bowen.

By the end of his trilogy, Burroughs has outlined a complex explanation for the evolutionary processes on Caprona. All creatures, including humans, lay eggs in pools and streams; these eggs drift south to the most primeval area of the continent, where they hatch as the most primitive member of their species. As time passes, each individual physically changes to represent more and more advanced levels of evolution, much as a frog goes from an egg to a tadpole to a mature adult. Some individuals stop evolving at lower levels than others.

Like many of his contemporaries, Burroughs saw evolution as a step-by-step progression of a species from the primitive to the advanced. This view remained prevalent until the mid-1900s, when scientists began to realize that the process was more complex. (Burroughs 1946)

See also Burroughs, Edgar Rice; Environmental Fiction; Evolution.

Lathe of Heaven, The

Ursula LeGuin's 1971 futuristic novel *The Lathe of Heaven* offers a vision of environmental apocalypse. The work is significant because it was extremely popular during the early American environmental movement and reflects the fear of global destruction that was common at the time.

The story's main character is George Orr, a young man whose dreams sometimes change reality retroactively. For example, if he dreams that there has been a drought for several years, when he wakes the drought is reality. Everyone but George experiences this as a long-standing reality; only George knows that it was not true before he dreamed it. He refers to this skill as "effective dreaming."

Afraid of what he might do to the world, George uses drugs to stay awake. He is soon arrested and ordered to visit psychologist William Haber; George hopes that Haber will end his effective dreaming. Instead, Haber uses hypnosis and other techniques to encourage George to dream even more, believing that he can use George to benefit the world.

At the beginning of the novel, the earth is overpopulated and polluted. In Portland, Oregon, where George lives, the situation is particularly bleak:

> Rain was an old Portland tradition, but the warmth—70 F. on the second of March—was modern, a result of air pollution. Urban and industrial effluvia had not been controlled soon enough to reverse the cumulative trends already at work in the mid-Twentieth Century; it would take several centuries for the CO_2 to clear out of the air, if it ever did. New York was going to be one of the larger casualities of the Greenhouse Effect [global warming], as the polar ice kept melting and the sea kept rising. . . . San Francisco was already on the rise, and would end up covering all the hundreds of square miles of landfill and garbage dumped into it since 1848. . . .[In Portland] it rained ceaselessly, steadily, tepidly. It was like living in a downpour of warm soup, forever. . . . Undernourishment, overcrowding, and pervading foulness of the environment were the norm. There was more scurvy, typhus, and hepatitis in the Old Cities, more gang violence, crime, and murder in the New Cities. . . . George stayed in Portland because he had always lived there and because he had no reason to believe that life anywhere else would be better, or different. (LeGuin 1971, 31)

But soon life *is* different, because Dr. Haber makes it so. He forces George to dream that there is no more overpopulation, and as a result history changes. Several years earlier, a plague wiped out billions of people, and now the world isn't crowded anymore. George is horrified at the thought that he caused so many deaths. He begs Haber to stop making him dream, but the doctor refuses to listen. One by one, the doctor treats various environmental and social ills. However, things never work out quite the way he wants them to. For example, when he tells George to end war among human beings, a race of turtlelike aliens attacks Earth, thereby uniting mankind in a common cause.

Haber quickly becomes frustrated with George, and he invents a machine that will copy George's brain waves and allow the psychologist to perform effective dreaming himself. He tells George he doesn't need him anymore, and after George leaves he turns on the device. Earlier, George had confessed to a girlfriend that in April 1998 the world was destroyed by extreme pollution, disease, and war and that he was the one who dreamed it back into existence. He told her: "We are all dead, and we spoiled the world before we died. There is nothing left. Nothing but dreams." (105) Now Haber begins to dream the world of April 1998. He understands that his whole existence is a dream and immediately goes insane. Meanwhile, reality begins to change to accommodate his vision. For example, "the buildings of downtown Portland . . . were melting. They were getting soggy and shaky. . . .The corners had already run down the sides, leaving great creamy smears." (165) As George watches the world around him dissolve, he rushes to turn off Haber's dreaming machine. When he does so, he discovers that the psychologist is an empty shell. Fortunately, however, George is able to restore the world with the help of the aliens, which also have the power of effective dreaming.

See also Environmental Apocalypse; Environmental Fiction; LeGuin, Ursula.

Lawrence, D. H.

D. H. (David Herbert) Lawrence was an English poet, essayist, novelist, and travel writer who produced a large body of work, some of which discusses humans' relationship to nature. For example, in the essay "The Spirit of Place" (1918) he talks about the importance of remaining connected to the land; in a poetry collection, *Birds, Beasts, and Flowers* (1923) he extols nature. In *The Symbolic Meaning: The Uncollected Versions of Studies in Classic American Literature* (1962) he discusses the destruction not only of the land but also of native people:

> It is plain that the American is not one with the [Native Americans] whom he has perforce lodged in his own soul. It is a dangerous thing to destroy any vital existence out of life. For then the destroyer becomes responsible, in his own living body, for the destroyed. Upon the destroyer devolves the necessity of continuing the nature and being of the destroyed. . . . [The Native American] lives unappeased and inwardly destructive in the American. (Schubnell 1985, 83)

Lawrence was born in Eastwood, Nottinghamshire, England, on September 11, 1885. While working as a teacher he wrote short stories and novels; his first book, *The White Peacock*, was published in 1911. His other novels include *Sons and Lovers* (1913), *Women in Love* (1920), *The Plumed Serpent* (1926), and *Lady Chatterley's Lover* (1928), which many countries initially banned as obscene. His first volume of poems was *Love Poems and Others* (1913).

As a writer, Lawrence led a nomadic life, traveling extensively throughout Europe, Australia, Mexico, and the United States. His first travel book was *Twilight in Italy* (1916), followed by *Sea and Sardinia* (1921), *Mornings in Mexico* (1927), and *Etruscan Places* (1932). During the winter of 1924–1925, while living in Taos, New Mexico, he became seriously ill; he remained in poor health for the rest of his life. He died on March 2, 1930, in France.

Leakey, Louis

Louis Seymour Bazette Leakey was an anthropologist who made many important discover-

Louis B. Leakey (Archive Photos)

ies related to the evolution of early humans. His fossil discoveries did much to advance scientific knowledge regarding the appearance and behavior of prehistoric hominids. In addition, Leakey sponsored the work of Dian Fossey and Jane Goodall, who lived among wild animals (gorillas and chimpanzees, respectively) and wrote about their experiences.

Leakey was born on August 7, 1903, in Kabete, Kenya, where his parents were missionaries. In 1924, after attending the University of Cambridge in England, he returned to East Africa to perform archaeological fieldwork. In 1936 he married Mary Douglas Nicol, a skilled archaeologist and artist in her own right. Mary Leakey rendered many drawings of the stone tools she and her husband found.

The couple worked together in Kenya for some 30 years. They explored several archaeological sites, but many of their most significant discoveries came from an area known as the Olduvai Gorge. There they found fossil evidence of a previously unknown species of human, which they named *Homo habilis*. Leakey theorized that it was the evolutionary link between an apelike hominid, *Australopithecus,* and a later, more human-like one, *Homo erectus.* He wrote about his discoveries and theories in several books, including *Adam's Ancestors* (1934) and *Olduvai Gorge* (1952). Discussions of Leakey's theories also appear in wife Mary's book, *Olduvai Gorge: My Search for Early Man* (1979), and in son Richard's books, which include *Origins* (1977) and *The Sixth Extinction* (1995). Louis Leakey died in October 1972; Mary Leakey died in October 1997. (Poynter 1997)

See also *Adam's Ancestors;* Evolution; Leakey, Richard; *Sixth Extinction, The.*

Leakey, Richard

Born on December 19, 1944, in Nairobi, Kenya, Richard Leakey is the son of famous anthropologists Louis and Mary Leakey. As a young man he worked as a guide, leading tourists on African safaris. Eventually, however, he became interested in anthropology himself. He went to London to study the subject but returned to Africa without attaining a degree.

Nonetheless, he participated in a 1967 anthropological expedition to Kenya, during which he made several important discoveries related to early hominids. His subsequent work at the site of these discoveries near Lake Turkana is considered among the most significant in the field. He wrote several books based on his findings, many with science writer Roger Lewis. These include *Origins* (1977), *Origins Reconsidered* (1992), and *The Sixth Extinction* (1995).

In his works, Richard Leakey proposed new theories on human evolution. In addition, he created the Louis Leakey Memorial Institute for African Prehistory, which is dedicated to the study of hominid fossils. In 1968 he was named director of the National Museum of Kenya. He is currently active in Kenyan politics. (Poynter 1997)

See also Evolution; Leakey, Louis; *Sixth Extinction, The.*

Leconte, Joseph

Born in 1826, Joseph LeConte was a geologist and naturalist who explored and mapped the Sierra Nevada Mountains with John Muir. LeConte wrote about his adventures in *A Journal of Ramblings Through the High Sierra* (1870). He also joined Muir in founding the Sierra Club conservation group in 1892. LeConte died in 1901.

LeGuin, Ursula

Science fiction and fantasy writer Ursula LeGuin often uses fictional worlds to comment on the failings of the real world; some of her works contain environmental themes. For example, *The Lathe of Heaven* (1971) depicts a global environmental apocalypse, *Always Coming Home* (1985) features a future in which pollution has destroyed much of California, and *The Word for World Is Forest* (1972) is set on a lushly forested planet named Athshea, where a peaceful tribal culture is invaded by destructive humans.

Born on October 21, 1929, in Berkeley, California, LeGuin attended Radcliff College and then Columbia University in New York. Her first novel was the first in a trilogy involving an alien society on the planet Hain, which established human life on earth. She followed her trilogy with the first in a series of four children's books known as the Earthsea Quartet. At the same time, she published several novels for adults, including *The Left Hand of Darkness* (1969), which comments on human sexuality and morality, and *The Dispossessed* (1974), which depicts both an anarchist world and a world of capitalists and communists. LeGuin continues to write fiction as well as essays on fiction, feminism, and other topics. (Spivack 1984)

See also Environmental Fiction; *Lathe of Heaven, The.*

Leibnitz, Gottfried Wilhelm

Born in Leipzig, Germany, in 1646, Gottfried Wilhelm Leibnitz was primarily a mathematician and philosopher, but he also contributed to the natural sciences. He was a prolific writer. His works include *Protogaea* (1680), which discusses the formation of the earth, *Brevis Demonstratio Erroris Memorabilis Cartesii et Aliorum Circa Legem Naturae* (Brief

Demonstration of the Memorable Error of Descartes and Others About the Law of Nature, 1686), and *De Ipsa Natura* (On Nature Itself, 1698).

Leibnitz originally set out to be a lawyer. He studied law at the University of Leipzig, and in 1666 he applied for his doctor of law degree; because he was only 20 years old, the university refused to grant it. He left Leipzig in disgust and received his degree in another city, where he became involved in politics.

Eventually, however, he turned to scientific study. In 1673 he invented a calculator, and in 1675 he developed theories related to calculus. But his financial situation was poor, and in 1676 he began working for a Hanoverian duke. Once again he was involved in law and politics. He also continued his scientific work, studying mining, geology, mathematics, and physics while perfecting and inventing several mechanical devices, including a water pump powered by windmills. He began publishing his work, and by the late 1600s he was well known throughout Europe.

In 1700 Leibnitz was named a foreign member of the Academy of Sciences in Paris. For several years he traveled widely, still in the service of the duke's family, but in early 1716 he developed severe gout that rendered him bed-ridden. He died on November 14, 1716. (Boynton 1948; Spangenburg and Moser 1993)

See also Geological Research; *Protogaea*.

Leopold, Aldo

Wildlife scientist Aldo Leopold was a pioneer of the modern conservation movement. His book *A Sand County Almanac* is considered a major work of environmental literature. Born on January 11, 1887, he was the son of German immigrants and grew up in Burlington, Iowa, speaking both German and English. As a boy he enjoyed hiking and other outdoor activities.

Eventually Leopold decided to become a forest ranger. He attended the Sheffield Scientific School at Yale University, where he studied the sciences and mechanical drawing; upon earning his undergraduate degree he entered Yale's postgraduate forestry program. He graduated from Yale Forestry School in 1909 and immediately began working for the U.S. Forest Service. His first assignment was in Apache National Forest in Arizona. In 1911 he was transferred to Carson National Forest near Santa Fe, New Mexico, where he married in 1912.

Shortly thereafter Aldo was caught in a storm and took sick. While recuperating, he wrote articles for *Carson Pine Cone,* a local rangers' newsletter, tackling forestry management issues. Meanwhile, he lost his job with the Forest Service. When he was well enough to work, the only position available was in a district office and focused on grazing issues, but he did well at it and was later promoted to a job developing game protection and public recreation programs. He became interested in tourism issues as they related to wildlife management, and in 1915 he wrote the *Game and Fish Handbook,* a Forest Service guidebook for rangers on wildlife management, wilderness-related laws, and species identification. He also promoted good hunting practices among local sportsmen to help prevent the overdepletion of game animals. As a result of his efforts, in 1916 the New Mexico Game Protection Association was created to address animal conservation issues.

In 1919 Leopold turned his attention to the subject of soil erosion as it affected lakes and rivers. Leopold had noticed that muddy runoff often killed fish, a problem he addressed in his Forest Service book of that year, *Watershed Handbook.* His next project involved two wilderness areas, Gila Canyon in New Mexico and Trappers Lake in Colorado. He decided that these two areas needed complete protection from the damage that tourism, logging, mining, grazing, road building, and development can cause. He wanted these activities banned, not only from these two areas but from many other wilderness areas as well. Leopold's idea of leaving wildlands wild was contrary to the prevailing view that all land should be used or enjoyed. Nonetheless, in 1924 the Forest Service agreed to Leopold's restrictions for Gila Canyon. It was the first fully protected, truly wild wilderness area in the country.

That same year, Leopold took a job in the private sector, conducting research in timber use for the Forest Products Laboratory in Madison, Wisconsin. At the same time, he continued to be involved in conservation groups and activities. In 1928 he took a job with the Sporting Arms and Ammunition Manufacturers' Institute, investigating conservation practices as they related to game animals. He published the results of his work as *Report on a Game Survey of the North Central States* (1931). The following year he published a textbook, *Game Management,* using some of the same material.

Now a well-known expert in game and wildlife management, Leopold was in great demand as a teacher and lecturer. He became one of the first professors of game management at the University of Wisconsin and lectured on conservationism in the surrounding community. He also helped form a national conservation group, The Wilderness Society. In 1935 he bought some land in the sand counties area of Central Wisconsin, where he and his family could spend the weekends. There they learned to farm and live in a primitive setting. These experiences formed the basis of the classic *A Sand County Almanac,* which was published posthumously in 1949.

In 1938 Leopold was named to head the University of Wisconsin's new Department of Wildlife Management, where he taught wildlife ecology. He also served on the Wisconsin Conservation Committee. In that capacity he recommended that timber wolves, which once roamed the area but had been hunted nearly to extinction, be brought to Wisconsin to help control the deer population. Although this proposal was rejected, it represents one of the first attempts of a conservationist to restore the balance of nature by reintroducing a lost species. Until his death on April 21, 1948, Leopold often spoke about the balance of nature and the importance of humans living in harmony with the environment. (Lorbiecki 1996; Meine 1988)

See also Balanced Ecosystems; Conservationism; Forest Management; *Sand County Almanac, A.*

Letters from an American Farmer

Letters from an American Farmer was written by French naturalist J. Hector St. John de Crèvecoeur, who has been called an 18th-century Thoreau. The book is a collection of 12 essays on rural life in America that extol the virtues of living off the land. In writing about the work, scholar Hans Huth says that de Crèvecoeur's essays "set an example for future naturalists" because of the author's "sympathetic descriptions of natural scenery and his directness in reporting his observations and impressions." (Huth 1972, 22)

De Crèvecoeur expresses his emotional response to his land. At one point, for example, he praises his farm by saying:

I never return home without feeling some pleasing emotion, which I often suppress as useless and foolish. The instant I enter on my own land, the bright idea of property, of exclusive right, of independence exalt my mind. Precious soil, I say to myself, by what singular custom of law is it that thou wast made to constitute the riches of the freeholder? What should we American farmers be without the distinct possession of that soil? It feeds, it clothes us, from it we draw even a great exuberancy, our best meat, our richest drink, the very honey of our bees comes from this privileged spot. No wonder we should thus cherish its possession, no wonder that so many Europeans who have never been able to say that such portion of land was theirs, cross the Atlantic to realise that happiness. (de Crèvecoeur 1957, 20–21)

De Crèvecoeur relates his feelings about the land to the essence of what it means to be an American, continuing:

This formerly rude soil has been converted by my father into a pleasant farm, and in return it has established all our rights; on it is founded our rank, our freedom, our

Etching of a view from Bushongo Tavern, five miles from Yorktown, 1788 (Library of Congress)

power as citizens, our importance as inhabitants of such a district. These images I must confess I always behold with pleasure, and extend them as far as my imagination can reach: for this is what may be called the true and the only philosophy of an American farmer. (de Crèvecoeur 1957, 20–21)

De Crèvecoeur also offers many observations on nature, for example, in describing Nantucket:

This island furnishes the naturalist with few or no objects worthy of observation; it appears to be the uneven summit of a sandy submarine mountain, covered here and there with sorrel, grass, a few cedar bushes, and scrubby oaks; their swamps are much more valuable for the peat they contain, than for the trifling pasture of their surface; those declining grounds which lead to the seashores abound with *beach grass,* a light fodder when cut and cured, but very good when fed green. On the east side of the island they have several tracts of salt grasses, which being carefully fenced, yield a considerable quantity of that wholesome fodder. (92–93)

De Crèvecoeur discusses some of the region's animals as well, devoting an entire essay to the subject of snakes and hummingbirds. On snakes, he reports:

We have but two, whose stings are mortal, which deserve to be mentioned; as for the black one, it is remarkable for nothing but its industry, agility, beauty, and the art of enticing birds by the power of its eyes. I admire it much, and never kill it, though its formidable length and appearance often get the better of the philosophy of some people, particularly of Europeans. The most dangerous one is the *pilot,* or *copperhead;* for the poison of which no remedy has yet been discovered. . . . It lurks in rocks near the water, and is extremely active and dangerous. Let man beware of it! I have heard only of one person who was stung by a copperhead in this country. The poor wretch instantly swelled in a most dreadful manner; a multitude of spots of different hues alternately appeared and vanished, on different parts of his body. . . . In the space of two hours death relieved the poor wretch from his struggles. . . . The poison of the rattlesnake is not mortal in so short a space, and hence there is more time to procure relief; we are acquainted with several antidotes with which almost every family is provided. (169–170)

Some of de Crèvecoeur's essays describe American customs and people. One of them describes life in Nantucket. Another is devoted to praising a Pennsylvania botanist, John Bertram, whose farm is a model of good agricultural practices. De Crèvecoeur's final essay, "Distresses of a Frontier Man," laments the start of the American Revolution, which forced de Crèvecoeur to abandon his farm forever. (de Crèvecoeur 1957; Huth 1972)

See also Crèvecoeur, J. Hector St. John; Thoreau, Henry David.

Lewis and Clark Expedition

The Lewis and Clark Expedition, the first American overland journey to the Pacific, resulted in journals filled with new information about the vast landscape. Lasting three years (1804–1806), the expedition was led by Captain Meriwether Lewis and Lieutenant William Clark and had roughly 40 members, ranging in age from 29 to 33 years old. They were knowledgeable in such sciences as zoology, botany, and meteorology, and were also skilled outdoorsmen.

Lewis and Clark had been directed by President Thomas Jefferson, who initiated the expedition, to keep copious notes about their experiences. The journals tell of the explorers' many adventures and observations as they traveled up the Missouri River through what is today North Dakota, westward through Montana, and over the Continental Divide, whereupon they used canoes to travel the Clearwater, Snake, and Columbia Rivers to the Pacific Ocean in Oregon. In returning east the leaders split up, boating the Marias and Yellowstone Rivers to the Missouri River, eventually landing in St. Louis, Missouri. Only one member of the party died during the trip.

Life of Its Own, A

In *A Life of Its Own: The Politics of Power and Water* author Robert Gottlieb discusses the U.S. water industry, particularly in the West. Along with Mark Reisner's *Cadillac Desert,* it is the most thorough discussion of water issues in print. Gottlieb is an environmental activist who has participated in water policy discussions. He says:

To explore the way in which water has been used and misused becomes a way of ultimately exploring certain forms of politics and power in our society. It tells us how key decisions get made and who gets to make them. It suggests the limits of democratic participation when powerful public agencies and private interests merge. It reveals the nature of the values involved in the options selected. It can also tell us much about the prospects for change and the resistance to it. And if, as the Ute Indians say, water has a life of its own, it becomes crucial to understand how those who wish to control this basic resource can, by their actions, affect our lives. (Gottlieb 1988, xviii)

A Life of Its Own has four sections. The first is an introduction to water politics. The second focuses on the major participants in the water industry and discusses their relationships with the government, the agricultural industry, and developers. The third addresses environmental issues, such as pesticide use and pollution, and explains how environmentalists are affecting the water industry. It also discusses rural opposition to changes in water rights and irrigation practices. The last section of the book discusses problems within the water industry, including economic hardships, environmental restrictions, and changing government policies. It points out that water industry leaders in western states have different concerns than those in eastern states:

The key for the water industry has been how to control this elusive and valuable resource. In the West, such efforts have primarily involved policies designed to deal with scarcity, such as drought conditions, and the ways in which surpluses can be created by transferring water from one area to another. In the East, these efforts have largely referred to situations where there is an overabundance of supply, with such problems as flooding, and the ways in which water sources can be tamed and harnessed. The water industry arose in part to exercise this control. (272)

However, Gottlieb points out that the current emphasis is not on controlling water supplies but on providing water that is clean and safe to drink. He concludes with the statement that the way the water industry handles environmental issues will "tell us much about what things remain essential and in what kind of society we live." (280) (Gottlieb 1988)

See also Environmental Politics; Gottlieb, Robert; Water Pollution.

Life on Earth

Life on Earth is naturalist David Attenborough's attempt to trace the history of nature from its prehistoric beginnings to modern times. Published in 1979, it is a companion to the television series *Life on Earth*, which Attenborough created for the British Broadcasting Corporation over a three-year period. Consequently, the work was extremely popular and helped educate the public about animal species and evolution. Each of the book's 13 chapters represents a different episode of the television series and includes many color photographs of insect, plant, and animal species.

Attenborough describes the evolution of these species in great detail. Of his attempt to "survey the whole animal kingdom," he says: "The condensation of three thousand million years of history into three hundred pages, the description of a group of animals containing tens of thousands of species within one chapter, compels vast omissions. My method has been to try to perceive the single most significant thread in the history of a group and then concentrate on tracing that, resolutely ignoring other issues, no matter how enticing they may seem." (Attenborough 1979, pp. 7–8)

After explaining the theory of evolution proposed by British naturalist Charles Darwin during the 1800s, Attenborough speculates on how life might have emerged from earth's primordial pools. He then follows the development of life into more and more complex forms, ending with a discussion of human beings. However, he says that the structure of his book is not meant to imply that humans are the "ultimate triumph of evolution." Instead, he states:

There is no scientific evidence whatever to support such a view and no reason to suppose that our stay here will be any more permanent than that of the dinosaur. The processes of evolution are still going on among plants and birds, insects and mammals. So it is more likely that if men were to disappear from the face of the earth, for whatever reason, there is a modest, unobtrusive creature somewhere that would develop into a new form and take our place. (308)

Attenborough sees no reason why the process of evolution should cease simply because humans are currently the dominant species. (Attenborough 1979)

See also Attenborough, Sir David; Balanced Ecosystems; Evolution; Species Identification and Classification.

Limits to Growth, The

Written by a group of scientists and businessmen organized as the Club of Rome, *The Limits to Growth* caused a great deal of controversy when it was published in 1972. It uses mathematical models from the Massachusetts Institute of Technology to support the idea that overpopulation will eventually deplete the earth's natural resources and cause widespread starvation and other disasters. *The Limits to Growth* proposes that population growth be controlled before such disasters occur in order to ensure environmental and economic stability. Its authors state:

Our conclusions are:
1. If the present growth trends in world population, industrialization, pollution,

food production, and resource depletion continue unchanged, the limits to growth on this planet will be reached sometime within the next one hundred years. The most probable result will be a rather sudden and uncontrollable decline in both population and industrial capacity.

2. It is possible to alter these growth trends and to establish a condition of ecological and economic stability that is sustainable far into the future. The state of global equilibrium could be designed so that the basic material needs of each person on earth are satisfied and each person has an equal opportunity to realize his individual human potential.

3. If the world's people decide to strive for this second outcome rather than the first, the sooner they begin working to attain it, the greater will be the chances of success. (Meadows et al. 1983, 23–24)

The authors argue that the population is growing exponentially rather than linearly, which means that it increases at a much faster rate. They explain the difference between these two growth patterns:

A quantity is growing linearly when it increases by a constant amount in a constant time period. For example, a child who becomes one inch taller each year is growing linearly. If a miser hides $10 each year under his mattress, his horde of money is also increasing in a linear way. . . . A quantity exhibits *exponential* growth when it increases by a constant percentage of the whole in a constant time period. A colony of yeast cells in which each cell divides into two cells every ten minutes is growing exponentially. For each single cell, after ten minutes there will be two cells, an increase of 100 percent. After the next ten minutes there will be four cells, then eight, then sixteen. If a miser takes $100 from his mattress and invests it at 7 percent (so that the total amount accumu-

lated increases by 7 percent each year), the invested money will grow much faster than the linearly increasing stock under the mattress. The amount added each year to a bank account or each ten minutes to a yeast colony is not constant. It continually increases, as the total accumulated amount increases. Such exponential growth is a common process in biological, financial, and many other systems of the world. (26–28)

The authors believe that people's use of natural resources is also increasing exponentially and will therefore become rare and costly in the future. At the same time, they point out that human waste is also increasing and already poses a serious problem:

What happens to the metals and fuels extracted from the earth after they have been used and discarded? In one sense they are never lost. Their constituent atoms are rearranged and eventually dispersed in a diluted and unusable form into the air, the soil, and the waters of our planet. The natural ecological systems can absorb many of the effluents of human activity and reprocess them into substances that are usable by, or at least harmless to, other forms of life. When any effluent is released on a large enough scale, however, the natural absorptive mechanisms can become saturated. The wastes of human civilization can build up in the environment until they become visible, annoying, and even harmful. Mercury in ocean fish, lead particles in city air, mountains of urban trash, oil slicks on beaches—these are the results of the increasing flow of resources into man's hands. It is little wonder, then, that another exponentially increasing quantity in the world system is pollution. (69)

When *The Limits to Growth* was published, its arguments created a great deal of controversy. They also caused a shift in public consciousness. According to Phil Shabecoff in *A Fierce Green Fire*:

The data and models used in *Limits* were widely challenged. But the possibility that humanity might exceed the earth's carrying capacity gained worldwide recognition and a prominent place on the American environmental movement's list of impending catastrophes.

Some environmental thinkers, however, rejected the notion of overpopulation and resource depletion as the sole or even chief cause of our environmental ills. They pointed instead at wasteful consumption, destructive technology, poor social and economic organization, and the power and privilege of corporations as the source of pollution and other strains on natural systems. (Shabecoff 1993, 96–97)

However, the Club of Rome largely ignored these critics. The group still exists today, although its members have changed, and it continues to meet regularly to discuss the relationship between population growth and environmental damage. (Meadows et al. 1983; Shabecoff 1993)

See also Club of Rome, The; Environmental Groups; Human Ecology.

Linnaeus, Carolus

Also called Carl von Linné, Swedish botanist and explorer Carolus Linnaeus developed the system by which scientists classify and name plants and animals. Under this system, two Latin words are used to identify the (1) genus and (2) species to which an organism belongs. For example, all human beings belong to the genus *Homo;* the modern human species is called *Homo sapiens,* or "wise men."

Carolus Linnaeus was born on May 23, 1707, and studied science and medicine at two universities in Sweden, Lund and Uppsala. He became a lecturer in botany at Uppsala in 1730, and in 1732 he conducted a university-sponsored study of the botany of Lapland. He published the results of his study as *Flora Lapponica* in 1737, which was translated into English as *Lachesis Lapponica* in 1811. In 1735 he published *Systema Naturae,* in which he introduced his system of classifi-

cation. By its 10th edition, in 1758, the book offered classifications for more than 4,000 animals. In 1737 Linnaeus published a classification of plants, *Genera Plantarum,* of which there were several subsequent editions. A second and more comprehensive book on plant classifications, *Species Plantarum,* appeared in 1753.

From 1738 to 1740 Linnaeus worked as a practicing physician in Stockholm, Sweden, but in 1741 he returned to teaching at Uppsala. He also continued to classify plant and animal species, as well as minerals, and categorized diseases. In 1761 he was granted the status of Swedish nobility, and he renamed himself Carl von Linné. He died on January 10, 1778, after a four-year illness. Ten years later, a wealthy medical student, James Smith, used Linnaeus's plant collection and library to establish the Linnean Society, which today is the oldest natural history society in Great Britain. (Bowler 1993; Glotfelty and Fromm 1996)

See also Species Identification and Classification; *Species Plantarum.*

Living Free

Living Free is the first-person account of author Joy Adamson's experiences with an African lioness named Elsa and her cubs. Written in 1960 and published in 1961, it is the sequel to Adamson's 1960 book, *Born Free,* in which she discusses how she raised Elsa from a cub. At the end of *Born Free,* Adamson and her husband, George, the senior warden of a government game preserve in Kenya, set the lioness free and watched her find a wild mate. *Living Free* takes up the story of Elsa from there; like its predecessor, it helped call public attention to African wildlife conservation issues.

The book begins in the fall of 1959, when Adamson visits Elsa in the African bush and discovers that she is pregnant. Lionesses who grow up in their family group, or pride, have an "auntie" lioness to provide them with food when they are too pregnant to hunt and to help them bear and rear their cubs. But because she was raised with humans, Elsa has no auntie, so Adamson is worried about her. She decides to remain camped near Elsa's wild home, willing to offer her assistance whenever needed.

Throughout her pregnancy, Elsa continues to visit Adamson's camp, and Adamson kills food for her. Finally, Elsa gives birth to three cubs; she does not allow the Adamsons to come near her den, but she does bring the cubs to see them on occasion. The humans are therefore able to document the animals' progression from babies to young adults. In addition to detailed descriptions of the lions' activities, *Living Free* has many black-and-white photographs of Elsa and her cubs.

However, a few incidents interfere with the Adamsons's contact with the lions. George, in his position as game warden, continually fights against poaching, and one day some poachers burn down his camp. He calls for help from the African government; despite their antipoaching efforts, the Adamsons continue to find illegal traps in the area. In addition, Elsa has begun to get into fights with a wild lioness who wants to take over her territory. Each time the Adamsons heal Elsa's wounds, she shows up at the camp with more.

Despite the threat of poachers and other lions, the Adamsons know they must leave Elsa to her life in the wild. Then someone begins spreading rumors that the lioness has been mauling people, and the Adamsons decide to move Elsa and her cubs to another area within the game preserve. Before they can do so, they receive an order from the government ordering them to remove Elsa from the game preserve altogether.

Living Free concludes with the Adamsons's receipt of this order. However, a publisher's note adds a postscript noting that a month later, Elsa contracted an illness and died. Her death was mourned throughout the world. Adamson's earlier book, *Born Free,* had made Elsa famous, and this fame only increased after the publication of *Living Free.*

Written in a conversational style, both books were extremely popular, and they raised public awareness about African poaching and wildlife conservation. Adamson's sequel to *Living Free,* entitled *Forever Free* (1962), was equally as popular. It concerns the fate of the cubs after Elsa's death. The publisher's postscript to *Living Free* explains that the cubs became wild and began attacking the goats of local tribesmen. The Adamsons decided to relocate them to an uninhabited area. This highly difficult operation was chronicled in *Forever Free,* along with the events surrounding Elsa's death. (Adamson 1961)

See also Adamson, Joy; Animal Behavior; *Born Free; Forever Free;* Wildlife Conservation.

Living Off the Country

Published in 1981, *Living Off the Country: Essays on Poetry and Place* is a collection of essays by poet and nature writer John Haines. The work emphasizes the importance that a particular place has on an individual's mind. For example, in his essay "The Writer as Alaskan: Beginnings and Reflections," Haines says:

As a poet I was born in a particular place, a hillside overlooking the Tanana River in central Alaska, where I built a house and lived for the better part of twenty-two years. . . . Many things went into the making of [my first] poems and the others I've written since: the air of the place, its rocks, soil, and water; snow and ice; human history, birds, animals, and insects. . . . Why I chose that particular place rather than another probably can't be answered completely. I might have gone elsewhere and become a very different poet and person. But there was, most likely, no other region where I might have had that original experience of the North American wilderness. (Lyon 1989, 366–367)

Haines continues to write and speak about his wilderness experiences and the deep connection between the human mind and nature. He currently lives on a homestead in Fairbanks, Alaska. (Lyon 1989)

Living Sea, The

The Living Sea was written by Captain Jacques-Yves Cousteau, an ocean explorer who popularized oceanography during the

French oceanographer Jacques Cousteau demonstrates his equipment on the deck of Calypso *at Cannes, 1956 (Archive France/Archive Photos)*

1960s with the help of research associate James Dugan. Published in 1963, the book was one of Cousteau's best-selling works. It describes his experiences exploring the seas aboard *Calypso,* his oceanographic research vessel, attempting to examine the ocean floor and marine life.

Cousteau dives underwater using his choice of three pieces of equipment: an Aqua-Lung, a forerunner to modern scuba gear that he himself invented; a bathyscaph; and the Cousteau Diving Saucer, a jet-propelled submarine with mechanical claws. Far beneath the surface he discovers underground shipwrecks and ancient artifacts, and at one point he experiences an undersea avalanche. He also observes many different sea creatures and discusses their behavior. For example, in describing an encounter with sperm whales, he says:

> Now there were at least a hundred of them, cruising west in pods at seven or eight knots. They were spread in all quarters around us. . . . From time to time, far on the horizon, we saw high geysers of water erupting from the placid ocean. They looked like explosions of depth charges. . . . I turned and saw an eruption as large as the Arc de Triomphe a few hundred feet away and heard a loud, splashy boom. "You missed it! It happened so fast," said [a crew member]. They had seen a sixty-foot sperm whale leaping straight up into the air, its tail clearing the water by fifteen feet. It fell back on its side and sent up the great splash, which was all I saw. (Cousteau 1963, 135–136)

Cousteau offers his own theory regarding this behavior, continuing:

> I conjectured [a] possible explanation for the giant leaps. Sperm whales are known to be the deepest divers among their order. Dead ones have been found entangled with submarine cables that were laid a mile deep. Specialists agree that they can dive at least three thousand feet. . . . Many captured sperm whales carry terrible scars, testifying to merciless fights with giant squids that take place in two or three thousand feet of water. I thought perhaps this was what produced the prodigious leaps out of the water. During a prolonged battle in the dark, a whale might overstay its time in that pressure, break away from the squid and, desperate for air, speed to the surface at twenty or twenty-five knots. The momentum could carry it high into the air where gravity would brake the vertical dash for life. If true, these geysers were merely incidents in the whale's daily feeding ordeal. As I pondered it, I felt that we would have to build deep, fast vehicles to accompany whales on their heroic dives and possibly witness the epic battle with [the squid]. (Cousteau 1963, 135–136)

What Cousteau eventually developed was an underwater camera, which he called the Deepsea Camera Sled. It could film while being dragged along the sea bottom at great depths. Cousteau reports: "We put all our know-how into the Deepsea Camera Sled. We were able to afford seven sleds, three with cinecameras. Knowing we would lose some of them, we designed for expendability, with rough, cheap welding and mass-produced tubing on the camera and flash cylinders." (252) Cousteau used these sleds extensively to study and film the ocean floor. Some of his footage was used to make movies and television specials, which furthered the public's interest in oceanography and ocean conservation. (Cousteau 1963)

See also Cousteau, Jacques-Yves.

Log from the Sea of Cortez, The

Published in 1951, *The Log from the Sea of Cortez* is the narrative portion of the book *Sea of Cortez* by John Steinbeck and E. F. Ricketts, which first appeared in 1941. Both works increased public awareness regarding the work of naturalists and marine biologists.

The Log includes an introduction by Steinbeck about friend Ricketts, a biologist immortalized in one of Steinbeck's most famous novels, *Cannery Row*. In 1940 Ricketts invited Steinbeck to accompany him on an expedition to the beaches along the Gulf of California, also known as the Sea of Cortez, where he intended to collect marine specimens. The two traveled together in a sardine boat, and *The Log* is a day-to-day first-person account of that trip and includes information about the way the scientific samples were gathered and catalogued. Steinbeck therefore considered it unique for its time, saying: "How does one organize an expedition: what equipment is taken, what sources read; what are the little dangers and the large ones? No one has ever written this. . . . We had read what books were available about the Gulf and they were few and in many cases confused." (Steinbeck 5)

The Log describes naturalist activities and discusses the marine environment and creatures of the Gulf of California. For example, Steinbeck reports:

> There are three ways of seeing animals: dead and preserved; in their own habitats for the short time of a low tide; and for long periods in an aquarium. The ideal is all three. It is only after long observation that one comes to know the animal at all. In his natural place one can see the normal life, but in an aquarium it is possible to create abnormal conditions and to note the animal's adaptability or lack of it. As an example of this third method of observation, we can use a few notes made during observation of a small colony of anemones in an aquarium. We had them for a number of months.

He continues the report:

> We brought a group of these on their own stone into the laboratory and placed them in an aquarium. Cooled and oxygenated sea water was sprayed into the aquarium to keep them alive. Then we gave them various kinds of food, and found that they do not respond to simple touch-stimulus on the tentacles, but have something which is at least a vague parallel to taste-buds, whatever may be the chemical or mechanical method. Thus, protein food was seized by the tentacles, taken and eaten without hesitation; fat was touched gingerly, taken without enthusiasm to the stomach, and immediately rejected; starches were not taken at all—the tentacles touched starchy food and then ignored it. (225–226)

Because Steinbeck was a popular novelist, his writings about these experiences were read by many people who had never before been exposed to naturalism or scientific study. In this way, the *Sea of Cortez* material made the public more knowledgeable about environmental sciences. (Steinbeck 1986)

See also Animal Behavior; Species Identification and Classification; Steinbeck, John.

Lopez, Barry

Barry Lopez is the author of several books about the relationship between humans and nature. His first was an essay collection entitled *Desert Notes: Reflections in the Eye of a Raven* (1976). His subsequent books include *River Notes: The Dance of Herons* (1979), *Winter Count* (1981), *Crossing Open Ground* (1988), and *Field Notes: The Grace Note of the Canyon Wren* (1996). Two of his works have won prestigious awards: *Arctic Dreams: Imagination and Desire in a Northern Landscape* (1986) won the National Book Award and *Of Wolves and Men* (1978) won the John Burroughs Medal, a prize for nature writing.

Professor Thomas Lyon, in discussing *Arctic Dreams* in his book on nature writing, *This Incomperable Lande,* calls the work "highly self-conscious," because Lopez does not limit himself to describing his experiences traveling through the Arctic. Instead, the author "has attempted to go beyond recording events and observations into an investigation of the mentality of seeking itself." (Lyon 1989, 90) However, Lyon adds that this approach to the material is not self-indulgent, explaining:

> Lopez's consciousness of self and nature is meant to be representative, and what develops is an exposition of two paths, two ways of seeing. We can approach the wild world (which is to say, *the* world) with designs on it, projections and preconceptions; or we can try to simply perceive it, to let it be whatever it is. Lopez's exposition becomes then a contemporary statement . . . of what may be the major ethical motif in American nature literature, the choice between domination and democratic membership. The alternatives frame the great question of how we should live. (Lyon 90)

Lopez was born in New York in 1945 but moved to Southern California shortly thereafter. He returned to New York in 1956. After graduating from a Jesuit high school, he attended Notre Dame University and subsequently began writing magazine articles and essays. He currently lives along the McKenzie River in Oregon.

Losing Ground

In *Losing Ground: American Environmentalism at the Close of the Twentieth Century* (1995), journalist Mark Dowie provides a thorough discussion of American environmental history and politics. Consequently Dowie's work is often cited as a valuable reference for both supporters and opponents of the environmental movement who wish to examine its ideology in depth.

Dowie divides American environmentalism into three periods, which he calls "waves": "The first began with the conservation/preservationist impulse of the late nineteenth and early twentieth centuries and coincided with the closing of the frontier. The second wave came in the brief era of environmental legislation that began in the mid-1960s and was abruptly halted by the Reagan administration in the 1980s. The third wave, a relatively fruitless and hopefully brief attempt to find a harmonious ('win-win') conciliation between conservative environmentalists and corporate polluters, is with us as we approach the mid-1990s." (Dowie 1995, 8)

Dowie describes each wave in great detail, discussing naturalists such as Henry David Thoreau, John Muir, and Gifford Pinchot as well as early environmentalists like Rachel Carson and Aldo Leopold and modern ones like Barry Commoner and Bill Devall. In explaining the origins of environmentalism, he says:

> The agenda of the American environmental movement did not emerge ready made during the 1960s. A vast tradition existed before [Rachel] Carson set pen to paper, under several different names, none of which included the *e*-word. What became known as environmentalism was an amalgam of resource conservation, wilderness preservation, public health reform, population control, ecology, energy conserva-

tion, anti-pollution regulation, and occupational health campaigns. All had become separate public concerns and developed as self-contained mini-movements during previous decades and, even, centuries. The modern environmental movement evolved from these many issues and causes in the context of a post–World-War-II urban environment whose degradation had become insistently obvious to people of all classes and races. (23–24)

Dowie then traces the development of modern environmental groups, explaining their connection to mainstream culture and to other movements of the period:

> Unlike the other new social movements of the 1960s and 1970s (women's, peace, civil rights, and gay liberation), which are essentially radical, the ecology movement was saddled from the start with conservative traditions formed by a bipartisan, mostly white, middle-class, male leadership. The culture they created has persisted until very recently and hampered the success of the movement. There has always been something very safe and unthreatening about conservationists. From time to time they have aggravated ranchers, strip miners, and timber barons. But rarely have they challenged the fundamental canons of western civilization or the economic orthodoxy of welfare capitalism—the ecologically destructive system that gives the nation's resources away to any corporation with the desire and technology to develop them. (28)

Yet Dowie credits the second wave, despite its origins, for accomplishing a great deal in the name of environmentalism. For example, he reports:

> During the 1970s the environmental movement became a political force to be reckoned with. Attempts were made to recruit millions of card-carrying "enviros" into a powerful national voting block—a

broad new bipartisan constituency spanning every imaginable ideology and party. Pollsters began to advise candidates that the "environmental vote" would be a major factor in elections. Candidates who had ever recycled a beer can, slept in a tent, or seen a deer outside of the zoo declared themselves environmentalists. A significant number were elected to both sides of the aisle [i.e., both Democrat and Republican], and a bipartisan environmental legislative strategy became feasible. In the years before the election of Ronald Reagan [to the U.S. presidency] new environmental issues were codified into laws and regulations and a new species of lawyer evolved to enforce them. (34)

After discussing the issues of the second wave in depth, Dowie turns to the successes and failures of the current third wave. He particularly praises the passion of grass-roots activists and criticizes national environmental groups for being too eager to compromise with business and government leaders, explaining:

When government and the environmental movement both . . . compromise on environmental issues, it is left to "radicals" to create the extreme position to counter the mega-technological position, be it preservation of pristine wilderness or a toxic-free world. Between two such extremes some degree of environmental protection can, hopefully, be brokered through compromise. But when radicals are excluded from the process, as they are by both government and mainstream environmentalists, there is no extreme against which to negotiate. Government, polluters, and environmentalists are then negotiating in relative harmony. The result is scant progress. (77)

Moreover, Dowie argues, because large national environmental groups are "mostly male, white, and patrician" they are unable to address the important environmental health and safety concerns of a multiethnic society.

(31–32) He therefore predicts that the third wave of American environmentalism will eventually give way to a more passionate, aggressive form of activism:

I believe . . . that a fourth wave is forming and that before the end of the century it will become the heart of a new American environmental movement. As it builds, the polite, effectual white gentleman's club that defined American environmentalism for almost a hundred years will either shrink into historical irrelevance or become an effective but equal player in the new movement. After so many decades of polite activism, the movement is becoming appropriately rude and decidedly American. If it becomes truly American by adopting new, wider strategies and a democratic ethos, it will prevail. (8)

Losing Ground concludes with an epilogue expressing hope for the future because "every poll that asks about it testifies that environmentalism is deeply rooted in the American psyche." (260) He believes that "the American environmental imagination is deep, and it is hard-wired to the American dream." (260) Accordingly, although "the movement we now support may fail . . . environmentalism itself will survive." (263) However, he believes that first "environmentalism needs to penetrate every institution, ideology, and religious faith in our culture. It needs to be seen as a social as well as a political movement." (263) (Dowie 1995)

See also Dowie, Mark; Environmental Groups; Environmental History; Environmental Politics.

Lost World, The
Published in 1912, *The Lost World* by Sir Arthur Conan Doyle was one of the first popular novels of the 20th century to tackle evolutionary theory. The work was inspired by *Extinct Animals,* a 1905 nonfiction book by E. Ray Lankester, the director of London's Natural History Museum; it included information about recent fossil discoveries.

The novel opens with the narrator, Edward Dunn Malone, attempting to convince his girlfriend, Gladys, to marry him. She refuses because he is not adventurous enough for her. He therefore decides to do something exciting to win her love. A reporter for London's *Daily Gazette* newspaper, he asks his editor for a risky assignment, and the editor suggests that he interview a famous zoologist and paleontologist, professor George Edward Challenger, known as a violent man.

Two years earlier, Challenger had gone to the Amazon jungles of South America and made a startling discovery. In a native village he encountered a dying American, Maple White, and looked in the man's knapsack. There he found a sketchbook filled with drawings of dinosaurs, along with what looked like dinosaur bones—but recent ones rather than fossilized ones. He set out to find where White had been, and on the way he spotted a living, flying pterodactyl. He took photographs of it, but they were ruined in a boating accident. When he returned to London, his bones were called a fraud and his story a fake.

When Malone visits Challenger, the two get into a fistfight because the scientist hates reporters, but in the end Malone wins Challenger's trust and accompanies him to a meeting of the London Zoological Institute, where Challenger argues that dinosaurs really do exist. The other scientists at the meeting decide to send an expedition to investigate Challenger's claims. When they ask for volunteers, Malone raises his hand. Also on the team are Mr. Summerlee, who is a professor of comparative anatomy, and Lord John Roxton, a world-famous sportsman. They meet Challenger in South America, where they hire some native packers and set out to retrace Maple White's steps. After finding signs of his path, they see a pterodactyl on a plateau that seems inaccessible. Eventually they find a fallen tree that acts as a bridge across the chasm. The three explorers cross it, whereupon one of their packers destroys the bridge to exact revenge on Roxton, who had killed his brother years earlier.

Now stranded on the plateau, the explorers investigate their surroundings. They discover many different kinds of dinosaurs and collect samples of strange insects. One day, while Malone is out walking, the explorers' camp is attacked by apemen. Challenger, Summerlee, and Roxton are taken prisoner, but Roxton soon escapes, and he and Malone rescue the others. They then join with a band of primitive humans who are at war with the apemen and help them conquer their enemies. One of these humans later shows Malone a way off the plateau. Unfortunately, the route is treacherous and the explorers cannot carry much with them. They return to the London Zoological Institute with seemingly no proof of their adventures, whereupon they are ridiculed at a public meeting. They then produce a live pterodactyl, which Roxton took from a hatchery before they left the lost world. Now they are lauded, even though the pterodactyl escapes out an open window.

A short time later, Malone visits Gladys and learns she has married another man during his absence. He subsequently discovers that Roxton found precious gems in the lost world and is giving each member of the expedition a portion. When Roxton announces that he is using his money to fund another expedition to the Amazon, Malone volunteers to go along.

The journalist Malone and the hunter Roxton are the heroes of *The Lost World;* in contrast, the novel portrays scientists in a negative light. Those at the zoological institute are depicted as ignorant fools, and even the scientists on the expedition are shown to be incompetent when compared with the hunter and journalist. When they are captured by the apemen, for example, Challenger and Summerlee are so busy arguing about what primitive species of man their captors represent that they fail to defend themselves, whereas Roxton easily manages to escape. Interestingly, the most popular modern novel related to evolutionary theory, Michael Crichton's *Jurassic Park,* also portrays scientists in a negative light. However, it criticizes them for being too competent rather than not competent enough, arguing that scientists should not tamper with the natural world just because they have the requisite knowledge to do so. (Crichton 1990; Doyle 1959)

See also Crichton, Michael; Doyle, Arthur Conan; Evolution; *Jurassic Park*.

Lovelock, James

British scientist and inventor James Lovelock was the originator of the Gaia hypothesis, which suggests that the earth's biosphere, atmosphere, oceans, and soil are part of a complex entity with its own life force. Gaia refers to an ancient Greek earth goddess.

Lovelock developed his hypothesis during the 1960s. At the time, he was studying the planet Mars for the National Aeronautics and Space Administration in California. While looking for signs of life on Mars, he evaluated the chemicals within that planet's atmosphere. He then compared these chemicals with those on earth and realized that a lifeless planet has different qualities than a living one. Moreover, he discovered that much about the earth's atmosphere was in "violation of the rules of chemistry." (Dobson 266) Lovelock began to suspect that some greater force was at work in maintaining the balance of life on earth. He wrote about his theory in a 1979 book, *Gaia: A New Look at Life on Earth.* This work immediately came to the attention of American environmentalists, some of whom developed the theory farther. One was Michael Allaby, who worked with Lovelock for a time and describes his theory in terms of the modern environmental movement in his 1990 book, *A Guide to Gaia.* Lovelock's other works include *The Ages of Gaia: A Biography of Our Living Earth* (1988) and *Healing Gaia* (1991). (Allaby 1989; Dobson 1991)

See also *Gaia;* Gaia Hypothesis; *Guide to Gaia, A.*

Lovins, Amory

American scientist Amory Lovins has written several books about energy issues, including *Is Nuclear Power Necessary?* (1979), *World Energy Strategies: Facts, Issues, and Options* (1975), and *Brittle Power: Energy Strategy for National Security* (1982). He believes that the United States should stop using nuclear power and fossil fuels and instead develop nonpolluting, renewal sources of power such as solar energy. He founded the Rocky Mountain Institute to promote his views and has won several awards for his conservation efforts.

Lucretius

The Roman philosopher and poet Lucretius, whose full name was Titus Lucretius Carus, was born in approximately 95 B.C. He is famous for his long poem, *De Rerum Natura* (On the Nature of Things), in which he discusses such topics as atomic structure, evolution, and thunder and lightning. The details of Lucretius's life are largely unknown, although some scholars believe he committed suicide circa 54 B.C. (Sikes 1971)

See also *De Rerum Natura;* Evolution.

Lyell, Charles

Scottish baronet Sir Charles Lyell was a geologist who advanced important concepts regarding the formation of earth's geological features. Born on November 14, 1797, in Kinnordy, Forfarshire, Scotland, he first became interested in science as a boy. His father was a naturalist who taught Lyell a great deal about the scientific study of plants, insects, and animals.

In 1816 Lyell enrolled at Oxford University, where he became interested in geology. He began studying geological formations and fossil evidence, making extensive notes on his findings and developing theories on how ancient natural processes might have created the landscape. But when he received his undergraduate degree in 1819 he decided to study law instead. He continued to study geology as a hobby, taking several vacations to explore interesting geologic sites even after being admitted to the bar in 1825.

That year, Lyell published his first articles based on his geologic work. In 1830 he published the first volume of his major book on the subject, *Principles of Geology.* The second volume was published in 1831, the third in 1833. By this time he had married Mary

Horner, who shared his interest in geology. She encouraged his work and helped him revise *Principles of Geology* several times. This book remained extremely popular for many years, and Lyell was consequently in great demand as a lecturer, first in Europe and later in the United States and Canada. He was also highly regarded in the scientific community. In 1838 his prominence increased with the publication of *Elements of Geology,* which identified and discussed rocks.

During the 1840s Lyell wrote books about his world travels. At the same time, he became involved in a variety of causes. For example, he helped plan Queen Victoria's Great Exhibition (1851–1852), and in 1852 he worked to change instructional methods at Oxford University. He was knighted in 1848 and received many scientific awards.

Lyell continued to research geologic formations throughout the 1850s, becoming interested in their relationship to evolution after his friend, Charles Darwin, published a book on the subject, *Origin of Species* (1859). In 1863 Lyell published his own work on evolution, *The Geological Evidence of the Antiquity of Man,* in which he supported many aspects of Darwinism. He furthered this support in an 1865 revision of *Principles of Geology.* Lyell died while working on yet another revision of that book in February 1875. (E. Bailey 1963; Lyell 1872; L. Wilson 1972)

See also Darwin, Charles Robert; Evolution; Geological Research; *Principles of Geology.*

M

Machinery of Nature, The

The Machinery of Nature was written by Paul Ehrlich, one of the foremost experts on overpopulation. However, the book is not about population but rather the science of ecology. Published in 1986, it offers one of the most thorough discussions of the subject ever provided for laypersons. Ehrlich defines *ecology* by saying:

> In addition to standard topics such as how populations change in size and how ecosystems are organized, it includes evolutionary biology and certain aspects of behavioral biology. It is a combination of disciplines that is sometimes called "population biology" (to distinguish it from molecular, cellular, and organismal levels of biological science). But *ecology* is the best-known term for the combination of disciplines that comprises the science behind life on earth; it is also the shortest. (Ehrlich 1986, 14)

Ehrlich says that his book's purpose is not to argue a particular position on an environmental issue. Instead, he seeks to explain and explore ecology as a scientific pursuit:

> I will explore a face of ecology that is unfa-

miliar to most people. I will not dwell on red-hot environmental issues such as overpopulation, extinction, desertification, acid rain, toxic waste disposal, whale and seal hunting, energy policy, and the ecology of nuclear war, although I will mention current issues when the context is pertinent. Rather I'm going to lead a frankly personalized tour of the principles of the scientific discipline that, among other things, provides a basis for formulating and evaluating policies to deal with those practical issues. Our tour proceeds from the simple to the complex. It starts with the relationships of individual organisms to their physical environments. . . . It moves on to the properties of populations—groups of individuals of the same species (kind) living in the same area. We'll see how and why populations grow, shrink, and evolve. Then we'll look at the interactions, such as mating behavior and the formation of schools and herds, of individuals within populations. That is followed by an examination of relationships between individuals of different species. . . . The properties of communities, which are the assemblages of different species found together in the same area, come next. . . . We look at such questions as why there are no living dinosaurs and what limits the number of species that populates an oceanic island. And finally, we explore ecosystems, the combination of communities and their physical surroundings. This is the ultimate level of ecological complexity, the one that is most often discussed on the political side of ecology. (14–15)

Ehrlich also discusses the scientists who work in the field of ecology. He talks about early ones such as Charles Darwin and Thomas Malthus, who developed theories regarding evolution and overpopulation, respectively, as well as modern ones. In regard to the latter, he says:

Ecologists find pleasure in their work in many ways. Ecology is a broad discipline, and its practitioners vary in their backgrounds, training, interests, and esthetic senses. The greatest pleasure for some is to be in the field, trying to discover nature's secrets. For others, it lies in creating an intellectually satisfying mathematical model that can assist in thinking about a complex natural phenomenon. Still others find great satisfaction in designing meticulous experiments in the laboratory to test raw theory or ideas developed during field observations. Some ecologists are driven by an intense desire to understand how the world works; others by an equivalent desire to apply ecological knowledge for the good of humanity. (15)

Ehrlich says that such diversity "is healthy for ecology as a whole" because the field will benefit from having several different approaches to the same environmental problem. (15–16) However, he also questions whether specialization might make it difficult to put solutions to those problems into practice, because communication between disciplines is limited or fraught with conflict. He believes that all people interested in ecology need to understand its general concepts.

In addition, Ehrlich argues that the only real way to solve environmental problems is to change the way people think. To this end, he supports the deep ecology movement, which does not mean that he is antiscience. He explains:

I am convinced that such a quasi-religious movement, one concerned with the need to change the values that now govern much of human activity, is essential to the persistence of our civilization. But agreeing that science, even the science of ecology, cannot answer all questions . . . does not diminish the absolutely crucial role that good science must play if our overextended civilization is to save itself. . . . Given the present level of human overpopulation, only a combination of changes in basic values *and* advances in science and technology seems to provide much hope for avoiding unprecedented calamities. And only an appreciation of how nature's machinery functions can provide the basis for the necessary changes in attitude and the guidelines for the safe deployment of new technology. (17–18)

Ehrlich hopes that his book will provide this appreciation and has kept his explanations of ecological principles easy to understand. He also includes photographs of several species of plants and animals. (Ehrlich 1986)

See also Ehrlich, Paul and Anne.

Mackaye, Benton

Born in 1879, U.S. regional planning expert Benton Mackaye wrote about land conservation in works such as *From Geography to Geotechnics* (1968) and *Expedition Nine: A Return to a Region* (1969), which concerns conservation in Massachusetts. He was one of the founders of the Wilderness Society and developed the idea for the Appalachian Trail in 1921. He also worked for conservationist Gifford Pinchot in the U.S. Forest Service. Mackaye died in 1975.

See also Pinchot, Gifford.

Magazines, Environmental

There are dozens of magazines covering nature and environmentalism. The most popular are published by major environmental groups such as the National Wildlife Federation, which produces *National Wildlife* and *International Wildlife* magazines, and the Sierra Club, which publishes *Sierra.* However, environmental magazines are also published by smaller environmental groups, as well as by individuals interested in promoting various aspects of environmentalism.

For example, the relatively small group Earth First! publishes *Earth First! Journal* to support radical environmentalism; a nonprofit Oregon group, Orlo, publishes *Bear Deluxe* to support the use of the creative arts in exploring environmental issues. The American Society for Environmental History and the Forest Historical Society jointly publish *Environmental History* to explore human interactions with the natural world, and the Massachusetts Institute of Technology publishes three environmental magazines: *Ecologist, Journal of Industrial Ecology,* and *Terra Nova: Nature and Culture.*

Other environmental magazines include *Environmental Ethics,* a leading forum for serious work in environmental philosophy; *Environment and History,* which brings scholars in the humanities and the biological sciences together to discuss environmental issues; *International Journal of Wilderness,* which focuses on wilderness research, planning, and management; and *International Journal of Ecoforestry,* which promotes responsible forest use. Two significant Canadian journals are *Trumpeter,* which deals with ecological philosophy, or ecosophy, and *Women and Environment,* which discusses environmental issues from a feminist perspective.

See also *International Wildlife; National Wildlife; Sierra.*

Make Room! Make Room!

The 1966 novel *Make Room! Make Room!* by Harry Harrison warns of the dangers of overpopulation. It is significant because it was the basis of a popular movie, *Soylent Green* (1973), which brought these dangers to the attention of people throughout the world. Moreover, Harrison's vision of an overpopu-lated future has been deemed realistic by overpopulation expert Paul Ehrlich, and the novel includes a bibliography of nonfiction works on overpopulation.

Make Room! Make Room! concerns a detective's attempts to track down a killer in New York City. It is a crowded place, where 35 million people are forced to live primarily on fortified seaweed crackers. As the detective moves through society looking for his suspect, the novel presents a society of physical and moral decay. Meanwhile, an old man recalls the past and wonders how the world went wrong. In the movie version, an extra twist was added: The detective discovers that the crackers are made not of seaweed but of recycled human beings, and the old man voluntarily dies to become food for someone else. (Stover 1990)

See also Ehrlich, Paul and Anne; Harrison, Harry; Human Ecology.

Malthus, Thomas Robert

Born in Rookery, England, on February 14, 1766, the Reverend Thomas Robert Malthus was one of the first people to argue that overpopulation was not good for society. In *An Essay on the Principle of Population,* first published anonymously in 1798, Malthus expressed his belief that as population increased the earth's food supply would no longer sustain it, which in turn would result in famine, disease, war, and death. Therefore, according to Malthus, any attempts to improve society were pointless so long as population growth remained uncontrolled.

This theory gained immediate attention, because it ran counter to the prevailing view that large families were desirable. However, many interpreted it to be an argument against the social reforms of that period. Malthus later tried to clarify his views; by 1826 he had written six more versions of his book, each one longer than the last. He published other works as well, including the 1820 book *Principles of Political Economy Considered with a View to Their Practical Application,* which discussed his ideas regarding thrift and economic depression.

Malthus came from a wealthy liberal family and was educated at home until 1784, when

Thomas Robert Malthus (Archive Photos)

he attended Jesus College in Cambridge. He received a master of arts degree there in 1791 and became a fellow of the college in 1793. He took holy orders in 1790. In 1805, after marrying Harriet Eckersall, he became a professor at the East India Company College in Haileybury, Hertfordshire. At Haileybury he taught history and political economy and expounded on his economic theories. However, according to R. Buckminster Fuller in *Utopia or Oblivion,* Malthus's employers at first tried to repress his writings, considering them the property of the East India Company.

After his work became known, Malthus became a member of several prestigious organizations, including the Political Economy Club and the Royal Society of Literature. In 1834 he helped found the Statistical Society of London. He died on December 23, 1834, but his theories continued to influence British society. In 1877 the Malthusian League was created as part of a movement to encourage birth control among the lower classes; the

group disbanded in 1927. (Bowler 1993; Fuller 1969; Malthus 1976; Shabecoff 1993)

See also *Essay on the Principle of Population, An;* Fuller, R. Buckminster; Human Ecology; *Utopia or Oblivion.*

Man and Nature

Man and Nature, or Physical Geography as Modified by Human Action, later retitled *The Earth Modified by Human Action,* was published in 1864. It was the first book in America to advocate true conservationism. Its author, diplomat George Marsh, suggested changes not only in wilderness practices but also in people's attitudes toward nature as well. For example, Marsh writes:

Man has too long forgotten that the earth was given to him for usufruct alone, not for consumption, still less for profligate waste. Nature has provided against the absolute destruction of any of her elementary matter, the raw material of her works; the thunderbolt and the tornado, the most convulsive throes of even the volcano and the earthquake, being only phenomena of decomposition and recomposition. But she has left it within the power of man irreparably to derange the combinations of inorganic matter and of organic life, which through the night of aeons she had been proportioning and balancing to prepare the earth for his habitation, when, in the fulness of time, his Creator should call him forth to enter into its possession. (McHenry 1972, 343)

Marsh offers many suggestions for the protection and wise use of wilderness areas. He also reports on the status of these areas in America:

The earth is fast becoming an unfit home for its noblest inhabitants, and another era of equal human crime and human improvidence, and of like duration with that through which traces of that crime and that improvidence extend, would reduce it to such a condition of impoverished productiveness, of shattered surface, of climatic excess, as to threaten the depravation, barbarism, and perhaps even extinction of the species.

True, there is a partial reverse to this picture. On narrow theatres, new forests have been planted; inundations of flowing streams restrained by heavy walls of masonry and other constructions; torrents compelled to aid, by depositing the slime with which they are charged, in filling up lowlands, and raising the level of morasses which their own overflows had created; ground submerged by the encroachments of the ocean, or exposed to be covered by its tides, has been rescued from its dominion by diking; swamps and even lakes have been drained, and their beds brought within the domain of agricultural industry; drifting coast dunes have been checked and made productive by plantation; seas and inland waters have been repeopled by fish, and even the sands of the Sahara have been fertilized by artesian fountains. These achievements are more glorious than the proudest triumphs of war, but, thus far, they give but faint hope that we shall yet make full atonement for our spendthrift waste of the bounties of nature. (281–282)

Marsh's words were highly influential, partially because of the social and political climate in which it appeared. As scholar Hans Huth explains in *Nature and the American:* "The era . . . was one of reorienting industry and reevaluating the potential of natural resources. It was therefore time to take stock of an entire continent. Marsh's book, because of its wide scope, offered abundant material on which to base a judgment about the future of the nation's resources." He continues: "No one before Marsh had realized the basic importance of conservation and the nature of its extraordinary and complex pattern, and no one had ever presented overwhelming facts of this kind. The book made an extraordinary impression and was reprinted many times; an enlarged edition was published in 1874.

Through many years to come, *Man and Nature* was to remain both a point of departure from old ways of thinking and a rallying point for new." (Huth 1972, 168–169) Consequently, as a direct result of Marsh's book, the U.S. government began to examine forestry management issues and created a forestry commission to address them. Public response to *Man and Nature* eventually led to the establishment of protected wilderness areas. (Cox 1971; Huth 1972; McHenry 1972)

See also Conservationism; Forest Management; Marsh, George Perkins.

Managing the Commons

Published in 1977, *Managing the Commons* was coedited by Garrett Hardin and John Baden, who have studied the way people use commonly held land, or commons. Issues related to commons gained prominence with environmentalists during the 1970s, and Hardin and Baden's book is a collection of articles on the subject.

One essay in particular is often cited by those discussing the pros and cons of creating commons within communities. Entitled "The Tragedy of the Commons," it was first published in *Bioscience* magazine and offers Hardin's thoughts on how easily shared land is destroyed. The article argues that a great deal of environmental damage is caused by a combination of personal freedom and natural selfishness, which leads people to exploit commons for their own gain. As Hardin explains:

The tragedy of the commons develops in this way. Picture a pasture open to all. It is to be expected that each herdsman will try to keep as many cattle as possible on the commons. Such an arrangement may work reasonably satisfactorily for centuries because tribal wars, poaching, and disease keep the numbers of both man and beast well below the carrying capacity of the land. Finally, however, comes the day of reckoning, that is, the day when the long-desired goal of social stability becomes a reality. At this point, the inherent logic of the commons remorselessly generates tragedy.

He continues:

> As a rational being, each herdsman seeks to maximize his gain. . . . The rational herdsman concludes that the only sensible course for him to pursue is to add another animal to his herd. And another. But this is the conclusion reached by each and every herdsman sharing a commons. Therein is the tragedy. Each man is locked into a system that compels him to increase his herd without limit—in a world that is limited. Ruin is the destination toward which all men rush, each pursuing his own best interest in a society that believes in the freedom of the commons. Freedom in a commons brings ruin to us all. (Hardin and Baden 1977, 20)

Therefore Hardin recommends that restrictions be placed on personal freedom. He argues that only by "closing the commons" can the earth be protected. These commons can be parcels of land, which can be restricted by fencing, or the global atmosphere, which can be "closed" by limiting pollution, pesticide use, the construction of nuclear energy facilities, and similar practices. Hardin suggests that restrictions of this kind are in the public's best interest:

> Every new enclosure of the commons involves the infringement of somebody's personal liberty. Infringements made in the distant past are accepted because no contemporary complains of a loss. It is the newly proposed infringements that we vigorously oppose; cries of "rights" and "freedom" fill the air. But what does "freedom" mean? When men mutually agreed to pass laws against robbing, mankind became more free, not less so. Individuals locked into the logic of the commons are free only to bring on universal ruin; once they see the necessity of mutual coercion, they become free to pursue other goals. (28–29)

Hardin also applies this argument to the problem of overpopulation, stating: "Freedom to breed will bring ruin to us all." He adds: "The only way we can preserve and nurture other and more precious freedoms is by relinquishing the freedom to breed, and that very soon. 'Freedom is the recognition of necessity'—and it is the role of education to reveal to all the necessity of abandoning the freedom to breed." (29) Hardin suggests that unless people curtail excessive reproduction in particular, and personal freedoms in general, the earth faces serious environmental destruction. (Hardin and Baden 1977)

See also Hardin, Garrett.

Manes, Christopher

Christopher Manes is a longtime environmental activist. A member of the radical environmental group Earth First!, he has served as the associate editor of *Earth First! Journal* and has written many articles expressing his views on environmental issues and activism. However, he is perhaps best known for *Green Rage: Radical Environmentalism and the Unmaking of Civilization* (1990). *Green Rage* defends the philosophy and practices of radical environmentalism, which advocates civil disobedience, and discusses the concept of deep ecology, which questions the right of humans to control nature. Manes has a doctorate in English from the University of Oregon and is the author of *Other Creations: Rediscovering the Spirituality of Animals* (1997). (Manes 1990)

See also Environmental Activism; Environmental Groups; *Green Rage*.

Manual of the Ornithology of the United States and Canada, A

Written by Thomas Nuttall, *A Manual of the Ornithology of the United States and Canada* was a major reference source for bird-watchers during the late 19th century, in part because it was more reasonably priced than similar works. The first volume appeared in 1823; subsequent editions were published in 1840, 1891, 1896, and 1903. The work not only offers physical descriptions of many bird species but also discusses their behaviors and habitats. In addition, the work makes general observations and comparisons between birds and other creatures. For example, Nuttall writes:

> Comparing animals with each other, we soon perceive that smell, in general, is much more acute among the quadrupeds than among the birds. Even the pretended scent of the Vulture is imaginary, as he does not perceive the tainted carrion, on which he feeds, through a wicker basket, though its odor is as potent as in the open air. This choice also of decaying flesh, is probably regulated by his necessities, and the deficiency of his muscular powers to attack a living, or even tear in pieces a recent prey. The structure of the olfactory organ, in birds, is obviously inferior to that of quadrupeds. (Lyon 1989, 149)

See also Nuttall, Thomas.

Maps and Dreams

Published in 1981, *Maps and Dreams* recounts the adventures of author Hugh Brody, who spent 18 months mapping the lands of northwestern British Columbia and studying the Native Americans who live there. Brody contrasts the Indian lifestyle with those of white ranchers, sports hunters, and oil pipeline workers who also live in the region. He also discusses the history of white exploration and Indian conflicts.

Marsh, George Perkins

George Perkins Marsh was one of the first American conservationists. Born on March 15, 1801, in Woodstock, Vermont, he attended Dartmouth College, New Hampshire, where he studied French, Spanish, Italian, German, and Portuguese. He intended to become a college professor, but after graduating in 1820 he decided to study law instead; he became a lawyer in 1825. Yet he continued to study other subjects, including literature and the science of soil conservation, and eventually became fluent in 20 languages. He also earned money as a farmer and lumber dealer, and consequently he began considering land management issues. Beginning in 1842, he served two terms in Congress, during which he promoted more careful use of the nation's natural resources. He later became a diplomat and served first as minister of Turkey and then as minister of Italy. While abroad he studied geography and agriculture, and in 1863 he wrote *Man and Nature, or Physical Geography as Modified by Human Action,* which discussed not only geography but also ecology and resource management. Published in 1874, the book raised public interest in conservation problems and influenced later conservationists such as John Muir and John Burroughs. Marsh died in July 1882. (Cox 1971; Curtis 1982)

See also Agriculture; Burroughs, John; Conservationism; Forest Management; *Man and Nature;* Muir, John.

Marshall, Bob

Born in 1901, Bob Marshall was a conservationist who traveled throughout the Arctic between 1929 and 1939 and wrote about the land and its people in *Arctic Village: A 1930s Portrait of Wiseman, Alaska* (1933). He campaigned for the protection of wilderness areas; a wilderness area in Montana is named after him. In addition, he helped found the Wilderness Society and worked as a professional forester, directing the U.S. Forest Service's Division of Recreation and Lands. Marshall was found dead on an overnight train from Washington, D.C. to New York City, New York in 1939. Only 39 years old, he died of either heart trouble or leukemia, according to an autopsy.

Matthew, William Diller

Born on February 19, 1871, in Saint John, New Brunswick, Canada, William Diller Matthew received his Ph.D. in paleontology from New York's Columbia University in 1895. As curator-in-chief of paleontology at the Museum of Natural History in New York City, he discovered several animal species and developed new theories about mammalian evolution. He published several books and articles about his work, including *Climate and Evolution* (1915). Matthew died on September 24, 1930. (Matthew 1939)

See also *Climate and Evolution;* Climate Changes; Evolution; Species Identification and Classification.

Matthiessen, Peter

Born in New York City on May 22, 1927, Peter Matthiessen writes fiction and nonfiction. He graduated from Yale University in 1950, moved to Paris, and helped found *The Paris Review,* a literature journal, in 1951. Later he returned to the United States, where he worked in Long Island as a commercial fisherman. He subsequently was hired by *The New Yorker* to explore wildlife issues throughout the world, and many of his works are the result of these experiences. His nonfiction books include *Wildlife in America* (1959), *The Cloud Forest: A Chronicle of the South American Wilderness* (1961), *The Snow Leopard* (1978), *African Silences* (1991), and *East of Lo Monthang* (1995). His novels include *Race Rock* (1954) and *At Play in the Fields of the Lord* (1965). He has won several awards for his writings, including a John Burroughs Medal (1982) and a gold medal from the Philadelphia Academy of Science (1984). (Caufield 1970; Matthiessen 1991; Trimble 1995)

See also *African Silences;* Burroughs, John; Nature Writing; Wildlife Conservation; *Wildlife in America.*

Maury, Matthew Fontaine

Matthew Fontaine Maury was a pioneer in the field of oceanography. Born on January 14, 1806, in Spotsylvania County, Virginia, he entered the U.S. Navy in 1825; from 1826 to 1830 he circumnavigated the globe. In 1836 he was made a lieutenant, but in 1839 he was injured in a stagecoach accident and forced off active duty.

Placed in charge of the Depot of Charts and Instruments, which eventually became the U.S. Naval Observatory and Hydrographic Office, Maury began gathering information on the earth's winds and currents, and in 1847 and 1848 he published collections of maps based on his research. He also studied the ocean floor, and in 1855 he published the first modern oceanography text, *Physical Geography of the Sea.*

When the Civil War broke out in 1861, Maury was made a captain in the Confederate Navy and placed in charge of coastal defenses. In addition, he conducted research in torpedo and mine technology. After the war, he went to Mexico to establish a Confederate colony there but soon returned to the United States to become a professor of meteorology at the Virginia Military Institute, a position he retained until his death on February 1, 1873. (Bowler 1993)

See also Geological Research; *Physical Geography of the Sea.*

McKibben, Bill

A former staff writer for *The New Yorker* and a frequent contributor to the *New York Review of Books,* Bill McKibben writes books, essays, and articles on nature and contemporary environmental issues. He is best known for his first book, *The End of Nature* (1989), in which he warns that environmental destruction is threatening all life on earth. His additional works include *The Age of Missing Information* (1992), *The Comforting Whirlwind: God, Job, and the Scale of Creation* (1994), and *Hope, Human and Wild: True Stories of Living Lightly on the Earth* (1995). (McKibben 1989)

See also *End of Nature, The;* Environmental Apocalypse.

McPhee, John

John McPhee is the author of several books that concern the relationship between humans and the environment, including *The Pine Barrens* (1968), *Coming into the Country* (1977), *Basin and Range* (1981), *In Suspect Terrain* (1983), *The Control of Nature* (1989), and *Rising from the Plains* (1986). His book *Encounters with the Archdruid* (1971) is a series of conversations with David Brower, a radical environmentalist.

Born in 1931 in Princeton, New Jersey, McPhee graduated from Princeton University. In 1964 he became a writer for *The New Yorker;* shortly thereafter he began writing books. McPhee currently teaches journalism at Princeton University. (McPhee 1989; Trimble 1995)

See also *Control of Nature, The.*

Mills, Enos

Born in 1870, Enos Mills was a naturalist, conservationist, and mountaineer who wrote about his adventures and observations in several books. They include *The Spell of the Rockies* (1911), *In Beaver World* (1913), *The Rocky Mountain Wonderland* (1915), *The Adventures of a Nature Guide* (1920), and *The Rocky Mountain National Park* (1924). Mills's work expressed his belief that wilderness areas should be protected for the good of humanity. He died in 1922.

Mitchell, John G.

John G. Mitchell has written books and articles on a variety of subjects, including education and religion. However, his best-known works are related to environmental issues. Among these are *Ecotactics: The Sierra Club Handbook for Environmental Activists* (1970), which he coedited with Constance L. Stallings; *The Man Who Would Dam the Amazon and Other Accounts from Afield* (1990), a collection of articles first published in *Audubon* and *Wilderness* magazines; and *Dispatches from the Deep Woods* (1992), a discussion of old-growth forests. He has also served as editor-in-chief of *Sierra* magazine and was once a science writer for *Newsweek*. (Mitchell 1970)

> See also *Ecotactics;* Environmental Groups; Environmental Politics.

Mivart, St. George Jackson

Biologist St. George Jackson Mivart was a major opponent of Charles Darwin's theories regarding evolution and natural selection. In particular, he could not accept the idea that human intelligence developed via a random process rather than through the direct intent of God. Born on April 1, 1900, in London, Mivart taught at St. Mary's Hospital from 1862 to 1884, during which he wrote a major work of biological study, *The Cat: An Introduction to the Study of Backboned Animals* (1881). His first book on evolution was *On the Genesis of Species,* published in 1871. His subsequent works include *Nature and Thought* (1882) and *The Origin of Human Reason* (1889). In later years, he wrote several scientific articles that displeased the Catholic Church. As a result, although he had been a teacher of natural history at a Catholic university in Belgium from 1890 to 1893, he was excommunicated from the Church in 1900. He died that same year. (Glass, Temkin, and Straus 1968)

> See also Darwin, Charles Robert; Evolution; *On the Genesis of Species.*

Momaday, N. Scott

Kiowa poet, novelist, and essayist N. Scott Momaday features landscape in his works. As Matthias Schubnell explains in *N. Scott Momaday: The Cultural and Literary Background* (1985):

> Nature and the American landscape are central features of Momaday's writings. The desert and canyons of the Southwest, where he grew up, and the Great Plains, where the culture of his Kiowa ancestors blossomed and declined, are more than mere settings for his works. They have deep cultural meaning for his understanding of an indigenous identity. Attachment to their homelands has been a powerful source of strength among American Indian peoples. They see their existences shaped and sustained physically and spiritually by the land. . . . This peculiarly native attitude is reflected in much of Momaday's work. (Schubnell 1985, 63)

Schubnell cites the 1968 novel *House Made of Dawn,* which won the Pulitzer Prize, as being one of Momaday's most significant works of nature writing. It is the story of Native Americans who lose touch with their heritage, become estranged from the land, and suffer both spiritually and physically as a result of their isolation; one of them eventually commits murder. Schubnell explains that Momaday's work expresses the belief "that individuals and cultures are molded by their homelands and that they must maintain a close relationship to them," (69) pointing out that all of the major characters in the novel "undergo changes and reach new insights under the influence of the spirit of place." (85)

Similarly, Momaday's book *The Way to Rainy Mountain* (1969), which includes poems as well as mythical, historical, and personal narratives, shows how a tribe is affected by changes in landscape. Momaday writes of the nomadic Kiowa's migrations across the Great Plains; he himself traveled the migration route to understand his heritage. The author expresses a piety both for his ancestors and for their environment.

Born on February 27, 1934, in Lawton, Oklahoma, Momaday grew up on various Indian reservations. He graduated from the University of New Mexico with a degree in political science in 1958. Shortly thereafter he was awarded the Wallace Stegner Creative Writing Scholarship, a grant that offered him the opportunity to study with Stegner at Stanford University in California for a year. Momaday remained a graduate student at Stanford until 1963, when he received his Ph.D. in English literature. He then taught in California for several years, first at Stanford and then at the University of California–Berkeley. In 1981 Momaday moved to Tucson, Arizona, where he currently teaches at the University of Arizona. In addition to *House Made of Dawn* and *The Way to Rainy Mountain,* his nature-related writings include a 1973 sketchbook on Colorado entitled *Colorado: Summer, Fall, Winter, Spring* and a collection of paintings, dialogues, poems, and poetic prose on the spirit of the wilderness entitled *In the Bear's House* (1999). Momaday is also an accomplished artist.

Moment on the Earth, A

Published in 1995, *A Moment on the Earth* by environmental reporter Gregg Easterbrook presents the author's reasons for feeling optimistic about the solution of environmental problems. In this regard, the book is part of a movement that developed during the 1990s to counter the warnings of environmental apocalypse that prevailed during the late 1980s. As Easterbrook points out: "Pessimism is the main current in contemporary environmental thought, and its refutation is the main concern of this book." (Easterbrook 1995, xx) To achieve balance in environmental discussions, he advocates "ecorealism," which is the unbiased evaluation of environmental facts. He explains:

> One reason I propose ecorealism is to create a language in which environmental protection can be discussed without descending into the oratorical quicksand of instant doomsday on the [political] left and bulldozer apologetics on the [political] right. Ecorealism offers a guiding ideal for those who care about the integrity of nature yet hold no brief for the extreme positions on either side. People sharing those values—a group that I figure at about 90 percent of the American population—need a vocabulary and a platform for reasoned ecological debate. Ecorealism will provide it. Such a debate will make environmental protection clearheaded and rational, and thus ultimately stronger still. (xx)

A Moment on the Earth offers lengthy essays on acid rain, air and water pollution, toxic waste, the spotted owl and other endangered species, chemicals and clean technology, climate (global warmth and cold), economics, energy, environmental groups, farming, forestry, land use, environmental politics, overpopulation, radiation (both natural and artificial), and the Third World. It also discusses environmentalism in terms of its place in earth's history. Easterbrook explains that before discussing individual issues he talks about "how nature might rank the problems humanity has caused in comparison to other problems faced by the natural world," adding:

> Of course the problems we experience in our own lives concern us more than the perspective of the past or the promise of the future. But I am convinced that full understanding of environmental issues cannot be obtained from consideration of the present alone. Hence the book begins by thinking backward to ages gone by and

Acid rain causes a denuded forest near Teplice, Czechoslovakia (© Dennis Degnan, Greenpeace)

ends by thinking forward to ages to come. Life is a river whose source is in the far past and whose delta—the point where the river suddenly spreads—may lie near at hand. We must attempt to fathom the entire expanse of that river to project where we will be carried on its currents. (xx-xxi)

Easterbrook therefore ends with a section entitled "The Green Future," in which he suggests changes in environmental thinking and predicts a time when "the whole great breathing heart-thumping enterprise of life may be more secure than today—protected by technical bulwarks against natural ecological devastation, by conservation strategies that stop extinctions, rendered unendable by expansion across distances that are astronomical in the true sense." (698) Easterbrook believes that space exploration and the colonization of other planets will ultimately spread earth's plants and animals to other worlds, where they will expand "to numbers vastly greater than they could have achieved on their own." (698) (Easterbrook 1995)

See also Antienvironmentalism; Easterbrook, Gregg; Environmental Apocalypse; Environmental Groups.

Monkey Wrench Gang, The

The Monkey Wrench Gang is the most famous and influential work of environmental fiction ever published. Written by environmental activist Edward Abbey and published in 1975, it concerns the escapades of a band of activists who use ecological sabotage, or ecotage, to fight development in the deserts of the American Southwest. The book inspired the environmental group Earth First! to adopt similar tactics in real life. Today these tactics, which include damaging roads, bridges, and industrial equipment, are called "monkeywrenching."

The Monkey Wrench Gang begins with a fictional act of ecotage: the dynamiting of a new bridge across Glen Canyon, intended to connect Utah and Arizona. The novel then flashes back to an earlier episode: Dr. A. K. Sarvis and his assistant, Bonnie Abbzug, setting fire to billboards along a desert highway. Sarvis considers it one of his "nighttime highway beautification projects." (Abbey 1975, p. 47) Shortly thereafter, Sarvis and Abbzug go on a river-rafting trip. Their guides are Joseph Fielding "Seldom Seen" Smith and his new assistant, a Vietnam veteran and former Green Beret named George Washington Hayduke. Both Smith and Hayduke believe that the government is destroying the desert. After Smith tells Sarvis and Abbzug that the Glen Canyon Dam has diminished the power of the Colorado River and ought to be dynamited, the group begins to discuss environmental activism. By the time they leave the river, the Monkey Wrench Gang has been born.

Sarvis is a wealthy surgeon and agrees to finance the operation. The group's first act of ecotage is against some bulldozers clearing a forest. Of this operation, Abbey writes:

The little pinyon pines and junipers offered no resistance to the bulldozers. The crawler-tractors pushed them all over with nonchalant ease and shoved them aside, smashed and bleeding, into heaps of brush, where they would be left to die and decompose. No one knows how sentient is a pinyon pine, for example, or to what degree such woody organisms can feel pain or fear, and in any case the road builders had more important things to worry about, but this much is clearly established as scientific fact: a living tree, once uprooted, takes many days to wholly die. (75–76)

After nightfall, the Monkey Wrench Gang uses a variety of methods to damage the bulldozers' engines, and they succeed in delaying the clear-cutting. Emboldened by this success, they undertake more difficult acts of ecotage. They move surveying stakes for a government road project, damage power lines and geological sensors, and blow up an electric train at a coal company, leaving behind clues that suggest a Native American activist group is responsible. Eventually, however, a local Mormon bishop named Love begins to suspect that Smith is involved in these activities.

Bishop Love is the leader of a desert search-and-rescue team, and after Hayduke and Smith drive an untended bulldozer off a cliff in broad daylight, he and his team chase them. The two monkeywrenchers escape, but afterwards Love continues to look for them.

Pursued by Bishop Love and law-enforcement officials, the gang temporarily splits up. Dr. Sarvis returns to work, Smith stays out of sight, and Hayduke and Abbzug head for a forest near the Grand Canyon to destroy clear-cutting equipment. Abbzug was once Dr. Sarvis's lover, but now she is in love with Hayduke. At the Grand Canyon the couple encounters another ecoteur, a masked horseman whom Hayduke calls the Lone Ranger. The man helps them destroy some bulldozers and rides off without telling them his name.

Hayduke and Abbzug return to the desert, where they commit another act of ecotage, but two helicopter pilots catch Abbzug in the act. Hayduke rescues her and sets the helicopter on fire. Now Bishop Love increases his efforts to find the monkeywrenchers, and one night he discovers all four trying to blow up a bridge. He and his posse chase the gang into a desert wilderness area. The terrain is difficult, and the monkeywrenchers have little water. Still, they keep hiking, until Bishop Love falls ill and his team calls on Dr. Sarvis for help.

Unable to let Love die, Sarvis and Abbzug turn themselves in, but Hayduke and Smith keep going. Eventually the two men split up. Smith is captured when he tries to steal food from some campers. Hayduke is cornered at the edge of a cliff, and law-enforcement officials literally shoot his body to pieces. Later Sarvis's lawyers manage to keep Sarvis, Abbzug, and Smith from serving time in prison. The group settles along the Colorado River and appears to lead a quiet life. Then Hayduke and the Lone Ranger show up at their door, and Hayduke explains that it was not he who was killed but a dummy. Hayduke accuses the monkeywrenchers of being responsible for blowing up the new bridge across Glen Canyon, but the book ends without the monkeywrenchers admitting their involvement. (Abbey 1975)

Inspired by *The Monkey Wrench Gang*, Earth First! decided to stage its first major act of ecotage at the Glen Canyon Dam. They snuck on top of the dam and unfurled a plastic "crack" across its face, symbolically destroying the concrete. Abbey was present during the event. (Abbey 1975; Glotfelty and Fromm 1996)

See also Abbey, Edward; Environmental Activism; Environmental Fiction; Environmental Movement.

Mora, Pat

Chicana poet Pat Mora writes about the desert landscape of the American Southwest. Much of her work is bilingual (English and Spanish), and she has written several books for children. Her publications include *Chants* (1984), *Borders* (1986), *Communion* (1991), *Listen to the Desert/Oye Al Desierto* (1994), *The Desert is My Mother/El Desierto Es Mi Madre* (1994), *Agua Santa/Holy Water* (1995), and *This Big Sky* (1998).

Mother Earth News

Mother Earth News is the one of the foremost magazines of the American "simple living" movement. Unlike most environmental periodicals, it is not published by an environmental group, and it does not ask for donations. Instead, it presents articles on such topics as solar heating, farming, building log homes, and alternative lifestyles. These articles are expressions of personal experience rather than reports on scientific research.

See also Environmental Groups; Simple Living Movement.

Mountaineering in the Sierra Nevada

Published in 1872, *Mountaineering in the Sierra Nevada* by explorer Clarence King (1842–1901) is a narrative about the author's adventures in the Sierra Mountains of the American West. King was a Yale-educated scientist who would later help establish the U.S. Geological Survey. His book therefore offers detailed information about all aspects of the mountains, along with personal comments about his reactions to his surroundings. King describes the origin of the mountains:

It appears most likely that the Sierra region was submerged from the earliest Palaeozoic, or perhaps even the Azoic, age. Slowly the deep ocean valley filled up, until, in the late Triassic period, the uppermost tables were in water shallow enough to drift the sands and clays into wave and ripple ridges. With what immeasurable patience, what infinite deliberation, has nature amassed the materials for these mountains! Age succeeded age; form after form of animal and plant life perished in the unfolding of that great plan of development, while the suspended sands of that primeval sea sunk slowly down and were stretched in level plains upon the floor of stone. (Finch and Elder 1990, 317)

King describes the view in a less scientific manner, saying: "Spread out below us lay the desert, stark and glaring, its rigid hill-chains lying in disordered grouping, in attitudes of the dead. The bare hills are cut out with sharp gorges, and over their stone skeletons scanty earth clings in folds, like shrunken flesh; they are emaciated corpses of once noble ranges now lifeless, outstretched as in a long sleep. Ghastly colors define them from the ashen plain in which their feet are buried." (324)

King's work has often been compared to that of John Muir, who also extolled the virtues of such mountains.

See also Muir, John.

Mowat, Farley

Canadian naturalist and environmentalist Farley Mowat has written several books chronicling his personal experiences with wild animals; he is one of the most famous writers in that genre. His books include *Never Cry Wolf* (1963), in which he talks about his research study on wolves in the Canadian Arctic, and *A Whale for the Killing* (1972), in which he describes his attempts to save a whale trapped in a pond. He has also written essays and books on environmental issues, including the book *Sea of Slaughter* (1984), which advocates stricter environmental protections for marine mammals. In addition,

Mowat has published a biography on Dian Fossey as well as several autobiographies, including *And No Birds Sang* (1980) and *Aftermath: Travels in a Post-War World* (1996), which discuss his experiences as a soldier during World War II. Mowat was born in Belleville, Ontario, Canada, on May 12, 1921. (Mowat 1963; Mowat 1972; Mowat 1984)

See also Animal Behavior; *Never Cry Wolf; Sea of Slaughter; Whale for the Killing, A.*

Muir, John

The writings of naturalist John Muir helped inspire the American conservation movement of the late 1800s and early 1900s. He was instrumental in the establishment of California's Sequoia and Yosemite National Parks as well as a national conservation program, and he promoted the protection of wilderness areas at every opportunity. He also wrote several popular books about his experiences in nature, including *The Mountains of California* (1896) and *My First Summer in the Sierra* (1911), with the aim of encouraging others to experience nature as well.

Born in Dunbar, East Lothian, Scotland, on April 21, 1838, Muir and his family emigrated to the United States in 1849 and settled in Wisconsin, where he spent his days clearing the forest, plowing land, and digging wells on the family farm. Later he would write that this upbringing prepared him for life as a naturalist, because as he worked with the earth he paid attention to its most minute details.

As a young man he attended the University of Wisconsin. He left in 1863 to travel through the United States and Canada but eventually took a factory job in Indiana. A talented inventor, he considered making inventing his career until an industrial accident blinded him. Although he gradually recovered his vision, the time spent in a dark sickroom changed his life; he vowed to spend the rest of his life outdoors. Shortly thereafter, he went on a 1,000-mile walk from Louisville, Kentucky, to the Gulf of Mexico, an experience he documented in a journal that was later published as *A Thousand Mile Walk to the Gulf*

(1916). In 1868 he journeyed to San Francisco, California, then to nearby Yosemite.

During his first summer in Yosemite, Muir worked as a shepherd. Then he became a guide for visitors to the region, which included American author Ralph Waldo Emerson. At the same time, Muir studied the area's geology and geography, and he is credited as being the first person to realize that Yosemite's rock formations were caused by ancient glaciers.

Although he would later travel to other parts of the country, Muir kept returning to Yosemite. Even after settling in Martinez, California, in 1880, he continued to visit the region, and he began urging the government to preserve it, believing that sheep grazing and human use were gradually destroying the area. Finally, largely because of Muir's urgings, the government established Sequoia and Yosemite National Parks in 1890.

Muir turned his attention to forest conservation elsewhere. In 1892 he founded the Sierra Club, devoted to promoting wilderness concerns and activities, and he wrote extensively on the issue of wilderness preservation. He was extremely effective in promoting his ideas. Two of his articles, "Forest Reservations and National Parks" (published in *Harper's Weekly* in 1897) and "The American Forests" (published in *Atlantic Monthly*, also in 1897), are often cited as the reason Congress voted to preserve more forest land shortly after their publication. Also effective in this regard was *Our National Parks*, published in 1916. It was one of the first books to focus public attention on problems in U.S. forestry management. Moreover, the work first appeared in a series of sketches in *Atlantic Monthly* in 1901, and these articles helped convince people of the importance of wilderness conservation.

Consequently, in 1903 President Theodore Roosevelt established a national conservation program, and during Roosevelt's administration more than 148 million forest acres were declared protected. In 1908, in honor of Muir's contributions in promoting wilderness preservation, a redwood forest near San Francisco was named Muir Woods. In 1914 he developed pneumonia; he died on December 24 in a Los Angeles hospital. (Cox 1971)

> See also Conservationism; Forest Management; *Our National Parks.*

Mumford, Lewis

Lewis Mumford was an urban planner and historian who criticized society's belief that science and technology could control nature. In such works as *Technics and Civilization* (1934), *The Culture of Cities* (1938), *The Condition of Man* (1944), *The Conduct of Life* (1951), *The City in History* (1961), and *The Myth of the Machine* (1970), he argued that machines were enslaving human beings rather than helping them; he went so far as to suggest that technology would ultimately destroy modern civilization.

Born on October 19, 1885, in Amenia, New York, Mumford studied at the New School for Social Research, where he studied urban planning. Shortly thereafter he began writing about architecture and urban planning issues. He also taught at several major universities and received numerous awards, including the Knight of the Order of the British Empire (1943) and the U.S. Medal of Freedom (1964). Mumford died on January 26, 1990.

Murie, Adolph

Naturalist Adolph Murie spent 25 years observing wolves and grizzlies in Mount McKinley National Park (now Denali National Park) in Alaska, meticulously recording details about individual animals and their family groups. During the early 1940s his work appeared in two government publications, *The Grizzlies of Mount McKinley* and *The Wolves of Mount McKinley.* Together these books were considered among the most important studies on North American wildlife, but they were not readily available to the general public until 1985, when they were reprinted in popular editions. Two other popular editions of his writings have also been published in recent years: *A Naturalist in Alaska* (1990) and *The Mammals of Denali* (1994).

Murie, Margaret

Born in Seattle, Washington, in 1902, conservationist Margaret Murie, commonly known as "Mardy," grew up in Fairbanks, Alaska, as the daughter of a sea captain. As an adult she traveled throughout Alaska with her husband, Olaus, a wildlife biologist. She wrote about her experiences in *Island Between* (1977) and *Two in the Far North* (1978). She also worked to protect the Arctic National Wildlife Refuge and to pass the Wilderness Act of 1964. She lives in Moose, Wyoming.

N

Nabhan, Gary Paul

Born in 1952, biologist Gary Paul Nabhan is an expert not only in the native plants of the American Southwest but also in the way in which Native Americans have traditionally used them. He has written several books about native people and plants, including *Wild Plants of the Pueblo Province: Exploring Ancient and Enduring Uses* (1995), *The Forgotten Pollinators* (1996), *At the Desert's Green Edge: An Ethnobotany of the Gila River Pima* (1997), and *Cultures of Habitat: On Nature, Culture, and Story* (1997).

Nabhan's best-known books on desert naturalism are *The Desert Smells Like Rain* (1982) and *Gathering the Desert* (1985), the latter of which won the John Burroughs Medal for excellence in nature writing. Both of these books are based on Nabhan's naturalist studies of the Papago Indians of southwestern Arizona. Nabhan is also the author of *Songbirds, Truffles, and Wolves: An American Naturalist in Italy* (1993), and he coauthored *The Geography of Childhood* (1994) with nature writer Stephen Trimble.

Nader, Ralph

Ralph Nader is a lawyer, consumer advocate, and environmental activist who ran for U.S. president in 1996 on the environmental platform of the Green Party. Born in Winsted, Connecticut, on February 27, 1934, he attended Princeton University and Harvard Law School. In 1965 he wrote *Unsafe at Any Speed,* in which he argued that automobiles were structurally unsafe. The following year, he testified before Congress on automobile design flaws, and legislators consequently passed the National Traffic and Motor Vehicle Act to put auto design under federal control.

Nader then turned his attention to other safety issues. In 1967 he helped bring about the Wholesome Meat Act, and in 1971 he established Public Citizen Inc., a group dedicated to consumer activism. He also became increasingly involved in environmental issues and wrote several books on environmental problems, including *Vanishing Air* (1970), *The Menace of Atomic Energy* (1977), and *Who's Poisoning America: Corporate Polluters and their Victims in the Chemical Age* (1981). (Nader et al. 1981; Shabecoff 1993)

See also Environmental Politics; *Who's Poisoning America.*

Naess, Arne

Norwegian philosopher Arne Naess is credited with developing the concept of deep ecology during the 1970s. In 1969 he resigned his position as a philosophy professor after teaching the subject for more than 30 years. According to David Rothenberg in the introduction to Naess's *Ecology, Community, and Lifestyle,* Naess took this action because "the threat of ecocatastrophe had become too apparent—there was much public outcry and protest. Naess believed philosophy could help chart a way out of the chaos. Because for him it had always been not just a 'love of wisdom' but a love of wisdom related to action." (Naess 1)

Thereafter Naess focused his attention on developing and writing about deep ecology, which suggests that humans are not separate from nature but an interconnected part of it. He says that in contrast to "the shallow ecology movement," whose aim is to "fight against pollution and resource depletion" with the objective of improving "the health and affluence of people in the developed countries," the deep ecology movement embraces "a deep-seated respect, even veneration, for ways and forms of life" (28) and promotes an "ideological change [that] is mainly that of appreciating *life quality* . . . rather than adhering to a high standard of living." (29) For this reason, Naess is also credited with contributing a great deal to the modern frugality movement, which advocates simple lifestyles and opposes materialism.

Naess is the author of many articles on ecological philosophy, or ecosophy, in general and deep ecology in particular. His first major work on the subject was the book *Ecology, Community, and Lifestyle,* first published in Norway in 1976. It inspired further discussions of the philosophy in such books as *Deep Ecology* (1985) by George Sessions and Bill Devall and *Is It Painful to Think?* by David Rothenberg (published in Norway in 1992 and in the United States in 1993), based on Rothenberg's interviews with Naess. These works in turn helped create the deep ecology movement. As Robert Gottlieb explains in *Forcing the Spring:*

> The concepts of deep ecology were popularized during the late 1970s and early 1980s through the publication of books and articles that sought to elaborate on Naess's original writings. These ideas influenced the development of a range of different conceptual approaches and organizations, such as bioregionalism (the notion that human societies—and environmental organizations—should be established according to patterns set by the natural environment) and the various kinds of spiritual and animal liberation groups that had direct lineage with the counterculture. Though many of these groups were small in terms of participants and often sectarian in their organization style, they nevertheless helped define an emerging Nature-centered movement. (Gottlieb 196)

According to scholar David Pepper, one such nature-centered movement concerns James Lovelock's Gaia hypothesis, which suggests that the earth is a single, living entity with a will to survive. Pepper sees many connections between Naess's work and Lovelock's work. In *Modern Environmentalism* he says:

> Whereas "shallow" ecologists consider that humans and nature are separate and humans are most important, deep ecologists deny any separation. They claim a "*total field view*" where every living being is part of Gaia, and has value. As Naess puts it, all organisms are "knots in the biospherical net or field of intrinsic relations," and the very notion of a world composed of discrete separate things is denied. What this means is not easy to grasp, but it does mesh with Eastern mysticism and some interpretations of contemporary physics, both of which influence deep ecologists. It implies that the universe is made of one basic spiritual or material entity or 'stuff,' and that different organisms or parts of nature are but different forms of this. (Pepper 22–23)

Because Pepper believes that this concept is an integral part of Eastern mysticism, he suggests that Naess's work was heavily influenced by the environmental poetry of Gary Snyder, whom Pepper calls "an interpreter of Eastern philosophy." (116) (Dobson 1991; Naess 1989; Pepper 1996; Rothenberg 1992)

> See also Deep Ecology Movement; *Is It Painful to Think?;* Rothenberg, David; Sessions, George; Snyder, Gary.

Nash, Roderick Frazier

Roderick Frazier Nash is a professor of history and environmental studies at the University of California–Santa Barbara. He has written several books on U.S. environmentalism and history, including *Wilderness and the American Mind* (1986) and *The Rights of Nature: A History of Environmental Ethics* (1989). (Nash 1989)

> See also Environmental History; Environmental Movement; *Rights of Nature, The.*

National Wildlife

National Wildlife is one of several magazines published by the National Wildlife Federation (NWF), an environmental group. It has one of the highest circulations of any environmental periodical and can be found at newsstands throughout the United States.

The bimonthly magazine addresses American conservation issues but confines itself to animal rather than human ecology. In other words, it discusses the impact of environmental problems on animals, not people. For example, the June/July 1998 issue includes articles such as "Return of the Jaguar" by Peter Friederici, which concerns the resurgence of the jaguar population in the United States; "This Prison is for the Birds" by Lisa Drew, which discusses bird species at the old prison site of Alcatraz Island off the coast of San Francisco; and "Listening to Wildlife in the Everglades" by Ted Levin, which examines five endangered species in South Florida. These articles are highly detailed yet written in a popular style, with many quotes from experts in various conservation fields.

In addition to offering information on environmental issues, the magazine also acts as a fund-raising tool for NWF. For example, accompanying Levin's article is a note that calls for donations to further NWF's conservation efforts in Florida.

> See also Environmental Groups; Habitat Protection; *International Wildlife;* Wildlife Conservation.

Natural History

Completed in 77 A.D., *Natural History* is an encyclopedic collection of 37 books by the Roman author Pliny. Book 1 introduces Books 2 through 36 and includes the sources on which Pliny based his work. Book 2 focuses on astronomy, Books 3 through 6 on geography, Books 7 through 11 on zoology, Books 12 through 19 on botany, Books 20 through 32 on medicines, drugs, and diet, and Books 33 through 37 on mineralogy and metallurgy. The work as a whole summarizes known facts and offers new details on a range of topics; it is significant for its discussions of animal, insect, and plant species, as well as its information on ancient cities and agricultural practices.

Until the 17th century, *Natural History* was viewed as an important resource. However, by the end of that century scientists had dismissed the collection as riddled with errors. In addition, in *The Norton History of the Environmental Sciences,* Peter J. Bowler says that Pliny "copied many passages almost wholesale" from the Greek author Theophrastus and questions the originality of *Natural History.* (Bowler 1993, 55) (Beagon 1992; Bowler 1993; French and Greenaway 1986; Whalley 1982)

> See also Pliny the Elder; Species Identification and Classification; Theophrastus.

Natural History and Antiquities of Selbourne, The

Published in England in 1789, *The Natural History and Antiquities of Selbourne* is a collection of letters written by pastor Gilbert White to two naturalists, Thomas Pennant and Daines Barrington, describing White's observations on daily walks through the countryside of his parish, Selbourne. White often wrote about animal behavior; his subjects include hedgehog eating habits, nesting habits in birds, and the activities of a pet land tortoise. He also commented on the relationship between animals and their environment. For example, on earthworms:

> Worms probably provide new soil for hills and slopes where the rain washes the earth away; and they affect slopes, probably to avoid being flooded. Gardeners and farmers express their detestation of worms; the former because they render their walks unsightly, and make them much work: and the latter because, as they think, worms eat their green corn. But these men would find that the earth without worms would soon become cold, hard-bound, and void of fermentation; and consequently sterile. (Finch and Elder 1990, 45)

White's work influenced many subsequent naturalists, including Charles Darwin and Henry David Thoreau. In fact Robert Finch and John Elder, in *The Norton Anthology of Nature Writing* (1990), call White "the patron saint of English nature writing." (22) In discussing *The Natural History and Antiquities of Selbourne,* they say: "White's book evokes days of hunting for echoes, nights of testing the hoots of owls with pitch-pipes. . . . White is always walking around looking and poking into things. . . . Gilbert White's letters show us an amateur scientist carrying out original research, in the open air, that is indistinguishable from recreation." (21)

See also Darwin, Charles Robert; Thoreau, Henry David; White, Gilbert.

Natural History of Carolina, Florida, and the Bahama Islands, A

Published in two volumes and an appendix between 1731 and 1747, *A Natural History of Carolina, Florida, and the Bahama Islands* was written by Englishman Mark Catesby after his second visit to America between 1722 and 1726; his first visit took place between 1712 and 1719. Catesby traveled extensively in the southeastern United States and took copious notes on his observations. He also sketched what he saw; because he knew engraving, he created his own illustrations for the books (200 engravings in all).

The first volume (1731) focuses on birds and includes information on 113 species; the second (1743) concentrates on fish, snakes, and plants. The works also exhibit an early understanding of habitat zones; Catesby discusses Carolina in terms of four vegetation regions: rice country, oak and hickory country, pine barrens, and scrub oak lands. (Lyon 1989)

Nature

Nature was first published anonymously as a 95-page book in 1836. However, its author, Ralph Waldo Emerson, soon became well known. The work expresses Emerson's views on a controversial 19th-century philosophy that he helped create—Transcendentalism, which suggests in part that God could best be found in nature and within the human soul rather than in a church. Emerson writes:

> The stars awaken a certain reverence, because though always present, they are inaccessible; but all natural objects make a kindred impression, when the mind is open to their influence. Nature never wears a mean appearance. Neither does the wisest man extort her secret, and lose his curiosity by finding out all her perfection. Nature never became a toy to a wise spirit. The flowers, the animals, the mountains, reflected the wisdom of his best hour, as much as they had delighted the simplicity of his childhood. . . .
>
> To speak truly, few adult persons can see nature. Most persons do not see the sun. At least they have a very superficial seeing. The sun illuminates only the eye of the man, but shines into the eye and the heart of the child. The lover of nature is he whose inward and outward senses are still truly adjusted to each other; who has retained the spirit of infancy even into the era of manhood.. . . . In the presence of nature a wild delight runs through the man, in spite of real sorrows. . . . In the woods, we return to wisdom and faith. There I feel that nothing can befall me in life,—no disgrace, no calamity . . . which

nature cannot repair. Standing on the bare ground . . . all mean egotism vanishes. I become a transparent eyeball; I am nothing; I see all; the currents of the Universal Being circulate through me; I am part or parcel of God. . . . In the wilderness, I find something more dear and connate than in streets or villages. (Whicher 1957, 23–24)

Nature encouraged others to seek out the wilderness, thereby helping to spread naturalism among the general public. Moreover, Emerson's work gradually changed people's attitudes toward nature by giving them a new philosophy to apply to naturalism. In *Nature and the American* Hans Huth explains:

Sentimental [nature] literature was still read for decades after Emerson's [book] was first published, and it is only just to admit that at least some of that literature channeled public interest in the direction of nature appreciation. Yet it gradually became apparent that the current of romantic sentimentalism could not keep up its force indefinitely unless a more rational and more substantial basis could be found for it. Rational minds would soon reject worn-out classifications such as sublimity, grandeur, and picturesqueness for interpreting the relationship between man and nature. . . . Emerson was determined to draw moral implications from his way of studying nature. . . . [His work] focused on the beginning conflict between the traditional way of life and industrialism. (Huth 1972, 88–89)

Nature argued that the traditional way of life was superior to industrialism. By encouraging people to live off the land, it supported the so-called simple living movement, and many transcendentalists began experimenting with simple living. One of them, George Ripley, created a transcendental community called Brook Farm, which was dedicated to this lifestyle. (Huth 1972; Miles 1964; Whicher 1960; Woodberry 1968)

See also Emerson, Ralph Waldo; Simple Living Movement; Thoreau, Henry David.

Nature Conservancy Magazine, The

The Nature Conservancy Magazine is a bimonthly publication of The Nature Conservancy (TNC), one of the wealthiest environmental groups in the United States. It is a popular periodical and has done much to interest nonscientists in conservation issues, particularly habitat protection. Land conservation is the primary focus of TNC, and many of its articles offer in-depth articles on the subject. For example, in the September/October 1997 issue, the article "How Green is My Valley?" by Martha Hodgkins Green discusses the efforts of private landowners, working with TNC, to protect an Idaho valley from development.

In this and many other articles, the value of TNC's help is highlighted. This is because magazines like *The Nature Conservancy Magazine* are intended not only to disseminate information about environmental problems but also to act as fund-raising tools for environmental groups that publish them. Two other examples of such periodicals are *National Wildlife*, published by the National Wildlife Federation, and *Sierra*, published by the Sierra Club.

See also Environmental Groups; Habitat Protection; *National Wildlife*; *Sierra*.

Nature Writing

Nature writing is a genre of environmental literature that expresses the author's personal relationship with wildlife and the land. It typically describes a specific experience in a particular place, often organized around seasons or a calendar year. For example, *The Inland Island* (1969) by Josephine Winslow Johnson reports her observations on her land during each month of the year, and *Epitaph for a Peach* by David Mas Masumoto describes his experiences during four seasons on a peach farm.

A particularly prevalent form of contemporary nature writing tells of the so-called back-to-nature experience, whereby an urban individual or family abandons the city to take up a rural lifestyle. For example, *Bean Blossom Dreams: A City Family's Search for a Simple Country Life* by Sallyann J. Murphy tells of her move from Chicago, Illinois, to a 42-acre farm in Brown County, Indiana. *A Family Place: A Man Returns to the Center of His Life* by Charles Gaines recounts his decision to move from New Hampshire to Nova Scotia, an experience he equates with that of 19th-century author Henry David Thoreau, who tells of his own back-to-nature experience in *Walden.*

Such works speak of nature as a utopia, extolling the virtues of the land and reporting on its spiritual benefits to humankind. Other nature writers, however, choose not only to share their wilderness experiences but also to discuss human threats on the natural world. During the conservation and environmental movements of the 20th century, nature writing increasingly expressed authors' personal philosophies on environmentalism. For example, John Muir not only wrote about his encounters with a bear but also argued that the bear's habitat needed to be preserved; Edward Abbey promoted environmental activism against wilderness destruction; and Farley Mowat argued in favor of wildlife conservation.

In many cases, modern nature writers will detail scientific facts and historical information. For example, Ann Zwinger's 1995 book, *Downcanyon,* which describes her adventures rafting the Colorado River, discusses the history of environmental destruction in the region. Terry Tempest Williams's 1991 book on Utah's Great Salt Lake, *Refuge: An Unnatural History of Family and Place,* uses a similar approach. Modern writers also tend to link the personal to the general. As Robert Finch and John Elder explain in *The Norton Anthology of Nature Writing:*

> Contemporary nature writers characteristically take walks through landscapes of associations. Beginning with a closely observed phenomenon, they reflect upon its personal meaning for them. Or, beginning with an argumentative point of view, they venture out into a natural setting that has no vested interest in their opinions and that contradicts or distracts as often as it confirms. In an age that has learned that any theory is subject to almost constant revision, a hallmark of the modern nature essay is its insistent open-endedness. (Finch and Elder 1990)

Because of this associative approach, many nature writers mention the work of other nature writers in their books. This practice often leads a reader on a path of discovery through the full offerings of the genre.

See also Abbey, Edward; Burroughs, John; Dillard, Ann; *Downcanyon;* Mowat, Farley; Muir, John; *Refuge;* Williams, Terry Tempest; Zwinger, Annie.

Nelson, Richard K.

Born in 1941, cultural anthropologist Richard K. Nelson spent several years living in the Far North, studying the region's native people and writing about them in books such as *Hunters of the Northern Ice* (1969), *Hunters of the Northern Forest: Designs for Survival Among Alaskan Kutchin* (1973), *Shadow of the Hunter: Stories of Eskimo Life* (1980), and *Make Prayers to the Raven: A Koyukon View of the Northern Forest* (1983). His book *The Island Within* (1989) is also set among the Koyukon Indians of Alaska, but it is a more personal account of his experiences and environment. For example:

> At the age of twenty-two, I went to live with Eskimos on the arctic coast of Alaska. It was my first year away from home . . . and the Eskimos . . . taught me their hunter's way.
>
> The experience of living with the Eskimos made very clear the direct, physical connectedness between all humans and the environments they draw existence from. Some years later, living with Koyukon Indians in Alaska's interior, I encountered a rich new dimension of that connectedness, and it profoundly changed my view of the world. Traditional

Charles Martin Smith is a young biologist studying wolves in the Arctic wilderness in the Carroll Ballard film Never Cry Wolf, *based on the book by Farley Mowat (Photofest)*

Koyukon people follow a code of moral and ethical behavior that keeps a hunter in right relationship to the animals. They teach that all of nature is spiritual and aware, that it must be treated with respect, and that humans should approach the living world with restraint and humility. Now I struggle to learn if these same principles can apply in my own life and culture. (Finch and Elder 1990, 794)

Nelson explores his own culture's hunting practices in *Heart and Blood: Living with Deer in America* (1997), which also describes North American deer species and discusses controversies regarding their management. In addition to such books, Nelson has written numerous articles for such magazines as *Harper's* and *Outside.*

Never Cry Wolf

Farley Mowat's *Never Cry Wolf* (1963) is a humorous yet informative first-person account of the Canadian naturalist's research on wolves during an earlier summer spent in the Arctic. Mowat also coauthored a 1983 film version of *Never Cry Wolf.*

The book begins with Mowat's childhood, his developing interest in biology, and his decision to become a biologist for the Canadian government, which sends him into the Arctic wilderness to investigate wolf behavior and determine how many caribou the wolves are eating. The caribou population has dramatically decreased, and the government is convinced that the wolves are responsible and should be reduced in number themselves.

Mowat reports that the government is concerned about the caribou because local fish and game clubs and the manufacturers of ammunition are upset "that the wolves are killing all the deer, and more and more of our fellow citizens are coming back from more and more hunts with less and less deer." (Mowat 1963, 15) He depicts Canadian officials as uncaring bureaucrats with no sense of humor and criticizes his fellow scientists, who "tended to shy as far away from living things as they could get, and chose to restrict themselves instead to the aseptic atmosphere of laboratories where they used dead—often very dead—animal material as their subject matter." (9)

Mowat prefers live contact with his research subjects. After receiving an assignment, he hires someone to fly him and his equipment into the wilderness, where he soon stumbles upon a wolf den inhabited by a mated pair of wolves, their cubs, and another male who takes turns babysitting the pups. Mowat dubs the extra male "Uncle Albert" and the mated wolves "George" and "Angeline."

Throughout the book, Mowat anthropomorphizes the animals' behavior, discussing them in terms of human emotions and intelligence and suggesting that the wolves are smarter than he is. He lives in a tent near the wolf den and, after observing a full summer of their lives, is convinced that the animals are not ferocious. In several instances, they have an opportunity to attack him and do not. He writes:

> Inescapably, the realization was being borne in upon my preconditioned mind that the centuries-old and universally accepted human concept of wolf character was a palpable lie. On three separate occasions in less than a week I had been completely at the mercy of these "savage killers"; but far from attempting to tear me limb from limb, they had displayed a restraint verging on contempt, even when I invaded their home and appeared to be posing a direct threat to the young pups. (76)

Moreover, Mowat learns that the wolves respect the boundaries of his tent and are careful not to bother him. He also discovers that they have an intricate and loving family relationship and that they communicate with wolves from other clans. Most importantly, he finds that they live primarily on mice and other rodents rather than caribou.

When Mowat does encounter a caribou slaughter, he sees marks that indicate a ski plane has landed there. He reports: "These deer had not been pulled down by wolves, they had been shot—some of them several times. One had run a hundred yards with its intestines dragging on the ice as a result of a gut wound." (237)

Mowat tells his superiors that people and not wolves are responsible for decimating the caribou population, but the Canadian government does not accept his findings, because its own tourist bureau supports hunting expeditions. Instead, the government organizes a wolf extermination program. In an epilogue to *Never Cry Wolf,* Mowat says that poisonous bait was set out for his wolf family in May 1959, and no one went back to check on whether it was eaten. Readers are left to wonder about George and Angeline's fate.

Popular at the beginning of the environmental movement, Mowat's book raised public awareness about the plight of wolves everywhere. One of his subsequent works, *Sea of Slaughter* (1984), touches on the same subject, but it does not display the humor of *Never Cry Wolf.* Instead, it is a blunt attack on humanity for decimating a variety of animal species. (Mowat 1963)

See also Animal Behavior; Mowat, Farley; *Sea of Slaughter; Whale for the Killing, A;* Wildlife Conservation.

New England Rarities Discovered

Published in 1672, *New England Rarities Discovered* by naturalist John Josselyn is significant because it is one of the first works to note that travelers could accidentally import nonnative species. In particular, the book lists 22 weeds that were brought to the Americas by Europeans. Josselyn, an Englishman who visited New England in 1638 and 1663, also commented on the loss of native plant and animal species during that time; for example, he reports on the decline of wild turkey populations.

New England's Prospect

Published in 1634, *New England's Prospect* is one of the first comprehensive descriptions of the North American environment. The book's author, naturalist William Wood, lived in Massachusetts between 1629 and 1633 and recorded his observations during that period. Otherwise, little is known about Wood's life.

New England's Prospect not only provides information about the types of animals that Wood encountered in North America but also comments on their behavior. For example, in discussing various small mammals, Wood says:

> The ounce or wildcat is about as big as a mongrel dog. This creature is by nature fierce and more dangerous to be met withal than any other creature, not fearing either dog or man. He useth to kill deer, which he thus effecteth: knowing the deer's tracts, he will lie lurking in long weeds, the deer passing by he suddenly leaps upon his back, from thence gets to his neck and scratcheth out his throat. . . . The English kill many of those [wildcats], accounting them very good meat. Their skins be a very deep kind of fur, spotted white and black on the belly. (Lyon 1989, 99)

Many subsequent nature writers have praised Wood's work, among them Henry David Thoreau in 1855. However, as Thoreau himself noted, *New England's Prospect* does not always provide correct information. For example, Wood declared that wolves "have no joints from their head to the tail, which prevents them from leaping, or sudden turning." (Lyon 99) Wood came to this conclusion after observing a captive wolf, saying:

> A certain man having shot a wolf as he was feeding upon a swine, breaking his leg only, he knew not how to devise his death on a sudden. The wolf being a black one, he was loath to spoil his fur with a second shot, his skin being worth five or six pound sterling. Wherefore he resolved to get him by the tail and thrust him into a river that was hard by; which effected, the wolf being not able to turn his jointless body to bite him, was taken. That they cannot leap may appear by this wolf, whose mouth watering at a few poor im-

paled kids, would needs leap over a five-foot pale to be at them; but . . . fell short of his desire. (Lyon 99–100)

Scholars have noted that such flaws are insignificant when compared to the importance of Wood's approach to his subject. Thomas Lyon, a professor of English at Utah State University, explains:

> Wood . . . declared that the aim of his stay in New England . . . had been observation pure and simple, which is certainly unusual, if not unique, among the first waves of Europeans coming to these shores. . . . His natural history catalog, as might be expected and forgiven, is incomplete—he lists only two species of owl, for instance, apparently the screech owl and the great horned owl—but his obvious feeling for animals and his care in description mark him as having something of the poetic-scientific temperament of many later, more accomplished nature writers. (Lyon 26)

Consequently, Wood's work is not typical of his era. (Lyon 1989)

See also Thoreau, Henry David.

New Exploration, The

Published in 1928, *The New Exploration: A Philosophy of Regional Planning* was written by Benton MacKaye, one of the first environmental engineers in America. As such he believed in careful environmental planning and management of natural resources. His book places natural resources into three classes: material resources such as soils, forests, and metallic ores; energy resources, which he defines as the mechanical energy produced by falling water or similar natural means; and psychological resources, which he defines as the human happiness induced by a particular environment.

MacKaye discusses all types of resources at length and argues that regional planners should attempt to maintain the natural world whenever possible, pointing out that iron, coal, timber, and petroleum have a "high potential—for human happiness or human misery." He adds that they "may be the seeds of freedom or seeds of bitterness; for in them is the latent substance of distant foreign wars as well as deep domestic strife." (MacKaye 1928, 228) Moreover:

> It takes more than towns and railroads and corn fields to make a nation and a pleasant land to live in. These are enough for the "material fact," but not for the "spiritual form." They are enough for a mechanical state of "civilization," but not for a living "culture." Man needs more than this to cover God's green earth, if he would be a *soul*. He needs just one thing further. He needs it in his home and dooryard; he needs it within his community; he needs it throughout his country and his planet. It is the right kind of environment. (29)

MacKaye recognized that people need to feel a part of nature rather than detached from it. (MacKaye 1928)

New Voyage to Carolina, A

Published in 1709, *A New Voyage to Carolina* reports on a two-month survey expedition through the American colony of Carolina by author John Lawson, one of the area's first college-educated naturalists. The book provides a natural history of the New World, thoroughly describing the land and its inhabitants, and it includes Lawson's own detailed drawings of plants.

A New Voyage to Carolina also offers Lawson's personal comments on his environment. Professor Thomas Lyon, in *This Incomperable Lande,* has this to say: "[Lawson's] writing shows not only a ready responsiveness to the scenes before him but also a certain flair, a recognition of some of the responsibilities of authorship to tell a story and present information in unified fashion." (Lyon 1989, 30) (Lyon 1989)

Night Country, The

Published in 1971, *The Night Country* is one of the best-known books by Loren Eiseley, who was among the first modern American scientists to write specifically for laypersons. An anthropologist, he calls himself "one of those few persons who pursue the farther history of man on the planet earth, what Darwin once called 'the great subject.'" (Eiseley 1971, 153)

Eiseley discusses such topics as evolution, the human mind, and the role of science in society. He also includes a great deal of autobiographical material in his work, because his writing is a personal expression of his beliefs rather than a mere recitation of facts. During the 1970s this brought him a great deal of criticism from peers. As Eiseley relates in *The Night Country:*

> A few years ago I chanced to write a book in which I had expressed some personal views and feelings upon birds, bones, spiders, and time, all subjects with which I had some degree of acquaintance. Scarcely had the work been published when I was sought out in my office by a serious young colleague. With utter and devastating confidence he had paid me a call in order to correct my deviations and to lead me back to the proper road of scholarship. He pointed out to me the time I had wasted—time which could have been more properly expended upon my own field of scientific investigation. The young man's view of science was a narrow one, but it illustrates a conviction all too common today: namely, that the authority of science is absolute.
>
> To those who have substituted authoritarian science for authoritarian religion, individual thought is worthless unless it is the symbol for a reality which can be seen, tasted, felt, or thought about by everyone else. Such men . . . reject the world of the personal, the happy world of open, playful, or aspiring thought. (139)

Eiseley returns to this theme again and again in *The Night Country.* He frequently criticizes the scientific community for trying to destroy individuality and creativity and for putting science above personal satisfaction.

Moreover, he suggests that most modern scientists study things like nuclear energy not to learn about the world or to benefit humankind but to gain power over others. He says: "Governments expend billions upon particle research, cosmic-ray research, not because they have been imbued suddenly with a great hunger for truth, but for the very simple, if barbarous, reason that they know the power which lies in the particle. If the physicist learns the nature of the universe in his cyclotron, well and good, but the search is for power." (140–141) Eiseley believes that this quest for power has changed the field of science for the worse, continuing:

> We have lived to see the technological progress that was hailed in one age as the savior of man become the horror of the next. We have observed that the same able and energetic minds which built lights, steamships, and telephones turn with equal facility to the creation of what is euphemistically termed the "ultimate weapon." It is in this reversal that the modern age comes off so badly. It does so because the forces which have been released have tended to produce an exaggerated conformity and, at the same time, an equally exaggerated assumption that science, a tool for manipulating the outside, the material universe, can be used to create happiness and ethical living. Science can be—and is—used by good men, but in its present sense it can scarcely be said to create them. Science, of course, in discovery represents the individual, but in the moment of triumph, science creates uniformity through which the mind of the individual once more flees away. (140–141)

Eiseley discusses earlier scientists who were naturalists in touch with their environment, quoting Henry David Thoreau: "If you would learn the secrets of nature, you must practice more humanity than others." (146) Eiseley believes that most modern scientists have become too distant from nature and from the spirituality it inspires. In fact he says that spirituality is an important part of science, pointing out that early naturalists were able "to glimpse eternity" through their scientific observations and research. (148)

Eiseley adds that "there is a natural history of souls, nay, even of man himself, which can be learned only from the symbolism inherent in the world about him." (148) Similar discussions of the relationship between spirituality and science appear in many other works of the period, but Eiseley was one of few scientists to address the issue. (Eiseley 1971)

See also Darwin, Charles Robert; Eiseley, Loren; Nature Writing; Nuclear Energy; Thoreau, Henry David.

No Turning Back

Published in 1994, *No Turning Back: Dismantling the Fantasies of Environmental Thinking* was written by environmentalist Wallace Kaufman, who had become dissatisfied with American environmentalism. His work has been embraced by the antienvironmental movement, which opposes current U.S. environmental policies.

Kaufman believes that environmentalists have become too pessimistic about environmental problems and have allowed their pessimism to blind them to scientific and economic truths. He says: "After thirty years in the environmental movement, I am worried that as it gains power, it cares less and less about reason and science. . . . In short, I believe the environmental movement has almost lost touch with reality." (Kaufman 1994, 7)

Kaufman gives many examples in support. He lists predictions of environmental catastrophes that did not come true, such as the statement in the 1972 book *The Limits to Growth* that the world's petroleum supplies would be exhausted by 1992, as well as catastrophes that are unlikely to come true, such as Barry Commoner's 1969 statement that "earth's life-support systems would be exhausted in fifty years." (25) He explains how these kind of doomsday predictions created the environmental movement and now threaten to end scientific objectivity. In this regard, he says:

Popular horse-racing tabloids are much more scientific than the environmental press. People who write the racing sheets know the uncertainty and risk in their predictions. News on the environment features experts who claim to be almost entirely certain about their predictions. Claiming to be certain, especially about a future disaster, can sell books and raise funds. (71)

Kaufman suggests that some environmentalists intentionally distort the truth to gain money and political power. He criticizes them for manipulating the American public and disputes many aspects of environmental thinking. For example:

Both children and adults hear over and over again that we are running out of landfill space. The popular children's book *Fifty Simple Things Kids Can Do to Save the Earth* has sold almost a million copies and claims that "we are making so much garbage that in many places there is not enough room to bury it all." But most garbage does not pollute. It consists of paper, yard clippings, stumps, dirt, concrete, tin, aluminum, and plastic. We are not running out of space at all. The problem is more economic and psychological. Who wants to live near a dump? And how much will we have to pay to haul garbage to a dump site? (86–87)

Kaufman criticizes many environmental books, including Al Gore's *Earth in the Balance,* the Sierra Club's *Ecotactics,* the works of Paul Ehrlich, Carl Sagan, and Stephen Schneider, and the media for distorting the truth about environmental issues. He advocates a new approach to environmentalism that embraces optimism for the future and doesn't mourn or romanticize the past:

We are in no worse position than humans ever were. We have lost some things and gained much. We may regret the loss of . . . the forests of Manhattan Island or the clouds of passenger pigeons that once darkened midwestern skies. But we don't regret the passing of yellow fever, malaria, or bubonic plague. Few people really want a simpler life. We may turn down the thermostat five degrees, but we won't take out the heat pump. We all want more, for ourselves and for the rest of the world, because that is the way to peace. (181)

Kaufman concludes that "the freedom of the human mind is more important than the quantities of any natural resource." (181) Moreover, he believes that "Western-style democracy, with its ever expanding protection of individual freedom, offers invaluable opportunities and incentives to pursue creative answers to environmental problems," provided that people consider such problems rationally. (15)

(Kaufman 1994)

See also Antienvironmentalism; Commoner, Barry; *Earth in the Balance; Ecotactics;* Ehrlich, Paul and Anne; Gore Jr., Albert; *Limits to Growth, The;* Sagan, Carl.

Nuclear Energy

Nuclear energy is produced by splitting atoms. This energy can be used to generate electrical power or to bomb cities. In either case, the type of atoms required for the process is dangerous. Only the highly unstable, or radioactive, elements release energy in a way that provides nuclear fuel. The most common radioactive materials used in nuclear reactors are uranium and plutonium, and before they can be used they must be mined and turned into pellets. At this phase of production, radioactive waste products are created; waste requires disposal. Radioactive waste is also created when the nuclear fuel loses its effectiveness after a few years of use and must be replaced.

Various methods to handle radioactive waste have been tried. Prior to 1983 it was typically sealed in containers and dropped into the ocean, but today such containers are buried. Concerns that radioactive material would consequently contaminate water and

A sodium-cooled breeder reactor, Richland, Washington (U.S. Department of Energy)

soil was a major impetus to the American environmental movement during the 1960s, and nuclear energy continues to be a controversial environmental issue today. Many authors have addressed the subject, including Carl Sagan, Murray Bookchin, Rachel Carson, Isaac Asimov, and Frederik Pohl. Pohl wrote not only nonfiction on the dangers of nuclear energy but also a novel. Entitled *Chernobyl,* it mixes fiction with facts to depict a real nuclear disaster at the Chernobyl nuclear power plant in Russia.

See also Asimov, Isaac; Bookchin, Murray; Carson, Rachel Louise; Pohl, Frederik; Sagan, Carl.

Nuttall, Thomas

English naturalist and botanist Thomas Nuttall is best known for his writings on North American plants and birds. His book *A Manual of the Ornithology of the United States and Canada* was an extremely popular bird-watching guide during the late 19th century.

Nuttall was born on January 5, 1786, in Long Preston, Yorkshire, England; he was raised in Blackburn, Lancashire. In 1808 he traveled to the United States, where he was hired by botanist Benjamin Smith Barton of the University of Pennsylvania to explore various regions of Delaware, Pennsylvania, New York, North Carolina, Virginia, Missouri, and Arkansas and collect plants for identification. In 1818 Nuttall published *The Genera of North American Plants* to present much of his work to the public. He also kept journals of his expeditions, but only one—*Journal of the Travels into the Arkansas Territory During the Year 1819*—was published during his lifetime (1821).

In 1822 Nuttall became a lecturer at Harvard University, and there he became interested in birds. He also became curator of the Harvard Botanic Garden. In 1830 he traveled throughout the southeastern United States, observing bird species; two years later the first volume of *A Manual of the Ornithology of the United States and Canada* appeared. In 1834 he resigned from Harvard to join an overland expedition, first to the Columbia River and then to the Pacific Coast; he eventually joined a sea expedition to the Hawaiian Islands. He returned to the United States in 1835.

In 1842 Nuttall returned to England, where he lived out his life as a gentleman farmer on an inherited estate in Lancashire. He visited the United States once (1847–1848) before his death on September 10, 1859.

See also *Manual of the Ornithology of the United States and Canada, A.*

O

Observations Made During a Voyage Round the World

Observations Made During a Voyage Round the World was written by German naturalist Johann (known as "John" in England) Reinhold Forster, who sailed with British explorer Captain James Cook during his second expedition around the globe. Published in 1778, the book is a lengthy, detailed record of Forster's observations and theories about earth's geography and life-forms; it advanced 18th-century knowledge.

The work is divided into six parts: The Earth and Its Strata, Water and the Ocean, The Atmosphere, The Changes of the Globe, Organic Bodies, and The Human Species. The last section, which discusses the social principles, manners, customs, languages, arts and sciences, and religious beliefs of a variety of native cultures, is significantly larger than the rest, and Forster considered it the most important. He states that in writing his book:

> My object was nature in its greatest extent; the Earth, the Sea, the Air, the Organic and Animated Creation, and more particularly that class of Beings to which we Ourselves belong. The History of Mankind has often been attempted; many writers have described the manners and characters of individuals, but few have traced the history of men in general, considered as one large body. . . . None of these authors ever had the opportunity of contemplating mankind in this state, and its various stages from that of the most wretched savages, removed in the first degree from absolute animality, to the more polished and civilized inhabitants of the Friendly and Society Isles. (Forster 1778, ii)

However, many scholars believe that Forster's observations on climate and plant and animal species are equally important. For example, Peter J. Bowler, in *The Norton History of the Environmental Sciences,* credits Forster as being one of the first naturalists to recognize that the number of species in a given region was dependent on temperature. Bowler writes:

> [Forster] noted that the plants and animals of a region form a unit defined by the environment. . . . The units succeeded one another in a regular sequence as one passed from the tropics to the frigid zones, with the tropics always having the most numerous and the most spectacular species. In addition, though, there were biological provinces defined by longitude

rather than latitude. The Pacific islands, for instance, saw an intermingling of the typical Asian and the American species. Islands in general had species similar (but often not identical) to those of the nearest continental land mass. Forster extended these generalizations to include the human inhabitants of the biological provinces. (Bowler 176)

Observations also presents significant theories related to physical geography. For example, it explores the relationship between volcanoes and the formation of islands. However, in discussing these theories, Forster acknowledges the assistance of the Count de Buffon, a French naturalist who wrote extensively on geographic phenomena. He also thanks several lesser scientists for helping him examine ocean salinity and temperature, as well as other physical properties of water, soil, and air. (Bowler 1993; Forster 1778)

See also Buffon, Georges Louis Leclerc, Comte de; Climate Changes; Comte de Buffon; Forster, Johann Reingold; Geological Research; Species Identification and Classification.

Olson, Sigurd

Born in 1899, nature writer Sigurd Olson wrote of his experiences amid nature in the Upper Midwest. His books include *The Singing Wilderness* (1956), *Listening Point* (1958), and *The Lonely Land* (1961). Olson lived in Ely, Minnesota, where he worked to preserve the nearby Quetico-Superior Wilderness Area. He died in 1982.

On the Genesis of Species

Published in 1871, *On the Genesis of Species* expresses the anti-Darwinian views of its author, British biologist St. George Jackson Mivart. Mivart did not believe that natural selection was part of the evolutionary process. Instead, he felt that new species appeared by preordination through an inner power he called "individuation." In addition, he could not accept that human intelligence evolved at all. He felt it was given by God to modern human beings. Mivart countered many of Darwin's views, in-

cluding the concept that similar species must share a common ancestor. (Bowler 1993)

See also Darwin, Charles Robert; Evolution; Mivart, St. George Jackson.

On the Origin of Springs and Rivers

On the Origin of Springs and Rivers by French lawyer Pierre Perrault was first published anonymously in Paris in 1674. It is based on Perrault's careful study of the Seine River, during which he disproved the prevailing theory that rivers were replenished by water from rocks or other underground sources. Perrault used precise measurements and careful arguments to prove instead that rainwater is enough to keep rivers flowing. Acknowledging that rainfall might not be an adequate source of replenishment in some regions, he nonetheless did not view that as a disputation of his work:

There are hardly any countries in the world where it never rains. The torrid zone, where this is more nearly true than anywhere else, is watered abundantly twice a year, possibly more than France is in the summer, and at least with greater abundance at certain times. But when we speak of regions where it never rains, we do not deny the possibility that there are large rivers there which may have their sources in other regions where it does rain, as, for example, the Nile, which flows through Egypt where it does not rain. There are countries in the world which do not produce wine, where not much of it could be produced, and business and commerce bring it from afar; similarly the great rivers make a kind of commerce of their waters to irrigate the provinces not watered ordinarily from heaven. (Boynton 1948, 354)

Because Perrault's work was so thorough, his theory was widely accepted by the scientific community. (Boynton 1948)

See also Perrault, Pierre.

Origin of Humankind, The

Published in 1994, *The Origin of Humankind* presents Richard Leakey's theories

Richard Leakey with a 2-1/4-million-year-old skull, 1972 (Popperfoto/Archive Photos)

on human evolution and prehistoric life. The son of a legend—and a noted paleontologist in his own right—Leakey is responsible for many important discoveries in the field. This book provides information about his own work and those of other scientists studying human fossils. Some of the theories he discusses are controversial, but he is careful to offer both sides of each debate along with his own views. For example, in mentioning the controversy regarding where man first originated, he says:

> The important issue of the origin of modern humans remains unresolved, despite the welter of information that has been brought to bear. My sense of it, however, is that the multiregional-evolution hypothesis is unlikely to be correct. I suspect that modern *Homo sapiens* arose as a discrete evolutionary event, somewhere in Africa; but I suspect, too, that when descendants of these first modern humans expanded into Eurasia, they intermixed with the populations there. Why the

genetic evidence, as currently interpreted, doesn't reflect this, I don't know. Perhaps the current reading of the evidence is incorrect. Or perhaps . . . [the genetic evidence] will turn out to be right, after all. This uncertainty is more likely to be resolved when the clamor of debate ebbs and new evidence is found in support of one or another of the competing hypotheses. (Leakey 99)

The Origin of Humankind is important not only because it summarizes current research on human origins; it also acknowledges the uncertainties in this field. This is in marked contrast to the first book on the subject, by Richard's father, anthropologist Louis Leakey. Entitled *Adam's Ancestors,* it summarized evolutionary science of the 1930s in a confident, definitive manner; it did not directly discuss controversies within the field that were prevalent at the time. (Leakey 1994)

See also *Adam's Ancestors;* Evolution; Leakey, Louis; Leakey, Richard.

Origin of Species, The

Charles Darwin's classic treatise—officially entitled *The Origin of Species by Means of Natural Selection, or the Preservation of Favoured Races in the Struggle of Life*—presented momentous theories on species evolution and natural selection. Published in November 1859, it was a controversial work that countered other theories prevalent at the time, particularly those of Jean-Baptiste Lamarck. As Darwin explains in his autobiography, "My views have often been grossly misrepresented, bitterly opposed and ridiculed, but this has been generally done, as I believe, in good faith." (Bates 28)

Despite criticism from the scientific community, the work was extremely popular. Darwin reports that the first edition (1,250 copies) was sold on the day it was published; 3,000 additional copies were sold shortly thereafter. Within the next 20 years, more than 16,000 copies were sold in England, and the book had been translated into almost every European language. Moreover, *The Origin of Species* was frequently discussed. According to Darwin: "The reviews were very numerous; for some time I collected all that appeared on the *Origin* and on my related books, and these amount (excluding newspaper reviews) to 265; but after a time I gave up the attempt in despair. Many separate essays and books on the subject have appeared." (26)

Darwin published some work on evolutionary theory prior to writing *Origin*. In fact he believes that this is one reason the book was so well received. He explains:

> The success of the *Origin* may, I think, be attributed in large part to my having long before written two condensed sketches, and to my having finally abstracted a much larger manuscript, which was itself an abstract. By this means I was enabled to select the more striking facts and conclusions. I had, also during many years, followed a golden rule, namely, that whenever a published fact, a new observation or thought came across me, which was opposed to my general results, to make a

> memorandum of it without fail and at once; for I had found by experience that such facts and thoughts were far more apt to escape from the memory than favourable ones. Owing to this habit, very few objects were raised against my views which I had not at least noticed and attempted to answer. (26–27)

Darwin responded to criticism of his work by including additional information in subsequent editions. For example, the second edition includes a discussion of the historical precedents for his ideas, which some reviewers considered a serious omission from the first edition. Darwin's original version of *The Origin of Species* began with a discussion of the variation of organisms, and this discussion was included in subsequent editions. It calls attention to the way humans have manipulated animal species via selective breeding, then shows how this artificial process relates to the natural processes that cause species to change. He says:

> We cannot suppose that all the breeds were suddenly produced as perfect and as useful as we now see them; indeed, in many cases, we know that this has not been their history. The key is man's power of accumulative selection: nature gives successive variations; man adds them up in certain directions useful to him. In this sense he may be said to have made for himself useful breeds. The great power of this principle of selection is not hypothetical. It is certain that several of our eminent breeders have, even within a single lifetime, modified to a large extent their breeds of cattle and sheep. . . . Breeders habitually speak of an animal's organisation as something plastic, which they can model almost as they please. (122–123)

Darwin next describes species variation in the wild: "I am convinced that the most experienced naturalist would be surprised at the number of the cases of variability, even in important parts of structure, which he could collect on good authority, as I have collected, during a course of years." (130) He then sets out to explain this variability, moving into a discussion of natural selection. He analyzes species competition and "the struggle for existence," which places species in direct competition with their own kind as well as others. (137) For example, he says:

> As the species of the same genus usually have, though by no means invariably, much similarity in habits and constitution, and always in structure, the struggle will generally be more severe between them, if they come into competition with each other, than between the species of distinct genera. We see this in the recent extension over parts of the United States of one species of swallow having caused the decrease of another species. The recent increase of the missel-thrush in parts of Scotland has caused the decrease of the song-thrush. How frequently we hear of one species of rat taking the place of another species under the most different climates! . . . We can dimly see why the competition should be most severe between allied forms, which fill nearly the same place in the economy of nature; but probably in no case could we precisely say why one species has been victorious over another in the great battle of life. (146)

Darwin then offers his theories as to why one species succeeds and another fails:

> Can it . . . be thought improbable, seeing that variations useful to man have undoubtedly occurred, that other variations useful in some way to each being in the great and complex battle of life, should occur in the course of many successive generations. If such do occur, can we doubt (remembering that many more individuals are born than can possibly survive) that individuals having any advantage, however slight, over others, would have the best chance of surviving and of procreating their kind? On the other

hand, we may feel sure that any variation in the least degree injurious would be rigidly destroyed. This preservation of favourable individual differences and variations, and the destruction of those which are injurious, I have called Natural Selection, or the Survival of the Fittest. Variations neither useful nor injurious would not be affected by natural selection, and would be left either a fluctuating element, as perhaps we see in certain polymorphic species, or would ultimately become fixed, owing to the nature of the organism and the nature of the conditions. (148–149)

In discussing natural selection more fully, Darwin counters the theory that cataclysmic events are necessary to cause a new species to appear:

> Nor do I believe that any great physical change, as of climate, or any unusual degree of isolation to check immigration, is necessary in order that new and unoccupied places should be left, for natural selection to fill up by improving some of the varying inhabitants. For as all the inhabitants of each country are struggling together with nicely balanced forces, extremely slight modifications in the structure or habits of one species would often give it an advantage over others; and still further modifications of the same kind would often still further increase the advantage, as long as the species continued under the same conditions of life and profited by similar means of subsistence and defence. No country can be named in which all the native inhabitants are now so perfectly adapted to each other and to the physical conditions under which they live, that none of them could be still better adapted or improved; for in all countries, the natives have been so far conquered by naturalised productions, that they have allowed some foreigners to take firm possession of the land. And as all foreigners have thus in every country beaten some of the natives, we may safely conclude that the

natives might have been modified with advantage, so as to have better resisted the intruders. (150)

Darwin also discusses the influence of geology and geography on the evolution of species, and he directly addresses many of the arguments he anticipates will be raised to counter his work. He also mentions his critics in his concluding chapter, which summarizes his thoughts on natural selection and evolution:

Although I am fully convinced of the truth of the views given in this volume under the form of an abstract, I by no means expect to convince experienced naturalists whose minds are stocked with a multitude of facts all viewed, during a long course of years, from a point of view directly opposite to mine. It is so easy to hide our ignorance under such expressions as the "plan of creation," "unity of design," &c., and to think that we give an explanation when we only re-state a fact. Any one whose disposition leads him to attach more weight to unexplained difficulties than to the explanation of a certain number of facts will certainly reject the theory. A few naturalists, endowed with much flexibility of mind, and who have already begun to doubt the immutability of species, may be influenced by this volume; but I look with confidence to the future,—to young and rising naturalists, who will be able to view both sides of the question with impartiality. Whoever is led to believe that species are mutable will do good service by conscientiously expressing his conviction; for thus only can the load of prejudice by which this subject is overwhelmed be removed. (261–262)

Darwin's work was indeed accepted by the next generation of naturalists, many of whom applied the theory of natural selection to human evolution. Darwin did not mention human development in *The Origin of Species,* but his subsequent work, *The Descent of Man,* did address the subject and consequently was even more controversial than *Origin.* (Bates and Humphrey 1957; Bowler 1996; Mayr and Mayr 1985; Ridley 1996)

See also Darwin, Charles Robert; *Descent of Man, The;* Evolution; Lamarck, Jean-Baptiste.

Ortiz, Simon J.

Simon J. Ortiz is a leading Native American poet; much of his work expresses feelings about the land. His books include *Going for the Rain* (1976), *A Good Journey* (1977), *From Sand Creek: Rising in This Heart Which Is Our America* (1981), *Fightin': New and Collected Stories* (1983), *Fight Back: For the Sake of the People, for the Sake of the Land* (1990), *After and Before the Lightning* (1994), and *Woven Stone* (1992), which is a compilation of poetry included in earlier volumes. He is also the editor of *Earth Power Coming: Short Fiction in Native American Literature* (1983) and *Speaking for the Generations: Native Writers on Writing* (1998).

Our Angry Earth

Written by Isaac Asimov and Frederik Pohl, *Our Angry Earth* (1991) discusses a range of environmental problems and suggests ways to solve them. It is typical apocalyptic environmental literature, which suggests that monumental disasters are threatening to destroy mankind. Yet Asimov states that "this book is not an opinion piece. It is a scientific survey of the situation that threatens us all—and it says what we can do to mitigate the situation. . . . It is a description of what we face and what we can do about it"; coauthor Pohl argues that "it is already too late to save our planet from harm." (Asimov and Pohl 1991, viii and ix) Pohl writes:

Too much has happened already: farms have turned into deserts, forests have been clear-cut to wasteland, lakes have been poisoned, the air is filled with harmful gases. It is even too late to save ourselves from the effects of other harmful processes, for they have already been set in motion, and will inevitably take their course. The global temperature will rise.

The ozone layer will continue to fray. Pollution will sicken or kill more and more living creatures. All those things have already gone so far that they must now inevitably get worse before they can get better. The only choice left to us is to decide how *much* worse we are willing to let things get. (ix)

Our Angry Earth has four sections: "The Background," "The Problems," "The Techno-cures," and "The Way to Go." In the first, the authors offer an overview of environmental theory and politics. For example, they discuss the Gaia hypothesis, a concept developed by English scientist James Lovelock (and named after Gaia, an ancient earth goddess). Asimov and Pohl explain:

Lovelock's insight was that life—all terrestrial life combined—was interactive and had the capacity to maintain its environment in such a way that its own continued existence was possible. If some environmental change should threaten life, life would then act to counter the change, in much the same way that a thermostat acts to keep your home comfortable when the weather changes, by turning on the furnace or the air conditioner. (15)

Asimov and Pohl say that in Lovelock's view "the entire biosphere of the planet Earth—which is to say, every last living thing that inhabits our planet, from the bacteria to the whales, the elephants, the redwood trees and you and me—could usefully be described as one single, planet-wide organism, each part of it almost as related and interdependent as the cells of our body. Lovelock felt that this super-being deserved a name of its own . . . 'Gaia.'" (14) The authors give several examples of Gaia's manifestation. For example:

Perhaps Gaia shows herself most clearly in the way she has kept Earth's temperature constant. . . . In the early days of Earth the Sun's radiation was about a fifth less than it is now. With so little warming sunlight the oceans should have frozen over, but that didn't happen. . . . The reason is that then the Earth's atmosphere contained more carbon dioxide than it does now. And there, Lovelock says, Gaia is at work. For plants came along to reduce the proportion of carbon dioxide in the air. As the Sun warmed up, the carbon dioxide, with its heat-retaining qualities, diminished—in exact step, over the millennia. Gaia worked through the plants (Lovelock suggests) to keep the world at the optimum temperature for life. (16–17)

However, Asimov and Pohl state that those who accept the Gaia hypothesis as true should not assume that environmental problems will solve themselves and that human beings will continue to thrive. They quote Lovelock as explaining that "people sometimes have the attitude that 'Gaia will look after us.' But that's wrong. If the concept means anything at all, Gaia will look after *herself.* And the best way for her to do that might well be to get rid of us." (21)

Asimov and Pohl then present information about a range of environmental threats, including global warming, acid rain, and air and water pollution. On air pollution, they state:

The deadliest poisons are invisible to us. No one yet knows how many cancers will be caused by the cloud of radioactive gases that the exploding Chernobyl nuclear power plant spewed out in the spring of 1986; estimates range into the hundreds of thousands from this single accident. Nor is there any accurate measure of how many will die as the result of poisons from the incineration of plastics and industrial wastes. Among the chemicals that are produced in this way—and that we breathe in—are the notorious PCBs and, still worse, the dioxins. These are so deadly that scientists have been unable to find a level, down to parts per *trillion* (think of it as a single drop in a large swimming pool), at which they are *not* dangerous. And even airborne lead is still a threat to the brains and bodies of young children in some places. We thought when we outlawed lead additives in gasoline that we had, at least, that problem solved. In fact, the level of lead in America's air has dropped by nine-tenths since 1970, but serious amounts remain. (87)

Asimov and Pohl offer solutions for such problems in the section entitled "The Technocures." They analyze new sources of energy, different types of fuel, and alternate methods of transportation. They also offer changes that individuals can make on a personal level. For example:

> The appliances in an average American home use so much electricity that the fossil-fuel plant that supplies them produces *five tons* of carbon dioxide a year to make them go. . . . As always, the quickest way to cut down on the pollution we cause with our household appliances is to use less energy to run them. A four-slice toaster uses more electricity than a two-stack, and if you are only toasting one or two slices at a time you are wasting most of that extra electricity. That means, of course, that you are forcing your local power plant to generate that much extra pollution. The way you use your appliances makes a big difference in how much energy they use. (224)

The idea that individuals can make a difference concerning environmental problems is continued in the last section, "The Way to Go." Asimov and Pohl discuss environmental activism and politics, demonstrating how people can become personally involved in environmentalism. They conclude with two appendices: a list of resources and organizations where readers can get further information about environmental causes, and a guide to help people set up their own environmental group. (Asimov and Pohl 1991)

See also Air Pollution; Asimov, Isaac; Environmental Activism; Environmental Apocalypse; Environmental Groups; Environmental Politics; Gaia Hypothesis; Lovelock, James; Nuclear Energy; Pohl, Frederik; Waste Management; Water Pollution.

Our National Parks

Written by naturalist John Muir, *Our National Parks* did much to publicize the national park system in America and encourage people to enjoy wilderness areas. It was published in 1916 but is made up of sketches first printed in *Atlantic Monthly* in 1901. The work contains 10 chapters, six of which discuss various aspects of Yosemite National Park. Yosemite was Muir's home for many years, and he was responsible for its addition to the national park system in 1890. In writing about its forests, he has this to say:

> The coniferous forests of the Yosemite Park, and of the Sierra in general, surpass all others of their kind in America or indeed in the world, not only in the size and beauty of the trees, but in the number of species assembled together, and the grandeur of the mountains they are growing on. Leaving the workaday lowlands, and wandering into the heart of the mountains, we find a new world, and stand beside the majestic pines and firs and sequoias silent and awe-stricken, as if in the presence of superior beings new arrived from some other star, so calm and bright and godlike they are. (Muir 1917, 108)

In addition to such descriptive passages, Muir offers highly detailed first-person narratives about his adventures in Yosemite. In discussing the park's animals, he writes:

> I was encamped in the woods about a mile back of the rim of Yosemite, beside a stream that falls into the valley by way of Indian Canyon. Nearly every day for weeks I went to the top of the North Dome to sketch; for it commands a general view of the valley, and I was anxious to draw every tree and rock and waterfall. . . . One morning in June, just as the sunbeams began to stream through

Sequoia National Park, California (National Archives)

the trees, I set out for a day's sketching on the dome; and before we had gone half a mile from camp [my dog] Carlo snuffed the air and looked cautiously ahead, . . . saying plainly enough, "There is a bear a little way ahead." I walked carefully in the indicated direction, until I approached a small flowery meadow that I was familiar with, then crawled to the foot of a tree on its margin, bearing in mind what I had been told about the shyness of bears. Looking out cautiously over the instep of the tree, I saw a big, burly cinnamon bear about thirty yards off, half erect, his paws resting on the trunk of a fir that had fallen into the meadow, his hips almost buried in grass and flowers. He was listening attentively and trying to catch the scent, showing that in some way he was aware of our approach. After examining him at leisure . . . I foolishly made a rush on him, throwing up my arms and shouting to frighten him, to see him run. He did not mind the demonstration much; only . . .

looked at me sharply as if asking, "What now? If you want to fight, I'm ready." Then I began to fear that on me would fall the work of running. But I was afraid to run, lest he should be encouraged to pursue me; therefore I held my ground. . . . Under these strained relations the interview seemed to last a long time. Finally, the bear, seeing how still I was, calmly withdrew his huge paws from the log, gave me a piercing look, as if warning me not to follow him, turned, and walked slowly up the middle of the meadow into the forest. . . . I was glad to part with him, and greatly enjoyed the vanishing view as he waded through the lilies and columbines. (191–3)

Muir discusses the other mammals of Yosemite, as well as its birds, trees, flowers, and streams. He also includes a chapter about Yellowstone National Park, and another on Sequoia and General Grant National Parks, touching on conservation and forestry management issues. For example, in discussing Sequoia National Park's giant redwood trees, he says:

> No unfavorable change of climate, so far as I can see, no disease, but only fire and the axe and the ravages of flocks and herds threaten the existence of these noblest of God's trees. In Nature's keeping they are safe, but through man's agency destruction is making rapid progress, while in the work of protection only a beginning has been made. . . . Perhaps more than half of all the Big Trees have been sold, and are now in the hands of speculators and mill men. Even the beautiful little Calaveras Grove of ninety trees, so historically interesting from its being the first discovered, is now owned, together with the much larger South or Stanislaus Grove, by a lumber company. (354–355)

In his concluding chapter, Muir discusses the destruction of forests throughout America and compares U.S. forestry practices with those in other countries throughout the world. In discussing techniques in America, he has this to say:

> The legitimate demands on the forests that have passed into private ownership, as well as those in the hands of the Government, are increasing every year with the rapid settlement and upbuilding of the country, but the methods of lumbering are as yet grossly wasteful. In most mills only the best portions of the best trees are used, while the ruins are left on the ground to feed great fires, which kill much of what is left of the less desirable timber, together with the seedlings, on which the permanence of the forest depends. Thus every mill is a center of destruction far more severe from waste and fire than from use. (379)

Muir also discusses U.S. politics and argues for better laws to protect wilderness areas. He criticizes the railroads for cutting through some of the most beautiful forests and leaving the timber to waste; he accuses the government of woefully mismanaging public lands. He concludes:

> All sorts of local laws and regulations have been tried and found wanting, and the costly lessons of our own experience, as well as that of every civilized nation, show conclusively that the fate of the remnant of our forests is in the hands of the Federal Government, and that if the remnant is to be saved at all, it must be saved quickly. Any fool can destroy trees. They cannot run away; and if they could, they would still be destroyed,—chased and hunted down as long as fun or a dollar could be got out of their bark hides, branching horns, or magnificent bole backbones. Few that fell trees plant them; nor would planting avail much towards getting back anything like the noble primeval forests. . . . Through all the wonderful, eventful centuries since Christ's time—and long before that—God has cared for these trees, saved them from drought, disease, avalanches, and a thousand straining, leveling tempests and floods, but he cannot save them from fools—only Uncle Sam [i.e., the U.S. government] can do that. (392–393)

Our National Parks was one of the first books to call public attention to the plight of American forests. By the time it was published, Muir had already done much to promote his conservation views. He established the Sierra Club, a group devoted to promoting wilderness concerns and outdoor recreation, in 1892. Consequently, his work was extremely popular, particularly because it included narratives of his adventures and information about the parks along with his discussions of conservation issues. (Gottlieb 1993; Muir 1917; Pepper 1996)

See also Animal Ecology; Conservationism; Environmental Politics; Forest Management; Muir, John; Waste Management.

Our Natural History

Environmental scientist Daniel B. Botkin's *Our Natural History: The Lessons of Lewis and Clark* (1995) presents information gathered during several research projects on environmental problems. However, it takes a unique approach, using the journals of 19th-century explorers Meriwether Lewis and William Clark to discuss the modern state of the American environment. Botkin explains that he decided "to explore our real wilderness heritage as reported by Lewis and Clark, and to revisit that wilderness and see how it had changed." (Botkin xvii) His book thus "describes the wilderness of the American West as seen by Lewis and Clark during their journey of 1804–1806, and compares it to today's American West as shaped by industrial civilization." (xvii) Botkin quotes liberally from the explorers' journals to describe their wilderness and uses these quotes to embark on lengthy discussions of modern environmentalism. For example, after discussing Lewis and Clark's wolf sightings, Botkin looks at today's wolf conservation efforts and explains why they are important:

> To understand what might be an essential ecological role of a species, we have to look at a broader picture, at the biological diversity of the Earth as a whole. About a million and a half species have been named, and speculations as to the total number vary from three to thirty million and beyond. Is it necessary to have all these species if life is to continue on the Earth? . . . I am reminded about all the parts in the small, single engine airplanes that I have flown. Think just about the instruments in the cockpit. Are all of them necessary? . . . The answer depends on one's point of view about redundancy. . . . Even with something as carefully designed and purposefully designed as an airplane, there is some ambiguity about how much redundancy of function is necessary. . . . In an airplane . . . there are necessary and in-use parts, and redundant parts—spare parts

that are on-line or off-line. There are also accessories that make flying more pleasant, such as well-designed earphones and microphones for hands-off radio communication, rather than a hand-held microphone and a loudspeaker; there is a heater and sometimes an air conditioner. Some would argue that these are not merely conveniences, but necessities for the safest kinds of flight. (148–151)

Botkin continues his comparison of the earth to an airplane when he adds:

> If determining what is necessary and what is merely convenient is this difficult for a small airplane with perhaps a few hundred to a few thousand parts, then what can we say about life on the Earth? At least people have made airplanes and they have specific purposes, so we know both the design and the purpose. Ecological justifications for the conservation of species seem to require that all species are necessary in one of the ways I have described for an airplane—either on-line and in use or as redundant, back-up equipment for safety—in the case of life on the Earth, the safety is in terms of the persistence of life within some specific area, or all life on the Earth. . . . But since we don't know the function of every species, it would be foolish to throw away something that might be an essential part just because we didn't know what it does. (148–151)

In addition to such discussions, Botkin also provides information about environmental history and mentions the work of noted conservationists and environmentalists, such as Aldo Leopold. He concludes with a chapter bemoaning the loss of America's native wilderness lands, particularly prairies that have succumbed to modern development. On this point, he says this: "Our alterations of the prairie leave us without large stretches of prairie land . . . so that we no longer have direct contact, a direct feel for these aspects of our environment." He adds:

We tend to think that solutions to environmental problems are simply a matter of an accumulation of facts, simply a technical inquiry; we leave it to laboratory technicians to tell us what river is polluted or what species is disappearing. But in my work attempting to help solve environmental issues, I had become convinced that the way that we deal with our environment has a lot to do with our cultural heritage and our myths about nature. As we become an increasingly urbanized and suburbanized people, more and more of us lose our direct contact with the land. As we remove the remnants of our natural environment, we lose contact with an important part of our heritage. We try to solve environmental problems from myths that seem to make sense from both the farmhouse and the apartment house. It is as if we were trying to navigate the prairie ocean without knowing where we had started, without a compass, or a path. (270)

Botkin points out that Lewis and Clark "searched for and found nature, observing it as it was, describing it with great accuracy and detail, seeing its beauty, experiencing its dangers, knowing its changeableness"; he suggests that modern people acquire the same "knowledge of nature" in order to solve the environmental problems of the world. (271) (Botkin 1995)

See also Botkin, Daniel; Conservationism; Environmental History; Leopold, Aldo.

Our Plundered Planet

Published in 1948, *Our Plundered Planet* typifies the earliest apocalyptic environmental literature, in which human beings are seen as destroyers of the natural world. Author Fairfield Osborn explains why he decided to write the book during the latter part of World War II:

It seemed to me, during those days, that mankind was involved in *two* major conflicts—not only in the one that was in every headline, on every radio, in the minds, in the hearts and in the sufferings of people the world over. The other war, the silent war, eventually the most deadly war, was one in which man has indulged for a long time, blindly and unknowingly. This other world-wide war, still continuing, is bringing more widespread distress to the human race than any that has resulted from armed conflict. It contains potentialities of ultimate disaster greater even than would follow the misuse of atomic power. This other war is man's conflict with nature. (Osborn vii)

Our Plundered Planet is divided into two parts, "The Planet" and "The Plunderer." In "The Planet," Osborn discusses evolution in terms of man's relationship to his environment. He explains that humans, who once had many characteristics that enabled them to survive and be content in any environment, had evolved into creatures with "mind-restlessness" that need and cause constant change. Accordingly:

In this metamorphosis [man] has almost lost sight of the fact that the living resources of his life are derived from his earth-home and not from his mind-power. With one hand he harnesses great waters, with the other he dries up the water sources. He must change with changing conditions or perish. He *conquers* a continent and within a century lays much of it into barren waste. He must move to find a new and unspoiled land . . . but where? His numbers are increasing, starvation taunts him—even after his wars too many are left alive. He causes the life-giving soils for his crops to wash into the oceans. He falls back on palliatives and calls upon a host of chemists to invent substitutes for the organized process of nature. Can they do this? . . . He hopes so. Hope turns to conviction—they *must*, or else he perishes. (Osborn 30–31)

Osborn warns of the dire consequences of overpopulation, suggesting that people will soon run out of inhabitable land. He adds that a "very large proportion of the originally habitable areas have already been so misused by man that they have lost their productive capacity. . . . [They] have been robbed of so much of their value that they are barely worth cultivation; the products from these lands possess little energy content; the people are undernourished." (36–37) He views soil erosion due to poor agricultural and land management practices as the greatest danger to mankind.

Osborn believes that scientists will be unable to remedy this problem, whether through the use of fertilizers or other means; he also predicts eventual doom if the earth is not treated with more care. In fact in the second part of *Our Plundered Planet,* he offers examples of environmental destruction throughout history and shows their dire consequences for civilizations and regions. For instance, he suggests that "the old Mayan Empire came to its end principally because its people employed faulty systems of agriculture and denuded their land of its forests" (168). In discussing modern Greece, he states:

> Originally at least 60 percent of the country was covered by fine forests. Now little more than 5 percent is so covered. Centuries of cutting and burning and overgrazing by sheep and goats have brought desolation to the hillsides. . . . Practically all wood needed for shipbuilding and building materials, and even charcoal, is imported, a situation that has prevailed for several centuries. A recent observer of the land situation in Greece reports . . . that during all his travels through the mountain section of the country he saw only two pair of partridges and one rabbit—all the natural wildlife having been killed off. He was struck by the complete absence of bird life. (104–105)

Such gloomy portraits permeate the remainder of the book. Moreover, although in his conclusion Osborn states that "there are real grounds for hope" because "within the last decade more has been accomplished than in all the previous years of our history" to improve the environmental health of the earth (196), he calls upon the U.S. government to pay more attention to conservation issues. He adds that other countries should do so as well and concludes: "Man must recognize the necessity of cooperating with nature. He must temper his demands and use and conserve the natural living resources of this earth in a manner that alone can provide for the continuation of civilization." (201)

In short, Osborn believes that civilization will end if environmental problems are left unsolved. His book was one of the first to take this tone, foreshadowing the doomsday predictions that proliferated during the American environmental movement of the 1960s and 1970s. (Osborn 1948)

See also Agriculture; Environmental Apocalypse; Environmental History; Environmental Movement; Evolution; Wildlife Conservation.

Our Synthetic Environment

Our Synthetic Environment was the first major work of noted social ecologist Murray Bookchin. Published in 1962, it warns of the dangers of pesticide use, but its popularity was eclipsed by Rachel Carson's *Silent Spring,* a book on the same subject published the same year. Nonetheless, historians often refer to Bookchin as one of the founders of the modern environmental movement, particularly as it relates to public health issues and radical activism.

Our Synthetic Environment contains a survey of health problems that became prevalent after World War II, contending they were caused by the overuse of chemicals, as well as nuclear weapons, pollution, and other synthetic dangers. In addition, Bookchin complains that society has allowed technology and economic concerns to become more important than human health, "to bring the laws of the biosphere into accordance with those of the marketplace," as evidenced by the proliferation of industrial facilities that create harmful pollution and waste products. (Bookchin 1994, p. 217)

Bookchin urges society to develop "technologies according to ecologically sound

Karen Blixen (Meryl Streep) assumes responsibility for running the coffee plantation in the film Out of Africa *(Photofest)*

principles . . . based on nonpolluting energy sources such as solar and wind power, methane generators, and possibly liquid hydrogen that will harmonize the world." (Bookchin lvii) He adds that "there can be no sound environment without a sound, ecologically oriented social environment" and suggests that society be restructured to replace large cities with smaller, economically independent, environmentally friendly cooperatives. (xix) Bookchin followed up the topic of social restructuring in later works, including *The Ecology of Freedom* (1982). (Bookchin 1994)

> See also Bookchin, Murray; Environmental Activism; Nuclear Energy; Waste Management.

Out of Africa

Published in 1937 as *Den Afrikanske farm,* *Out of Africa* by Isak Dinesen describes the author's life on an African farm. It also recounts her struggle to save the farm from bankruptcy, an effort that eventually fails. In 1914 Dinesen (the pseudonym of Karen Blixen) went to Africa to marry Baron von Blixen, a hunter

who owned a 6,000-acre coffee plantation. Her husband often left her alone to deal with the workers and make decisions regarding the harvest. In 1921 the couple divorced. Dinesen continued to own and manage the plantation until 1931, when drought and financial difficulties forced her to sell the place and return to her native Denmark.

In discussing the book, Matthias Schubnell compares it to the work of N. Scott Momaday, a Native American novelist who once called *Out of Africa* "one of the great books of our time." (Schubnell 1985, 70) Schubnell says:

> Dinesen and Momaday both believe that man is ultimately a manifestation of the soil. Dinesen declares that "the Natives were Africa in flesh and blood. . . . We ourselves, in boots, and in our constant hurry, often jar with the landscape. The Natives are in accordance with it." She sees both the native people and the animals as "weighty with such impressions of the world around them as have been slowly gathered and heaped up in their

dim minds; they are themselves features of the land." She describes geographical formations, plants, trees, and the indigenous people as "different expressions of one idea, variations upon the same theme." . . .Momaday, too, sees man and land as inseparable. . . . Momaday and Dinesen also share the belief that the unity between a landscape and its inhabitants prevails beyond death, when the land receives man and makes him part of itself. Dinesen's description of the burial of her friend Denys in the hills of Kenya and Momaday's story of the unmarked grave of an Indian woman are expressions of their mindfulness of the presence of the dead in the soil. (71–72)

See also Dinesen, Isak.

Outermost House, The

Published in 1928, *The Outermost House* by poet-philosopher Henry Beston (1888–1968) describes the author's experiences during a year living on the Great Beach at Cape Cod, Massachusetts. Beston not only expresses his appreciation for his surroundings but also discusses the nature of solitude, which he suggests is a human need. For example: "The world to-day is sick to its thin blood for lack of elemental things, for fire before the hands, for water welling from the earth, for air, for the dear earth itself underfoot." (Lyon 1989, 82)

Beston himself found his isolation restorative. He concludes his work by saying that "whatever attitude to human existence you fashion for yourself, know that it is valid only if it be the shadow of an attitude to Nature. . . . Do no dishonour to the earth lest you dishonour the spirit of man. . . . Touch the earth, love the earth, honour the earth, her plains, her valleys, her hills, and her seas; rest your spirit in her solitary places." (Lyon 83)

Professor Thomas Lyon, in discussing the "literature of solitude" in his own book, *This Incomperable Lande,* argues that Beston's work was the last significant book published in the genre in the United States until Edward Abbey's *Desert Solitaire* in 1968. Lyon calls *The Outermost House* a "talismanic book of solitude in American nature." (Lyon 83) Because of the significance of Beston's work, the cottage in which he lived while writing *The Outermost House* was declared a National Literary Landmark in 1964. It was destroyed by a storm in 1978. (Lyon 1989)

See also Abbey, Edward; *Desert Solitaire.*

Overpopulation
See Human Ecology.

P

Panda's Thumb, The

The Panda's Thumb: More Reflections in Natural History is a collection of essays by paleontologist Stephen Jay Gould expressing his theories on evolution. Published in 1980, it is a sequel to his 1977 book, *Ever Since Darwin.* As such, it discusses various evolutionary principles and examines the work of Charles Darwin. It also discusses the writings of Jean Baptiste Lamarck, Louis Agassiz, and other scientists in the field of evolution. (Gould 1980)

> **See also** Agassiz, (Jean) Louis (Rodolphe); Darwin, Charles Robert; Evolution; Gould, Stephen Jay; Lamarck, Jean-Baptiste.

Pandell, Karen

Born in 1950, Karen Pandell has won numerous awards for her children's books, which promote environmentalism. Her works include *Animal Tracks of the Pacific Northwest* (1981), *Land of Dark, Land of Light: The Arctic National Wildlife Refuge* (1993), and *I Love You Sun, I Love You Moon* (1994). Pandell has won numerous awards from librarians, teachers, and environmentalists. She is particularly concerned about biodiversity and the protection of wilderness areas.

Path Where No Man Thought, A

A Path Where No Man Thought: Nuclear Winter and the Ends of the Arms Race (1990) by noted scientist Carl Sagan discusses the effect of nuclear explosions on the environment. Sagan, a professor of astronomy and space sciences, cowrote the book with Richard Turco, a professor of atmospheric sciences. Both authors had been honored during the early 1980s for developing the theory of nuclear winter, and their book consequently carried a lot of weight with the public when it was published.

A Path Where No Man Thought defines and discusses nuclear winter. According to its authors:

> It describes what determines the global climate of the Earth, and how nuclear war could change that climate; what the long-term consequences of nuclear war would be like, for individuals and societies; and how nuclear winter can help chart a path to take us from the present obscenely bloated nuclear arsenals into a world which, if not wholly freed from the scourge of nuclear war, at least is far safer than our present world—which is a world made in almost total ignorance of the most serious consequences of actually using the

weapons that, at great cost, we have painstakingly accumulated in order to keep us "secure." (Sagan and Turco 1990, 6–7)

Sagan and Turco explain how a nuclear war would send dust and smoke into the atmosphere:

The high-altitude dust particles reflect additional sunlight back to space and cool the Earth a little. More important are the dense palls of black smoke high in the atmosphere; they block the sunlight from reaching the lower atmosphere, where the greenhouse gases mainly reside. These gases are thereby deprived of their leverage on the global climate. The greenhouse effect is turned down and the Earth's surface is cooled much more. (23–24)

Sagan and Turco discuss alternative weapons strategies and offer suggestions for reducing the number of nuclear weapons—even eliminating them altogether. They also provide color photographs of nuclear explosions and their aftermath, as well as computer models of the effects of nuclear war on Earth. In addition, *A Path Where No Man Thought* offers detailed notes and references; almost half of the book is supporting material. (Sagan and Turco 1990)

See also Climate Changes; Nuclear Energy; Sagan, Carl.

Peacock, Doug

Cinematographer Doug Peacock is the chairman of Round River Conservation Studies, an environmental organization. He has written several nature books, including *Grizzly Years: In Search of the American Wilderness* (1990) and *Baja!* (1991). Peacock is an expert on grizzly bears and advocates their natural restoration to wilderness areas, as opposed to reintroducing grizzlies from a popluated area into an unpopulated one.

Perrault, Pierre

Born in Paris, France, circa 1611, Pierre Perrault is considered one of the founders of the science of hydrology. Through careful study, he determined that precipitation is sufficient to maintain a river's flow. His most important work on this subject is *On the Origin of Springs and Rivers,* which was first published anonymously in 1674. Despite his scientific achievements, Perrault made his living as a lawyer and, subsequently, as a government administrator. He died in Paris in 1680. (Boynton 1948)

See also *On the Origin of Springs and Rivers.*

Pesticides and Chemicals

Pesticides are substances that poison organisms. The three most common types are insecticides, which kill insects, herbicides, which kill weeds, and fungicides, which kill fungi. Farmers use pesticides to protect their crops; homeowners use them to protect their lawns. However, as crops and lawns are watered, some pesticides drain into nearby water sources. Others eventually work down into the soil, affecting the groundwater beneath. In either case, pesticides can contaminate drinking water and threaten human health. Pesticides can also leave a residue on food, which some scientists believe is harmful.

One of the first people to raise public awareness of the dangers of pesticide use, Rachel Carson, thanks to her 1962 book, *Silent Spring,* is often credited with inspiring the American environmental movement. But Carson was not the first to write about the problem. Murray Bookchin discussed health risks posed by pesticides in a 1952 article, "The Problem of Chemicals in Food," as well as in his 1962 book, *Our Synthetic Environment.*

And in 1925 Dr. Alice Hamilton exposed the occupational hazards related to industrial chemicals in *Industrial Poisons in the United States.* Industrial chemicals, which are used to manufacture products or are by-products of the manufacturing process, can threaten the health of factory workers and cause air and water pollution. Hamilton was the first to address the issue of worker health in regard to chemical use and is considered to be a pioneer in the field of human ecology.

Discarded pesticide cans in rural California, 1972 (National Archives)

More recently, Wendell Berry, Paul and Anne Ehrlich, and many other authors have considered the dangers of pesticide and chemical use while examining agricultural practices and their impacts on land and water. Critics of environmentalism, such as Michael Fumento, have also discussed pesticides and chemicals, as there are several cases where environmentalists misidentified the potential harm. The most notorious example involved the use of Alar, a chemical sprayed on apples to alter growing time and to improve appearance. After an environmental group incorrectly reported that Alar posed a serious, immediate risk to human health, consumers stopped buying apples, and the industry suffered severe economic loss. Fumento reports on this event in his 1993 book, *Science Under Siege*. More recently, however, the dangers of pesticide use have not received as much public attention as other aspects of environmentalism such as species loss.

See also Agriculture; Berry, Wendell; Bookchin, Murray; Carson, Rachel Louise; Ehrlich, Paul and Anne; Environmental Groups; Fumento, Michael; Hamilton, Alice; Human Ecology; *Industrial Poisons in the United States; Our Synthetic Environment; Science Under Siege; Silent Spring.*

Philosophie Zoologique

Philosophie zoologique (Zoological Philosophy) by Jean-Baptiste Lamarck was first published in 1809 to express the author's view on how animals adapt to their environments. Lamarck believed that an animal's muscles and organs could be physically altered by overuse and underuse. For example, a giraffe's legs and neck could be made longer and stronger by repeatedly reaching to grab leaves atop taller trees. Moreover, Lamarck thought that use-related physical changes could be passed along genetically to the next generation. These two suppositions formed the basis of Lamarckism, a theory that would later be in direct opposition to Darwin's theory of evolution.

When Darwin's *The Origin of Species* was published in 1859, many opponents of evolutionary theory disputed it—primarily with Lamarckism. It remained a viable theory until the 1930s, when the science of genetics advanced enough to disprove it. However, Peter J. Bowler, in *The Environmental Sciences,* points out that Lamarck's work was seriously flawed, even given the constraints of 18th- and 19th-century science. He explains:

> The evidence he presented was unsatisfactory because it never occurred to him that another process (natural selection) might produce similar results. More important, he did not link his concept of progress to the evidence that was now beginning to emerge from the fossil record. Lamarck was convinced that Nature would allow no species to become extinct, and interpreted the supposedly extinct fossils as evidence that old species have changed into something quite different in the modern world. There was also no attempt to explore the geographical dimension of evolution. Lamarck was a museum naturalist, not a traveler, and his concept of adaptation was devised from theoretical principles, not from a close observation of how animals and plants actually survive in the world. (Bowler 191–192)

Nonetheless, Bowler credits Lamarck for helping to advance "the idea of evolution as a means of challenging the traditional image of a static world designed by God." (191) The concept that species can change would be important to later work on evolutionary theory. (Bowler 1993; Lamarck 1984)

See also Darwin, Charles Robert; Evolution; Lamarck, Jean-Baptiste.

Physical Geography of the Sea

Published in 1855, *Physical Geography of the Sea* by Matthew Maury offered the first detailed information on ocean floors; it also identified Maury's methods for obtaining that information. He developed a way to determine ocean depths by using sound echoes, and he was able to create accurate maps based on his work. However, *Physical Geography of the Sea* did not address scientific principles exclusively. According to Peter J. Bowler in *The Environmental Sciences,* Maury's work "was based on the assumption that the earth had been designed for the benefit of humankind by a wise and benevolent God." (Bowler 210) (Bowler 1993)

See also Geological Research; Maury, Matthew Fontaine.

Pilgrim at Tinker Creek

Pilgrim at Tinker Creek by Annie Dillard is one of the most famous works of modern American nature writing. Published in 1974, it is her first-person account of observations and experiences while exploring nature around Tinker Creek in Virginia's Blue Ridge Mountains. It also discusses her relationship to the land and, by extension, the relationship of humankind to the land. For example, Dillard talks about losing oneself in the wilderness:

> *Self*-consciousness . . . does hinder the experience of the present. It is the one instrument that unplugs all the rest. So long as I lose myself in a tree, say, I can scent its leafy breath or estimate its board feet of lumber, I can draw its fruits or boil tea on its branches, and the tree stays tree. But the second I become aware of myself at any of these activities—looking over my own shoulder, as it were—the tree vanishes, uprooted from the spot and flung out of sight as if it had never grown. And time, which had flowed down into the tree bearing new revelations like the floating leaves at every moment, ceases. It dams, stills, stagnates. Self-consciousness is the curse of the city and all that sophistication implies. It is the glimpse of oneself in a storefront window, the unbidden awareness of reactions on the facets of other people— the novelist's world, not the poet's. I've lived there. I remember what the city has to offer: human companionship, major-league baseball, and a clatter of quickening stimulus like a rush from strong drugs that leaves you drained. I remember how you bide your time in the city, and think, if

you stop to think, "next year . . . I'll start living; next year . . . I'll start my life. . . ." If you wish to tell me that the city offers galleries, I'll pour you a drink and enjoy your company while it lasts; but I'll bear with me to my grave those pure moments . . . where I stood planted, open-mouthed, born, before . . . [a] river, up to my neck, gasping, lost, receding into a watercolor depth and depth to the vanishing point, buoyant, awed, and had to be literally hauled away. These are our few live seasons. Let us live them as purely as we can, in the present. (Dillard 1974, 81–82)

Dillard relates her nature experiences during all four seasons of the year, describing in poetic detail her activities, her surroundings, and the animals she encounters. She also provides scientific and historical information related to her subjects. For example, in discussing the muskrat, she says:

Someday, I had been telling myself for weeks, someday a muskrat is going to swim right through that channel in the cattails, and I am going to see it. That is precisely what happened. I looked up into the channel for a muskrat, and there it came, swimming right toward me. Knock; seek; ask. It seemed to swim with a side-to-side, sculling motion of its vertically flattened tail. . . .

   Muskrats are the bread and butter of the carnivorous food chain. They are like rabbits and mice: if you are big enough to eat mammals, you eat them. Hawks and owls prey on them, and foxes; so do otters. . . . Men kill them, too. One Eskimo who hunted muskrats for a few weeks each year strictly as a sideline says that in fourteen years he killed 30,739 muskrats. The pelts sell, and the price is rising. Muskrats are the most important fur animal on the North American continent. . . . Keeping ahead of all this slaughter, a female might have as many as five litters a year, and each litter contains six or seven or more muskrats. (192–193)

In addition to such descriptive exposition, *Pilgrim at Tinker Creek* includes expressions of Dillard's spirituality, which is perhaps why she calls herself a pilgrim. She speaks of "catching God's eye with the easy motions of praise" (259) and the prayerfulness inspired by nature. In her concluding chapter, she says this:

Divinity is not playful. The universe was not made in jest but in solemn incomprehensible earnest. By a power that is unfathomably secret, and holy, and fleet. There is nothing to be done about it, but ignore it, or see. And then you walk fearlessly, eating what you must, growing wherever you can, like the monk on the road who knows precisely how vulnerable he is, who takes no comfort among death-forgetting men, and who carries his vision of vastness and might around in his tunic like a live coal which neither burns nor warms him, but with which he will not part. (270)

Dillard explores many aspects of nature: its history, its science, its appearance, its deeper meanings to humankind. In this respect, her work is similar to most modern nature writing, combining introspective comments with descriptive details and facts. (Dillard 1974)

   See also Dillard, Annie; Nature Writing.

Pinchot, Gifford

Born on August 11, 1865, in Simburg, Connecticut, Gifford Pinchot was a politician and conservationist who encouraged the preservation of wilderness areas. He wrote two influential books on forestry management, *Primer of Forestry* (1899) and *The Training of a Forester* (1917), as well as books and articles on conservation.

   Pinchot first studied forestry in France, Austria, and Switzerland, where he traveled after graduating from Yale University in 1889. After he returned to the United States in 1892, he conducted the country's first systematic forestry study. He decided that American forests were not being managed well by the Department of Interior, which was responsi-

Gifford Pinchot, 1943 (Archive Photos)

ble for the resources of publicly held wilderness areas. He convinced the government to place all forest lands under the control of the Department of Agriculture, thereby creating the U.S. Forest Service.

Pinchot served as chief of the Forest Service from 1898 to 1910 and was the chief adviser to President Theodore Roosevelt on conservation issues. In this capacity he was receptive to conservationist John Muir's arguments in favor of establishing more government-protected wilderness areas and worked toward creating more national parks. In addition, in 1903 Pinchot founded the School of Forestry at Yale, which was attended by such notable conservationists as Aldo Leopold. In 1908 Pinchot became chair of the National Conservation Commission; he served as governor of Pennsylvania from 1923 to 1927 and again from 1931 to 1935. He died on October 4, 1946, in New York City. (Cox 1971)

See also Conservationism; *Fight for Conservation, The;* Forest Management; Leopold, Aldo.

Planet of the Apes

Published in 1963, the science fiction novel *Planet of the Apes* by Pierre Boulle contains a plot based on evolutionary theory. It is representative of fiction from the early environmental movement, in that it suggests humanity is destroying itself.

The novel's first-person narrator, a French journalist named Ulysse Merou, travels to the planet Soror from earth in the year 2500 and finds it inhabited by unintelligent, mute humans and intelligent, speaking primates. Captured and taken to a research laboratory, Merou is frustrated when his guards do not understand his language. They believe that he has been taught to mimic speech as some ape's pet. However, one of the scientists, a female chimpanzee named Zira, suspects that Merou might have some form of intelligence.

Eventually Zira learns Merou's language and he learns hers. Together they discuss his journey from earth and the differences between earth and Soror. Zira introduces Merou to her fiancé, Cornelius, who arranges for the man to appear at a scientific gathering. There he delivers a speech about his journey from earth and the wonders of technology he can show them; the apes decide to release Merou to work with Cornelius.

Shortly thereafter Merou and Cornelius find archeological evidence that an advanced human culture existed on the planet more than 10,000 years before. Cornelius manipulates human brains to extract collective memories of the race and discovers that humans were once masters over apes. Gradually the apes learned to mimic their oppressors and took over the planet, whereas the humans descended into a primitive state.

Cornelius's discoveries about ape evolution are revolutionary, and he is afraid to reveal them to his superiors. At the same time, the government has decided that Merou is a threat to the apes' way of life. Merou has produced a child with a woman named Nova, and the boy has demonstrated intelligence and an ability for speech. Fearing that the family could create a new race of clever humans, government officials plot to kill Merou

Charlton Heston as an astronaut-turned-slave in Planet of the Apes *(Archive Photos)*

and Nova and imprison their baby in a research institution.

Before this can happen, however, Zira and Cornelius switch the family with three humans who are to be sent into space on an experimental satellite. Merou then pilots the satellite to his spaceship and takes off for earth. When he arrives there, he discovers that gorillas are running the airport. He takes off again, planning to find a safe planet somewhere. Meanwhile, he places his story in a sealed bottle and jettisons it into space.

The main plot of *Planet of the Apes* is framed by the discovery of the bottle by a young couple, Phyllis and Jinn, who are taking a holiday in space. They are not from earth, but Jinn attended school there in the past and so can read the manuscript. At the end of the novel, they express disbelief over Merou's story—and the reader learns they are chimpanzees!

Planet of the Apes blames the deterioration of the human race on its loss of interest in mental pursuits. In the section describing the collective memory of the race, Merou quotes one woman as saying: "What is happening could have been foreseen. A cerebral laziness has taken hold of us. No more books; even detective novels have now become too great an intellectual effort. No more games; at the most a hand or two of cards. Even the childish motion picture does not tempt us any more. Meanwhile the apes are meditating in silence. Their brain is developing in solitary reflection." (116)

In discussing this mental laziness, Merou criticizes humans for writing too many books that merely repeat the same ideas over and over. The orangutans in Soror's ape society are also prolific authors, writing countless derivative works, and they are rigid, unreasonable thinkers. Nonetheless, they are given control of the scientific community, even though the chimpanzees make most of the scientific and technical discoveries. Meanwhile, the gorillas are masters at exploiting those discoveries and making them profitable. In this way, each type of ape fulfills a designated role in society, exhibiting racism toward those unlike themselves.

By showing the flaws in its fictional ape society, *Planet of the Apes* is actually criticizing real-life human society. However, many aspects of this criticism were missing from a movie version of the novel, released in 1968. The movie attributed humanity's downfall not to a loss of intellectualism but to nuclear war. The film is set entirely on earth, although that fact is not revealed until the end of the story. (Boulle 1963; Becker 1996)

See also Boulle, Pierre; Environmental Apocalypse; Environmental Fiction; Evolution; Nuclear Energy.

Plato

An ancient Greek philosopher, Plato wrote on a range of topics, including nature, the environment, and the origin of the universe. For example, in his work *Timaeus,* Plato attempts to describe earth's physical laws; in its unfinished sequel, *Critias,* he discusses how deforestation has led to soil erosion on Greek hillsides:

What now remains compared with what then existed is like the skeleton of a sick man, all the fat and soft earth having wasted away, and only the bare framework of the land being left. . . . There are some mountains which now have nothing but food for bees, but they had trees not long ago. . . . There were many lofty trees of cultivated species and . . . boundless pasturage for flocks. Moreover, it was enriched by the yearly rains from Zeus, which were not lost to it, as now, by flowing from the bare land into the sea; but the soil it had was deep, and therein it received the water, storing it up in the retentive loamy soil, and . . . provided all the various districts with abundant supplies of springwaters and streams, whereof the shrines still remain even now, at the spots where the fountains formerly existed. (Ponting 1991, 76–77)

Born in Athens, Greece, circa 428 B.C., Plato came from a prominent family and might have been destined for a political career. However, he became disenchanted with the Greek government after it condemned the philosopher Socrates to death for corrupting young minds. Socrates was a mentor to Plato, who followed many of his teachings; after his mentor's death Plato left the country. His subsequent travels are undocumented until 388 B.C., when he arrived in Sicily and befriended the ruler of Syracuse, Dionysius I.

In 387 B.C. Plato returned to Athens and founded a research and educational center for people interested in philosophy, law, mathematics, and science. Called the Academy, it was the forerunner of the modern university and consequently a place where issues related to the environment could be discussed. Plato remained at the Academy for the rest of his life, although on two occasions he returned to Syracuse to try to educate Dionysius II, the successor of the first Dionysius. Both attempts ended in failure.

Nonetheless, Plato was considered one of the best teachers of his time, and for ages after his death (ca. 347 B.C.) his published writings influenced human thought. Most of his 36 works (Plato's letters are typically deemed to be a single work) were dramatic dialogues, so named because of their conversational style. Scholars typically divide these dialogues into three categories: early, middle, and late. Plato's early dialogues were written before he founded the Academy and primarily concern the life and teachings of Socrates. Plato's middle dialogues, written during the early years of the Academy, discuss such topics as justice, politics, reason, and virtue. His late dialogues, written after he failed in his attempts to teach Dionysius II, address issues like theology, cosmology, and natural laws and therefore are the most significant in terms of the environmental sciences. *Timaeus* and its unfinished sequel *Critias* are late dialogues. (Ponting 1991)

See also Aristotle; *Timaeus.*

Playing God in Yellowstone

Playing God in Yellowstone: The Destruction of America's First National Park (1986), by Alston Chase, is highly critical of the way in which environmentalists address wilderness issues; it also makes the case that the National Park Service has mismanaged Yellowstone National Park. When it was published in 1986, the book created a controversy regarding proper management of federal lands. Its author, Alston Chase, is the former chair of the Yellowstone Library and Museum Association, which publishes books on the park and sponsors the Yellowstone Institute, an educational program.

Chase divides *Playing God in Yellowstone* into four sections: "The Range," "The Wildlife," "The Rangers," and "The Environmentalists." In the first section, he traces the development of park policy and explains that early conservationists used to kill animals to control overpopulation, whereas the American environmental movement of the 1960s and 1970s made such activities unpopular. He says:

> The environmental awakening . . . made the public less tolerant of the policy of direct reductions. . . . For [environmentalists] Rachel Carson, Paul Ehrlich, Barry Commoner, and others taught that nature's problems were caused by humanity. The way we lived, grew food, drank water, dumped sewage, built houses, drove cars was destroying the earth. And the silent victims of our greed and waste were the dumb and innocent animals of the world. (Chase 1987, 43–44)

As a result of this philosophy, the National Park Service adopted a hands-off policy toward park management and stopped thinning overpopulated elk herds. This led to overgrazing, which reduced food supplies not just for the elk but for other animals in the park. Consequently, some species became endangered, and soil erosion threatened many regions in Yellowstone. Compounding this problem was the fact that elk were not allowed to migrate outside the park boundaries, as they had during primitive times.

Therefore, Chase argues, the Park Service was wrong to assume that Yellowstone could be "self-regulating." He points out that primitive people had always kept elk populations in check through hunting:

> The policy of natural regulation was born in the heat of enthusiasm for the new environmental awareness, . . . an ecology that had no place for humanity. Yellowstone biologists conceived a theory that sustained this view: Primitive people may have been predators . . . but predation had no significance in the ecosystem. . . .If primitive people had no biological significance in the ecosystem, then pristine conditions could be defined without them. If the park were in original condition, if man had never counted in the ecosystem, then the way to preserve the park would be to keep man and nature apart. In so defining their mission, park scientists were, of course, ignoring volumes of evidence about the Indian's past, but this evidence was historical and archaeological, and the scientists—all biologists—were not trained to understand it. (113–114)

Chase calls this approach to wilderness preservation "bad ecology," and in "The Wildlife" section of his book he explains how it also harmed the wolf and the bear. During the 1920s and 1930s, park rangers systematically trapped and killed animal predators, and wolves became extinct in Yellowstone. However, according to Chase, "the Park Service . . . was reluctant to admit that this natural treasure had been lost. Rather, they argued, wolves continued to live in the park in small numbers." (136) When some scientists suggested that wolves from elsewhere be trapped and reintroduced into Yellowstone, park officials said this was unnecessary. Chase explains: "Never having admitted that it had destroyed these animals, the Park Service could not say loudly that they must return. . . . Touting the ecosystem as essentially intact and claiming that predators had no essential part in it, the Service saw no emergency in their absence." (140–141)

Buffalo crossing the road, Yellowstone National Park, 1962 (National Archives)

Chase believes that the Park Service similarly mismanaged the bear population. He reports that since the late 1880s bears in Yellowstone had been allowed to feed on park garbage. As a result their population increased, along with human-bear interactions. When people began to be injured by bears, rangers decided to close the garbage dumps. Chase says:

> Government scientists believed . . . that the bear problem had been the result of failure to manage the park according to good ecological principles. To manage the bears scientifically required weaning them of garbage so that, rather than concentrating around the dumps and campgrounds, they would disperse throughout the park, and rather than continuing to grow to artificially high numbers the population would drop to the "natural carrying capac-

ity" of the range. Thus the ecosystems approach, by thinning out the bears, would cure the park manager's headache. The bear problem would disappear, naturally. (149)

However, Chase reports that after the garbage dumps were closed many bears starved to death. Others raided campers' supplies in an attempt to find food, sometimes injuring or even killing campers. Park rangers responded to this situation by trapping, tagging, and relocating to deep wilderness any bear seen near a campground. Relocated bears that returned to a campsite were destroyed, as were other animals that caused a problem. In fact Chase says:

> Since the Park Service had assumed authority in 1916, not a year had passed that officials did not kill an animal in Yellow-

stone. Wolf, cougar, lynx, bobcat, wolverine, fox, martin, fisher, pelican, coyote, elk, bison, antelope, beaver, ground squirrel, mole, rat, mouse—and now black and grizzly bear—had, at one time or another, fallen victim to a program of removal. And each had been dispatched in the name of an environmental ideal. (193)

Therefore, Chase asks: "How could environmentalism, the movement of Thoreau, Muir, Aldo Leopold, and Rachel Carson, dedicated to the highest ideals of wildlife preservation, remain silent as it witnessed the slow decay of our natural heritage? How could any group dedicated to conservation actually become an unwitting partner with the government in promoting practices that were bringing about this decline?" (194)

Chase explores possible answers to these questions in the last two sections of his book. In "The Rangers" he discusses the politics of tourism and states that the Park Service has spent more money on tourist-related projects than on scientific research. In "The Environmentalists," he examines environmental thinking in America and suggests that environmentalism has become more a religion than a science; therefore, environmentalists make decisions based on ideology rather than scientific data. He criticizes this ideology, saying it undermined efforts to create a true science of ecology; he concludes that "if Yellowstone dies its epitaph will be: 'Victim of an Environmental Ideal.'" (375)

In the second edition of *Playing God in Yellowstone,* published in 1987, Chase added an epilogue that compared Yellowstone's problems to those in other national parks. He talks about new efforts to improve wildlife management and offers his own suggestions in this regard. Specifically, he suggests that the National Park Service be made into an independent agency, separate from the Department of the Interior, and says: "To reduce the power of special-interest groups [such as environmentalists] and enhance the professional stature of the agency, anyone appointed director of the National Park Service should be subject to Senate confirmation, and his or her credentials clearly established." (390) Moreover, according to Chase, the National Park Service should emphasize scientific research and that in order "to make management more sensitive to the contributions of science, the ranger corps should be completely professionalized. That is, the Service should create a cadre of resource managers who would be required to have graduate training in relevant academic disciplines to advance through the ranks. . . . Qualifications for superintendents and their staffs should be similar to those we expect of college administrators or museum directors." (390) However, he says these changes will not occur unless Americans reject the idea that wilderness areas thrive without human intervention. (Chase 1987; Glotfelty and Fromm 1996)

See also Animal Ecology; Balanced Ecosystems; Biodiversity; Carson, Rachel Louise; Chase, Alston; Commoner, Barry; Conservationism; Ehrlich, Paul and Anne; Environmental Politics; Habitat Protection; Leopold, Aldo; Muir, John; Thoreau, Henry David; Wildlife Conservation.

Pliny the Elder

Pliny the Elder, or Gaius Plinius Secundus, was a Roman scholar and soldier who lived from approximately 23 A.D. to 79 A.D. He held a variety of official positions and wrote at least seven books, including a history of Rome, a biography, and a book on throwing lances, but only *Natural History* survives in its entirety. This encyclopedic work is divided into 37 separate books concerning such topics as astronomy, geography, anthropology, zoology, botany, geology, and mineralogy. According to letters written by his nephew, Pliny the Younger, Pliny the Elder died while investigating the eruption of Mt. Vesuvius, overcome by volcanic fumes. (Beagon 1992; French and Greenaway 1986)

See also *Natural History.*

Pohl, Frederik

Best known for his science fiction work, Frederik Pohl has written or coauthored such novels as *The Space Merchants* (1953), *Day Mil-*

lion (1970), *Gateway* (1977), *JEM* (1979), *The Years of the City* (1985), and *Chernobyl* (1986). His novels and short stories typically show the possible future consequences of current social problems, such as overpopulation and pollution. In addition, he has coauthored nonfiction books that address such problems. For example, *Our Angry Earth,* cowritten with Isaac Asimov, addresses a range of global environmental issues. Pohl has also edited several science fiction anthologies, and in 1978 he published his memoirs, entitled *The Way the Future Was.* He was born in New York City on November 26, 1919. (Asimov and Pohl 1991)

See also Asimov, Isaac; *Chernobyl;* Environmental Fiction; *Our Angry Earth.*

Population Explosion, The

The Population Explosion by Paul R. Ehrlich and Anne H. Ehrlich is one of the foremost examples of apocalyptic environmental nonfiction. It was published in 1990 as the sequel to Paul Ehrlich's *The Population Bomb* (1968). Whereas *The Population Bomb* warned of the disasters that would occur if population growth continued at its current rate, *The Population Explosion* argues that those disasters are already apparent. As Paul and Anne Ehrlich explain in the preface to *The Population Explosion:*

The Population Bomb tried to alert people to the connection of population growth to such events [as food-supply depletion and starvation-related diseases]. The book also warned about the greenhouse warming and other possible [environmental] consequences of "using the atmosphere as a garbage dump." It concluded: "In short, when we pollute, we tamper with the energy balance of the Earth. The results in terms of global climate and in terms of local weather could be catastrophic. Do we want to keep it up and find out what will happen? What do we gain by playing 'environmental roulette'?" . . . A 1990s primer on population by necessity looks very different from our original work. *The Population Explosion* is being written as ominous changes in the life-support systems of civilization become more evident daily. It is being written in a world where hunger is rife and the prospects of famine and plague ever more imminent. (Ehrlich and Ehrlich 1990, p. 10)

The Ehrlichs explain that during the time between the publication of *The Population Bomb* and that of *The Population Explosion,* the world's population had increased by 1.8 billion people. Given such rapid expansion, they title the first chapter of *The Population Explosion* "Why Isn't Everyone as Scared as We Are?" In it they offer statistics regarding population growth rates as well as an overview of the kinds of problems that overpopulation causes. In subsequent chapters they go into greater detail about such problems, using historical facts to support their view that the earth cannot sustain an unlimited amount of people. For example:

Historians trying to explain why past civilizations rose, flourished for a time, then usually declined or fell prey to some conquering outside force have customarily looked for causes in social, economic, or political factors. Rarely have they considered population pressures, and their contributions to environmental deterioration and depletion of resources, as underlying causes of a civilization's downfall. Yet numerous contemporary accounts documented problems with soil erosion, recurring floods and droughts associated with deforestation, and so forth. The Greek philosophers described such processes and warned of the consequences of continued deforestation and of overgrazing, especially by goats. The warnings went unheeded; Greece today is nearly a desert, its soils thin and poor, the vast majority of its original forests long vanished. (53)

The Ehrlichs then discuss the ecology of agriculture, explaining that attempts to increase food production often hurt the environment. Conversely, environmental damage can decrease food production:

Poster in China advocating one child per family (Owen Franken/Corbis)

In the Soviet Union, the ill-advised diversion of water for irrigation from rivers that fed the inland Aral Sea has led to a regional ecological disaster. The sea, once a productive fishery, has shrunk in area by a third; two thirds of its former volume is gone. Shoreline towns have been stranded far inland, and the fishery has been destroyed. Worse, the irrigated cropland has been turned into a salt desert. . . . Salt, dust, and dried pesticide residues have been carried and deposited thousands of miles away by winds and rain, causing health problems for the population and affecting agriculture over vast areas. (94)

The Ehrlichs offer details about such health problems, as well as diseases that are spread when too many people try to occupy too small an area. They explain that "high densities in human populations [make] them—all else being equal—subject to high rates of disease." (153) Moreover, they argue that there are no benefits to having a dense population, not even when economics are considered. They contend that economists commonly believe population growth results in economic growth but that such an assumption is wrong. They advocate the establishment of a new science, called "ecological economics":

> Those being trained in ecological economics would first be given the baseline understanding that society's first priority must be to keep nature's house in order. They would learn that the key to doing this is to reduce the number of people to a quantity that can be properly sheltered without destroying the house. Considerable instruction on the basics of how the physical-biological world works must be included in the training of all economists. Otherwise they will continue to whisper the wrong messages into the ears of politicians and businessmen. (168)

The Ehrlichs offer other solutions to the problem of overpopulation, through government policies and individual actions. For example, they advocate that governments offer unrestricted access to birth control and that parents limit themselves to having no more than two children. They add: "Individuals have a responsibility not just to restrain their reproduction, but wherever possible to make choices that help to preserve Earth's habitability." (228) For example, they suggest that people eat less meat and more vegetables, wear sweaters instead of turning up their thermostats, and ride a bike instead of driving a car. In addition, they provide sample letters to show how people can influence politicians on environmental issues and provide a list of environmental organizations. (Ehrlich and Ehrlich 1990; Shabecoff 1993)

See also Agriculture; Climate Changes; Ehrlich, Paul and Anne; Human Ecology.

Powell, John Wesley

Geologist and ethnologist John Wesley Powell conducted studies based on both areas of expertise. He wrote about geology in *Exploration of the Colorado River of the West and Its Tributaries* (1875), which was later revised as *Canyons of Colorado* (1895), and about Native American languages in *Introduction to the Study of Indian Languages* (1877). He also wrote about the need for land conservation in *Report on the Lands of the Arid Region of the United States* (1878).

Born on March 24, 1834, in Mount Morris, New York, Powell served in the Civil War before becoming a professor of geology at Illinois Wesleyan University. From 1871 to 1879 he worked for the federal government, surveying lands in the American West. In 1879 he was named the first director of the U.S. Bureau of Ethnology of the Smithsonian Institution; he continued his association with the organization until his death on September 23, 1902. Powell also served as director of the U.S. Geological Survey from 1881 to 1892, during which time he worked on water irrigation projects.

Practice of the Wild, The

The Practice of the Wild (1992) is a collection of nine essays on wilderness issues and attitudes by American author-poet Gary Snyder, who helped shaped the environmental movement of the 1960s and 1970s. In the first essay, "The Etiquette of Freedom," Snyder discusses the relationship between civilizations and wilderness, noting that at one time these two entities were intertwined. He explains:

> When we think of wilderness in America today, we think of remote and perhaps designated regions that are commonly alpine, desert, or swamp. Just a few centuries ago, when virtually *all* was wild in North America, wilderness was not something exceptionally severe. . . . There has been no wilderness without some kind of human presence for several hundred thousand years. Nature is not a place to visit, it is *home*—and within that home territory

there are more familiar and less familiar places. Often there are areas that are difficult and remote, but all are *known* and even named. (Snyder 1990, 6–7)

Snyder then points out that elements of wilderness continue to exist in the most civilized places:

Wilderness is now—for much of North America—places that are formally set aside on public lands—Forest Service or Bureau of Land Management holdings or state and federal parks. Some tiny but critical tracts are held by private nonprofit groups like The Nature Conservancy or the Trust for Public Land. . . . But wildness is not limited to . . . formal wilderness areas. Shifting scales, it is everywhere: ineradicable populations of fungi, moss, mold, yeasts, and such that surround and inhabit us. Deer mice on the back porch, deer bounding across the freeway, pigeons in the park, spiders in the corners. . . . Exquisite complex beings in their energy webs inhabiting the fertile corners of the urban world in accord with the rules of wild systems, the visible hardy stalks and stems of vacant lots and railroads, the persistent raccoon squads, bacteria in the loam and in our yogurt. (14–15)

In his second essay, "The Place, the Region, and the Commons," Snyder explores the concept of wilderness as a place, saying that he wants to "talk about place as an experience and propose a model of what it meant to 'live in place' for most of human time." (25) He states:

For most Americans, to reflect on "home place" would be an unfamiliar exercise. Few today can announce themselves as someone *from* somewhere. Almost nobody spends a lifetime in the same valley, working alongside the people they knew as children. Native people everywhere (the very term means "someone born there") and Old World farmers and city people

share this experience of living in place. (25–26)

Snyder then discusses land management throughout history, including the development of commons, or common wilderness areas shared by all. He talks about the difficulty of managing modern commons, which he defines to include oceans and air as well as forests, and mentions the efforts of environmentalists such as John Muir, John Wesley Powell, Aldo Leopold, and David Foreman to stop abuses on public lands.

Snyder's third essay, "Tawny Grammar," concerns native culture and language, as well as the language of nature in the form of animal tracks and other signs. His fourth essay, "Good, Wild, Sacred," discusses the sacredness of wilderness areas and the spread of environmentalism. His fifth essay, "Blue Mountains Constantly Walking," focuses on the sacredness of mountains. In his sixth essay, "Ancient Forests of the Far West," Snyder becomes more political. He discusses how his experiences as a logger during the 1950s influenced his environmental beliefs, traces the history of various logging practices, and argues for changes in forestry management: "There should be *absolutely no more logging* in the remaining ancient forests. In addition we need the establishment of habitat corridors to keep the old-growth stands from becoming impoverished biological islands." (134)

Snyder's next two essays, "On the Path, Off the Trail" and "The Woman Who Married a Bear," concern knowledge and spirituality. In "On the Path," he talks about his discovery of Zen Buddhism and how it has affected his life. In "The Woman Who Married a Bear," he relates a story that appears in many Native American cultures, concerning a woman who marries a bear, learns her husband's ways, and eventually becomes a bear herself. Both essays deal with people who are struggling to live in two different worlds.

In his final essay, Snyder ties together many aspects of his book. He talks about Buddhism, nature, civilization, wilderness issues, and environmentalism, explaining the deep ecology movement and citing the work of deep ecologists George Sessions and Bill Devall. He also mentions the environmental activist group Earth First!, whereby "direct-action techniques that go back to the civil rights and labor movement days are employed in ecological issues." (180) In the end, Snyder recommends that all people become more active in environmental issues, suggesting that environmental awareness is a sign of personal enlightenment. (Glotfelty and Fromm 1996; Snyder 1990)

> See also Animal Ecology; Deep Ecology Movement; Devall, Bill; Environmental Groups; Environmental History; Environmental Politics; Foreman, Dave; Forest Management; Habitat Protection; Leopold, Aldo; Muir, John; Powell, John Wesley; Sessions, George.

Priestley, Joseph

Joseph Priestley was an 18th-century clergyman who left behind a large body of work tackling a range of religious and scientific subjects. In terms of the environment, however, his most significant contribution was the discovery of the components of the atmosphere, particularly oxygen. *Experiments and Observations on Different Kinds of Air* (six volumes, 1774–1786) discusses his research.

Priestley was born near Leeds, Yorkshire, England, on March 13, 1733. He studied history, philosophy, and science before becoming an assistant minister in 1755. In 1758 he opened his own school, where he provided his students with scientific equipment. In 1761 he accepted a teaching position at a prominent academy in Lancashire, England, and wrote some of his own grammar and history textbooks.

Priestley also embarked on scientific study. His experiments with electricity brought him a membership in the Royal Society of London in 1766, and the following year he was appointed minister of a chapel in Yorkshire. He continued his scientific research, however, and began concentrating on gases, eventually discovering nitric oxide, nitrogen dioxide, nitrous oxide, hydrogen chloride, ammonia, sulfur dioxide, silicon tetrafluoride, nitrogen, carbon monoxide, and oxygen. He also invented a technique to add air to water, which later inspired the invention of soda water.

In 1772 Priestley became a librarian and tutor in the household of an earl. He remained in this position until 1779, when he became a minister in Birmingham, England. There he met scientist and naturalist Erasmus Darwin, who offered him financial assistance so he could continue his scientific studies. However, Priestley was forced from Birmingham in 1791 because of his unpopular political views; a mob burned down his house after he expressed support for the French Revolution, which had occurred two years earlier.

Priestley then took a teaching position near London, but after the French king, Louis XVI, was executed in 1793, he feared that the public would again attack him. Consequently, in 1794 he moved to the United States, settling in Pennsylvania. He died there on February 6, 1804. (Boynton 1948)

> See also Darwin, Erasmus; *Experiments and Observations on Different Kinds of Air.*

Principles of Animal Ecology

Principles of Animal Ecology, written in 1949 by ecologist Warder C. Allee and fellow Chicago zoologists Orlando and Thomas Park, Alfred E. Emerson, and Karl P. Schmidt, is one of the first textbooks on the study of ecology, which it defines as "the science of the interrelation between living organisms and their environment . . . emphasizing interspecies as well as intraspecies relations," or, in a broader sense, as "the science of communities." A community is "a natural assemblage of organisms which, together with its habitat, has reached a survival level such that it is relatively independent of adjacent assemblages of equal rank; to this extent, given radiant energy, it is self-sustaining."

The book is divided into five sections: "The History of Ecology," "Analysis of the Environment," "Populations," "The Community," and "Ecology and Evolution." In discussing the first topic, the authors outline a progression of changes regarding how people have approached the environmental sciences. In ancient Greece, the authors explain, individuals learned about nature by studying it firsthand, but during the Middles Ages they primarily studied it through books. Gradually people began to learn not only through books but through the study of laboratory animals, either living or preserved. Then they observed wild animals in the field as well.

In keeping with this approach, *Principles of Animal Ecology* combines its discussion of how various animals affect and are affected by their environment with facts extrapolated from field and laboratory observations. The second section contains information about environmental properties such as heat, light, air and water currents, atmospheric gases, and soil composition. Section 3 discusses principles of population growth, as well as the organization of insect societies. Section 4 focuses on the way that animal communities develop and function, and the fifth section presents issues of evolutionary theory, such as genetic variation, adaptation, and natural selection. The book offers no formal conclusion, but at the end of the sixth section the authors suggest that an individual animal or an animal community has the best chance of survival if it is in harmony with its companions and its environment. (Allee 1949; Bowler 1993)

See also Allee, Warder Clyde; Animal Ecology; Environmental History; Evolution; Habitat Protection.

Principles of Geology

This three-volume work (published in July 1830, December 1831, and April 1833), entitled *Principles of Geology, Being an Attempt to Explain the Former Changes of the Earth's Surface by Reference to Causes Now in Operation,* advanced new theories regarding geological processes. The author, Charles Lyell, was a geologist who suggested that slow, natural processes, as opposed to sudden, violent events, created earth's geological features. For example, he suggested that mountains were formed by a series of small earthquakes over an extremely long period rather than by a few catastrophic ones.

Because he believed in such slow processes, Lyell theorized that the earth was far more ancient than was commonly believed. This aspect of his work greatly influenced other scientists of the period. For example, Charles Darwin studied *Principles of Geology* and made his own observations of the geological facts it presented. As a result he decided that Lyell was correct in stating that the earth's features had been formed gradually. He then applied the concept of gradualism to his own theories on species evolution.

However, *Principles of Geology* offers more facts and examples than theories. Before writing the work, Lyell explored geological features such as caves, lake sediments, and volcanoes throughout Europe; he gave detailed accounts of his findings. He continued these studies after *Principles of Geology* was published and used that research in revising the work. Several editions of his book appeared during the ensuing years. The 11th edition (1872) was published in two volumes as *Principles of Geology, or The Modern Changes of the Earth and Its Inhabitants.* Lyell was working on the 12th edition when he died in 1875. (Lyell 1872; L. Wilson 1972)

See also Darwin, Charles Robert; Evolution; Geological Research; Lyell, Charles.

Protogaea

Published in 1680, *Protogaea* by Gottfried Wilhelm Leibnitz was the first work to propose that the earth was originally a mass of molten lava. The book also suggests that water vapors helped form the earth's crust. Leibnitz writes:

It is readily believed that at the origin of things, before the separation of the opaque material from the luminous, *when our globe was incandescent,* the fire drove the humidity into the air, acting like a distillation. That is to say, as a result of the lowering of the temperature, it was converted into aqueous vapors. These vapors, findings themselves in contact with the chilled surface of the earth, condensed to water. The water, working over the debris of the recent conflagration, took up the fixed salts, giving rise to a . . . [solution] which soon formed the sea. (Boynton 1948, 358)

Leibnitz's work had a significant impact on subsequent geologic studies. (Boynton 1948)

See also Geological Research; Leibnitz, Gottfried Wilhelm.

Ptolemy

Claudius Ptolemaeus, more familiarly known as Ptolemy, was an ancient Greek scholar whose work in the fields of mathematics, astronomy, and geography greatly influenced scientific thought. He lived in Alexandria from approximately 127 A.D. to 145 A.D.; he left behind little information about his life. He did, however, write extensively about his scientific work.

Ptolemaeus's 13-volume book on astronomy, *Almagest,* identifies and discusses more than 1,000 stars, talks about the nature of planets, and offers theories regarding planetary motion. It also argues that the earth is the center of the solar system. In addition to *Almagest,* Ptolemy wrote books on geometry and other mathematical subjects. His most important work related to the environmental sciences is his *Guide to Geography,* an eight-volume work that details information on geographical locations, maps, and mapmaking. It remained a valuable resource for several hundred years after Ptolemy's death and was later used by Renaissance explorers. (Dreyer 1953)

See also Geological Research; *Guide to Geography.*

Pyle, Robert Michael

Ecologist Robert Michael Pyle is best known for a collection of essays entitled *Wintergreen* (1986), which won the John Burroughs Medal for excellence in nature writing. His other works include *The National Audubon Society Field Guide to North American Butterflies* (1981), a collection of first-person nature essays entitled *The Thunder Tree: Lessons from an Urban Wildland* (1993), *Insects* (1993), and *Where Bigfoot Walks: Across the Dark Divide* (1995), which presents fieldwork supported by a 1989 Guggenheim Fellowship.

Born in Denver, Colorado, in 1947, Pyle worked for The Nature Conservancy before becoming a full-time writer. He currently lives on a homestead in Washington State.

Q

Quammen, David

Conservationist David Quammen has written books and articles on a range of nature-related subjects and is a regular contributor to *Outside* magazine. His columns often make connections between animal and human behaviors. His books include *Natural Acts: A Sidelong View of Science and Nature* (1985), which addresses the issue of animal rights, *The Flight of the Iguana: A Sidelong View of Science and Nature* (1988), *The Song of the Dodo: Island Biogeography in the Age of Extinctions* (1996), and *Wild Thoughts from Wild Places* (1998). Born in Cincinnati, Ohio, in 1948, Quammen currently lives in Montana.

R

Rafinesque, Constantine Samuel

Nineteenth-century naturalist Constantine Samuel Rafinesque traveled throughout the United States and wrote extensively about his experiences and observations, thereby furthering naturalism among the American public. As Hans Huth reports in *Nature and the American:*

> The results of [Rafinesque's] studies, published in magazines, seemed so meritorious to European learned societies that they bestowed many honors on him.
> Rafinesque must be considered one of the most advanced spirits of his time, contributing to the stimulation of interest in American science and dissemination of knowledge about it.
> Rafinesque's four hundred papers scattered through the magazines of the period give favorable account of the quality and quantity of papers made accessible to the public through the many periodicals that were being published at this time. Essentially differing in quality from contributions to the "department of poetry," articles on natural history and travel were with few exceptions sent in by experts. The public reached through these periodicals was much larger than the actual number of subscribers, for ever copy was undoubtedly handed around among friends and neighbors. The most widely read publications were the *Columbian Magazine,* the *American Museum,* the *Massachusetts Magazine,* the *New York Magazine,* and the *Port Folio;* but there were others, like the *Boston Magazine* and the *Ladies' Magazine,* which are of interest because they specialized in articles on travel and nature. (Huth 1972, 26)

Rafinesque was born on October 22, 1783, in Galata, Turkey. His first trip to the United States lasted from 1802 to 1805. In 1815 he returned to America and settled in Kentucky, where he became a university professor and studied botany, classifying many species of plants. In 1826 he moved to Philadelphia, Pennsylvania. He died there on September 18, 1840. (Fitzpatrick 1982)

Rape of the Wild

Published in 1988, *Rape of the Wild: Man's Violence Against Animals and the Earth* by Andrée Collard with Joyce Contrucci is an important work of ecofeminism. As scholar Mary Daly reports in a foreword to the book:

Andrée Collard Names with uncompromising Courage the evil wrought by the patriarchal rapers of Earth. *Rape of the Wild* . . . makes absolutely clear the connections between ecology and Radical Feminism. Its author was able to do this because she Lived both of these causes to the utmost. (Collard 1988, x–xi)

Collard explains her position in the introduction:

In patriarchy, nature, animals and women are objectified, hunted, invaded, colonised, owned, consumed and forced to yield and to produce (or not). The violation of the integrity of wild, spontaneous Being is rape. It is motivated by a fear and rejection of Life and it allows the oppressor the illusion of control, of power, of being alive. As with women as a class, nature and animals have been kept in a state of inferiority and powerlessness in order to enable men as a class to believe and act upon their "natural" superiority/dominance. . . . I have taken the position that it is morally wrong to kill for pleasure, to inflict pain for the thrill of discoveries nobody needs, to colonise other creatures' minds and bodies, to make a fetish of those very animals the culture as a whole is bent on eliminating, and to conserve wild animals in parks, zoos and game reserves, thereby destroying their integrity of being. (1–2)

Collard is particularly harsh toward those who would use animals for scientific research, but she also criticizes animal breeders and others who make a profit at animals' expense, as well as people who pollute the earth with pesticides in order to control nature. In discussing the latter, she praises Barry Commoner's *The Closing Circle,* because its author recognizes "the interconnectedness of all organisms in nature." (147) However, she criticizes him for stating "the environmental crisis is hardly a 'motherhood' issue." (148) Collard counters:

Ecology is very much a motherhood issue since woman and nature have been linked in our consciousness since prehistory. To delve into the environmental crisis is to begin to see how fundamental this connection is to social justice and political goals. Commoner points to blacks and the poor first as primary victims of environmental degradation, then as powerful allies in the fight against it. I would add that all women are victims of degradation. All women are experts in the art of survival. (147–148)

Collard argues that it is time for feminists to become more concerned with ecology and concludes her book by saying:

Historically, our destiny as women and the destiny of nature are inseparable. It began within earth/goddess-worshipping societies which celebrated the life-giving and life-sustaining powers of woman and nature, and it remains despite our brutal negation and violation in the present. Women must re-member and re-claim our biophilic power. Drawing upon it we must make the choices that will affirm and foster life, directing the future away from the nowhere of the fathers to the somewhere that is ours—on this planet—now. (168)

See also *Closing Circle, The;* Commoner, Barry.

Rarest of the Rare, The

Diane Ackerman's *The Rarest of the Rare* (1995) is a collection of essays and poems on endangered species and habitats, some of which first appeared in such magazines as *Life* and *National Geographic*. The author is well known for making environmental issues accessible to the general public and has consequently helped popularize the natural sciences in recent years. *The Rarest of the Rare* focuses on endangered species. However, Ackerman argues that "so many plants and animals are endangered that it would be impossible to write an exhaustive book on the subject." For this reason, she has confined her discussion to "three delegate animals (monk seals, short-tailed albatrosses, and golden lion tamarins), two endangered ecosystems (the Amazon and the Florida scrublands), and an "endangered phenomenon" (the migration of the monarch butterfly). (Ackerman 1995, xix)

In discussing endangered species and habitats, Ackerman describes efforts to save them and quotes experts in environmental issues. For example, she talks about the Golden Lion Tamarin Reintroduction Project, which reintroduces captive tamarins (a primate) into the wild, and she reports on her interviews with the head of the project. But she also offers her own opinions on environmental issues and relates them to personal experiences. For example, she states that she was involved in a movement to save the California habitat of the monarch butterfly and explains:

> The world would be a poorer place without butterflies. So I joined forces with Chris Nagano of the Los Angeles Museum's Monarch Project, to help persuade California to pass legislation protecting the monarchs. In 1987 such a law was passed. There are many other conservation success stories—tougher problems to solve, bigger animals to protect, more complex obstacles than ignorance and greed to overcome. But it reassures me to know that a small animal, whose "usefulness" can't be proven, can be saved through the determined efforts of a few people. (131–132)

Ackerman's book offers no conclusion to summarize her positions on environmental issues. However, the introduction does explore some of her beliefs on endangered species and the efforts to save them. For example, she says:

> As more and more species become rare, angles of color will be deleted from this living kaleidoscope, reducing the possible combinations. Variety is not only the spice of life, it's the indispensable ingredient. So should we preserve the last remaining

smallpox virus? . . . I'm glad it's locked up safe, and I pray it never escapes from its prison; but it may one day offer us an insight into, or solution to, a biological trauma we can't now imagine. . . . I cherish life's variety and would like as much of it around as possible. (xvii)

Ackerman advocates the preservation of as many species as possible. (Ackerman 1995)

See also Ackerman, Diane; Animal Ecology; Balanced Ecosystems; Biodiversity; Habitat Protection; Wildlife Conservation.

Rawlings, Marjorie Kinnan

Novelist and short story writer Marjorie Kinnan Rawlings offers rich descriptions of landscapes in her work. Her best known novel is *The Yearling* (1938). Awarded the Pulitzer Prize, it concerns the relationship between a boy and an orphaned fawn. An autobiographical work, *Cross Creek* (1942), tells of Rawlings's experiences in the remote village of Cross Creek, Florida, where she lived for 13 years on a farm containing a 72-acre orange grove.

Born in Washington, D.C., on August 8, 1896, Rawlings graduated from the University of Wisconsin in 1918 and worked as a newspaper reporter before moving to Cross Creek in 1928. In backwoods Florida she found a setting for her novels. Her first was *South Moon Under* (1933), followed by *Golden Apples* (1935). Rawlings's final book was *The Sojourner,* published shortly before her death on December 14, 1953.

Ray, Dixy Lee

Zoologist Dixy Lee Ray was considered to be one of the most prominent critics of environmental politics. She headed the Atomic Energy Commission under President Richard Nixon, served as governor of Washington State (1977–1981), and received many awards during her career, including the United Nations Peace Prize. One of her primary concerns was that the media report scientific facts objectively. Her 1995 book, *Environmental Overkill: Whatever Happened to Common Sense?,* which she wrote with reporter Lou

Scene from The Yearling, *1946 (Archive Photos)*

Guzzo, argues that environmentalists often distort facts to give themselves more power in American society.

This position brought her harsh criticism from environmentalists. For example, David Helvarg, in *The War Against the Greens,* at-tacks Ray for being "the unofficial standard bearer for an emerging counterscience that attempts to discredit as 'environmental hysteria' commonly accepted research on acid rain, pesticides, ozone depletion, climate change, toxic waste, radiation, and all other human-originated sources of pollution." (Helvarg 1994, 229) Ray addressed such issues in *Trashing the Planet: How Science Can Help Us Deal with Acid Rain, Depletion of the Ozone, and Nuclear Waste* (1990), also cowritten with Guzzo. She died on January 3, 1994. (Helvarg 1994; Ray and Guzzo 1993)

> See also Antienvironmentalism; Climate Changes; *Environmental Overkill;* Pesticides and Chemicals.

Ray, John

During the 17th century, English botanist John Ray recognized that what defined an animal's species was its ability to produce offspring with other members of that species. Prior to this idea, scientists incorrectly believed that animals were related because of their general appearance or behaviors. Ray's definition of a species was a critical advance in scientific thinking.

Ray was born on November 29, 1627, in Black Notley, Essex, England. He attended the University of Cambridge on a scholarship, receiving a bachelor's degree in 1648 and a master's in 1651. Until 1662 he held a fellowship at Trinity College but was forced to leave for religious and political reasons. With the help of patrons, he then became a naturalist, publishing information about plants in England, Wales, and Europe.

Ray's most important books were *Methodus Plantarum Nova* (1682), which added new categories to the botanical species classification system, the three-volume *Historia Plantarum* (1686–1704), which identified many types of plants and discussed their anatomical similarities, and *Synopsis Methodica Anamalium Quadrupedum et Serpentini Generis* (1693), which focused on similarities among quadrupeds. His work aimed to group lifeforms into species. When he died on January 17, 1705, Ray was writing *Historia Insectorum,* a discussion of insect species. (Boynton 1948; Spangenburg and Moser 1993)

> See also Species Identification and Classification.

Raymo, Chet

Born in 1936, nature writer Chet Raymo is best known for his science columns in the *Boston Globe* and for a 1985 book entitled *The Soul of the Night: An Astronomical Pilgrimage,* in which he discusses earth's relationship to the universe. For example, he says:

> Let us connect the multimillion-dollar telescopes to our kitchen radios and convert the radiant energy of the stars into sound. What would we hear? The random crackle of the elements. The static of electrons fidgeting between energy levels in the atoms of stellar atmospheres. The buzz of hydrogen. The hiss and sputter of matter intent upon obeying the stochastic laws of quantum physics. Random, statistical, indifferent noise. It would be like the hum of a beehive or the clatter of shingle slapped by a wave. (Finch and Elder 1990, 789)

Raymo teaches astronomy and physics at Stonehill College in Eaton, Massachusetts. His other works include *Biography of a Planet: Geology, Astronomy, and the Evolution of Life on Earth* (1984) and *Honey From Stone: A Naturalist's Search for God* (1987).

Refuge

Published in 1991, *Refuge: An Unnatural History of Family and Place* was written by Terry Tempest Williams, one of America's preeminent nature writers. The work describes her observations regarding an unusual and disastrous rising of Utah's Great Salt Lake, which occurred between 1983 and 1985. The phenomenon caused environmental damage and reduction of wildlife throughout the area. Williams worked to evaluate the extent of this damage and reports the historical and scientific significance of her discoveries. For example, she says:

> Snowy plovers [a type of bird] have shown a 50 percent decline in abundance on the California, Oregon, and Washington coasts since the 1960s, due to the loss of coastal habitats. The National Audubon

Society petitioned the U.S. Fish and Wildlife Service in March 1988 to list the coastal population of the western snowy plover as a threatened species. The present population estimate for the western United States, excluding Utah, is ten thousand adult snowy plovers, rising to thirteen thousand individuals after breeding season. A knowledge of inland population numbers and distribution is essential to our understanding of the status of the species as a whole. That's why we are counting them in Utah.

I have been combing the salt flats . . . for them since early morning. So far, my count is zero. (Trimble 1995, 375)

Williams relates such destruction to her own personal tragedy. While she was studying the Great Salt Lake, her mother was dying of ovarian cancer, and she discusses her feelings of loss in her work. (Knowles 1992; Trimble 1995)

See also Nature Writing; Williams, Terry Tempest.

Reisner, Marc

Marc Reisner began writing extensively on environmental issues while working as a staff reporter for the newsletter of the Natural Resources Defense Council, a group devoted to U.S. environmental politics. Reisner held that position from 1972 till 1979, when he was awarded a journalism fellowship that provided him with the resources to investigate water-use issues in the western United States. His research was later incorporated into *Cadillac Desert,* published in 1986. This work is considered to be one of the most important analyses of water conservation issues in the United States. Reisner has written several other books on environmental issues, including *Overtapped Oasis: Reform or Revolution for Western Water* (1990) and *Game Wars: The Undercover Pursuit of Wildlife Poachers* (1991). (Reisner 1986)

See also *Cadillac Desert;* Environmental Politics.

Rights of Nature, The

Published in 1989, *The Rights of Nature* by environmental historian Roderick Frazier Nash is an important and often cited reference work for environmentalists. It traces the history of environmental ethics, discussing major conservationists, environmentalists, and environmental scientists as diverse as Aldo Leopold, Edward Abbey, John Muir, Rachel Carson, Murray Bookchin, Charles Darwin, and Arne Naess. Nash analyzes the ideology of their writings, connecting them to historical periods and political climates. He also offers his own views on environmentalism. For example, in his concluding chapter he says:

Nuclear war and nuclear winter have the potential of focusing attention on the rights of both humans and nature as no other recent issue. The environmental movement has begun to recognize that what is at stake in disarmament is nothing less than the fate of the planet. Philosophers and scientists agree that the rights of any individual organism have no significance apart from the existence of a habitat, which alone assures existence, liberty, and the opportunity to pursue happiness. Some raise questions about the rights of the habitat itself. Ending the threat of nuclear holocaust is likely to become a major moral imperative for future liberators of nature as well as people. (Nash 1989, 198)

Nash examines environmentalism primarily in philosophical terms. He explains that his book "concerns the history and implications of the idea that morality ought to include the relationship of humans to nature," adding:

Focusing on American intellectual history, it traces the relatively recent emergence of the belief that ethics should expand from a preoccupation with humans (or their gods) to a concern for animals, plants, rocks, and even nature, or the environment, in general. One way to think of this is as an evolution of ethics from the natural rights of a limited group of humans to the rights of parts or, in some theories, all of nature. (4)

Accordingly, he finds similarities between America's modern environmental movement and the 19th-century abolition movement:

A century and a half ago a group of American reformers proposed a change in thought and action that, for its time, was no less radical than that mandated by biocentric ethics. The problem then was slavery, an institution socially and legally predicted on the denial of moral standing to black people. An initially tiny group of radical reformers known as abolitionists found this practice morally wrong. After exhausting other alternatives, they succeeded in persuading a majority of Northerners to support a civil war that ended the institution. What is intriguing for the present purposes is that the abolitionists faced an ethical and political situation directly comparable to that presently confronting the radical environmentalists. In both instances we find reformers who have identified an oppressed minority that they think possesses rights and is therefore entitled to liberty from exploitation. In each case we hear the argument that the laws and institutions supporting such exploitation are morally wrong and must be changed, legally if possible; otherwise if necessary. (200)

In discussing how he came to examine environmentalism in terms of ethics, Nash credits the influence of environmentalist George Sessions, who has written extensively on the concept of deep ecology. Nash says that it was Session's comment that "a philosophically perceptive history of the shift from 'conservation' to 'ecological consciousness' in the 1960s and 1970s has yet to be written" that inspired him to examine the subject himself. (xii) (Nash 1989)

See also Abbey, Edward; Bookchin, Murray; Carson, Rachel Louise; Conservationism; Darwin, Charles Robert; Deep Ecology Movement; Environmental Activism; Environmental History; Environmental Movement; Leopold, Aldo; Muir, John; Naess, Arne; Nash, Roderick Frazier; Nuclear Energy; Sessions, George.

Ring of Bright Water

Published in 1961, *Ring of Bright Water* by naturalist Gavin Maxwell recounts the author's experiences with a wild otter that becomes his pet. However, the book is not merely the story of one man's relationship with an animal. It also describes the Scottish coast near the Hebrides, offering many details about the area's land, sea, and wildlife. The remainder of the book focuses on otters, reporting their behavior in the wild and telling of Maxwell's adventures with Mij, the otter who shares his home.

River Runs Through It, A

Published in 1976, *A River Runs Through It, and Other Stories* by Norman Maclean features the novella "A River Runs Through It," which is set in 1937 on the Big Blackfoot River in Montana. Although it is about family relationships, it also expresses the author's love of nature in general and fly-fishing in particular. The novella's distinctive opening line is: "In our family, there was no clear line between religion and fly fishing." (Maclean 1992, 1) But neither can save the life of the narrator's brother, who has a problem with alcohol and gambling; he is found dead shortly after failing to pay a debt.

Throughout the story, "A River Runs Through It" includes many descriptions related to the river and fly-fishing, which provides the male family members an opportunity to bond with one another. The turbulent river is also a metaphor for life. As the narrator explains:

As the heat mirages on the river in front of me danced with and through each other, I could feel patterns from my own life joining with them. It was here, while waiting for my brother, that I started this

The Reverend Maclean inculcates his sons with a religious love of nature in A River Runs Through It *(Photofest)*

story, although, of course, at the time I did not know that stories of life are often more like rivers than books. But I knew a story had begun, perhaps long ago near the sound of water. And I sensed that ahead I would meet something that would never erode so there would be a sharp turn, deep circles, a deposit, and quietness. (69)

Rogers, Pattiann

Poet Pattiann Rogers writes primarily about nature and spirituality. Milkweed Editions, the publisher of her poetry book *Firekeeper: New and Selected Poems* (1994), introduces the collection thus: "Rogers's poems incorporate the details of a field guide and the reverence of a hymnal."

Rogers has received many awards and grants for her work, which has appeared not only in poetry collections but also in magazines such as *Prairie Schooner* and *American Poetry Review*. In addition to *Firekeeper*, her books include *The Expectations of Light* (1981), *Legendary Performance* (1987), *Splitting and Binding* (1989), *Geocentric* (1993), *Eating Bread and Honey* (1997), *A Covenant of Seasons* (1998, with Joellyn Duesberry), and *The Dream of the Marsh Wren: Writing as Reciprocal Creation* (1999).

Roosevelt, Theodore

Theodore "Teddy" Roosevelt served as U.S. president from 1901 to 1909; a longtime conservationist, he actively supported conservation issues throughout his lifetime. He helped to enact new laws and policies to protect natural resources, expanded the national park system, and protected some 194 million acres of federal land from development. An avid outdoorsman and naturalist, he wrote about wilderness experiences in *Hunting Trips of a Ranchman* (1885), *Ranch Life and the Hunting Trail* (1888), *The Wilderness Hunter* (1893), *Outdoor Pastimes of an American Hunter* (1905), *African Game Trails* (1910), and *A Book-Lover's Holiday in the Open* (1916). He

President Teddy Roosevelt was responsible for creating the U.S. national park system (Archive Photos)

also wrote articles in favor of wilderness preservation and befriended conservationist John Muir.

Born on October 27, 1858, Roosevelt attended Harvard and, for a brief time, Columbia Law School. He was elected to the New York State Assembly in 1881. After failing to win reelection, he retired from public life and became a rancher. In 1889, however, he accepted an appointment to the U.S. Civil Service Commission, and in 1895 he became president of the New York Board of Police Commissioners. He remained in that position until 1897, whereupon he became assistant secretary of the U.S. Navy.

One year later, he resigned his post in order to fight in the Spanish-American War, leading the legendary Rough Riders. When he returned from Cuba as a hero, he was elected governor of New York and quickly became famous for fighting corruption. In 1900 he was elected U.S. vice president on the Republican ticket with William McKinley; after President McKinley was assassinated in September 1901, Roosevelt succeeded him in office. He served out the original term and was reelected in 1904.

When his administration ended, Roosevelt spent nearly a year hunting in Africa, then toured Europe before returning to America and politics. He continued to enjoy wilderness activities, including an expedition to the Brazilian jungles, and to write about his experiences. He died in Oyster Bay, New York, on January 6, 1919.

In discussing Roosevelt's conservation writings, scholar Paul Schullery argues that Roosevelt's works had more significance than did other works from the period. Schullery says:

> Roosevelt was all of these: adventurer, sportsman, and naturalist. But he is set apart from other wilderness writers because he was more than even these things—he was also a politician. Other writers of great influence in his time, such as [John] Muir and [John] Burroughs, exerted most of their influence as private citizens either through their writings or through independent organizations such as the Sierra Club. Theodore Roosevelt, on the other hand, was able to convert his beliefs directly into legal entities. It is to our benefit that, unlike most political figures, he was also an able, lively writer. Thus, besides his actual legislative and executive achievements, we have his own words on why those achievements mattered to him. By his own example he shows how he thinks national parks and similar reserves should be enjoyed. He tells us, and shows us, why they are important. He even gives us firsthand accounts of how other great writers (Burroughs in Yellowstone, Muir in Yosemite) enjoyed them. His writings on wilderness preservation . . . amount to his personal testimonial on the worth of the wilderness, just as the areas he discusses testify by their existence to the effectiveness of his fight. In his pleas for wildlife conservation, or a bureau to manage all national parks (finally established in 1916), or to leave the Grand Canyon "as it is," he expresses the spirit of his executive ambitions. (Schullery 1986, 18–19)

Roosevelt encouraged conservationism on both a political and personal level. (Schullery 1986)

See also Burroughs, John; Conservationism; Muir, John; *Wilderness Hunter, The.*

Roszak, Theodore

A professor of history in California, Theodore Roszak is the author of essays and books expressing his view that technology is splintering society and should be replaced with more holistic approaches to life. His works include *Person/Planet* (1978), *Where the Wasteland Ends* (1973), and *The Voice of the Earth: An Exploration of Ecopsychology* (1993), which examines such issues as the Gaia hypothesis and the relationship between nature and religion. Roszak also edited *Ecopsychology: Restoring the Earth, Healing the Mind* (1995), a collection of essays on how the health of the planet is related to humans' mental health. In addition, he is a skilled artist whose work has received public acclaim. Roszak was a Guggenheim Fellow from 1971 to 1972.

Rothenberg, David

David Rothenberg has written and edited several books on ecology, including *Hand's End: Technology and the Limits of Nature* (1993) and *Is It Painful to Think?* (1992), a book based on his interviews with Norwegian ecologist Arne Naess. He has also translated Naess's *Ecology, Community, and Lifestyle: Outline of an Ecosophy* from Norwegian to English. He is considered one of the foremost experts on Naess's philosophy of deep ecology and has been involved in the movement that developed from it.

> See also Deep Ecology Movement; *Is It Painful to Think?*; Naess, Arne.

Rubbish! The Archaeology of Garbage

Rubbish! by William Rathje and Cullen Murphy is often cited by environmentalists in the context of recycling issues. Published in 1992, the book presents information from one of the most in-depth studies of an environmental problem ever undertaken. Its authors were involved in the Garbage Project, which began in 1972 to evaluate the contents of garbage dumps.

Rubbish! shares some of their findings. It also traces the history of garbage archaeology and discusses human attitudes toward waste, consumption, and consumerism. It exposes myths regarding biodegradation, saying:

> Misconceptions about the interior life of landfills are profound—not surprisingly, since so very few people have actually ventured inside one. There is a popular notion that in its depths the typical municipal landfill is a locus of roiling fermentation, of intense chemical and biological activity. That perception is accompanied by a certain ambivalence. A landfill is seen, on the one hand, as an environment where organic matter is rapidly breaking down—biodegrading—into a sort of rich, moist, brown humus, returning at last to the bosom of Mother Na-

ture. Biodegradation, in this view, is something devoutly to be desired, an environmentally correct outcome of the first order, perhaps even part of God's plan. Romantic thinking about biodegradation is widespread. . . .

> On the other hand, coexisting with the romance of biodegradation, there is the view of a landfill as an environment from which a toxic broth of chemicals leaches into the surrounding soil, perhaps to pollute groundwater and nearby rivers and lakes. What both views of landfills have in common is the assumption that a great deal of biodegradation is taking place. (Rathje and Murphy 111–112)

The authors reveal the real way that a landfull functions, continuing: "The truth is, however, that the dynamics of a modern landfill are very nearly the opposite of what most people think. Biologically and chemically, a landfill is a much more static structure than is commonly supposed. For some kinds of organics, biodegradation goes on for a little while, and then slows to a virtual standstill. For other kinds, biodegradation never really gets under way at all" (Rathje and Murphy 111–112).

Such findings from the 1972 Garbage Project contributed to calls for recycling programs throughout the United States. However, *Rubbish!* points out that the practice is not a new one:

> Americans tend to think of "recycling" as a relatively modern concept that has only recently gained broad public acceptance, and whose practical benefits have only just begun to be realized. Among some environmentalists, the need for recycling seems to be viewed as the conceptual outgrowth of a series of propositions that gained wide currency some two decades ago. These are: First, that the United States was potentially on the verge of a new political-cum-spiritual-cum-environmental awakening (a proposition embodied in Charles Reich's *The Greening of America,* 1970); second, that it was about time that something like

A city garbage dump, Washington, D.C. (U.S. Department of Energy)

this occurred, because people were wolfing down the planet's resources far too quickly (a proposition embodied in the 1972 Club of Rome report, *Limits to Growth*); and third, that the new awakening, should it come, ought to be characterized by an ecologically conservative and individually responsible lifestyle. . . . This sort of thinking may very well have helped to encourage the emergence of a certain kind of recycling, but recycling itself is probably as old as—indeed, seems to be a fundamental characteristic of—the human species. The archaeological record is crowded with artifacts that display the results of recycling behavior. (191–192)

Rubbish! offers several examples of such artifacts and discusses modern recycling efforts outside the United States. It concludes with several suggestions for America. For example, its authors suggest that government should "encourage modest changes in household behavior," because "a few relatively simple changes in standard operating procedure

could, over time, have a beneficial effect on the overall solid-waste situation. Although it makes no sense for governments to promulgate a wide and complex array of suggested household reforms in this regard—which would no doubt be as confusing as the surfeit of advice about health and diet has now become—they could usefully hammer away on two or three fronts [such as food waste, composting, and hazardous waste]." (243)

Rubbish! concludes with a list of corporations and individuals who supported the Garbage Project. The study conducted 11 landfill excavations that yielded results included in the book; findings from an additional four studies had not yet been analyzed when the work was published. (Rathje and Murphy 1992)

See also Club of Rome; *Greening of America, The; Limits to Growth, The.*

Rural Hours

Published in 1850 and revised in 1887, *Rural Hours* is one of the first nature books by an American woman. Its author, Susan Fenimore

Cooper, was the daughter of novelist James Fenimore Cooper; her work was extremely popular in America and England.

Rural Hours describes the flora and fauna around New York's Otsego Lake. It also discusses the preservation of the area's forests, criticizing clear-cutting and other destructive practices. As Karen Knowles points out in *Celebrating the Land: Women's Nature Writings, 1850–1991,* this mention of conservationism predates the work of male naturalists like Henry David Thoreau and John Muir. According to Knowles, "Cooper's work reflects her belief in stewardship of the land, a rather long-sighted view considering America's expansionist and exploitative mood during the nineteenth century. She offers an important woman's perspective on nature at a time when men's experiences were more widely published." (Knowles 1992, 3) To illustrate this perspective, Knowles quotes Cooper from *Rural Hours:*

> The first colonists looked upon a tree as an enemy, and to judge from appearances, one would think that something of the same spirit prevails among their descendants at the present hour. It is not surprising, perhaps, that a man whose chief object in life is to make money should turn his timber into bank-notes with all possible speed; but it is remarkable that any one at all aware of the value of wood, should act so wastefully as most men do in this part of the world. Mature trees, young saplings, and last year's seedlings, are all destroyed at one blow by the axe or by fire; the spot where they have stood is left, perhaps, for a lifetime without any attempt at cultivation, or any endeavor to foster new wood. One would think that by this time, when the forest has fallen in all the valleys—when the hills are becoming more bare every day—when timber and fuel are rising in prices, and new uses are found for even indifferent woods— some forethought and care in this respect would be natural in people laying claim to common sense. (Knowles, 10–11)

(Cooper 1968; Knowles 1992)

See also Muir, John; Nature Writing; Thoreau, Henry David.

S

Sagan, Carl Edward

A professor of astronomy and space sciences, Carl Edward Sagan authored several nonfiction books about scientific and environmental issues, as well as a science fiction novel entitled *Contact* (1985). He is also credited with several important scientific discoveries, including developing the theory of nuclear winter. Sagan discusses the theory of nuclear winter, which hypothesizes that nuclear explosions will cause global cooling, in *A Path Where No Man Thought: Nuclear Winter and the End of the Arms Race* (1990).

Born on November 9, 1934, in Brooklyn, New York, Sagan earned his doctorate at the University of Chicago in 1960 and subsequently taught at both the University of California–Berkeley and Harvard University. From 1962 to 1968 he worked at the Smithsonian Astrophysical Observatory. In 1968 he became a professor of astronomy at Cornell University and began directing its Laboratory for Planetary Studies.

Carl Sagan (Archive Photos/Monitor)

Sagan worked on several space missions, researching planetary surfaces and atmospheres, and received several prestigious awards for his research into nuclear winter, as well as a Pulitzer Prize for his 1978 nonfiction book *The Dragons of Eden: Speculations on the Evolution of Human Intelligence*. His other works include *The Cosmic* (1979), *Comet* (1985), *Pale Blue Dot* (1995), and *The Demon-Haunted World* (1996). In addition, he hosted a popular television series entitled *Cosmos*. Sagan died on December 20, 1996, of a rare bone-marrow disease. A collection of his essays, entitled

Billions and Billions: Thoughts on Life and Death at the Brink of the Millennium, was published posthumously in 1997; in it he discusses a variety of issues, including environmental issues. (Cohen 1987; Sagan and Turco 1990)

> See also Climate Changes; Environmental Politics; Nuclear Energy; *Path Where No Man Thought, A.*

Sale, Kirkpatrick

American essayist and author Kirkpatrick Sale is an avowed Luddite, which means that he opposes all technology. His books include *Dwellers in the Land* (1985) and *Rebels Against the Future—The Luddites and their War on the Industrial Revolution: Lessons for the Computer Age* (1995). His articles opposing technology have appeared in such magazines as *The Nation,* and at some of his lectures he smashes a computer on stage.

Sand County Almanac, A

Published posthumously by the author's son, *A Sand County Almanac* by Aldo Leopold is one of the most famous books on conservation and ecology ever written. It is a collection of essays about Leopold's experiences and observations in the sand counties area of central Wisconsin, where he and his family bought an abandoned farm as a weekend retreat. During their visits they lived in a shack, a chicken house/cowshed that they fixed up themselves.

A Sand County Almanac was published in two versions. The original 1949 version contains three parts. The first, "A Sand County Almanac," is Leopold's month-by-month recounting of a year's worth of experiences on the farm. The second part, "Sketches Here and There," describe various episodes in his life that led him to explore conservation issues. The third part, "The Upshot," expresses his conservation philosophy, which he summarizes as follows:

> Conservation is getting nowhere because it is incompatible with our Abrahamic concept of land. We abuse land because we regard it as a commodity belonging to us.

When we see land as a community to which we belong, we may begin to use it with love and respect. There is no other way for land to survive the impact of mechanized man, nor for us to reap from it the esthetic harvest it is capable, under science, of contributing to culture. (Leopold 1966, x)

Leopold develops this concept at length in an essay entitled "The Land Ethic," in which he says: "There is as yet no ethic dealing with man's relation to land and to the animals and plants which grow upon it. Land . . . is still property. The land-relation is still strictly economic, entailing privileges but not obligations." (218) Leopold believes that applying ethics to land use is "an evolutionary possibility and an ecological necessity." (218) He criticizes the conservation movement of his time as being inadequate because it does not engage people's sense of right and wrong, saying: "Obligations have no meaning without conscience." (225)

Leopold discusses conservation in terms of morals, an approach that was still relatively new at the time. Scholar J. Baird Caldicott explains that although the environmental literature of Henry David Thoreau, John Muir, and Charles Darwin introduced ethical elements into discussions of the environment, Leopold's work was "the first self-conscious, sustained, and systematic attempt in modern Western literature to develop an ethical theory which would include the whole of terrestrial nature and terrestrial nature *as a whole* within the purview of morals." (Callicott 157)

This type of discussion formed the basis of America's environmental movement. For this reason, *A Sand County Almanac* has been called "the environmentalist's bible." (Callicott 3) Scholar Curt Meine explains: "The enduring contribution of 'The Land Ethic' to environmental philosophy is its clear conviction that the free individual must be responsible for and responsive to the land he or she lives upon." (180)

Leopold argues against both commercial and personal exploitation of the land. In the final essay of *A Sand County Almanac,* entitled "Conservation Esthetic," he criticizes people for destroying wilderness areas with roads, trails, and public campgrounds, whether for economic gain or private enjoyment. Scholar Wallace Stegner reports:

> Unlike many early conservationists, Leopold was as suspicious of recreation as he was of logging and agriculture. He noted that the impulse to refresh ourselves out of doors has damaged many of our remaining wild places—and he wrote before off-road vehicles had carried damage close to ruin. The lure of tourist money, he said, is a gun pointed at the heart of the wild, and he was right. (Callicott, 236)

In a July 31, 1947, foreword to *A Sand County Almanac,* Leopold explains the reason for his beliefs. He discusses his background in forestry and wildlife management and describes his evolution as a conservationist. However, when Leopold's son published the book in 1948, he rejected that foreword in favor of much shorter version written on March 4, 1948. He also changed the book's title from *Great Possessions* and edited portions of the text. In a second edition of *A Sand County Almanac,* published in 1966, he renamed the second part of the book "The Quality of Landscape" and inserted an additional section, entitled "A Taste for Country." It is a collection of eight Leopold essays on conservation topics, originally published in a 1953 book, *Round River.* Many scholars believe that the addition of the *Round River* essays disrupts the structure of the original *Almanac,* which was carefully crafted to move from the concrete, personal, and experiential (Leopold's adventures on the farm) to the abstract, universal, and intellectual (a conservation philosophy). (Glotfelty and Fromm 1996; Leopold 1966; Shabecoff 1993)

See also Animal Ecology; Conservationism; Darwin, Charles Robert; Environmental Movement; Forest Management; Leopold, Aldo; Muir, John; Thoreau, Henry David.

Saro-Wiwa, Ken

Born in 1941, Nigerian author Ken Saro-Wiwa sought to protect Ogoni tribal lands in his native country against oil exploration and development. He wrote about Nigeria's problems in *Nigeria: The Brink of Disaster* (1991). Four years later he was arrested by the Nigerian government after a public protest and executed. His other works include *A Forest of Flowers: Short Stories* (1986).

Schneider, Stephen H.

Stephen H. Schneider, Ph.D., is a climatologist who has written many books and articles on environmental issues and policies. His books include *The Genesis Strategy: Climate and Global Survival* (1976), *The Primordial Bond: Exploring Connection Between Man and Nature Through the Humanities and Sciences* (1981), *The Co-Evolution of Climate and Life* (1984), *Global Warming: Are We Entering the Greenhouse Century?* (1989), and *Laboratory Earth: The Planetary Gamble We Can't Afford to Lose* (1997). Schneider has also headed the Interdisciplinary Climate Systems at the National Center for Atmospheric Research in Boulder, Colorado. (Schneider 1989)

See also Climate Changes; *Global Warming.*

Science Under Siege

Published in 1993, *Science Under Siege: How the Environmental Misinformation Campaign Is Affecting Our Laws, Taxes, and Our Daily Life* is one of the books most frequently cited by people who oppose environmentalism. Its author, Michael Fumento, is a journalist who set out to expose the field's myths, particularly those related to human health issues. In the introduction he says:

> Activists have compared the environmental health problems of today with the scourge of communicable and infectious diseases in earlier ages. As one activist put it, "Earlier generations lived in fear of polio and smallpox. Nowadays, the most deadly epidemics we face are man-made. Chemical dumpsites, radioactive wastes, acid rain, toxic shock syndrome . . . food

additives and more. These are the perils that most threaten our health today. . . ." But is what they are telling us accurate? Or does the real assault on the public come not so much from chemicals, computer terminals, and electricity as it does from the media, environmental activists, government bureaucrats and politicians, and industry opportunists who warn us that modern life carries with it a multitude of new risks of death? . . . Is it possible that by concentrating so much attention and money on preventing slight or unverifiable risks we are diverting attention and other resources away from the many real risks in life? (Fumento 14)

In examining the accuracy of environmentalism, Fumento focuses on the issues of global warming, the ozone layer, acid rain, and overpopulation, offering in-depth information about each problem and the way environmentalists and the media have reported it. For example, in discussing the theory that most cancers are caused by environmental problems, he says:

> For the longest time, the assertion held that the vast majority—perhaps as much as 90 percent—of cancer deaths are attributable to the synthetic products developed by the chemical industry after World War II. . . . This extreme view, promoted by many persons and organizations including the NRDC [Natural Resources Defense Council], seems to have been abandoned . . . but it remains "common knowledge" that much cancer is caused by industrial chemicals, including both pollutants and pesticides. . . . In fact, surveys of cancer incidence tend to show that when the aging of the American population is taken into account, industrial countries do not suffer higher rates of cancer. Such highly respected epidemiologists as Richard Doll and Richard Peto of Oxford University, both influential in establishing the link of cigarette smoking to disease, have stated clearly that there is no con-

vincing evidence that there is a general increase in cancer related to the conditions of the modern world. (58–59)

However, Fumento's work does not simply impart facts and statistics. It also includes passionate views on environmental subjects. For example, in concluding his chapter on cancer he states:

> The day will come, not too long from now, when dosing animals with massive amounts of chemicals and then declaring that this predicts cancer in humans at low doses will be literally laughed at, in the same way we now laugh at witch doctoring and entrail reading. Our current cancer prevention scheme will be classified alongside leeching with the great medical follies of history. The only question is, how many hundreds of billions of dollars will be spent before then and how many lives will be needlessly cut short by policies focused on the trivial and unlikely, rather than the real dangers and truly preventable risks? (77)

Fumento is particularly critical of environmental activists who work to influence public policy, suggesting that many of them intentionally misstate risk statistics and facts to create a climate of fear and achieve their goals. However, he acknowledges that the media might also be to blame for these inaccuracies:

> Sheer sloppiness and the crunch of deadlines . . . cannot be ruled out as factors in media misinformation. Often, for example, journalists will eschew reading a science or medical magazine article in favor of simply reading the abstract. Thus, after the *New England Journal of Medicine* *(NEJM)* published a study on AIDS virus infections on college campuses, some reporters . . . declared that it was a new study that showed an "alarming increase" in infections over those reported in an old one. In fact, this *was* the old study, which *NEJM* had simply decided to take eigh-

teen months to publish. . . . The assertion that a study could show an "alarming increase" over what turned out to be the same study merely illustrates the ability of the media to find something new and alarming in absolutely anything. (341)

Fumento adds: "The average reporter works toward two things because the average newspaper cares about two things. The first is making deadlines; the second is being interesting. Accuracy is not high up in the hierarchy." (341)

Fumento also criticizes the public's attitude. In his final chapter, he points out that the greatest risks to human health are smoking, drinking, and overeating, and yet people are more afraid of environmental ills than of those controllable behaviors. He concludes that "we are a nation that desperately needs to reevaluate its priorities in terms of health risks. Industrial pollutants should be on the list, but the list's order must be determined by the scope and severity of the risk and the cost of alleviating it, not by the latest [television] exposé or the latest direct mail drive of the Natural Resources Defense Council." (371) He adds: "It is time to begin shaping policies on the basis of science, rather than shaping science to fit policies. It is time to go back to the good ideas of the early environmentalists and conservationists and to reject those of the fanatics and faddists who have since jumped aboard the bandwagon." (372) (Fumento 1993)

> See also Antienvironmentalism; Environmental Activism; Environmental Politics; Fumento, Michael; Human Ecology; Pesticides and Chemicals.

Sea Around Us, The

Written in 1950 and translated into more than 20 languages, *The Sea Around Us* was on the nonfiction best-seller list for 39 weeks after its publication and won the National Book Award for nonfiction in 1952. Its author, Rachel Carson, is considered one of the most important environmentalists in American history. Her writings on environmental issues increased public interest in the science of ecol-

ogy and helped spur the environmental movement of the 1960s and 1970s.

The Sea Around Us concerns the ecology of the ocean. It is divided into three parts. The first, entitled "Mother Sea," explains how the sea was formed and how volcanic activity creates islands. It also talks about various forms of sea life and the ocean's intricate food chain. Part 2, "The Restless Sea," describes the interaction between wind and water, as well as the way the earth's rotation affects the tides. Part 3, "Man and the Sea About Him," discusses the ocean's effects on the earth's climate. All three parts contain historical information about sea exploration; Part 3 focuses on people's attempts to remove minerals and petroleum from the sea.

In discussing such attempts, *The Sea Around Us* does not condemn people for exploiting the sea's resources. However, in a 1960 revised edition of the book, Carson includes a preface that does criticize people's careless treatment of the ocean. She says: "Although man's record as a steward of the natural resources of the earth has been a discouraging one, there has long been a certain comfort in the belief that the sea, at least, was inviolate, beyond man's ability to change and to despoil. But this belief, unfortunately, has proved to be naïve." (Carson 1961, p. xi) She then condemns the practice of depositing barrels of nuclear waste on the ocean floor, arguing that "it is only a matter of time until the contents of all such containers already deposited at sea will be free in the ocean waters, along with those yet to come as the applications of atomic science expand. To the packaged wastes so deposited there is now added the contaminated run-off from rivers that are serving as dumping grounds for atomic wastes, and the fall-out from the testing of bombs, the greater part of which comes to rest on the vast surface of the sea." (xii) She points out that scientists do not yet know all of the consequences that radioactive wastes will have on sea life.

Carson's 1961 preface also explains that researchers are only beginning to understand the complicated dynamics of the sea. When

The Sea Around Us was first published, the science of oceanography was in its infancy, but subsequent developments in submarine technology allowed people to travel deeper beneath the ocean surface than ever before. Carson's revised edition of the book therefore includes newer research regarding the geology of the ocean floor, along with black-and-white photographs of oceanographic research equipment as well as photographs of sea life and surface events such as storms and volcanic activity. However, in the final chapter to both editions, she says that researchers still have much to learn about the ocean. After a historical discussion of navigation and mapmaking, she says: "It took centuries to chart the surface of the sea; our progress in delineating the unseen world beneath it seems by comparison phenomenally rapid. But even with all our modern instruments for probing and sampling the deep ocean, no one now can say that we shall ever resolve the last, the ultimate mysteries of the sea." (209) (Carson 1961)

> See also Balanced Ecosystems; Carson, Rachel Louise; Climate Changes; Environmental Movement; Geological Research; Nuclear Energy; *Silent Spring;* Waste Management; Water Pollution.

Sea of Slaughter

Published in 1984, *Sea of Slaughter* is the work of Canadian naturalist Farley Mowat, one of the most popular nature writers addressing conservation issues today. The book is written in first-person narrative but has an extensive bibliography of scientific material. Like Mowat's earlier works, including *Never Cry Wolf* (1963) and *A Whale for the Killing* (1972), it mixes personal commentary with historical facts and statistics to discuss humanity's assault on nature. By the time *Sea of Slaughter* was written, however, Mowat had become more deeply involved in the environmental movement; therefore the book is a far more serious work than its predecessors, offering a long list of atrocities that human beings have committed against a variety of animals, such as birds, bears, otters, wild dogs and cats, fish, and whales.

Sea of Slaughter opens with a discussion of how Mowat became interested in the endangered species of oceans and seashores. For a time he lived in Newfoundland, where he witnessed human attacks on whales and seals. Later he realized that the populations of these animals and many others were decreasing along the Atlantic Coast. He found himself wondering three things: "If the natural life in the eastern seaboard had lost so much ground during a single human generation, how much might it have lost since European men began their conquest of this continent? And, if that loss had been on a scale comparable to what was happening now, what did it portend for the ongoing existence of all life on this planet—human and non-human—since, in the last analysis, life is indivisible? Finally, if animate creation was indeed being done to death by man, what could we do to halt the slaughter before it was too late?" (Mowat 1984, 12)

In *Sea of Slaughter* Mowat attempts to answer these questions by presenting a history of natural life in North America. He limits himself to the eastern coastline because he is most familiar with it. Moreover, he says: "This is a comparatively small portion of the earth's surface, but it had an incredibly rich natural history, and the destruction of its creature life reflects in miniature the history of the exploitation of such life throughout the entire domain of modern man, a domain that has now come to encompass almost the entire surface of this planet." (13) Mowat also restricts his discussion to birds, fish, and sea mammals, "because if we *should* change our attitude . . . the sea mammals seem to have the best chance for recovery and survival in a world where many terrestrial mammals are being physically squeezed out of existence by our destruction of their habitats and by our burgeoning appetites." (13)

However, although *Sea of Slaughter* is a chronicle of assaults on animals, Mowat stresses that it is "not a book about animal extinctions." (13) He explains: "It is about a massive diminution of the entire body corporate of animal creation. Although a number of the chapters tell the stories of animals that have indeed been extirpated, the greater part of the book is concerned with those species that still survive as distinct life forms but have suffered horrendous diminishment. Many have been reduced to little more than relic populations that continue to exist by whatever grace and favour mankind sees fit to extend to them." (13–14)

In discussing this diminishment, Mowat quotes historical first-person accounts of hunters, researchers, and other observers of nature. Some of these accounts are quite graphic. For example, one 1778 description of a polar bear hunt includes the following passage:

I shot the [female bear] through the head and killed her dead. The cub perceiving this and getting sight of me made at me with great ferocity; but just as the creature was about to revenge the death of his dam, I saluted him with a load of large shot in his right eye, which not only knocked that out, but also made him close the other. He no sooner was able to keep his left eye open than he made at me again, quite mad with rage and pain; but when he came to the foot of the bank, I gave him another salute with the other barrel, and blinded him most completely; his whole head was then entirely covered with blood. (100)

In addition to such accounts, Mowat himself meticulously describes each species' typical manner of death, sparing no details. He therefore suggests that some readers might be disturbed by his book, which documents a "pit of horrors" caused by "the consequences of unbridled greed unleashed against animate creation." (14) But he explains that his aim in sharing these descriptions is to "help to change our attitudes and modify our future activities so that we do not become the ultimate destroyers of the living world." (14)

To that aim, Sea of Slaughter also includes Mowat's opinions on a variety of political issues related to the environmental movement. For example, in his chapter on wild cats and

dogs, he criticizes the Canadian Wildlife Federation, which he explains was created by hunting and fishing groups and is not related to the federal government's Canadian Wildlife Service. He states that this group "proclaims it is devoted to 'enhancing wildlife population' . . . [but] this 'enhancement' is, to a very considerable degree, intended to provide living targets to satisfy its sportsmen members." To prove his point, Mowat says that the group raised money by raffling off "a ten-day hunting safari to Zimbabwe, where the lucky winner would have the opportunity to shoot his fill of African animals." (159)

Sea of Slaughter is particularly noted for its thorough discussion of harp seal slaughters. After its publication, Mowat was credited as being one of the first naturalists to expose this practice to public scrutiny, and the issue remains important to the author. In 1996, for example, he became involved with an effort to make living seals more profitable than dead ones. As part of an environmental group called the Sea Shepherds, he flew to Quebec's Magdalen Islands to collect shed seal hair, which was then sold as stuffing for comforters.

Sea of Slaughter lauds this kind of activity and offers many comments in support of environmentalists everywhere. In its concluding paragraphs, it commends "individuals who, revolted by the frightful excesses to which we have subjected animate creation, are beginning to revolt against the killer beast man has become. Banding together in groups of ever-increasing potency, they are challenging the licence of vested interests to continue savaging the living world for policy, profit, or pleasure." (405) (Mowat 1984)

See also Animal Behavior; Conservationism; Environmental Activism; Environmental Movement; Habitat Protection; Mowat, Farley; Wildlife Conservation.

Sessions, George

Ecophilosopher George Sessions coauthored *Deep Ecology: Living as If Nature Mattered* (1985) with Bill Devall. It was the first North American book on deep ecology, an environmentally centered philosophy originated by

Norwegian philosopher Arne Naess; as such it helped to define the deep ecology movement in the United States.

See also *Deep Ecology;* Deep Ecology Movement; Devall, Bill.

Shabecoff, Philip

Philip Shabecoff has written numerous articles on environmental issues. For 14 years he was chief environmental reporter for *The New York Times;* later he became executive editor of *Greenwire,* an environmental news service. He is the author of a comprehensive history of the American environmental movement, *A Fierce Green Fire: The American Environmental Movement* (1993), an important reference source for anyone studying American environmentalism. (Shabecoff 1993)

See also Environmental History; Environmental Movement; *Fierce Green Fire, A.*

Shepard, Paul

A professor of natural philosophy, Paul Shepard is the author of several books about the connection between humans and their environment. In particular, he believes that people's contact with animals influences brain development and, consequently, sanity. His works include *Man in the Landscape* (1967), *Environ/mental: Essays on the Planet as a Home* (1971), *Thinking Animals: Animals and the Development of Human Intelligence* (1978), *Nature and Madness* (1982), and *The Others: How Animals Made Us Human* (1996).

Shiva, Vandana

Director of the Research Foundation for Science, Technology, and Natural Resource Policy in Dehradun, India, physicist Vandana Shiva promotes environmentalism among women's groups in her native country. She is the author of several books on environmental issues, including *Forestry Crisis and Forestry Myths: A Critical Review of Tropical Forests* (1987), *Staying Alive: Women, Ecology, and Development* (1988), and *Ecology and the Politics of Survival: Conflicts Over Natural Resources in India* (1991).

Sierra

The magazine *Sierra* is published bimonthly by the Sierra Club, the oldest and one of the largest environmental groups in the United States. The periodical is significant not only because it has a large circulation but because it presents the latest research and offers environmentalists' views on a range of environmental problems. For example, the July/August 1997 issue discusses forestry conservation, the January/February 1998 issue focuses on environmental politics, and the July/August 1998 issue is devoted to the ocean, offering articles on pollution, endangered species, fishing practices, and coastal habitats. In addition to providing such information, *Sierra* functions as a fund-raising tool for the group, encouraging people to donate to environmental causes. In this respect it is like many other magazines published by environmental groups, such as *National Wildlife* and *The Nature Conservancy Magazine.*

See also Environmental Groups; Environmental Politics; Forest Management; Habitat Protection; *National Wildlife; Nature Conservancy Magazine, The;* Water Pollution; Wildlife Conservation.

Silent Spring

Written by biologist Rachel Carson, *Silent Spring* warns about the dangers of indiscriminate pesticide use and helped inspire the American environmental movement during the 1960s and 1970s. As Philip Shabecoff reports in *A Fierce Green Fire:*

Silent Spring . . . is now recognized as one of the truly important books of this century. More than any other, it changed the way Americans, and people around the world, looked at the reckless way we live on this planet. Focusing on a specific problem—the poisoning of the earth by chemical pesticides—*Silent Spring* was a broad examination of how carelessly applied science and technology were destroying nature and threatening life, including human life. Beautifully written and a bestseller, it sounded a deep chord which af-

Grape vines are dusted with pesticides, California, near Fresno, 1972 (National Archives)

fected people emotionally and moved them to act. It may be the basic book of America's environmental revolution. (Shabecoff 1993, 107)

Silent Spring was published in 1962, first in serial form in *The New Yorker Magazine* and subsequently as a book. It opens with a description of a town suffering from "a strange blight." Carson writes:

Some evil spell had settled on the community: mysterious maladies swept the flocks of chickens; the cattle and sheep sickened and died. Everywhere was a shadow of death. The farmers spoke of much illness among their families. . . .

There was a strange stillness. The birds, for example—where had they gone? . . . The few birds seen anywhere were moribund; they trembled violently and could not fly. It was a spring without voices. . . . On the farms the hens brooded, but no chicks hatched. The farmers complained that they were unable to raise any pigs— the litters were small and the young survived only a few days. The apple trees were coming into bloom but no bees droned among the blossoms, so there was no pollination and there would be no fruit. The roadsides, once so attractive, were now lined with browned and withered vegetation as though swept by fire. These, too, were silent, deserted by all living things. (Carson 1962, pp. 2–3)

Carson then states that this town does not exist but is representative of the type of environmental destruction taking place across America. The cause of this destruction is excessive pesticide use. Carson explains:

Since the mid-1940s over 200 basic chemicals have been created for use in killing insects, weeds, rodents, and other organisms. . . . These sprays, dusts, and aerosols are . . . applied almost universally to farms, gardens, forests, and homes—nonselective chemicals that have the power to

kill every insect, the "good" and the "bad," to still the song of birds and the leaping of fish in the streams, to coat the leaves with a deadly film, and to linger on in soil—all this though the intended target may be only a few weeds or insects. (7)

Carson discusses the reasons behind this increase in pesticide use and says: "It is not my contention that chemical insecticides must never be used. I do contend that we have put poisonous and biologically potent chemicals indiscriminately into the hands of persons largely or wholly ignorant of their potentials for harm." (12) She then offers several chapters of information on how chemicals damage air, water, soil, insects, plants, animals, and people. She particularly condemns the use of DDT (dichloro-diphenyl-trichloroethane), a chemical she believes can cause cancer in humans.

When *Silent Spring* was published, Carson's comments about the relationship between pesticides and cancer had an enormous impact on the American public. According to Roderick Frazier Nash in *The Rights of Nature: A History of Environmental Ethics:* "The realization that insecticides menaced human health made *Silent Spring* headline news." (Nash 1989, p. 79) Nash explains that this response was exactly what the author intended, saying: "Carson intended the book to shock Americans into awareness and action. She was angry. Her objective was to outlaw insecticides or at least greatly constrain their use." (79)

To this aim, in addition to discussing health risks, *Silent Spring* gives examples of places where pesticide spraying has failed to save crops, either because the sprayed insects eventually became resistant to chemicals or because once one insect was eliminated another arrived to take its place. Carson emphasizes the impact these failures had on agricultural profits and offers alternative methods for managing pesticides. (Carson 1962; Nash 1989; Shabecoff 1993)

See also Carson, Rachel Louise; Environmental Activism; Environmental Movement; Pesticides and Chemicals.

Silko, Leslie Marmon

Poet and novelist Leslie Marmon Silko features the land in her work. As Gregory Salyer says in *Leslie Marmon Silko,* his book on the author's writings: "More than any other writer, Silko gives the earth a voice by making her the heroine of nearly every story. Whether she is speaking through women, men, or animals, the earth is embodied in these voices and calls us back to the very ground on which we stand." (Salyer 1997, 133)

Of Native American heritage, Silko was born on March 5, 1948, in Albuquerque, New Mexico, and grew up on an Indian reservation in nearby Laguna. She attended the University of New Mexico, graduating with a B.A. in English in 1969. Her first story, "The Man to Send Rain Clouds," was published that same year in *New Mexico Quarterly* and was later featured in a collection (*The Man to Send Rain Clouds,* 1974).

Silko spent a few years after graduation exploring different lifestyles. She took some graduate English courses, taught briefly on an Indian reservation, and was married and divorced twice. In 1973 she moved to Alaska, where she wrote a novel, *Ceremony* (1977), a collection of poetry, *Laguna Woman* (1974), and several short stories. In 1976 she returned to Laguna; two years later she accepted a teaching position at the University of Arizona–Tucson. In 1981 she published a collection of poems, short stories, and photographs entitled *Storyteller,* and in 1991 her novel *Almanac of the Dead* appeared.

Between major works Silko published nonfiction and produced a film, *Estoyehmuut and the Gunnadeyah,* and a videotape, *Running on the Edge of the Rainbow.* Her other works include *Sacred Water: Narratives and Pictures* (1993), *Yellow Woman and a Beauty of the Spirit: Essays on Native American Life Today* (1996), and *Garden in the Dunes* (1997). Silko continues to live and write in Tucson.

Simple Life, The

The 1973 book *The Simple Life: The Christian Stance Toward Possessions* by theologian Vernard Eller illustrates the merging of environmentalism, the simple living movement, and religion that occurred during the late 1960s and early 1970s. At that time, people increasingly began to examine environmental issues in terms of lifestyle and spirituality, and Eller's work represents one of the foremost examples of this trend. He argues the need for simple living by saying:

Today an urgent new rationale for simple living has obtruded upon us. Unless we voluntarily discipline our present runaway rate of consumption, we shortly will bring disaster upon the race either through the contamination of our environment, through the depletion of essential natural resources or, most likely, through both at once. . . . And what makes the situation even more difficult regarding the environmental crisis is that very many people will need to act before the action has any effect on the problem at all. Thus, if I look around and do not see that anyone else is hurting himself to save the situation, I draw the natural conclusion that it would be stupid for me to give up my piece of the pie to no purpose. (Eller 1973, 35–38)

He then relates simple living to Christianity, saying:

Christians, however, . . . have a rationale for the simple life that is infinitely superior to mere self-interest. And even more to the point, they have a gospel that goes far beyond man's saving himself by pulling at his own ecological bootstraps: it includes a God who can and will . . . give man what it takes to discipline their rate of consumption, first of all as a way of getting themselves correctly positioned to enjoy this God, and then—as an entirely free bonus—as an effective way of meeting the environmental crisis as well. . . . The ecologists themselves should be the first to applaud the fact that Jesus asks for loyalty to himself even before loyalty to the environment; his demand is the best possible guarantee that the environment will get what it needs. (Eller 1973, 35–38)

Other religionists of the period argued the same points from their own theological perspectives. For example, Dr. Fritz Schumacher discusses the connection between environmentalism and Buddhism in *Small Is Beautiful;* and the works of Gary Snyder often speak of environmentalism in terms of Taoism. Many authors of the 19th century, particularly Ralph Waldo Emerson, also talked about the religious aspects of nature, but they did not typically analyze their topic in terms of environmental problems. Instead, they focused on spiritual needs and the emotional satisfaction derived from wilderness pursuits. (Eller 1973)

See also Emerson, Ralph Waldo; Simple Living Movement; *Small Is Beautiful;* Snyder, Gary.

Simple Living Movement

The simple living movement is an offshoot of the modern environmental movement. Not all participants in the simple living movement are environmentalists. However, they do typically adhere to a lifestyle that is ecologically sound.

People who advocate simple living seek to reduce dependence on modern technology. They shun the materialism and wastefulness of technologically advanced societies. Many have gone back to nature, so to speak, living modestly off the land. One of the people credited with inspiring this trend is 19th-century essayist Henry David Thoreau, whose book *Walden* concerns his own experiences with simple living. Although it was published in 1854, *Walden* was not fully appreciated until the 1900s, when conservationists and environmentalists decided that Thoreau's call for a more simple lifestyle was worth following.

As the environmental movement gained strength during the mid-1900s, ecologists increasingly supported simple living as a way to improve the environment. Wendell Berry spoke of the connection between simple living and environmentalism in *A Continuous Har-*

mony (1972); Vernard Eller did the same in *The Simple Life* (1973), which examines both issues from a religious perspective. Such works were widely read by environmentalists, many of whom decided to embrace a more primitive lifestyle. A major publication of the movement, *The Whole Earth Catalogue,* offered these people information on tools, kits, and other products designed for rural living. Today the magazine *Mother Earth News* provides similar information, publishing articles from individuals who want to share helpful advice based on their own experiences with simple living. (Shi 1985; Simple Living Collective 1977)

See also Berry, Wendell; *Continuous Harmony, A; Mother Earth News; Simple Life, The;* Thoreau, Henry David; *Walden; Whole Earth Catalogue, The.*

Sixth Extinction, The

Published in 1995, *The Sixth Extinction: Patterns of Life and the Future of Humankind* is a prominent example of the modern apocalyptic view on evolution. The book, by noted anthropologist and conservationist Richard Leakey and science writer Roger Lewin, argues that the earth has already gone through five great periods of extinction, the most recent of which occurred 65 million years ago when the dinosaurs disappeared; it suggests that a sixth period of extinction is now under way. The authors explain:

Life's flow is in a constant, dynamic change. Sometimes it is driven by a shift in climate, so that terrain that once was arid may become moist, bringing with it a shift in the cast of characters that are able to live there. Sometimes it is driven by a burst of evolutionary turmoil, so that creatures that once existed are no more, and new ones take their place. Bouts of extinction and speciation are a periodic force in changing life's flow, generating constantly shifting patterns. (Leakey and Lewin 1995, 5)

In the first two sections of the book, "Time and Change" and "The Engine of Evolution," they discuss the first five periods of extinction. They broach the evolutionary theories of such scientists as Charles Darwin and Stephen Jay Gould and offer their own opinions regarding evolution and the disappearance of species. They also discuss the importance of maintaining earth's biodiversity. In the last two sections of the book, "The Balance of Nature?" and "The Future," they suggest that human beings are causing a sixth period of extinction. They address the balance of nature and man's interference with it, discussing exploration, colonization, overpopulation, hunting, and other issues related to human expansion and species destruction. To illustrate the effect that humans can have on a single species, they offer detailed information on the plight of the elephant, which has been hunted for its ivory:

> Elephants, biologists now realize, are a key agency in the creation of mosaic habitats in which other species can thrive. . . . Biologists use the term *keystone herbivore* to describe this kind of species. And, just as an arch will collapse if the keystone is removed, so too will an ecosystem if its keystone herbivore goes extinct. [Biologist] Norman Owen-Smith . . . claims it is possible to see this on a grand scale in the not very distant past. Almost certainly, human predation was responsible for the extinction of the large herbivores in the Americas . . . ten thousand years ago. . . . But, he points out, many smaller mammals and birds became extinct too. . . . With the mega-herbivores eliminated, open forest glades closed up, bushland reverted to woodland, and grassland mosaics became uniform tall grassland. These vegetational changes . . . would have restricted the habitats available to smaller herbivores, causing the cascade of extinctions we see in the fossil record. (216)

Leakey and Lewin explain that there are three main ways that humans can cause species extinction. The first is hunting. The second is by introducing a foreign species into an ecosystem, whether accidentally or on purpose. The third is habitat destruction. They suggest that such actions can have serious consequences, arguing that without biodiversity human beings will probably become extinct, too. They state: "The daily cutting of tropical forests and encroachment on wild habitats is a less dramatic process than [an] asteroid impact, but in the end the effect is the same. Insidiously, a mass extinction is occurring. In pursuing our own ends, we treat the world of nature as if it can withstand each of our assaults without harm, but we do so at our own peril." (250) (Leakey and Lewin 1995)

See also Climate Changes; Darwin, Charles Robert; Environmental Apocalypse; Evolution; Gould, Stephen Jay; Habitat Protection; Leakey, Richard.

Small Is Beautiful

Published in 1974, *Small Is Beautiful* was written by Dr. Fritz Schumacher, who served as economic adviser to the British National Coal Board from 1950 to 1970. The book appeared during the early environmental movement and helped inspire later writings on social ecology and simple living. Moreover, its title became one of the catch phrases of the movement.

Small Is Beautiful addresses materialism, the overproduction of goods needed to support it, and the consequent depletion of the earth's resources. Schumacher calls these resources "natural capital," using economic terms to explain their intrinsic value. He says:

> Let us take a closer look at this "natural capital." First of all, and most obviously, there are the fossil fuels. No one, I am sure, will deny that we are treating them as income items although they are undeniably capital items. If we treated them as capital items, we should be concerned with conservation; we should do everything in our power to try and minimize their current rate of use; we might be saying, for instance, that the money obtained from the realization of these assets—these irreplaceable assets—must be placed into a

special fund to be devoted exclusively to the evolution of production methods and patterns of living which do *not* depend on fossil fuels at all or depend on them only to a very slight extent. These and many other things we should be doing if we treated fossil fuels as capital and not as income. And we do not do any of them, but the exact contrary of every one of them: we are not in the least concerned with conservation; we are maximizing, instead of minimizing, the current rates of use; and, far from being interested in studying the possibilities of alternative methods of production and patterns of living—so as to get off the collision course on which we are moving with ever-increasing speed— we happily talk of unlimited progress. (Schumacher 1974, 11–15)

Schumacher reports that this behavior has given many people cause for concern, saying: "The liquidation of these capital assets is proceeding so rapidly that even in the allegedly richest country in the world, the United States of America, there were many worried men, right up to the White House, calling for the massive conversion of coal into oil and gas, demanding ever more gigantic efforts to search for and exploit the remaining treasures of the earth." (Schumacher 1974, 11–15)

Schumacher discusses the reasons for such behavior, citing public attitudes and scientific advances as being the most to blame for it. Of the former, he says: "We are estranged from reality and inclined to treat as valueless everything we have not made ourselves." (11–12) Of the latter, he states:

Our scientists and technologists have learned to compound substances unknown to nature. Against many of them, nature is virtually defenceless. There are no natural agents to attack and break them down. It is as if aborigines were suddenly attacked with machine-gun fire: their bows and arrows are of no avail. These substances, unknown to nature, owe their almost magical effectiveness precisely to nature's

defencelessness—and that accounts also for their dangerous ecological impact. . . . The changes of the last twenty-five years, both in the quantity and in the quality of man's industrial processes, have produced an entirely new situation—a situation resulting not from our failures but from what we thought were our greatest successes. (12–15)

Consequently Schumacher argues that the only way to improve the environment is to change society's approach to the production of goods and to begin treating the earth's resources not as income, which can be replenished, but as capital, which must be conserved. Otherwise, "the modern industrial system consumes the very basis on which it has been erected." (16)

In discussing conservation, Schumacher points out the benefits of keeping human societies and their components small. He explains that by "small" he means "appropriate":

What scale is appropriate? It depends on what we are trying to do. The question of scale is extremely crucial today, in political, social and economic affairs just as in almost everything else. What, for instance, is the appropriate size of a city? . . . While one cannot judge these things with precision, I think it is fairly safe to say that the upper limit of what is desirable for the size of a city is probably something of the order of half a million inhabitants. It is quite clear that above such a size nothing is added to the virtue of a city. In places like London, or Tokyo, or New York, the millions do not add to the city's real value but merely create *enormous* problems and produce human degradation. So probably the order of magnitude of 500,000 inhabitants could be looked upon as the upper limit. (55)

Schumacher also suggests that societies should limit technology as well. He argues that advanced, complicated technology is not necessarily better for people to use:

Simple equipment is normally far less dependent on raw materials of great purity or exact specifications and much more adaptable to market fluctuations than highly sophisticated equipment. Men are more easily trained; supervision, control, and organization are simpler; and there is far less vulnerability to unforeseen difficulties. (151–152)

Along with simple machines, Schumacher advocates a simpler approach to life in general. In particular, he suggests that certain aspects of Buddhist philosophy be embraced by all human societies:

While the materialist is mainly interested in goods, the Buddhist is mainly interested in liberation. . . . It is not wealth that stands in the way of liberation but the attachment to wealth; not the enjoyment of pleasurable things but the craving for them. The keynote of Buddhist economics, therefore, is simplicity and nonviolence. From an economist's point of view, the marvel of the Buddhist way of life is the utter rationality of its pattern—amazingly small means leading to extraordinarily satisfactory results.

For the modern economist this is very difficult to understand. He is used to measuring the "standard of living" by the amount of annual consumption, assuming all the time that a man who consumes more is "better off" than a man who consumes less. A Buddhist economist would consider this approach excessively irrational: since consumption is merely a means to human well-being, the aim should be to obtain the maximum of well-being with the minimum of consumption. Thus, if the purpose of clothing is a certain amount of temperature comfort and an attractive appearance, the task is to attain this purpose with the smallest possible effort, that is, with the smallest annual destruction of cloth and with the help of designs that involve the smallest possible input of toil. The less toil there is, the more

time and strength is left for artistic creativity. It would be highly uneconomic, for instance, to go in for complicated tailoring, like the modern vest, when a much more beautiful effect can be achieved by the skilful draping of uncut material. It would be the height of folly to make material so that it would wear out quickly and the height of barbarity to make anything ugly, shabby or mean. What has just been said about clothing applies equally to all other human requirements. The ownership and the consumption of goods is a means to an end, and Buddhist economics is the systematic study of how to attain given ends with the minimum means. (45–50)

Schumacher also advocates a Buddhist attitude toward nature. He explains that under Buddhist philosophy "non-renewable goods must be used only if they are indispensable, and then only with the greatest care and the most meticulous concern for conservation. To use them heedlessly or extravagantly is an act of violence." (50–51) *Small Is Beautiful* asks that people embrace Buddhism's tenets regarding simple living, even if they do not embrace its religious teachings. For this reason, the book remains important for those involved in the simple living movement.

See also Simple Living Movement.

Snyder, Gary

Poet and essayist Gary Snyder has written extensively on man's relationship to nature; many of his ideas helped to shape the American environmental movement during the 1960s and 1970s. He was born on May 8, 1930, in San Francisco, grew up in the Pacific Northwest, and attended the University of California–Berkeley, where he studied linguistics and languages. He also worked as a seaman, a lumberjack, and a forest ranger. From 1956 to 1964 Snyder spent most of his time at a monastery in Kyoto, Japan, where he practiced Zen Buddhism; during the late 1960s he became an environmental activist and spokesperson.

Snyder's many works include *Turtle Island* (1974), for which he won the 1975 Pulitzer Prize, *No Nature: New and Selected Poems* (1992), and two collections of essays, *The Practice of the Wild* (1990) and *A Place in Space: Ethics, Aesthetics, and Watersheds* (1995). *The Practice of the Wild* contains nine essays on wilderness issues and attitudes; *A Place in Space* contains 29 essays exploring the importance of place in people's sense of self. In 1996 Snyder published a long poem, *Mountains and Rivers Without End,* performing readings of the work in several major cities. (Snyder 1990; Steuding 1976)

See also Environmental Activism; Environmental Movement; *Practice of the Wild, The; Turtle Island.*

Social Ecology

Ecology refers to the relationship of the earth's living and nonliving organisms to one another and to their environment. *Social ecology* refers to the way that human social systems impact earth's ecology. Social ecologists view social problems such as overpopulation and poverty as inseparable from ecological problems such as forest depletion and air pollution.

The concept of social ecology was first developed by Murray Bookchin, an environmentalist interested in pollution. As Bookchin studied the issue, he recognized that urbanization was responsible for many other ecological problems. He consequently decided that these problems would not be solved under a capitalist system. In *Which Way for the Ecology Movement?* (1994), he explains that "ecological degradation is, in great part, a product of the degradation of human beings by hunger, material insecurity, class rule, hierarchical domination, patriarchy, ethnic discrimination, and competition." (Bookchin 1994, 17) Similarly, in *The Closing Circle* (1971), social ecologist Barry Commoner states that the environmental crisis "is not the product of man's *biological* capabilities ... but of his *social* actions." (Commoner 1971, 299)

Social ecologists believe that the only way to solve ecological problems is to change human attitudes and lifestyles. Many suggest that people end their dependence on technology and return to a more simple way of life. This concept is part of the simple living movement. Other social ecologists advocate deeper changes in attitude. Some participate in the deep ecology movement, which not only embraces the concept of simple living but offers a complex philosophy regarding people's relationship to nature. Other social ecologists believe that the solution is found in politics rather than individual attitudes. Commoner, for example, supports socialism and argues that private corporations need to be under public control in order to end business practices that damage the environment.

See also Bookchin, Murray; *Closing Circle, The;* Commoner, Barry; Deep Ecology Movement; Simple Living Movement; *Which Way for the Ecology Movement?*

Solace of Open Spaces, The

The Solace of Open Spaces (1985) is a collection of essays in which author Gretel Ehrlich describes her experiences living as a Wyoming sheep rancher as well as her impressions of the land. For example, in an essay entitled "On Water," Ehrlich says:

Dryness is the common denominator in Wyoming. We're drenched more often in dust than water; it is the scalpel and the suit of armor that make westerners what they are. Dry air presses a stockman's insides outward. The secret, inner self is worn not on the sleeve but in the skin. It's an unlubricated condition: there's not enough moisture in the air to keep the whole emotional machinery oiled and working. . . . Cowboys have learned not to waste words from not having wasted water, as if verbosity would create a thirst too extreme to bear. If voices are raspy, it's because vocal cords are coated with dust. (Trimble 1995, 202)

Ehrlich is not a native of Wyoming; she was raised in Santa Barbara, California. She thus brings an outsider's perspective to her work. (Trimble 1995)

Species Identification and Classification

During ancient times, interest in the environment was expressed primarily through efforts to identify and classify the world's organic and nonorganic components. Some people studied nature in order to benefit from it, by finding medicinal plants or valuable ores, for example. Others sought to understand the order of the world by determining how its creatures are related to one another. One of the earliest scholars to engage in species classification was Aristotle (384–323 B.C.), who was the first person to identify the dolphin as a mammal rather than a fish. He also developed the concept that life was a hierarchy of lesser and greater creatures, all inferior to man.

Greek botanist Theophrastus expanded on Aristotle's work by describing more than 550 plants, and circa 50 A.D. Greek physician Dioscorides wrote *De Materia Medica* to discuss plants with medicinal uses. Roman scholar Pliny the Elder (27–79 A.D.) identified plant and animal species (including mythological beasts as well as real ones) in his 37-volume work *Natural History.*

During the Renaissance, knowledge of nature expanded with increased exploration and colonization, and works such as *Observations Made During a Voyage Round the World* (by Johann Reinhold Forster) spread such information to the general public. At the same time, the development of more powerful microscopes allowed men like Jan Swimmerdam to discover a new world at the bacterial level.

One of the most significant books of this period is Conrad Gesner's *Historia Animalium* (more than 4,000 pages in five volumes, 1551–1587). It provided information on hundreds of creatures and greatly advanced Renaissance knowledge. However, it listed animals alphabetically rather than using a classification system.

This type of arrangement became problematic as the number of known species grew. In the case of plants, for example, the number doubled from 6,000 to 12,000 during the 17th century. Fortunately, English naturalist John Ray developed the concept of species, suggesting that animals should be grouped according to their ability to reproduce with one another; in the 18th century Swedish botanist Carolus Linnaeus used this concept to create the species classification system that is still used today.

Around the same time, the Comte de Buffon (1707–1788) produced an encyclopedia of natural history that included information on all known species and discussed their origin. His work would later become important to Jean-Baptiste Lamarck, Georges Cuvier, Charles Darwin, and other scientists involved in the study of species evolution. These evolutionary theorists examined species and their fossils in order to discover how they might have changed over time. Lamarck also developed a system of organizing species for museum display; Cuvier refined Linnaeus's classification system.

During modern times, scientists continue to identify and classify new species. However, because most species have already been discovered, they are more concerned with determining which existing species are threatened or endangered. This focus on preservation began during the 19th century, when books on species identification, such as John James Audubon's *Birds of America,* were written with the intent of promoting conservationism. As the body of works of this type grew, so too did the public's concern for species preservation.

See also Aristotle; Audubon, John James; *Birds of America;* Buffon, Georges Louis Leclerc, Comte de; Conservationism; Cuvier, Georges; Darwin, Charles Robert; Dioscorides; Gesner, Conrad; *Historia Animalium;* Lamarck, Jean-Baptiste; Linnaeus, Carolus; *Natural History; Observations Made During a Voyage Round the World;* Pliny the Elder; Ray, John; Swimmerdam, Jan; Theophrastus.

Species Plantarum

Published in 1753, *Species Plantarum* introduced the modern system of naming and classifying botanical species. Its author, Carolus Linnaeus, was the first to give each known plant two Latin names, one for its genus and one for its individual species. He did the same for animals in the 10th edition of *Systema*

Naturae (orig. publ. 1735; 10th ed. 1758). Linnaeus's work was extremely important. His books were widely read, and his classification system was quickly adopted by scientists throughout the world. At first the specific names that Linnaeus created, as set forth in his books, were the only ones in existence, but as new species and genera were discovered other scientists created names in accordance with Linnaeus's guidelines. Moreover, this classification system caused scientists to carefully consider the similarities among species so that they could group them according to genus. (Larson 1971)

See also Linnaeus, Carolus; Species Identification and Classification.

Steensen, Niels

Born on January 10, 1638, in Copenhagen, Denmark, 17th-century physician Niels Steensen, also known as Nicolaus Steno, made major contributions to the field of geology. For example, he recognized that fossils were the remains of prehistoric creatures, and he studied the properties of the rocks that contained them, developing theories regarding rock formations and suggesting that strata could be used to trace the earth's geologic history. His work was published in 1669 as *De solido intra solidum naturaliter contento dissetationis prodomus* (Prodome to a Dissertation Concerning a Solid Naturally Enclosed Within a Solid).

Despite his success as a scientist, in 1675 Steensen abandoned his research altogether to become a Catholic priest. He lived out his life in the clergy, dying in Germany on November 26, 1686. (Boynton 1948; Spangenburg and Moser 1993)

See also Geological Research.

Stegner, Wallace

Born in 1909, award-winning novelist Wallace Stegner wrote several nonfiction books related to nature and the wilderness of the American West. They include *Big Rock Candy Mountain* (1943), *Beyond the Hundredth Meridian: John Wesley Powell and the Second Opening of the West* (1954), *Wolf Willow: A History, a Story, and a Memory of the Last Plains Frontier* (1962), *The Sound of Mountain Water* (1969), and *Where the Bluebird Sings to the Lemonade Springs: Living and Writing in the West* (1992). He also directed the writing program at Stanford University, where N. Scott Momaday was one of his students. Stegner died in 1993.

See also Momaday, N. Scott.

Steinbeck, John

American novelist John Steinbeck received the Novel Prize for Literature in 1962 and is perhaps best known for the novel *The Grapes of Wrath* (1939), about a poor Oklahoma farm family struggling against harsh environmental and economic conditions. However, he also wrote an important nonfiction book related to the environmental sciences. Entitled *The Sea of Cortez* (1941) and later reissued in part as *The Log from the Sea of Cortez* (1951), it chronicles Steinbeck's experiences gathering marine specimens for his friend, Ed Ricketts.

Steinbeck was born in Salinas, California, on February 27, 1902. In 1920 he enrolled at Stanford University as an English major, but his attendance was sporadic; he left in 1925

John Steinbeck (Archive Photos)

without a degree. He began working for a New York newspaper, the *American*.

In 1929 Steinbeck published his first novel, *Cup of Gold*. It was unsuccessful, as were his next two novels, *The Pastures of Heaven* (1932) and *To a God Unknown* (1933). His fourth novel, *Tortilla Flats* (1935), and a collection of stories entitled *The Red Pony* (1937) were more popular. However, it wasn't until the 1937 publication of the novel *Of Mice and Men* that Steinbeck became truly successful. *Of Mice and Men* earned him many prestigious awards, both as a novel and as a play adaptation; two years later he received the Pulitzer Prize and a National Book Award for *The Grapes of Wrath*, which was the top bestseller of 1939.

Shortly thereafter, Steinbeck became interested in documentary films. He traveled to Mexico for a movie on mountain villages, and during World War II he wrote propaganda films and literature for the U.S. government. The most significant work of that period is the novel *The Moon Is Down* (1942), about Nazi oppression in Norway. After the war he continued writing best-selling novels, including *Cannery Row* (1945), *The Pearl* (1947), and *East of Eden* (1952), as well as movie adaptations of his work. He also wrote nonfiction books, such as *Travels with Charley in Search of America* (1962), which documents a three-month trip through the United States with his poodle, Charley. Steinbeck died on December 20, 1968, in New York City. (Fontenrose 1964; French 1975)

See also *Log from the Sea of Cortez, The.*

Steinhart, Peter

Born in 1943, Peter Steinhart is a regular contributor to *Audubon* magazine and the author of such books as *California's Wild Heritage: Threatened and Endangered Animals in the Golden State* (1990) and *The Company of Wolves* (1995). He also provided the text for *Tracks in the Sky* (1987), Tupper Ansel Blake's photographic treatment of Pacific Coast wildlife and wetlands.

Robert Finch and John Elder, in *The Norton Anthology of Nature Writing* (1990), call Steinhart "one of our finest journalistic interpreters of environmental and scientific ideas," adding: "What distinguishes his essays is . . . his belief that 'when we change nature we change our hearts and minds.'" (811).

Stickley, Gustav

American furniture designer Gustav Stickley believed that the physical properties of a home would influence its owners. To that end, he argued that simple homes with simple furniture would promote conservationist thinking. In his 1909 book, *Craftsman Homes*, he writes: "We have wasted and misused so many of our natural resources. All we really need is a change in our point of view toward life and a keener perception regarding the things that count and the things which merely burden us. This being the case, it would seem obvious that the place to begin a readjustment is in the home." (Stickley 1909, 195–196)

Born on March 9, 1858, in Osceola, Wisconsin, Stickley worked at his uncle's chair factory and eventually became its owner, relocating it to Binghamton, New York. In 1900 he began manufacturing extremely simple yet solid furniture, and the following year he started publishing a magazine, *The Craftsman*, to promote his ideas on simple furniture and simple living. *The Craftsman* also featured architectural plans for simple homes that expressed Stickley's beliefs about nature.

Stickley says that "the healthiest and happiest life is that which maintains the closest relationship with out-of-doors"; accordingly, his houses have "outdoor living rooms, dining rooms and sleeping rooms, and many windows to let in plenty of air and sunlight." Moreover, he advocates that Craftsman homes be built away from the city, explaining:

We have planned houses for country living because we firmly believe that the country is the only place to live in. The city is all very well for business, for amusement and some formal entertainment,—in fact for anything and everything that, by its nature, must be carried on outside of the home. But the home itself should be in some place where there is peace and quiet, plenty of room and the chance to establish a sense of intimate relationship with the hills and valleys, trees and brooks and all the things which tend to lessen the strain and worry of modern life by reminding us that after all we are one with Nature. (195–197)

Stickley's work appeared just as America's conservation movement was gaining strength, and it reflects the attitudes that inspired that movement, speaking of nature primarily in terms of human enjoyment and spirituality. For example, Stickley says:

When we have turned once more to natural living instead of setting up our puny affairs and feverish ambitions to oppose the quiet, irresistible course of Nature's law, we will not need to turn hungrily to books for stories of a bygone Golden Age, nor will we need to deplore the vanishing of art and beauty from our lives, for when the day comes that we have sufficient courage and perception to throw aside the innumerable petty superfluities that hamper us now at every turn and the honesty to realize what Nature holds for all who turn to her with a reverent spirit and an open mind, we will find that art is once more a part of our daily life and that the impulse to do beautiful and vital creative work is as natural as the impulse to breathe. (203–204)

For a time *The Craftsman* was extremely popular, but by 1916 sales had fallen so low that Stickley stopped publishing it. Sales of Stickley furniture had declined as well, and when he died on April 21, 1942, he was facing financial difficulty. During the 1970s, however, interest in Craftsman products, particularly homes, revived, and today they are highly valued. (Stickley 1909)

See also Conservationism; Simple Living Movement.

Stone, Roger D.

In 1986 environmentalist and journalist Roger Stone decided to assess the ecological health of the Atlantic Seaboard in North and South America. He sailed the coast in a yacht called *The Sanderling,* making observations and comparing them to historical accounts of the region. Along the way he also spoke with conservationists and scientists about coastal environmental issues. In 1990 he published a first-person account of his experiences in *The Voyage of the Sanderling,* in which he notes that his journey was sponsored by an environmental group, the World Wildlife Fund (WWF). Stone was vice president of WWF from 1982 to 1986. He is also a former chief of the Rio de Janeiro bureau of Time-Life News. (Stone 1990)

See also Balanced Ecosystems; Conservationism; Habitat Protection; *Voyage of the Sanderling, The;* Water Pollution; Wildlife Conservation.

Stork and the Plow, The

Written by Paul Ehrlich, Anne Ehrlich, and Gretchen Daily, *The Stork and the Plow: The Equity Answer to the Human Dilemma* (1995) is the sequel to the Ehrlichs' *The Population Explosion* (1990). Like the Ehrlichs' other works, it warns of a future environmental apocalypse and is therefore often cited by antienvironmentalists who accuse environmentalists of using scare tactics to influence public policy.

Paul and Anne Ehrlich are experts on environmental policy and population problems who are on the faculty of Stanford University, where Gretchen Daily is a research scientist. In *The Stork and the Plow,* the authors expand on ideas presented in *The Population Explosion,* discussing the dangers of overpopulation. In particular, they analyze how population growth affects food production; the stork represents the birth rate and the plow represents agriculture. They explain the relationship:

The world population and food situation beautifully illustrates both the superficial simplicity and the underlying complexity of humanity's ties to the laws and limits of nature. No human activity causes as much direct environmental damage as agriculture, yet no other activity is more dependent for its success on environmental integrity. No lack of the material ingredients of well-being causes as much human suffering as lack of food. And no index so plainly measures failure of a population to remain within its carrying capacity [sustainability] as the extent of hunger-related disease and death. (Ehrlich and Ehrlich 1995, 6)

The Stork and the Plow details agricultural practices throughout the world, documenting facts with extensive notes. The authors also offer opinions regarding the ways that different countries try to control population and how these efforts relate to the feminist movement. For example, they believe that "an extreme wing of the feminist movement . . . has seized on the serious and real problems of abuse of women that exist in most (perhaps all) societies as justification for condemning national and international family planning programs. They view the programs as a racist and sexist plot by the rich and the white-skinned to suppress the poor and dark-skinned by forcing contraception on their women." (133)

The Stork and the Plow argues that, regardless of feminist fears, population growth must be controlled; otherwise, disasters will occur that will ultimately threaten women far more than family planning programs ever would. The authors list several environmental problems that seem to be connected to overpopulation and overfarming, including soil erosion, climate change, and rises in sea levels. They also offer suggestions for solving these problems. For example, they argue for global equity, saying that nations should cooperate to control global population and limit the amount of resources each country can use. In other words, "so many gallons of water will be extracted from rivers with international basins, so many cubic meters of lumber and tons of oil imported, etc. All trade agreements should be designed to allow for differences in

environmental and workers' welfare regulations without penalizing nations that have higher standards and strong controls. Similarly, each nation must pledge to control environmentally damaging emissions that have transborder impacts." (278) The authors insist that even though such global changes will be difficult to achieve, they are necessary if earth is to survive. (Ehrlich and Ehrlich 1995)

See also Agriculture; Antienvironmentalism; Climate Changes; Ehrlich, Paul and Anne; Environmental Apocalypse; Human Ecology; *Population Explosion, The.*

Studies on Glaciers

Published in 1837, *Studies on Glaciers* by Louis Agassiz was the first book to present the theory that the earth once experienced an ice age, when glaciers covered its surface. This theory was at odds with the prevailing scientific opinion that the earth had been cooling gradually since its beginning. As Peter J. Bowler explains in *The Norton History of the Environmental Sciences:*

By modern standards much of Agassiz's interpretation was in error, but in the eyes of his opponents the theory also flew in the face of all the evidence for a steady cooling of the earth through geological time. Agassiz himself accepted the cooling-earth theory, but argued that the process was not continuous. Like a good catastrophist he postulated occasional very sharp drops in the overall temperature interspersed between long periods of stable conditions. Nevertheless, the claim that the last drop in temperature had created conditions that were *colder* than those of today seemed to violate the basic logic of the cooling-earth theory. (Bowler 1993, 225)

A decade after the book's publication, most geologists still rejected the ice age theory. However, evolutionary theorist Charles Darwin partially supported Agassiz's work and wrote that because of it he had begun "examining the marks left by extinct glaciers" on Welsh soil. (226) (Bowler 1993)

See also Agassiz, (Jean) Louis (Rodolphe); Climate Changes; Darwin, Charles Robert; Evolution; Geological Research.

Suess, Eduard

Born in London on August 20, 1831, geologist Eduard Suess advanced the theory that the continents were once a single landmass that broke apart some 200 million years ago. He discussed many of his theories regarding prehistoric geology in *Das antlitz der erde* (The Face of the Earth), a multivolume work published between 1883 and 1888. He also wrote extensively on mountain formation, postulating that they were caused by volcanic activity and violent movements that disrupted the earth's crust. Prior to his geological writings, Suess published articles on fossils as an assistant at the Hoffmuseum in Vienna, Austria, a position he held from 1852 to 1857. From 1857 to 1901 he was a professor of geology at the University of Vienna. In addition, in 1869 he became involved in politics, and he remained active in that regard until shortly before his death on April 26, 1914. (Bowler 1993)

See also *Face of the Earth, The;* Geological Research.

Swammerdam, Jan

Seventeenth-century Dutch naturalist Jan Swammerdam is best known as the first person to examine red blood cells under a microscope and describe them in writing. However, in terms of the environmental sciences, his significance lies in his microscopic studies of insects and his contributions to the modern classification system of insect species. He is considered by many scholars to be the first true entomologist.

Swammerdam was born on February 12, 1637, in Amsterdam. He earned the status of physician in 1667 yet never practiced medicine, preferring instead to devote himself to his microscope. Supported largely by his father, he studied insects and, later, human subjects until 1673, when his father stopped supporting him. Shortly thereafter he joined a religious cult. In 1680 he fell ill and died at the age of 43. Although some of his work was published as *A General History of Insects* during his lifetime, his most important book, the two-volume *Biblia naturae,* was published posthumously (1737–1738).

See also Species Identification and Classification.

Sylva

Sylva: A Discourse of Forest Trees and the Propagation of Timber in His Majesty's Dominions by John Evelyn illustrates the type of environmental awareness that developed during the Renaissance and Restoration in Europe. Published in England in 1662, it advocates the establishment of conservation practices, including selective cutting and aggressive replanting, in order to save existing forests. England's forests were being threatened by overharvesting, in part due to the shipbuilding industry and the growing population's heating needs. Evelyn undertook his study of forest depletion for the Royal Navy, working on commission to identify and describe the country's trees. *Sylva* discusses the cultivation of and best uses for many different types of timber. The author continued to update his work for several years after its publication, and the book remained significant even after Evelyn's death in 1706. By 1825, 10 editions had been published for general use. Although *Sylva* raised awareness of the importance of preserving local forests, the English continued to exploit forests abroad.

See also Conservationism; Evelyn, John; Forest Management.

T

Tansley, Arthur G.

British ecologist Arthur G. Tansley coined the word "ecosystem" in an article describing a community of interconnected plants and animals. Born in 1871, he was a botanist who studied plant communities in Asia, Egypt, and Great Britain during the early 1900s. In 1912 he published *Types of British Vegetation,* based on his work. In 1913 he helped establish the British Ecological Society. Tansley advocated a scientific rather than an emotional approach to ecology, and his main interest continued to be vegetation. He remained active in the field until his death in 1955. (Bowler 1993; Nash 1989; Pepper 1996)

> **See also** Animal Ecology; Balanced Ecosystems.

Teaching a Stone to Talk

Teaching a Stone to Talk: Expeditions and Encounters is the work of Annie Dillard, one of the foremost nature writers in America. Published in 1982, the book not only offers her observations about flora and fauna but also expresses her personal relationship to her environment. For example:

> I alternate between thinking of the planet as home—dear and familiar stone hearth and garden—and as a hard land of exile in which we are all sojourners. Today I favor the latter view. The word "sojourner" occurs often in the English Old Testament. It invokes a nomadic people's sense of vagrancy, a praying people's knowledge of estrangement, a thinking people's intuition of sharp loss. . . . We don't know where we belong, but in times of sorrow it doesn't seem to be here, here with these silly pansies and witless mountains, here with sponges and hard-eyed birds. In times of sorrow the innocence of the other creatures—from whom and with whom we evolved—seems a mockery. Their ways are not our ways. We seem set among them as among lifelike props for a tragedy—or a broad lampoon—on a thrust rock stage. (Dillard 1982, 150–151)

Dillard mentions God, angels, and other aspects of religious belief as they relate to people's connection to nature. She also discusses the environmental sciences as well as early naturalists and explorers, devoting one chapter to polar expeditions and another to Charles Darwin's research on the Galapagos Islands. In the latter, she mentions the controversy Darwin generated and talks about "social Darwinists," whom she defines:

Social Darwinists seized Herbert Spencer's phrase, "the survival of the fittest," applied it to capitalism, and used it to sanction ruthless and corrupt business practices. A social Darwinist is unlikely to identify himself with the term; social Darwinism is, as the saying goes, not a religion but a way of life. A modern social Darwinist wrote the slogan "If you're so smart, why ain't you rich?" The notion still obtains, I believe, wherever people seek power: that the race is to the swift, that everybody is *in* the race, with varying and merited degrees of success or failure, and that reward is its own virtue. (121)

Dillard finds social Darwinists unappealing, and her writing reflects an approach to life that is more in touch with nature. In fact she says: "I could very calmly go wild. I could live two days in the [weasel's] den, curled, leaning on mouse fur, sniffing bird bones, blinking, licking, breathing musk, my hair tangled in the roots of grasses. Down is a good place to go, where the mind is single." (15–16) (Dillard 1982)

See also Darwin, Charles Robert; Dillard, Annie; Evolution; Nature Writing.

Teale, Edwin Way

Born in 1899, Pulitzer Prize–winning nature writer Edwin Way Teale was a contributing editor of *Audubon* magazine from 1942 to 1980. He also wrote about his wilderness activities in such books as *The Lost Woods* (1945), *North with the Spring* (1951), and *A Walk Through the Year* (1978) and was a noted nature photographer. Many of his nature writings concern the area around his home in Hampton, Connecticut. That home still exists, but today it is part of a 156-acre nature sanctuary. Teale died in 1980.

Theophrastus

Greek philosopher Theophrastus supervised research into the nature of plants and animals as head of the Lyceum, an academy founded by Aristotle. He wrote extensively about his findings as well as his theories and beliefs; not all of his works survived the ages. Of that which remains, perhaps the best known regarding the environmental sciences is *Historia Planetarium,* which describes and classifies animals, plants, and minerals. Theophrastus was born circa 372 B.C. in Eresus, on the island of Lesbos. He later went to Athens, where he studied under Aristotle at the Lyceum. In 323 B.C. Aristotle retired, and Theophrastus took over the school. He continued to support Aristotle's philosophical views and wrote extensively on Aristotelian subjects. In addition to *Historia Planetarium,* his works include *Peri Phyton Aiton* (*Plant Growth*), *Physikon Doxai* (Opinions on Natural Philosophers), and *Charakteres* (Characters), the latter of which describes and classifies 30 types of people according to their morals and behavior. Theophrastus is thought to have died in 287 B.C.

See also Aristotle; *Historia Planetarium.*

Thomas, Edward

Born in London in 1878, Edward Thomas wrote essays and poems about nature-related subjects. His best known work is *The South Country* (1909), which describes the English countryside and recognized that the Industrial Revolution threatened to alter the landscape permanently. Thomas's collection of poems, entitled *Poems,* was published in 1917, shortly after he died in World War I.

Thomas, Lewis

Lewis Thomas is a physician who writes essays about biology, the earth, and environmental issues. His first book was a collection of 29 essays on a variety of nature-related topics, entitled *The Lives of a Cell: Notes of a Biology Watcher* (1974); it won the National Book Award. Lewis's subsequent works include *The Medusa and the Snail* (1979) and *Late Night Thoughts on Listening to Mahler's Ninth Symphony* (1983).

Born on November 25, 1913, in Flushing, New York, Lewis attended Princeton University in New Jersey and Harvard Medical School, where he received his medical degree in 1937. After serving in the U.S. Navy, he taught medicine at various universities. In

1954 he took a teaching position at the New York University School of Medicine and eventually became the school's dean. In 1969 he left there to become a teacher at Yale; in 1973 he accepted the presidency of the Memorial Sloan-Kettering Cancer Center.

Thoreau, Henry David

Born on July 12, 1817, in Concord, Massachusetts, naturalist Henry David Thoreau warned that the Industrial Revolution would cause future environmental destruction and suggested that people learn to live off the land. His 1854 book, *Walden,* which offers information on how to live simply in a wilderness setting, was rediscovered by modern environmentalists who used it to popularize the back-to-nature movement during the 1960s and 1970s.

Thoreau graduated from Harvard University in 1837, whereupon he became a teacher at his former grammar school. Unable to control his students, he quit after two weeks and began working for his father, a pencil manufacturer. The following year he started his own school, which used new teaching techniques. However, he soon left it in the hands of his brother and became a poet.

By this time Thoreau had befriended writer Ralph Waldo Emerson, and the pair developed American Transcendentalism, a philosophy that, among other things, celebrated nature. In 1840 the transcendentalists established a magazine, *The Dial,* to advance their views. Thoreau contributed poems and nature essays to the periodical, and in 1842 he concluded that his future as a writer was bright enough to warrant a trip to New York. However, after spending a year trying to attract the notice of publishers, he returned to Concord and his father's pencil factory.

Immensely unhappy, Thoreau decided he needed a private weekend retreat. He began to build it beside a small lake known as Walden Pond, on land owned by Emerson, and he soon realized that he wanted to live there permanently, eating whatever the land was able to produce. He remained at Walden Pond from 1845 to 1847. He kept a journal of his

Henry David Thoreau (Archive Photos)

experiences with simple living there, and it became the basis of the 18 essays in *Walden.* He also spent some of his time writing *A Week on the Concord and Merrimack Rivers.* Published in 1849, that book describes Thoreau's observations and adventures during a seven-day New England boat trip. Thoreau also wrote an essay, "Civil Disobedience" (1849), about defending individual beliefs. Aside from *Walden,* it would become his most famous work.

However, Thoreau's writing brought him little recognition during his lifetime. *A Week on the Concord and Merrimack Rivers* was self-published; only 220 of its 700 copies sold. *Walden* sold only 2,000 copies after five years in print. Nonetheless, according to scholar Hans Huth, Thoreau did attract several followers, who in turn "continued to emulate the nature essay throughout the second half of the nineteenth century." (Huth 1972, 95)

After leaving Walden Pond Thoreau supported himself through surveying work and collecting plant and animal specimens for Harvard University. Later he took over his father's pencil factory. He also participated in the anti-slavery, or abolition, movement. He died on May 6, 1862. His posthumously published works include *Life Without Principle* (1863), *Excursions* (1863), *The Maine Woods* (1864), *Cape Cod* (1865), and *Faith in a Seed* (1993).

Thoreau was working on *The Maine Woods* when he died; the book chronicles three expeditions that the author made into the woods during 1846, 1853, and 1857. *Faith in a Seed* is a collection of Thoreau's late natural history writings, including "The Dispersion of Seeds," which supported Darwin's theory of natural selection by refuting the then-prevalent theory that some plants could spring spontaneously to life without seeds. (Cox 1971; Huth 1972)

See also Darwin, Charles Robert; Nature Writing; Simple Living Movement; *Walden.*

Through the Arc of the Rain Forest

Published in 1990, *Through the Arc of the Rain Forest* by Karen Tei Yamashita is a novella set in a Brazilian rain forest, as is a subsequent Yamashita work, *Brazil-Maru* (1992). Both describe the land and its exploitation by human beings. In *Through the Arc of the Rain Forest,* the forest is threatened with destruction as several characters seek to profit from one of its natural resources, Matacao. This story is narrated by a ball revolving near the head of one of the main characters, Kasumasa Ishimaru, who is asked to find the elusive Matacao for an American company.

See also *Brazil-Maru.*

Timaeus

Timaeus was written by Greek philosopher Plato sometime before 347 B.C. The work discusses mathematics, cosmology, physics, and biology, but in terms of the environmental sciences its most significant aspect is its view of God's relation to nature. Plato believed that God was an intelligence whose ideas became material. These ideas were the pure, ideal patterns upon which individual plants and animals were based. Plato thus believed that studying real plants and animals was not as important as thinking about their ideal forms in the abstract. In addition, *Timaeus* suggests

that God not only created the world but also periodically destroys it to start anew. Plato's concept of cyclical catastrophes influenced the views of later scientists regarding evolution, species extinction, and geological processes. (Bowler 1993)

See also Evolution; Geological Research; Plato.

Toward an Ecological Society

Toward an Ecological Society (1980), by noted social ecologist Murray Bookchin, contains one of his most frequently quoted essays, "Open Letter to the Ecology Movement." It criticizes environmentalists for putting self-interest ahead of environmental concerns:

> Ecology is being used against an ecological sensibility, ecological forms of organization, and ecological practices to "win" large constituencies, *not to educate them.* The fear of "isolation," of "futility," of "ineffectiveness" yields a new kind of isolation, futility and ineffectiveness, namely, a complete surrender of one's most basic ideals and goals. "Power" is gained at the cost of losing the only power we really have that can change this insane society— our moral integrity, our ideals, and our principles. This may be a festive occasion for careerists who have used the ecology issue to advance their stardom and personal fortunes; it would become the obituary of a movement that has, latent within itself, the ideals of a new world in which masses become individuals and natural resources become nature, both to be respected for their uniqueness and spirituality. (Bookchin 1980, 82)

Bookchin is an advocate of social ecology, which he believes is superior to modern environmentalism as it is practiced by large environmental groups. He explains:

> Ecology is now fashionable, indeed, faddish—and with this sleazy popularity has emerged a new type of environmentalist hype. From an outlook and movement that at least held the promise of challeng-

ing hierarchy and domination have emerged a form of *environmentalism* that is based more on tinkering with existing institutions, social relations, technologies, and values than on changing them. I use the word "environmentalism" to contrast it with ecology, specifically with social ecology. Where social ecology, in my view, seeks to eliminate the concept of the domination of nature by humanity by eliminating the domination of human by human, environmentalism reflects an "instrumentalist" or technical sensibility in which nature is viewed merely as a passive habitat, an agglomeration of external objects and forces, that must be made more "serviceable" for human use, irrespective of what these uses may be. Environmentalism, in fact, is merely environmental engineering. It does not bring into question the underlying notions of the present society, notably that man must dominate nature. On the contrary, it seeks to facilitate that domination by developing techniques for diminishing the hazards caused by domination. (77–78)

Bookchin argues that people, instead of trying to control nature or the amount of damage it receives, should be addressing the deeper issue of how they relate to one another and to the environment. He advocates sweeping social changes, suggesting that "the very concept of dominating nature stems from the domination of human by human, indeed, of woman by men, of the young by their elders, of one ethnic group by another, of society by the state, of the individual by bureaucracy, as well as of one economic class by another or a colonized people by a colonial power." (76) (Bookchin 1980)

See also Bookchin, Murray; Social Ecology.

Travels of William Bartram, The
Published in 1791 as *Travels Through North and South Carolina, Georgia, East and West Florida, the Cherokee Country, the Extensive Territories of the Muscogulges, or Creek Confederacy, and the Country of the Choctaws*, William

Bartram's *The Travels of William Bartram* describes four years in the wilderness of the southeastern United States beginning in 1773. Many scholars consider the work flawed yet ahead of its time because of Bartram's approach toward his subject matter. For example, in discussing Bartram's work in *This Incomperable Lande*, Professor Thomas Lyon says:

Bartram's account of these four blithe years . . . is rambling, diverse, florid, oddly put together in places, sketchy on dates and distances traveled, clogged in places with long lists of Latin names of plants, and probably more than a little repetitive, to most readers. But it is also the first fully developed nature essay in this country; it is a brilliant evocation of a mind and vision, and the land that inspired them. . . . Bartram's ready impressionability to whatever he happened upon, and his mind's quickness to recognize not only relationships but also the possibility that he himself might be included in them in some fashion, create his ecological style. He saw a grand, systematic patterning, all revealing the "Almighty hand," . . . so that whatever a man of sensibility and training looked upon, if he looked well, became meaningful. Simply walking through the woods, or catching an unexpected view of the ocean, could evoke from this sensitive man a spiritual excitement. (Lyon 1989, 38)

Bartram often connects his observations to spirituality. For example, in the introduction to *The Travels of William Bartram*, he says:

The animal creation . . . excites our admiration, and equally manifests the almighty power, wisdom, and beneficence of the Supreme Creator and Sovereign Lord of the universe; . . . how wonderful is the mechanism of these finely formed, self-moving beings, how complicated their system, yet what unerring uniformity prevails through every tribe and particular species! . . . We admire the mechanism of a watch, and the fabric of a piece of brocade, as being the production of art; these merit our admiration, and must excite our esteem for the ingenious artist or modifier, but nature is the work of God omnipotent: and an elephant, even this world is comparatively but a very minute part of his works. (Lyon 113–114)

Trimble, Stephen

Stephen Trimble is the editor of an important collection of nature writing, *Words from the Land: Encounters with Natural History Writing* (1989; revised 1995); he has also written several nature-related books, including *The Bright Edge: A Guide to the National Parks of the Colorado Plateau* (1979), *Window into the Earth: Timpanogos Cave* (1983), *The Sagebrush Ocean: A Natural History of the Great Basin* (1984), and *The Geography of Childhood (Why Children Need Wild Places)* with Gary Paul Nabhan (1994). Trimble is also an accomplished photographer and has contributed illustrations to such works as *Mud Matters* by Jennifer Owings Dewey (1998) and *Earth Tones* by Ann Ronald (1995).

Born in 1950 in Denver, Colorado, Trimble is the son of a field geologist; his first job was as a national park ranger in Utah, then in Colorado. While working for the park service, he wrote booklets on national parks. *The Bright Edge* was his first full-length work. After its publication, Trimble studied for and received a master's degree in ecology. In 1981 he became a full-time writer-photographer and moved to Santa Fe, New Mexico, where he wrote about the region's Native Americans. He now lives in Salt Lake City, Utah.

See also Nabhan, Gary Paul.

Turtle Island

A collection of poetry and essays by environmentalist Gary Snyder, *Turtle Island* was published in 1974 and won a Pulitzer Prize the following year. It expresses the author's environmental beliefs and advocates changes in the way American society approaches environmental concerns. For example, in one of the book's most frequently quoted essays, "Four Changes," Snyder advocates government ef-

forts to reduce global overpopulation, adding that individuals should "explore other social structures and marriage forms, such as group marriage and polyandrous marriage, which provide family life but many less children," as well as "share the pleasures of raising children widely, so that all need not directly reproduce to enter into this basic human experience." (Snyder 1974, 91–92) He suggests that each woman have no more than one child.

In addressing the issue of pollution, Snyder proposes equally aggressive measures to clean up the air. He argues against pesticide use, nuclear energy, and large automobiles, suggesting that people walk to work or share rides. He also advocates recycling programs and waste reduction, as well as communal living, in which resources are shared. He specifically supports the concept of simple living, saying: "Support handicrafts, gardening, home skills, mid-wifery, herbs—all the things that can make us independent, beautiful and whole. Learn to break the habit of unnecessary possessions—a monkey on everybody's back—but avoid a self-abnegating anti-joyous self-righteousness. Simplicity is light, carefree, neat and loving—not a self-punishing aesthetic trip." (98–100)

Snyder believes that people are capable of adopting his suggestions, because "we have it within our deepest powers not only to change our 'selves' but to change our culture." (100) He also has a great deal of hope for the future, provided that today's environmental activists both educate the public and learn from past cultures:

We can hope to use the media. Let no one be ignorant of the facts of biology and related disciplines; bring up our children as part of the wildlife. Some communities can establish themselves in backwater rural areas and flourish—others maintain themselves in urban centers, and the two types work together—a two-way flow of experience, people, money and home-grown vegetables. Ultimately cities may exist only as joyous tribal gatherings and fairs, to dissolve after a few weeks. Investigating new lifestyles is our work, as is the exploration of ways to explore our inner realms—with the known dangers of crashing that go with such. Master the archaic and the primitive as models of basic nature-related cultures, as well as the most imaginative extensions of science—and build a community where these two vectors cross. (101–102)

Snyder's beliefs were shared by many early environmentalists, and his prize-winning work helped disseminate their agenda to the general public. (Snyder 1974)

See also Environmental Activism; Simple Living Movement; Snyder, Gary.

U

Undiscovered Country, The

The Undiscovered Country is representative of the work of American nature writer John Hay. Published in 1982, the book is a collection of essays related to Hay's observations of nature in the Cape Cod area of Massachusetts. It discusses not only his own connection to nature but other people's as well. For example, Hay says:

> You have to suppose, with or without much knowledge, that we don't attach ourselves to a place merely to get away from another one. While human culture seems to be acquiring the role of a substitute for nature, I suspect we also learn from whatever reaches are left inside us to match the earth's, and whatever of its sensual messages we innately receive. Otherwise, why should we roll in the first snow, or rejoice all over again at being visited by the fragile, white blossoms of the shadblow in early spring? Have we not experienced them before? (Trimble 1995, 159)

Hay is not only an essayist but a poet, and his work is therefore highly descriptive and literary in style. It also includes historical and scientific information. (Trimble 1995)

See also Hay, John; Nature Writing.

Unsettling of America, The

The Unsettling of America was written by American farmer, poet, essayist, and ecologist Wendell Berry, who was instrumental in shaping the early environmental movement in the United States. The book argues that changing attitudes toward farming have caused many of today's environmental problems. Berry decided to write the book when he realized that large agricultural concerns, or agribusinesses, were displacing small family farms.

The Unsettling of America was published in 1977, although portions of it appeared earlier as magazine articles in *The Nation* and *Co-Evolution Quarterly*. It is divided into eight chapters. The first, entitled "The Unsettling of America," introduces the idea that there are two ways to use the land, as an exploiter or as a nurturer. Berry explains:

> The exploiter is a specialist, an expert; the nurturer is not. The standard of the exploiter is efficiency; the standard of the nurturer is care. The exploiter's goal is money, profit; the nurturer's goal is health—his land's health, his own, his family's, his community's, his country's. Whereas the exploiter asks of a piece of land only how much and how quickly it can be made to produce, the nurturer asks

Giant combines at work in the Midwest are an example of agribusiness (U.S. Department of Agriculture)

a question that is much more complex and difficult: What is its carrying capacity? (That is, how much can be taken from it without diminishing it? . . .) The exploiter wishes to earn as much as possible by as little work as possible; the nurturer expects, certainly, to have a decent living from his work, but his characteristic wish is to work *as well* as possible. . . . The exploiter typically serves an institution or organization; the nurturer serves land, household, community, place. The exploiter thinks in terms of numbers, quantities, "hard facts"; the nurturer in terms of character, condition, quality, kind. (Berry 1986, 7–8)

Berry adds that "the exploitive always involves the abuse or the perversion of nurture and ultimately its destruction." (8) For this reason, large agribusinesses are quickly replacing family farms in America today. (8) Berry laments the decline of family farming, sug-

gesting that this change reflects a deeper problem in society: the desire to avoid hard work. He says:

The growth of the exploiters' revolution on this continent has been accompanied by the growth of the idea that work is beneath human dignity, particularly any form of hand work. We have made it our overriding ambition to escape work, and as a consequence have debased work until it is only fit to escape from. . . . We have taken the irreplaceable energies and materials of the world and turned them into jimcrack "labor-saving devices. . . ." But is work something that we have a right to escape? And can we escape it with impunity? . . . All the ancient wisdom that has come down to us . . . tells us that work is necessary to us, as much a part of our condition as mortality; that good work is our salvation and our joy; that shoddy or dishonest or self-serving work is our curse and our doom. We have tried to escape the sweat and sorrow . . . only to find that, in order to do so, we must forswear love and excellence, health and joy. (12)

Berry believes that this antiwork attitude is the cause of many environmental problems, because people who want to "pursue . . . ideals of affluence, comfort, mobility and leisure indefinitely" cannot accept the fact that natural resources are exhaustible and therefore waste them. Consequently, he states that "the basic cause of the energy crisis is not scarcity; it is moral ignorance and weakness of character. We don't know *how* to use energy, or what to use it *for*. And we cannot restrain ourselves. Our time is characterized as much by the abuse and waste of human energy as it is by the abuse and waste of fossil fuel energy." (13)

Berry discusses the abuse of human energy more fully in his second chapter, entitled "The Ecological Crisis as a Crisis of Character." He explains that America has become a country of specialists, a system under which the average person "consigns the problem of food production to . . . 'agribusinessmen,' the problems of health to doctors and sanitation experts, the problems of education to school teachers and educators, the problems of conservation to conservationists, and so on." (19–20) Berry argues that because "specialization requires the abdication to specialists of various consequences and responsibilities that were once personal and universal," it leads to great unhappiness. (19) He explains:

The beneficiary of this regime of specialists ought to be the happiest of mortals. . . . *All* of his vital concerns are in the hands of certified experts. He is a certified expert himself and as such he earns more money in a year than all his great-grandparents put together. Between stints at his job he has nothing to do but mow his lawn with a sit-down lawn mower, or watch other certified experts on television. . . . The fact is, however, that he is probably the most unhappy average citizen in the history of the world. He has

not the power to provide himself with anything but money. . . . From morning to night he does not touch anything that he has produced himself, in which he can take pride. For all his leisure and recreation, he feels bad, he looks bad, he is overweight, his health is poor. His air, water, and food are all known to contain poisons. (20)

Berry believes that specialization removes accountability, which in turn leads to poor quality products. Moreover, the system destroys a sense of wholeness, cutting people off from each other and from the land. Berry says: "We have given up the understanding . . . that we and our country create one another, depend on one another, are literally part of one another; that our land passes in and out of our bodies just as our bodies pass in and out of our land; that as we and our land are part of one another, so all who are living as neighbors here, human and plant and animal, are part of one another, and so cannot possibly flourish alone." (22) Instead, specialization encourages the idea that "the rule is never to cooperate, but rather to follow one's own interest as far as possible." (22) Berry believes that this attitude is prevalent even among conservationists, who typically specialize in a single wilderness area or environmental issue.

Berry explores the problems of conservationism more fully in chapter 3, "The Ecological Crisis as a Crisis of Agriculture." He criticizes conservationists for not living a conservationist lifestyle, saying: "The typical present-day conservationist will fight to preserve what he enjoys; he will fight whatever directly threatens his health; he will oppose any ecological violence large or dramatic enough to attract his attention. But he has not yet worried much about the impact of his own livelihood, habits, pleasures, or appetites. . . . He does not have a definition of his relationship to the world that is sufficiently elaborate and exact." (28) Berry also criticizes conservationists for isolating nature from human society, saying: "We need places in reach of every community where children can imagine the prehistoric and the beginning of history: the unknown, the trackless, the first comer." (29–30) Although Berry recognizes that some wilderness areas need to be kept in their pristine state, he says: "We cannot hope—for reasons practical and humane, we cannot even wish—to preserve more than a small portion of the land in wilderness. Most of it we will have to use." (30) He then discusses the concept of "kindly use," whereby the land can be used for agricultural purposes without harming the environment.

In the next three chapters—"The Agricultural Crisis as a Crisis of Culture," "Living in the Future: The 'Modern' Agricultural Ideal," and "The Use of Energy"—Berry develops his ideas regarding sound agricultural practices more fully and criticizes trends in agribusiness. For example, he says:

The industrialization of animal husbandry is . . . seriously oversimplified. In addition to the ethical questions involved, the use of animals as machines—penning them in feed lots and cages—creates an enormous pollution problem [because of excessive manure]. . . . The dependence of our farmers on chemical fertilizers is not seen as a problem, and so the connection is missed. . . .. once plants and animals were raised together on the same farms—which therefore neither produced unmanageable surpluses of manure, to be wasted and to pollute the water supply, nor depended on such quantities of commercial fertilizer. The genius of American farm experts is very well demonstrated here: they can take a solution and divide it neatly into two problems. (62)

Berry also criticizes modern agriculture's overdependence on machines. He relates this practice to human character, saying: "The only logic of the machine is to get bigger and more elaborate. In the absence of *moral* restraint—and we have never imposed adequate moral restraint upon our use of machines—the machine is out of control by definition." (94) For

this reason, Berry believes that the Amish people have a better approach to agriculture and to life. He states: "They alone, as a community, have carefully restricted their use of machine-developed energy, and so have become the only true masters of technology." (95)

In his next chapter, "The Body and the Earth," Berry turns to questions of religion, discussing spiritual as well as physical health and their relationship to ecology. For example, he says: "Perhaps the fundamental damage of the specialist system . . . has been the isolation of the body. At some point we began to assume that the life of the body would be the business of grocers and medical doctors, who need take no interest in the spirit, whereas the life of the spirit would be the business of churches, which would have at best only a negative interest in the body." (104) Berry believes that this separation of body and soul leads to "misapprehension and folly," adding: "By dividing body and soul, we divide both from all else. We thus condemn ourselves to a loneliness for which the only compensation is violence—against other creatures, against the earth, against ourselves." (106) Moreover, Berry blames the division of body and soul for a host of other modern problems, such as infidelity.

In his last two chapters, "Jefferson, Morrill, and the Upper Crust" and "Margins," Berry returns to a discussion of agriculture, focusing on agricultural education, agribusinesses, family farms, and good farming practices. He also praises the writings of Barry Commoner, who suggests that farmers learn organic farming techniques. However, Berry adds: "Dr. Commoner is . . . willing to advocate only half the remedy that is called for. . . . He wishes to do away with agriculture's dependence on petroleum-derived fertilizers, pesticides and herbicides, but he will not contemplate the reduction of its dependence on petroleum fuels. . . . To suggest that anything besides a tractor could be used for motive power on the farm is like setting fire to the church—the righteous not only do not *do* it, they do not *think* about it." (199–200)

Berry concludes with a list of "public remedies" that advocates various changes in lifestyle and agricultural practices, as well as new laws regarding such issues as energy use, waste disposal, and farming price controls. However, he believes that most of these changes must be handled by individuals, saying: "To turn an agricultural problem over to the developers, promoters, and salesmen of industrial technology is not to ask for a solution; it is to ask for more industrial technology and for a bigger bureaucracy to handle the resulting problems of social upset, unemployment, ill health, urban sprawl, and overcrowding." (219)

Much of Berry's other environmental writings also advocate local solutions to environmental problems. According to literary scholar Dana Phillips (in his essay "Is Nature Necessary?") Berry has stated "that 'global' solutions to the problems of natural recovery cannot succeed." (Glotfelty and Fromm 1996, 220) Moreover, Phillips explains that Berry's work as a whole is "regional, historical, and collective," because although the author primarily writes about his own experiences as a Kentucky farmer he also "argues that the soil is our heritage, our history. That is, the soil is also to be read, interpreted, taught, learned from, handed down to the next generation, and kept from becoming mere dirt. For Berry, farming is the deliberate but restrained process of turning nature into culture—and culture into nature." (221) (Berry 1986; Glotfelty and Fromm 1996; Shabecoff 1993)

See also Agriculture; Berry, Wendell; Commoner, Barry; Conservationism; Environmental Movement; Pesticides and Chemicals; Waste Management; Water Pollution.

Urbanization
See Human Ecology.

Utopia or Oblivion

Utopia or Oblivion: The Prospects for Humanity was written by R. Buckminster Fuller, an inventor and philosopher noted for his development of geodesic dome houses. Published in 1969, it offers Fuller's views on a range of topics, including energy, technology, human creativity, and politics.

Fuller believes that advancing technology is the hope of the future. He says: "Take away all the inventions from humanity and within six months half of humanity will die of starvation and disease. Take away all of the politicians and all political ideologies and leave all the inventions in operation and more will eat and prosper than now while racing on to take care of 100 percent of humanity." (Fuller 1969, 348)

Fuller discusses many important inventions and speculates on future technology. For example, he envisions a time when large floating cities will be anchored in the ocean and talks about the impact such cities would have on the environment. As an inventor, he believes it is his duty "to employ the earth's resources and energy income in such a way as to support all humanity while also enabling all people to enjoy the whole earth, all its historical artifacts and its beautiful places without one man interfering with the other, and without any man enjoying life on earth at the cost of another." (348) (Fuller 1969)

See also Environmental Politics; Fuller, R. Buckminster.

V

Van der Post, Laurens

Born in South Africa in 1906, Laurens Van der Post was the author of several books related to his experiences in Africa and Java, including *Venture to the Interior* (1951), *The Lost World of the Kalahari* (1958), and *The Heart of the Hunter* (1961). Van Der Post was, at various times, a soldier, an explorer, a political adviser, and a farmer, and he possessed an appreciation of tribal cultures. He also wrote about other countries in such works as *A Portrait of All the Russias* (1967) and *A Portrait of Japan* (1968). He died in 1996 just after celebrating his ninetieth birthday.

Vegetable Staticks

Published in 1727, *Vegetable Staticks* is significant because it inspired a new approach to plant study. Its author, Stephen Hales, took careful measurements of plants and used those measurements to determine the amount of water they absorbed, the rate of absorption, and the speed and pressure of sap flow within the plant. Hales's methods influenced other scientists, who began to see the value of measurement as a research tool. As Stephen Hales writes:

> And since we are assured that the all-wise Creator has observed the most exact proportions, *of number, weight, and measure,*

in the making of all things; the most likely way therefore, to get any insight into the nature of those parts of the creation, which come within our observation, must in all reason be to number, weigh, and measure. And we have much encouragement to pursue this method of searching into the nature of things, from the great success that has attended any attempts of this kind. . . . And if we reflect upon the discoveries that have been made in the animal economy, we shall find that the most considerable and rational accounts of it have been chiefly owing to the statical examination of their fluids, viz., by inquiring what quantity of fluids, and solids dissolved into fluids, the animal daily takes in for its support and nourishment. And with what force and different rapidities those fluids are carried about in their proper channels, according to the different secretions that are to be made from them. . . . And since vegetables, their growth and the preservation of their vegetable life is promoted and maintained, as in animals, by the very plentiful and regular motion of their fluids, which are the vehicles ordained by nature to carry proper nutriment to every part; it is therefore reasonable to hope that in them also, by the same method of inquiry, considerable discoveries may in time be made, there being, in many respects, a great analogy between plants and animals. (Boynton 1948, 407–408)

Hales also discusses at length the circulation of sap, detailing his experiments with trees of various kinds. His work encouraged others to embark on careful studies of plants and to think of the similarities between plant and animal systems. In 1733, *Vegetable Staticks* reappeared as the first volume of Hales's *Statical Essay;* the second volume of this work deals with blood circulation and blood pressure. (Boynton 1948; Spangenburg and Moser 1995)

See also Hales, Stephen.

Verne, Jules

Jules Verne is the author of several famous science fiction novels, many of which tackle issues of science and technology. In terms of the environmental sciences, his most significant is his book *Le voyage au centre de la terre* (A Journey to the Center of the Earth, 1864), which depicts a scientific expedition into a volcano.

Verne was born on February 8, 1828, in Nantes, France. He studied law but later chose to become a playwright. His first success in this regard was *Les pailles rompues* (The Broken Straws), which was produced at the Theatre Historique in 1850. He worked as a secretary for that theater from 1852 to 1854; he later became a stockbroker but continued to write.

Verne's first novel, *Voyages extraordinaires—cinq semaines en ballon* (Five Weeks in a Balloon), was published in 1863. His other works include *De la terre à la lune* (From the Earth to the Moon, 1865), *Vingt mille lieus sous les mer* (Twenty Thousand Leagues Under the Sea, 1869), *Le tour du mond en quatre-vingt jour* (Around the World in Eighty Days, 1873), and *L'Île mystérieuse* (The Mysterious Island, 1874). All of his works were extremely popular, and they uncannily predicted many future inventions. Verne died on March 24, 1905, in Amiens, France. (Evans 1966)

See also Environmental Fiction; *Journey to the Center of the Earth, A.*

Vestiges of the Natural History of Creation

Vestiges of the Natural History of Creation was published anonymously in 1844 by Robert Chambers, an amateur naturalist who argued that new animal species appear not because of natural evolution but because their appearance was preordained by God. As part of this argument, he suggested that God had deigned for species to grow in intelligence and complexity, with man being the final result. However, this suggested that man was just an advanced animal, and as a result the publication of *Vestiges of the Natural History of Creation* caused an uproar in some circles.

Chambers's critics assailed the view that humans were in any way related to apes, even by divine plan. Others believed that Chambers's theory regarding God's progression of the species, from ignorant to intelligent, offered a comfortable way to explain the fossil evidence that existed at the time. This evidence, which was subsequently used by Charles Darwin to develop his theory of evolution, seemed to show a close relationship between humans and apes, suggesting that the former evolved from the latter.

Chambers discussed fossils in order to prove his point that the brain sizes of early apelike creatures increased as God brought them to higher and higher levels of intelligence. However, he did not explain the appearance of new species—a process that he and many of his contemporaries referred to as "transmutation"—in terms of any natural or environmental causes. Chambers also offered no observations of natural laws, although he did discuss animal classification systems in an attempt to show God's orderly process for making the world. Nonetheless, his views gradually gained acceptance, and because they presented a system whereby man was the end result of a long process, they made the public more receptive to Darwin's subsequent views on evolution. (Glass, Temkin, Straus 1968)

See also Chambers, Robert; Darwin, Charles Robert; Evolution; Species Identification and Classification.

Vogt, William

Born in 1902, economist William Vogt has argued that a desire to overuse the earth's resources is inherent in human nature and that people will find it difficult to stop such behavior even when they know it will destroy the environment. His best known work is *Road to Survival,* published in 1948.

Vonnegut, Kurt

Novelist Kurt Vonnegut uses science fiction and satire to criticize various aspects of modern society. One of his most famous novels, *Cat's Cradle* (1963), shows the total destruction of earth's environment because of carelessness involving a scientific discovery.

Born on November 11, 1922, in Indianapolis, Indiana, Vonnegut worked for an electric company until 1950, when he became a freelance writer and began selling his short stories to science fiction magazines. His first novel was published in 1952. Entitled *Player Piano,* it depicts a futuristic America in which the working man has been replaced by machines and society is beginning to crumble.

In addition to *Cat's Cradle,* one of Vonnegut's best-known novels is *Slaughterhouse Five* (1969), which also addresses war and global destruction. He continues to write novels, plays, short stories, articles, and autobiographical works. His most recent novels include *Galapagos* (1985), *Bluebeard* (1987), and *Hocus Pocus* (1990). (Schatt 1976)

See also *Cat's Cradle;* Environmental Apocalypse; Environmental Fiction.

Voyage of the Beagle, The

The Voyage of the Beagle was written by Charles Darwin, who became famous during the 19th century for his theory of evolution. The book is considered a classic of natural history. Published in 1839, it is a diary of his observations and experiences while acting as a naturalist on board HMS *Beagle* from 1831 to 1836. The ship left England for the South American coasts and the South Seas; the significance of *The Voyage of the Beagle* lies in Darwin's commentary on the way species differ from location to location. As scholar Walter Sullivan reports in a 1972 introduction to the work:

> Darwin . . . noticed that, as he journeyed south along the coasts of Brazil and Argentina, there was a gradual change in the characteristics of various plants and animals—a hint that geographical separation led to the evolution of variations.
>
> It was, however, the distribution of species among the islands of the Galapagos that most influenced him in this respect. He was deeply impressed by the manner in which the species differed slightly from one island to the next. The implication was strong that each island had evolved its own varieties. The idea of a simultaneous creation of all species was becoming increasingly absurd in Darwin's mind. (Darwin 1972, xiv)

For example, in discussing one particular family of birds in the Galapagos, Darwin writes:

> The most curious fact is the perfect gradation in the size of the beaks in the different species of Geospiza, from one as large as that of a haw-finch to that of chaffinch, and . . . even to that of a warbler. . . . The beak of the Cactornis is somewhat like that of a starling; and that of the fourth sub-group, Camarhynchus, is slightly parrot-shaped. Seeing this gradation and diversity of structure in one small, intimately related group of birds, one might really fancy that from an original paucity of birds in this archipelago, one species had been taken and modified for different ends. (328)

Darwin would later use such observations to develop his theory of evolution. However, *The Voyage of the Beagle* is not a book of theories; instead it offers detailed descriptions of the flora and fauna that Darwin encountered during his five-year voyage. It also discusses geological formations. While onboard the *Beagle,* Darwin read from Charles Lyell's book

Illustration of HMS Beagle *in the Straits of Magellan (Corbis)*

Principles of Geology, which inspired him to consider the subject of geology more fully. As Sullivan explains:

> Lyell was a proponent of "uniformism" in the evolution of geologic features. The mountains, valleys, and far-flung rock formations of the world, he said, were not formed by catastrophic events but gradually, by processes now in evidence on all sides.
>
> Time and again, during his exploration of South America, Darwin saw evidence to support this. Seashell deposits high above sea level showed that the Andes and fringing coastline had thrust up, but this had apparently occurred slowly, allowing wave action on beaches at successive heights to grind up most of the shells. (xiv)

Darwin described this phenomenon himself:

> I spent some days in examining the step-formed terraces of shingle, first noticed by Captain B. Hall, and believed by Mr. Lyell to have been formed by the sea, during the gradual rising of the land. This certainly is the true explanation, for I found numerous shells of existing species on these terraces. Five narrow, gently sloping, fringe-like terraces rise one behind the other, and where best developed are formed of shingle: they front the bay, and sweep up both sides of the valley. At Guasco, north of Coquimbo, the phenomenon is displayed on a much grander scale, so as to strike with surprise even some of the inhabitants. The terraces are there much broader, and may be called plains; in some parts there are six of them, but generally only five; they run up the valley for thirty-seven miles from the coast. . . . They have undoubtedly been formed by the denuding power of the sea, during long periods of rest in the gradual elevation of the continent. (296)

Sullivan reports that *The Voyage of the Beagle* was an immediate best-seller; even before its publication, scientists were reading excerpts from it at scientific meetings. However, Sullivan adds that when Darwin then used his work to propose evolution, in many cases "admiration turned to outrage." (ix) Darwin's subsequent book, *The Origin of Species,* was extremely controversial. (Darwin 1972)

> **See also** Darwin, Charles Robert; Evolution; Lyell, Charles; *Origin of Species, The; Principles of Geology.*

Voyage of the Sanderling, The

Published in 1990, *The Voyage of the Sanderling* is Roger D. Stone's first-person account of a two-year, 8,000-mile journey down the Atlantic Coast of North and South America on a yacht named *The Sanderling.* The trip was sponsored by the World Wildlife Fund; Stone's book is thus representative of the type of publications supported by modern environmental groups.

The author's task was to assess the ecological health of the Atlantic Coast from Maine to Rio de Janeiro. *The Voyage of the Sanderling* chronicles his adventures at sea and his observations on land. It also reports on several important coastal issues, quoting scientists and conservationists regarding their concerns about the environment. For example, according to Stone:

> Once a quiet area of fishermen and small farms, eastern North Carolina is experiencing rapid change and a proportionate increase in environmental difficulties. The arrival of industries such as a Texasgulf Chemicals Company phosphate plant and large corporate farms and a quickening of

residential development along the bays and estuaries have resulted in higher levels of all forms of water pollution. During the hot dry summer of 1987 the Pamlico and Pungo rivers both experienced unprecedented oxygen shortages, algal blooms, and fish die-offs. "We had eels, hog suckers, and crabs jumping out of the water and crawling up the bank," a scientist told the *Washington Post.* As further evidence of stress on the Pamlico, red sores and ulcers broke out among its finfish and even its crabs. On the outer islands, large-scale resort development activities have provoked concern about a variety of environmental issues, ranging from beach erosion to the effects of storm-water runoff on shellfishing areas in the bays between the islands and the mainland. Managing the region's rapid development is a challenging task. "You get yelled at no matter what you decide," said the legal services lawyer Dan Besse, chairman of the Governor's Coastal Resources Commission. (Stone 1990, 87)

The Voyage of the Sanderling also discusses the history of coastal exploration and development, comparing the current ecological condition of the Atlantic Coast with historical accounts of the region. It provides portraits of early explorers as well as photographs, maps, and other illustrations related to coastal history and Stone's experiences on *The Sanderling.* (Stone 1990)

> **See also** Balanced Ecosystems; Environmental Groups; Habitat Protection; Stone, Roger D.; Water Pollution; Wildlife Conservation.

W

Walden

The 1854 book *Walden* is considered one of the most important American simple-living or back-to-nature works ever published. Often reprinted, it is a collection of 18 essays written by Henry David Thoreau, who spent two years in a self-made retreat near Walden Pond in Concord, Massachusetts. Thoreau subsequently published *Walden* to describe his experiences living off the land, as well as to express his opinions on modern life and his beliefs regarding spirituality and nature. Many scholars believe that it is the latter aspects of *Walden* that have caused the work to endure. For example, E. B. White, in an essay on *Walden* entitled "A Slight Sound at Evening," says:

> If Thoreau had merely left us an account of a man's life in the woods, or if he had simply retreated to the woods and there recorded his complaints about society, or even if he had contrived to include both records in one essay, "Walden" would probably not have lived a hundred years. As things turned out, Thoreau, very likely without knowing quite what he was up to, took man's relation to nature and man's dilemma in society and man's capacity for elevating his spirit and he beat all these matters together, in a wild free interval of

> self-justification and delight, and produced an original omelette from which people can draw nourishment in a hungry day. "Walden" is one of the first vitamin-enriched American dishes. (Ruland 1968, 28)

In other words, the book doesn't merely describe nature, as was typical of many works of the period. Instead, it discusses nature and the environment in terms of modern lifestyles and human spirituality. Unfortunately, *Walden* was not fully appreciated in its own time; it sold only 2000 copies after five years in print. But it was later popularized by those in the American conservation movement, and by 1953 there had been 133 editions of the work.

The work's popularity increased during the 1960s with the arrival of the modern environmental movement; its adherents emphasized the spiritual and philosophical aspects of environmentalism as well as its scientific aspects. Modern environmentalists particularly embraced Thoreau's call for a more simple lifestyle, as in this passage from *Walden:*

> Most men appear never to have considered what a house is, and are actually though needlessly poor all their lives because they think that they must have such

a one as their neighbors have. As if one were to wear any sort of coat which the tailor might cut out for him, or, gradually leaving off palm-leaf hat or cap of woodchuck skin, complain of hard times because he could not afford to buy a crown! It is possible to invent a house still more convenient and luxurious than we have, which yet all would admit that man could not afford to pay for. Shall we always study to obtain more of these things, and not sometimes to be content with less? Shall the respectable citizen thus gravely teach, by precept and example, the necessity of the young man's providing a certain number of superfluous glow-shoes, and umbrellas, and empty guest chambers for empty guests, before he dies? Why should not our furniture be as simple as the Arab's or the Indian's? . . . At present our houses are cluttered . . . and a good housewife would sweep out the greater part into the dust hole, and not leave her morning's work undone. . . . The very simplicity and nakedness of man's life in the primitive ages imply this advantage, at least, that they left him still but a sojourner in nature. When he was refreshed with food and sleep, he contemplated his journey again. He dwelt, as it were, in a tent in this world, and was either threading the valleys, or crossing the plains, or climbing the mountain-tops. But lo! men have become the tools of their tools. The man who independently plucked the fruits when he was hungry is become a farmer; and he who stood under a tree for shelter, a housekeeper. We now no longer camp for a night, but have settled down on earth and forgotten heaven. . . . We have built for this world a family mansion, and for the next a family tomb. (Thoreau 26–28)

Thoreau decries materialism and the lifestyle necessary to support it. He criticizes the Industrial Revolution and the frantic pace of modern civilization:

Our life is frittered away by detail. . . . Simplicity, simplicity, simplicity! I say, let your affairs be as two or three, and not a hundred or a thousand; instead of a million count half a dozen, and keep your accounts on your thumb-nail. . . . Simplify, simplify. Instead of three meals a day, if it be necessary eat but one; instead of a hundred dishes, five; and reduce other things in proportion. . . . The nation itself, with all its so-called internal improvements, which, by the way, are all external and superficial, is just such an unwieldy and overgrown establishment, cluttered with furniture and tripped up by its own traps, ruined by luxury and heedless expense, by want of calculation and a worthy aim, as the million households in the land; and the only cure for it, as for them, is in a rigid economy, a stern and more than Spartan simplicity of life and elevation of purpose. (67–68)

To help others learn how to achieve such simplicity, Thoreau discusses day-to-day activities at Walden Pond and provides detailed information about farming practices and finances. He also describes his home and surrounding countryside at various times of the year. Although he left Walden because he "had several more lives to live, and could not spare any more time for that one," he considered his time there a worthwhile experience. (239) He believes "that if one advances confidently in the direction of his dreams, and endeavors to live the life which he has imagined, he will meet with a success unexpected in common hours." (240) He recommends that others experiment with simple living:

Cultivate poverty like a garden herb, like sage. Do not trouble yourself much to get new things, whether clothes or friends. Turn the old; return to them. Things do not change; we change. Sell your clothes and keep your thoughts. . . . Moreover, if you are restricted in your range by poverty, if you cannot buy books and newspapers, for instance, you are but confined to the most significant and vital experiences; you are compelled to deal with the material which yields the most sugar and the most starch. It is life near the bone where it is sweetest. (243)

Walden remains popular today, both within and outside of the simple living movement. (Ruland 1968; Thoreau 1965)

See also Environmental Movement; Simple Living Movement; Thoreau, Henry David.

Wallace, Alfred Russell

British naturalist Alfred Russell Wallace mounted two major expeditions, one to South America in 1848 and another to the Malay Archipelago during 1854–1862. He reported his observations from these journeys in *A Narrative of Travels on the Amazon and Rio Negro* (1853) and *The Malay Archipelago* (1868). He also corresponded with Charles Darwin; together they presented a paper on the theory of evolution to scientists in 1858. Darwin is given more credit for this theory because he developed it more fully and promoted it in public; however, Wallace's contributions to its inception were significant. In 1870 Wallace published two essays of his own on the subject in a collection entitled *Contributions to the Theory of Natural Selection,* in which he disagreed with Darwin's position that human intelligence was as subject to natural selection as the human body.

Born on January 8, 1823, in Usk, Monmouthshire, England, Russell was a schoolteacher before joining his first expedition. In addition to his work as a naturalist, he was a supporter of two social causes, women's suffrage and a movement to nationalize land ownership. In 1910 the British government honored him with the Order of Merit. He died on November 7, 1913.

Wallace, David Rains

Born in 1945, David Rains Wallace wrote *The Klamath Knot* (1983), which won the John Burroughs Medal for excellence in nature writing. It describes the various ecosystems of the Klamath Mountains in southern Oregon and discusses the area in terms of evolutionary theory. For example, Wallace writes:

Evolutionary humanity is a truer microcosm of nature than medieval philosophers dreamed. The human body does not merely resemble nature in its parts, it recapitulates the history of life, as much a living reenactment of evolutionary dramas as the Klamath Mountains. Corpuscles float in a primal nutrient bath of blood; intestines crawl about absorbing food in the manner of primitive works; lungs absorb and excrete gases as do gills and leaves. No human organ would look out of place if planted in some Paleozoic sponge bed or coral reef.... Humanity can't be defined apart from the intricacies of natural selection, mutation, symbiosis, preadaptation, and neoteny that formed it. It can't be defined apart from the millions of other species on the earth. (Finch and Elder 1990, 857)

Wallace wrote more than a dozen other books on nature-related topics. They include *The Dark Range: A Naturalist's Night Notebook* (1978), *Idle Weeds: The Life of an Ohio Sandstone Ridge* (1980), *The Untamed Garden and Other Personal Essays* (1986), *Life in the Balance: A Companion to the Audubon Television Specials* (1987), *The Quetzal and the Macaw: The Story of Costa Rica's National Parks* (1992), and *The Monkey's Bridge: Mysteries of Evolution in Central America* (1997).

War Against the Greens, The

Published in 1994 by the Sierra Club, an environmental group, *The War Against the Greens: The "Wise-Use" Movement, the New Right, and Anti-Environmental Violence* discusses antienvironmental forces in contemporary America. It is one of few books on the subject and is therefore considered a valuable resource for those studying American antienvironmentalism. The book's author, journalist and private investigator David Helvarg, interviewed many of the participants in the so-called Wise Use movement, which he believes is one of the greatest threats to modern environmentalism. He says:

At its core Wise Use/Property Rights is a counterrevolutionary movement, defining itself in response to the environmental revolution of the past thirty years. It aims to create and mold disaffection over environmental regulations, big government, and the media into a cohesive social force that can win respectability for centrist arguments seeking to "protect jobs, private property and the economy by finding a balance between human and environmental needs." (Helvarg 1994, 9)

Wise Use activists believe that environmental regulations are harming the U.S. economy and infringing on people's property rights, and they work to change environmental policies in that regard. Helvarg reports that the Wise Use movement has in fact been very successful

in its ability to mobilize a network of core activists to intervene in and politicize local conflicts. . . . Whenever a local election is turned in favor of a prodevelopment Republican, or a fax campaign skews a Sunday newspaper poll to suggest that a majority of readers think environmentalism has gone too far, or public land-use hearings are disrupted by hundreds of angry protesters, or the *New York Times* seeks out policy responses from "leaders of environmental, industrial, and property rights groups," anti-enviro leaders such as [Ron] Arnold and [Chuck] Cushman score it as a victory for their "guerrilla warfare tactics." (8–9)

Helvarg strongly opposes antienvironmentalism. *The War Against the Greens* criticizes those who support it and attacks their positions on a range of issues. For example, he offers an unflattering portrait of the late zoologist-politician Dixy Lee Ray, whom he painted as a "standard bearer" in the antienvironmental movement:

Among the list of environmental problems [Dixy Lee Ray] reviews and finds of no real consequence is the population explosion that has seen the number of people on the planet more than double since

1950, from 2.5 to 5.5 billion. "The population problem is based on present trends continuing in to the future, which they never do," she assures her audience. "Population growth goes up and down like global warming. If you looked at the growth rate of racquetball courts in the 1970s and extended it, the whole country would be covered by racquetball courts today. . . ." Three days before her death, she criticized as alarmist media reports about secret cold-war radiation experiments conducted on some eight hundred Americans without their knowledge during the 1940s and 1950s. . . . "Everybody is exposed to radiation," Dixy Lee told the Associated Press just before she passed on. "A little bit more or a little bit less is of no consequence." (242)

But Helvarg is also critical of the media, which he believes is not reporting a broad enough range of environmental stories. However, he believes he understands the reason for this, explaining:

The dramatic elements of conflict and disaster that play well on the news also guarantee a certain level of distortion in its environmental coverage. The *Exxon Valdez* oil spill got extensive play, particularly on the electronic media, in part because it provided such stark visual contrasts: images of Alaska's pristine Prince William Sound played against the apparent ravages of crude oil and its effect on shorelines, birds, bears, and otters. Bioaccumulation of toxics, loss of biodiversity, or depletion of marine resources, while potentially far more disastrous in their consequences, were incremental problems and therefore harder to illustrate. (275)

Helvarg quotes one media executive as saying: "How do you show soil or groundwater contamination? How do you illustrate important decision-making processes such as risk assessment and budgeting? . . . Sometimes there is no solution, and good stories go unreported because it is too difficult, time-consuming, or expensive to illustrate them." (275)

Interestingly, many of those who oppose the environmental movement, such as Michael Fumento, are equally critical of the media. In their case, however, they believe that the media is biased in favor of environmentalists. Helvarg insists that this is not accurate as to major news organizations but is true of the "specialized" environmental media created by environmental groups themselves. He says that such media mix "open political advocacy with nature writing, ecological perspectives, and factual, well-researched exposés." (276) As examples of this he cites magazines such as *Sierra, National Wildlife,* and *International Wildlife,* each of which is published by an environmental group. Helvarg also points out that antienvironmental magazines reach far fewer people than environmental ones, arguing this proves the antienvironmental movement is weaker than it claims. He explains:

If the environmental movement has been able to build a substantial specialized media, the anti-enviros' failure to create their own media may reflect just how fragile is their claim that they function as an independent social movement. The two largest-circulation anti-enviro publications being put out today are the tabloid newsletters of People for the West and the anti–animal rights group Putting People First, both of which claim press runs of around twenty thousand. . . . The anti-enviros' attempts to put out a slick national magazine foundered after one year. (277)

However, Helvarg notes that the antienvironmental movement has been successful in getting the support of conservative radio talk show hosts such as Rush Limbaugh, as well as some government officials and courts. These achievements disturb him. But he is even more upset over acts of violence that he believes have been committed against environmentalists by antienvironmental groups. He reports that environmentalists have received death threats and says that some have died under mysterious circumstances. He faults law enforcement agencies for not doing enough to protect environmentalists.

Helvarg calls for environmental groups to take a strong stand against antienvironmental violence. He also suggests that environmentalists work harder to counter antienvironmental thinking in America, saying: "To date the Wise Use/Property Rights backlash has been a bracing if dangerous reminder to environmentalists that power concedes nothing without a demand and that no social movement, be it ethnic, civil, or environmental, can rest on its past laurels." (458) (Helvarg 1994)

See also Antienvironmentalism; Environmental Movement; Environmental Politics; Fumento, Michael; Helvarg, David; Ray, Dixy Lee.

Warming, Johannes Eugenius Bulow

Danish botanist Johannes Eugenius Bulow Warming is considered the first modern plant ecologist because he wrote about plants in terms of their environment. His most important work on this subject is *Plantesamfund,* which was published in 1895 and translated into English as *Oecology of Plants* in 1909. In it he discusses plant communities, explaining:

The term "community" implies a diversity but at the same time a certain organized uniformity in the units. The units are the many individual plants that occur in every community, whether this be a beech-forest, a meadow, or a heath. Uniformity is established when certain atmospheric, terrestrial, and any other factors . . . are co-operating, and appears either because a certain, defined economy makes its impress[ion] on the community as a whole, or because a number of different growth-forms are combined to form a single aggregate that has a definite and constant guise. (Warming 1909, 91–92)

Warming was born in Mano, Denmark, on November 3, 1841. He received a Ph.D. from the University of Copenhagen in 1871 and

Industrial waste from the E. I. Dupont Company goes into the Arthur Kill River in the metropolitan New York area, 1974 (National Archives)

taught botany at the Royal Institute of Technology in Stockholm, Sweden, in 1885, whereupon he joined the faculty of the University of Copenhagen. In 1888 he published his first book on plants, *On the Vegetation of Greenland,* which was based on a scientific expedition he accompanied during 1884. Warming studied South American vegetation as well. He died in Copenhagen on April 2, 1924. (Warming 1909)

Waste Management

Waste management is the disposal of waste products, whether they be organic or inorganic, ordinary trash, or hazardous chemicals. It is an important global environmental issue because of the volume and nature of the waste created by millions of individuals and businesses each day. The topic is mentioned in most books addressing the health of a particular habitat or the earth as a whole. For example, Rachel Carson's *The Sea Around Us* examines the impact of waste disposal on oceans; Murray Bookchin's *Our Synthetic En-*

vironment and Ralph Nader's *Who's Poisoning America* discuss the threat that chemical and nuclear wastes pose for earth's atmosphere. Other works focus entirely on the issue of waste management, most notably William Rathje and Cullen Murphy's *Rubbish! The Archaeology of Garbage* (1992). This book reports on a study of landfill garbage and discusses the wasteful practices of modern society.

See also Bookchin, Murray; Carson, Rachel Louise; Nader, Ralph; Nuclear Energy; *Our Synthetic Environment; Rubbish! The Archaeology of Garbage; Sea Around Us, The; Who's Poisoning America.*

Wasted Ocean, The

The Wasted Ocean (1989) was published by the American Littoral Society, a nonprofit organization dedicated to preserving the littoral zone, the region where the sea meets the land. The group says that the book was "the first handbook of marine conservation" ever published (Bulloch 1989, *ix*). Its author, David

Dead fish are pulled out of the pesticide-contaminated Rhine River near Koblenz, Germany, 1969 (Archive Photos)

Bulloch, is a past president of the society. He presents a thorough discussion of the ocean-related environmental problems that were prevalent during the 1980s, which he outlines as follows:

> Critical coastal habitats are disappearing. More than one-half of all our marine wetlands have been destroyed—filled in for ports, marinas, or housing or used as dumps. . . . Whole ecosystems are collapsing under a bath of excess nutrients and strange new substances. This chemical bombardment flows from countless pipelines, leaches from dumps and fills, and runs off from streets and farms. . . . This wasting of our waters coincides with the increasing popularity of the pleasures of our coast and its seafood. Per capita consumption of fish and shellfish is at an all-time high. So too are visits to the beach, recreational fishing, boating, and the demand for nearby living space. (2)

A Wasted Ocean also discusses three important marine conservation laws enacted in

1972: the Clean Water Act, the Coastal Zone Management Act, and the Marine Protection, Research, and Sanctuaries Act. It lists more laws in an appendix and provides addresses for some 50 environmental groups involved in coastal conservation issues. (Bulloch 1989)

See also Balanced Ecosystems; Bulloch, David K.; Habitat Protection; Water Pollution; Wetlands Preservation.

Water Pollution

Water pollution and the politics related to it have been a concern for hundreds of years. In fact one of the earliest calls for environmental activism concerned water pollution: In 1882 Norwegian playwright Henrik Ibsen wrote about a town's efforts to keep their polluted water a secret in order to maintain their lucrative tourist trade. Two more recent examples of literature addressing this topic are Marc Reisner's *Cadillac Desert* and Robert Gottlieb *A Life of Its Own,* both of which primarily focus on the American West. Many other works discuss the quality of water in specific habitats. Roger Stone's *The Voyage of the Sanderling,* for instance, reports on water pollution along the East Coast of America, and Rachel Carson's *The Sea Around Us* and David Bulloch's *The Wasted Ocean* address the health of oceans worldwide.

See also Bulloch, David K.; *Cadillac Desert;* Carson, Rachel Louise; *Enemy of the People, An;* Gottlieb, Robert; Ibsen, Henrik; *Life of Its Own, A;* Reisner, Marc; *Sea Around Us, The;* Stone, Roger D.; *Voyage of the Sanderling, The; Wasted Ocean, The.*

Waterton, Charles

Charles Waterton is the author of *Wanderings in South America, the North-West of the United States, and the Antilles, in the Years 1812, 1816, 1820, and 1824,* which was published in 1825. The work is an account of Waterton's explorations through the Amazon jungle and other regions.

Waterton was born in Yorkshire, England, in 1782. In 1804 his family sent him to British Guiana to manage a plantation, and eight years later he made the first of four expeditions into the wilderness. He returned to England in 1825. By this time, he had already ordered the establishment of a bird sanctuary on the family estate; it was the first such conservancy in the country. Waterton died in 1865.

Wegener, Alfred Lothar

German geophysicist Alfred Lothar Wegener developed the theory that the earth's continent began as a single landmass that eventually separated and drifted apart. Earlier scientists had suggested that the continents were once joined; however, they theorized that this continent was broken by the formation of new oceans. Wegener was the first to believe in continental drift. He wrote a book on the subject, *Die entstehung der kontinente und ozeane* (The Origin of Continents and Oceans), which was published in 1915 and translated into English in 1924.

Wegener was born on November 1, 1880, in Berlin, Germany. He received a Ph.D. in astronomy from the University of Berlin in 1905; the following year he embarked on a two-year scientific expedition to Greenland to study air currents. He mounted another expe-

dition to Greenland before accepting a teaching position at the University of Graz, in Austria, in 1924. In 1929 and again in 1930 he returned to Greenland to conduct more scientific studies; he died there in November 1930. (Bowler 1993)

See also Geological Research.

Wetlands Preservation

Wetlands are water habitats, such as swamps and marshes, either inland or along coastlines. They host a huge variety of plants, insects, fish, birds, and mammals. They have also been subject to a great deal of environmental destruction. Wetlands preservation is therefore frequently mentioned in environmental literature on species endangerment and extinction, as well as in works concerning water pollution. For example, Roger Stone's *The Voyage of the Sanderling* examines coastal wetlands damage as it relates to species extinction along the Eastern Seaboard of the United States.

See also Animal Ecology; Stone, Roger D.; *Voyage of the Sanderling, The;* Water Pollution; Wildlife Conservation.

Whale for the Killing, A

Published in 1972, *A Whale for the Killing* was written by Canadian naturalist Farley Mowat, a popular nature writer who drew public attention to wildlife conservation issues during the 1970s and 1980s. The book is a first-person account of his attempt to rescue a Fin whale stranded on the southwestern coast of Newfoundland in January 1967. But it is also the story of Mowat's disillusionment with humanity—even in one of the most remote, rural parts of the world.

Mowat moved to the small Newfoundland fishing community of Burgeo in 1962, because he wanted to spend his life among "a natural people, living in at least some degree of harmony with the natural world." (Mowat 1972, 147) He idealizes his neighbors until a local fisherman tells him that a whale following a school of herring has become trapped in nearby Aldridges Pond and that some men have been harassing it. The pond is a shallow saltwater enclosure that connects with the At-

Wetlands in New Jersey (Rasmussen, W.C./USGS)

lantic Ocean only at extremely high tide, and the whale, which Mowat soon discovers is a pregnant female, will be unable to free herself until the water rises again. That event is at least a month away.

Meanwhile the residents of Burgeo have been using her for target practice. Over the next several days, they continue to fire hundreds of rounds of ammunition into her body and intentionally cut her with boat propellers. Some boaters also try to drive her ashore or into a treacherous area of sharp rocks. Although not everyone participates in this brutality, no one is willing to stop it. Mowat cannot believe the callousness of the people he once revered. He writes: "They are essentially good people. I know that, but what sickens me is their simple failure to resist the impulse of savagery. . . . They seem to be just as capable of being utterly loathesome as the [people] from the cities with their high-powered rifles and telescopic sights and their mindless compulsion to slaughter everything alive, from squirrels to elephants." (146–147)

Mowat shouts at the boaters, but they make fun of him. He begs town leaders and law enforcement officials to help him protect the whale, but they refuse. Finally he decides to alert the international media to her plight. He is already a well-known naturalist, and his report receives a great deal of attention; as a result, the citizens of Burgeo receive a barrage of negative publicity from around the world. Canadian officials declare the whale to be under government protection, and the worst attacks stop.

Local businesspeople now realize that the whale will attract tourist dollars to the town. They suddenly embrace the whale's cause, helping Mowat figure out how to feed her and keep the pond safe; some suggest that the whale never be set free. As one resident explains: "She's doing good in the pond. . . . We ought to keep her there. No place else in the world's got a tame Fin Whale. It'd be a sin to turn her loose when she can do so much for Burgeo." (191) Few seem concerned about the whale's emotional state, or that of her mate, who remains just outside the pond and continues to call to his stranded companion.

Moreover, not everyone in Burgeo is happy about Mowat's efforts to protect the whale. Some call him a troublemaker and advise him to leave town; when Mowat attempts to trap herring for the whale, someone cuts his nets. Mowat perseveres, but the whale's bullet and propeller wounds prove too much. She dies from massive infection, and her gangrenous, bloated body becomes a source of embarrassment for the town. Faced with new attacks from the media after the death, Burgeo's residents become defensive. Eventually, "even those who had been blameless in the tragedy or who had shown sympathy for the whale" began to insist that "the men who had killed the whale . . . had been justified in doing what they did." (227)

Throughout *A Whale for the Killing*, Mowat bemoans the whale's fate with great passion, and his descriptions of Burgeo's attacks on the helpless creature are graphic. He similarly describes a beached whale massacre several years earlier in St. Pierre, the industrialized capital of the French islands of St. Pierre–Miquelon near the southern coast of Newfoundland, where "the slashing and the hacking on that bloody foreshore continued long after all the whales had bled to death. A crowd of four or five hundred people drank in the spectacle with eager appetite. It was a great fiesta in St. Pierre." (68)

His work is therefore a powerful indictment of humanity's senseless abuse of nature. It is made even more powerful by Mowat's tendency to anthropomorphize the whales; in this and many of his other works, such as *Never Cry Wolf* (1963), he discusses animals in terms of their emotions and family relationships and suggests that they are as intelligent and worthy of respect as human beings. This was a new concept when *A Whale for the Killing* was published, at the beginning of the environmental movement. Consequently, the book evoked a new level of sympathy from readers and raised public awareness not only about Burgeo's doomed whale but about the plight of all whales throughout the world.

Moreover, Mowat included historical facts and 1972 statistics about whaling and whale extinction in his book, which encouraged people to think about the politics of whale conservation. He advocated a "world-wide embargo on trade in all whale products, otherwise many whaling companies will simply transfer their operations to flags of convenience so that their ships may join the growing fleet of pirate whalers." (237) He also offered a scathing indictment on the International Whaling Commission (IWC), arguing: "It is abundantly clear that if we are to save *any* of the whales, Great or Small, we must reject the I.W.C. as our instrument for preventing the ultimate commission of a crime against life which is of such magnitude that it has no equal in human history. The I.W.C. has never served the whales . . . it has only served the whalers." (Mowat 236) After his experience in Burgeo, he became more active in environmental politics and eventually wrote an even stronger indictment of humanity, *Sea of Slaughter* (1984). (Mowat 1972)

See also Animal Behavior; Environmental Movement; Environmental Politics; Mowat, Farley; *Never Cry Wolf; Sea of Slaughter;* Wildlife Conservation

Which Way for the Ecology Movement?

Which Way for the Ecology Movement? (1994) is a collection of essays by Murray Bookchin, a major figure in the modern environmental movement. A radical activist, he blames social causes for environmental destruction. Accordingly, his essays

emphasize that ecological degradation is, in great part, a product of the degradation of human beings by hunger, material insecurity, class rule, hierarchical domination, patriarchy, ethnic discrimination, and competition. Their focus, in short, is on the inseparability of social problems from ecological problems; hence my use of the name *social ecology.* They attempt to demystify mystical and deep ecology, neo-Malthusianism, and sociobiology, all of which serve to derail serious social critique and orient it toward celebrations of "wilderness," the worship of nature deities, primitivism, often a hatred of technology and science as such, and a denigration of reason and the belief that progress is *possible*—especially progress cast in humanistic or human terms. (Bookchin 1994, 17).

Bookchin is extremely critical of deep ecologists Arne Naess, Bill Devall, and George Sessions, as well as those who believe in James Lovelock's Gaia hypothesis, because he believes that they have turned environmentalism into a form of religious belief. He also criticizes radical environmentalists Edward Abbey, Dave Foreman, and Christopher Manes for putting the needs of the earth above the needs of people. He says:

Granted we must deal kindly—and for many individuals, lovingly—with nonhuman life-forms. Granted too that wilderness, insofar as this term has meaning nowadays when the biosphere has been irrevocably altered by human action, should be protected, even expanded, and that the integrity of the natural world should be a matter of profound concern. Yet let us not forget that wilderness preservation is an eminently *social* issue, and its future depends profoundly upon the type of social system as well as the values we develop. (11–12)

Bookchin argues that environmentalism must be accompanied by a concern for humanity continuing:

Cruelty to human beings, let me add, often goes hand in hand with a neglect of nonhuman life-forms and wild areas, despite Edward Abbey's statement in *Desert Solitaire* (page 20) that he would rather kill a man than a snake. . . . The ways in which we interact with each other as social beings profoundly influence attitudes we are likely to have toward the natural world. Any sound ecological perspective rests in great part on our social perspectives and interrelationships; hence, to draw up an ecological agenda that has no room

for social concerns is as obtuse as to draw up a social agenda that has no room for ecological concerns. Indeed, any attempt to distinguish one from the other, or to focus on one at the expense of the other, can and has led to an outright lack of concern for the ways animals we call human treat one another—and concomitantly, to an ugly misanthropic outlook. (11–12)

Moreover, Bookchin argues that "antihumanism" causes experts to ignore the real causes of human problems. He explains:

The burgeoning nationalism, xenophobia, parochialism, and tribalism that have claimed an inestimable number of lives in recent times cannot be attributed to Malthusian myths that blame wars and conflicts on overpopulation or a dwindling food supply. . . . Neo-Malthusians invoke "overpopulation," deep ecologists involve "anthropocentrism," ecotheologians invoke "avarice," ecofeminists invoke "male aggressiveness," ecomystics generally invoke "rationality," Jungians appeal to immutable archetypes, Freudians cite stages of human development—and inevitably, sociobiologists invoke intractable, even "selfish genes." What these modern, largely mystical attributions share is that they all regard social dislocations as the result of a biologically determined "human nature"—and only rarely, if ever, of social forces like capitalism, hierarchy, the market imperative of "grow or die," or corporate balance-sheets. That human beings are far from constituting a unified "humanity"—divided as they are by gender, ethnicity, nationality, skin color, status, wealth, and vocational privileges, in short, hierarchy and class, oppressed and oppressor, exploiter and exploited, tends to be swept under the carpet. (12–13)

These are the problems that Bookchin seeks to highlight through his work. He believes that if such social problems are solved so that human beings do indeed become one cooperative humanity, then environmental problems will also have a chance of being solved. Moreover, he sees environmental problems as a reflection of the immorality that has permeated all of human life. In "Sociobiology or Social Ecology," the final essay of *Which Way for the Ecology Movement?*, Bookchin incorporates material from *The Ecology of Freedom* and concludes:

> Civilization as we know it today is more mute than the nature for which it professes to speak and more blind than the elemental forces it professes to control. Indeed, civilization today lives in hatred of the world around it and in grim hatred of itself. Its gutted cities, wasted lands, poisoned air and water, and mean-spirited greed constitute a daily indictment of its odious immorality. A world so demeaned may well be beyond redemption, at least within the terms of its own institutional and ethical framework. The thermonuclear flames and the ecological disasters that may engulf our planet will render it irretrievably inhospitable to life—a dead witness to cosmic failure. If only because this planet's history, including its human history, has been so full of promise, hope, and creativity, it deserves a better fate than what seems to confront it in the years ahead. (75)

(Bookchin 1994)

See also Abbey, Edward; Bookchin, Murray; Deep Ecology Movement; *Desert Solitaire;* Environmental Movement; Foreman, Dave; Gaia Hypothesis; Lovelock, James; Malthus, Thomas Robert; Manes, Christopher; Naess, Arne; Nuclear Energy; Social Ecology.

White, Gilbert

Eighteenth-century clergyman Gilbert White wrote one of the first popular books on natural history in England. Entitled *The Natural History and Antiquities of Selbourne*, it was published in 1789 and became a classic shortly thereafter. The book is a collection of letters describing the flora and fauna of the English countryside and extolling the virtues of undeveloped lands.

White was born in Selbourne, Hampshire, England, on November 3, 1845. He attended Oriel College in Oxford from 1740 to 1743. In 1765 he published his first work related to naturalism, *Calendar of Flora and the Garden*, and in 1768 he published *Naturalist's Journal*. During this period he began writing letters to other naturalists; 110 of them were included in *The Natural History and Antiquities of Selbourne*. White died in Selbourne on June 26, 1793. (Christopher 1970; White 1880)

Whitman, Walt

American poet and essayist Walt Whitman wrote about nature in relation to the human spirit. In the poem "Wood Odors," for example, he speaks of the woods as a place of worship; the trees are "the myriad living columns of the temple." In "Miracles," he lists as miracles such things as "honeybees busy around the hive" and "animals feeding in the fields." In other works, he symbolically connects the regeneration evident in nature with the fate of the human soul after death.

Whitman was born on May 31, 1819, in West Hills, Long Island, New York. He grew up in Brooklyn and began working in a print shop when he was only 12; this led to a career as a newspaper reporter and editor. During the early 1850s he also built houses and sold real estate.

In 1855 Whitman decided to self-publish a volume of poetry, which he titled *Leaves of Grass*. A second edition appeared the following year; a third, expanded volume appeared in 1860. None of these books did well financially, and some of their poems were decried as immoral because of their sexual allusions.

When the Civil War broke out Whitman volunteered to visit wounded soldiers. He also worked as a government clerk. In 1865 he published two more volumes of poetry, *Drum Taps* and *Sequel to Drum Taps*, about the realities of war. Two years later he published a fourth edition of *Leaves of Grass*, replacing some of the original poems with new ones. Finally, Whitman's writing began to be noticed, particularly after popular author John Burroughs wrote *Notes on Walt Whitman as Poet and Person* (1867).

During the next several years, Whitman continued to revise *Leaves of Grass;* the book went through nine editions in all. A collection of his work, *The Complete Poems and Prose,* was published in 1888. By that time Whitman was making enough money from his writing to support himself in a simple cottage, where he remained until his death on March 26, 1892.

See also Burroughs, John.

Who's Poisoning America

Who's Poisoning America: Corporate Polluters and their Victims in the Chemical Age is a collection of essays edited by political activist Ralph Nader and two of his associates, Ronald Brownstein and John Richard. Published in 1981, it offers case studies of "chemical violence" perpetrated against the earth; it influenced public opinion regarding corporate environmental practices. (Nader et al. 1981, *vii*)

Nader, Brownstein, and Richard explain that the studies were "chronicled by writers in the affected communities" because "having lived through these toxic dramas, the writers have a deep understanding of the injustices these communities experienced." (*ix*) They add: "Their suffering is, in its own poignant language, a call to action for all Americans to save their country, protect the integrity of the air, land and water, and defend future generations. Their experiences should be appreciated as more than just a plea to arouse our conscience and assume our civic duties. They must also stimulate both a fundamental reassessment of technology in terms of human values and a commitment of our time and energy to connect our political economy to human health and happiness." (ix)

Perhaps the most famous case study in the book concerns Love Canal, a residential area in Niagara Falls, New York. During the late 1970s the inhabitants of Love Canal began developing serious illnesses, and eventually they discovered that their land had been contaminated by poisonous chemical wastes. They convinced public officials that the problem was serious, and eventually the federal government declared the area uninhabitable

and relocated the residents. Such successes lead Nader to conclude that "we are not helpless in the environmental crisis." (311) In the final essay of the book, he discusses local activism as well as environmental law and politics, suggesting various ways to end pollution. For example, he advocates harsh criminal penalties for corporate polluters and says that people need to reduce or even end their dependence on chemicals and fossil fuels. (Nader et al. 1981)

See also Environmental Activism; Environmental Politics; Nader, Ralph.

Whole Earth Catalogue

Created by environmentalist Stewart Brand, the *Whole Earth Catalogue* was one of the most important publications of the modern American environmental movement. According to Robert Gottlieb in *Forcing the Spring,* the first printing of the work had as many as a million readers and was consequently the most popular expression of the counterculture or back-to-the-land movement that "helped reaffirm the notion that environmentalism was also about constructing alternatives" to modern society. (Gottlieb 98–99) Moreover, Brand's friend Stephanie Mills, in *Whatever Happened to Ecology?,* points out that the *Whole Earth Catalogue* "has been associated in the public mind with the ecology movement from the beginning. . . . Stewart had blazoned on his covers (and was, I believe, the guy who had originally procured for public view), *the* great icon of the movement—NASA's image of the whole Earth as viewed from space." (Mills 86)

Like Gottlieb, Mills argues that Brand's work was more than just a catalog; it was an expression of environmental philosophy:

Stewart's greatest gift—and service—was to equip individual responsibility and local self-reliance. The *Whole Earth Catalogue* was an exaltation of the value of tools, and of durable goods. Between the lines was the unmistakably libertarian hint that if you didn't like the way things were going, you could always change it, beginning with your own household, homestead, or commune. What transpired on the material plane was of real consequence, although heavily conditioned by our ways of knowing. . . . One basic inference that could be drawn from the *Whole Earth Catalogue*'s quick success was that among its devotees were a great many people who felt lifestyle to be a pivotal ecological-moral issue, an explicit summation of values of beliefs. (85)

To that end, the catalog offers descriptions, recommendations, facts, advice, and purchasing information regarding a variety of books, kits, tools, and other merchandise related to simple living and environmentalism. Mills reports that the first edition of the *Whole Earth Catalogue,* published in 1968, features such items as

> geodesic domes, simplified carpentry, plumbing and wiring, tipis, cabins, adobe homes, Aladdin lamps, seed catalogues, bee books, gardening manuals, pruning handbooks, woodstoves and windmills, foraging, solar-energy use, hardware, knot-tying lore, woodcraft, pottery, weaver's and jeweler's supplies, buckskin, how to build your own furniture and how to make cowboy horse gear and how to construct a classic guitar, always a little math, self-publishing, filmmaking, theater production, mail-order food and flour mills, *A Manual of Simple Burial,* emergency medical guides, *A Handbook for Conscientious Objectors,* camping and mountaineering equipment, tents, auto repair manuals, aviation, and always maps, massage, education, child's play, and of course the *I Ching.* (87)

To supplement his work, Brand published additional *Whole Earth* material in a quarterly magazine, *Whole Earth Review,* which was originally called *CoEvolution Quarterly* and continues in print. Brand updated the *Whole Earth Catalogue* until 1971, when he announced he was finished with the project and published *The Last Whole Earth Catalogue.* Nonetheless, in 1974 *The Updated Last Whole Earth Catalogue* and *The Whole Earth Epilogue* appeared, and during the 1980s there were several editions of *The Next Whole Earth Catalogue* and *The Whole Earth Software Catalogue,* followed by *The Essential Whole Earth Catalogue.* In 1990 the *Whole Earth Ecolog: The Best of Environmental Tools and Ideas* was published. The book's newest incarnation is *The Millennium Whole Earth Catalogue: Access to Tools and Ideas for the Twenty-first Century* (1995), which was edited by Howard Reingold.

Throughout all the editions the publication kept with Brand's original intent, which was to support people's desire to go back to nature and live simply in a wilderness setting. However, the newest version, *The Millennium Whole Earth Catalogue,* acknowledges the importance of modern technology and provides a great deal of information about the use of computers and the Internet. (Brand 1986; Mills 1989)

See also Brand, Stewart; Environmental Movement; Simple Living Movement.

Wilderness Bill of Rights, A

Published in 1965, *A Wilderness Bill of Rights* was written by William O. Douglas, an active conservationist and a justice on the U.S. Supreme Court. He believed that nature had a right to protection under the law. In *A Wilderness Bill of Rights* he argues:

> Our Constitution not only spells out the authority of the majority; it also places restraints on them. It protects minorities, placing their rights beyond the reach of the majority—unless the Constitution is itself amended. The unpopular can speak and write as they wish and worship even in an unorthodox way. The majority cannot deprive the most depraved person of counsel in a criminal trial. Even a despised one is entitled to bail. . . . Wilderness values may not appeal to all Americans. But they make up a passionate cause for millions. They are, indeed, so basic to our national well-being that they must be

honored by any free society that respects diversity. We deal not with transitory matters but with the very earth itself. We who come this way are merely its short-term tenants. Our power in wilderness terms is only the power to destroy, not to create. Those who oppose wilderness values today may have sons and daughters who will honor wilderness values tomorrow. Our responsibility as life tenants is to make certain that there are wilderness values to honor after we have gone. (McHenry 368–369)

To this end, Douglas offers a "Bill of Rights" concerning the use of wilderness areas, to "guarantee that large areas of the original America will be preserved in perpetuity." (369) He states that wilderness areas should be enjoyed without being abused and believes that children have a right "to an understanding of their place in nature's community, of which they are a part." (369) (McHenry 1972)

See also Conservationism; Douglas, William O.

Wilderness Hunter, The

The Wilderness Hunter was written by Theodore Roosevelt, a dedicated conservationist who became president of the United States (1901–1909). Published in 1893, the book represents the prevailing philosophy of early conservationists: that wilderness areas should be preserved so that hunters would have ample opportunity to enjoy their sport. Roosevelt writes:

Hunting in the wilderness is of all pastimes the most attractive, and it is doubly so when not carried on merely as a pastime. Shooting over a private game preserve is of course in no way to be compared to it. The wilderness hunter must not only show skill in the use of the rifle and address in finding and approaching game, but he must also show the qualities of hardihood, self-reliance, and resolution needed for effectively grappling with his wild surroundings. The fact that the hunter needs the game, both for its meat and for its hide, undoubtedly adds a zest to the pursuit. Among the hunts which I have most enjoyed were those made when I was engaged in getting in the winter's stock of meat for the ranch, or was keeping some party of cowboys supplied with game from day to day. (Roosevelt 1986, 55–56)

However, Roosevelt's love of hunting was not at odds with his conservationism. As Paul Schullery explains in the introduction to an anthology of Roosevelt's work, *Wilderness Writings*:

Roosevelt's hunting is a knotty problem to some modern readers. Nature-lovers often forget that two of the greatest figures in American nature study, [John James] Audubon and [Aldo] Leopold, were also enthusiastic hunters. Because hunting is now morally repugnant to many people, modern nature enthusiasts have compartmentalized themselves into camps—some armed with binoculars, some with back packs, some with fishing rods, some with rifles, and so on; and often their rivalries and disagreements defeat their common goal of resource protection. Those who don't hunt can't understand those who do, or imagine how hunters can claim to appreciate things they kill. Historians, too, have struggled with Roosevelt's sporting interests; they shy away from that element of his character. . . . But any student of Roosevelt's writings knows he was nothing if not moral. Hunting was ridiculed by some in his time, as it always has been, but only a very few thought it immoral. Within the different social and cultural framework of Roosevelt's day, hunting was an acceptable and even commendable recreation. . . . By the standards of his day Roosevelt's attitudes were most enlightened. . . . Even those who disapprove of hunting . . . will find much of worth here. They will find a passionate ebullient lover of nature, a man whom the gentle Catskill nature writer John Burroughs defended as being such a great student of wildlife *because* he had hunted, thereby participating firsthand in the life struggles of poorly understood animals, and thereby accepting the responsibilities such deadly participation entailed: to kill cleanly and without waste, to learn all that could be learned, and to know gratitude for the opportunity. (19–20)

Roosevelt was a product of his era, but he was also ahead of his time with regard to many of his conservationist views. (Roosevelt 1986)

See also Burroughs, John; Conservationism; Muir, John; Roosevelt, Theodore.

Wildlife Conservation

Wildlife conservation is a common theme in environmental literature. The earliest writings on wildlife sought to identify and classify species. However, along with efforts to collect specimens for study came the realization that certain animals were being threatened with extinction. Slowly, naturalists like John James Audubon and Alexander Wilson, who worked to identify bird species, became interested in preserving species that were threatened.

In order to help such conservation efforts, scientists studied animal behavior to determine the forces threatening animals in native habitats. This science—animal ecology—gained popularity during the mid-1900s. African animals garnered the most attention, particularly after the publication of Joy Adamson's *Born Free,* which romanticized Adamson's research project on wild lions and inspired people to donate money to her efforts. Other scientists, noting the benefits of public interest on conservation efforts, decided to publish their own books about their work. Subsequent examples of such literature are Dian Fossey's *Gorillas in the Mist,* which concerns mountain gorillas, Jane Goodall's *In the Shadow of Man,* which focuses on chimpanzees, and Farley Mowat's *Never Cry Wolf* and *A Whale for the Killing,* on wolves and whales.

Modern works on wildlife conservation do not necessarily focus on a single species. Many undertake to study a range of species, typically in a single habitat. Sometimes the habitat is large, as with Peter Matthiessen's *Wildlife in America.* Others are much smaller, as with Alston Chase's *Playing God in Yellowstone,* which concerns the wildlife in America's most famous national park. There are also many books on endangered species throughout the world, such as Diane Ackerman's *The Rarest of the Rare.* Many environmental magazines are devoted to the issue of wildlife conservation; *National Wildlife* and *International Wildlife* are published by the National Wildlife Federation, an environmental group.

See also Ackerman, Diane; Adamson, Joy; Animal Ecology; Audubon, John James; *Born Free;* Chase, Alston; Environmental Groups; Fossey, Dian; Goodall, Jane; *Gorillas In the Mist; In the Shadow of Man; International Wildlife;* Matthiessen, Peter; Mowat, Farley; *National Wildlife; Never Cry Wolf; Playing God in Yellowstone; Rarest of the Rare, The; Whale for the Killing, A; Wildlife in America;* Wilson, Alexander.

Wildlife in America

Wildlife in America by Peter Matthiessen is a complete account of the history of wildlife destruction in America due to exploration, settlement, hunting, and other human practices. The book's publication in 1959 contributed to public awareness of wilderness conservation issues at the beginning of the modern environmental movement. It offers many historical details about individual species endangerment, as well as an appendix listing rare, endangered, and extinct species. This list was updated in a 1987 revised edition, which includes an epilogue discussing developments in wildlife conservation during the environmental movement. The epilogue concludes with the suggestion that much more needs to be done to protect animal species. Matthiessen writes: "Indifference to loss of species is, in effect, indifference to the future, and therefore a shameful carelessness about our children. . . . The loss of any species, particularly an obscure and little-known one, is unlikely to persuade most of us that the immediate and tangible benefits of a highway, dam, or shopping center should be foregone. Cumulatively, however, such decisions will bring about a cascade of extinctions unlike any previously experienced in human history." (280) (Matthiessen 1987)

See also Environmental Movement; Matthiessen, Peter; Wildlife Conservation.

Williams, Terry Tempest

Naturalist Terry Tempest Williams is one of the foremost nature writers in America today. Her best-known work is *Refuge: An Unnatural History of Family and Place* (1991). It relates an episode of environmental destruction in Utah to a personal tragedy in Williams's family; Williams's mother was dying of ovarian cancer at the same time the waters of the Great Salt Lake were threatening a bird sanctuary.

Williams was born in 1955 near the Wasatch Mountains in Utah. She was named naturalist-in-residence at the Utah Museum of Natural History after having worked as a teacher there for 15 years. She has also taught on a Navajo reservation, an experience she documents in *Pieces of White Shell* (1984). Her other works include a 1989 short-story collection (*Coyote's Canyon*) and a 1995 prose poem (*Desert Quartet*). (Knowles 1992; Trimble 1995)

See also Nature Writing; *Refuge*.

Wilson, Alexander

Naturalist Alexander Wilson was America's first major ornithologist; his eight-volume *American Ornithology* was the first work to provide substantial information on the country's bird species. He also gave naturalist John James Audubon the idea of creating his own book on the subject, *Birds of America*, which helped to popularize bird-watching. In addition, Wilson was an accomplished nature writer. Hans Huth, in *Nature and the American*, reports that Wilson's epic poem, "The Foresters, Description of a Pedestrian Tour to the Fall of the Niagara in the Autumn of 1804," was particularly successful and "opened a new path to the enjoyment of nature." (Huth 1972, 25) In discussing Wilson's verse, Huth says:

As a scientist Wilson has been remembered, but as a poet and writer he has been undeservedly forgotten. It may be that his lyrics were never really popular, but because of his radiant personality Wilson in his day had considerable influence in making his contemporaries aware of the beauties of nature. . . . Wilson well knew that the thing for which he was striving seemed quixotic to most of his contemporaries, but this did not prevent him from following his own designs and enjoying the "sight of the green meadows, the singing of birds, the fragrance of flowers and blossoms," which were in great contrast to "the burning streets, the growling oyster men, the stinking sewers and polite company of Philadelphia." (Huth 24)

Wilson was born in Paisley, Scotland, in 1766. As a boy he was apprenticed to a weaver, but he abandoned his trade to become a traveling salesman. In addition to selling fabric he marketed his own verse, and eventually he gained much renown as a poet. He used his fame to protest unfair labor practices and was publicly attacked for his views. Consequently, he moved to the United States, where he held a variety of jobs. He also befriended a naturalist and became interested in birds. While working as the assistant editor of an encyclopedia in 1806, he decided to write *American Ornithology*. Its first volume was published two years later. Wilson sold the book as he traveled across the country to study birds, offering subscriptions for the complete work to such notables as Thomas Jefferson and James Monroe. Wilson died in 1813 while finishing up the eighth volume. (Cox 1971; Huth 1972)

See also *American Ornithology;* Audubon, John James; Species Identification and Classification.

Wilson, Edward O.

Noted biologist Edward O. Wilson helped establish the controversial field of sociobiology, which suggests that many social behaviors have their origins in genetics. Wilson applied this concept to Charles Darwin's theory of evolution, arguing that social traits such as altruism—just as physical traits—are subject to natural selection.

Wilson was born on June 10, 1929, in Birmingham, Alabama. He attended the University of Alabama, where he studied ant behavior; he received his master's degree in 1950. He then attended Harvard University, graduating with a doctorate in 1955; he began teaching at Harvard the following year. His specialty continued to be ant behavior, and he did groundbreaking work in the field, discovering how ants communicate with one another and how they relate to their environment.

Wilson's first book, *The Insect Societies* (1971), confirmed his reputation as the world's foremost authority on ants. A later work, *The Ants* (1990), is the most comprehensive work on the subject ever written. Wilson's theories on sociobiology appear in *Sociobiology: The New Synthesis* (1975) and *On Human Nature* (1978), which won the Pulitzer Prize. His 1992 book, *The Diversity of Life,* also discusses environmental ethics, biodiversity, and endangered species.

Wilson became a professor of zoology at Harvard in 1964 and remained in the position until 1976, whereupon he became a professor of science. In 1972 he was named curator of entomology at Harvard's Museum of Comparative Zoology. He has won numerous awards for his work. (E. Wilson 1992)

See also Biodiversity; Darwin, Charles Robert; *Diversity of Life, The;* Evolution.

Wordsworth, William

English Romantic poet William Wordsworth not only described the natural world but also wrote about the relationship between humans and nature. He expressed the view—revolutionary during his day—that man is responsible for protecting nature. Consequently, liter-

William Wordsworth (Archive Photos)

ary scholars such as Karl Kroeber have called him a protoecologist.

In *Ecological Literary Criticism: Romantic Imagining and the Biology of Mind* (1994), Kroeber elaborates on this aspect of Wordsworth's work, using the poem "Nutting" as an example. Kroeber points out that the language of the poem equates the violation of the woods with a rape. On a search for hazel nuts, Wordsworth speaks of "forcing" his way through nature and discovering a hazel nook with "not a broken bough" that is a "virgin scene." After enjoying the nook's sweetness, the poet has to "ravage" it until it is "deformed and sullied" and forced to surrender. Kroeber argues that the poem is therefore about Wordsworth's moral conflict over the exploitation of nature; other scholars have viewed "Nutting" primarily as an expression of sexuality.

Wordsworth wrote numerous short poems on nature, as well as verse portraits of rural people. During his lifetime, his works appeared (with some of Samuel Taylor Coleridge's poetry) in a collection entitled *Lyrical Ballads* (1798, rev. 1800), as well as in *Poems, in Two Volumes* (1807). Wordsworth also wrote several long poems, including *Descriptive Sketches* (1793), *The White Doe of Rylstone* (1815), *Thanksgiving Ode* (1816), *The Borders* (1842), and the autobiographical *The Prelude, or, Growth of a Poet's Mind* (1850).

Born in Cockermouth, Cumberland, England, on April 7, 1770, Wordsworth was orphaned at age 13, whereupon he and his brothers were sent away to school; his sister, Dorothy, remained behind. He went to St. John's College in Cambridge in 1787 and spent the summer of 1790 in France, where he witnessed the French Revolution. After receiving his degree in England he returned to France, had an affair, and fathered a child. He then visited England; when war suddenly broke out between France and England he was unable to return to his mistress and daughter. This threw him into a depression, compounded by his sympathies for France and his inability to earn a living. His spirits lifted in 1795, when he received an inheritance and was reunited with Dorothy. Shortly thereafter, he and Coleridge became friends, and the two men began writing together. Wordsworth had devoted himself to poetry in college, but with Coleridge's encouragement he became more serious about the activity.

Thereafter, Wordsworth produced a large body of verse. However, he endured much criticism of his work until 1820, when his long poem, *The River Duddon,* was well received. In later years, his reputation grew, although toward the end he spent much of his time revising earlier work rather than producing new poems. In 1843 he was named poet laureate of Britain, a post he held until his death on April 23, 1850.

Wyndham, John

Science fiction writer John Wyndham wrote novels on human ethics. One of his most famous books, *Day of the Triffids* (1951), is representative of post–World War II attitudes toward the environment. Born John Wyndham Parkes Lucas Beynon Harris in Birmingham, Warwickshire, England, in 1903, he held several jobs before turning to writing in the 1920s. His other works include *The Kraken Wakes* (1953), *The Chrysalids* (1955), and *The Trouble with Lichen* (1960), in addition to several short stories.

See also *Day of the Triffids;* Environmental Fiction.

Z

Zakin, Susan

Susan Zakin is an environmental journalist whose articles have appeared in such publications as *Mother Jones, Sierra, The New York Times,* and *Newsday.* Her 1993 book, *Coyotes and Town Dogs: Earth First! and the Environmental Movement,* offers a detailed discussion of the history and activities of the radical environmental group Earth First! (Zakin 1993)

> See also *Coyotes and Town Dogs;* Environmental Activism; Environmental Groups; Environmental Movement.

Zoonomia

Published between 1794 and 1796, *Zoonomia, or the Laws of Organic Life* was written by English physician Erasmus Darwin, the grandfather of evolutionary theorist Charles Darwin. The book addresses the elder Darwin's own views on evolution. It proposes that living things change, or transmute, in accordance with their environment and that their adaptations are built upon by the next generation. A well-known poet, Erasmus Darwin also expressed his theory of transmutation in some of his verse. In *The Temple of Nature* (1803), for example, he writes that organisms "as successive generations bloom,/New powers acquire, and larger limbs assume." (Bowler 188) By proposing that creatures physically change in accordance with the demands of their environment, Darwin's work is closer to that of J. B. Lamarck than to that of his own grandson, who openly rejected many of the principles expressed in *Zoonomia.* (Bowler 1993)

> See also Darwin, Charles Robert; Darwin, Erasmus; Evolution.

Zwinger, Ann

Ann Zwinger is a prominent nature writer whose work describes American wildlife and habitats, particularly in the western United States, and touches on related conservation issues. For example, in *The Mysterious Lands* (1989) she writes of her experiences studying bighorn sheep in desert wildlife areas. Her other works include *Run, River, Run: A Naturalist's Journey Down One of the Great Rivers of the West* (1975), which won the John Burroughs Medal for nature writing, *Wind in the Rock* (1978), *A Conscious Stillness: Two Naturalists on Thoreau's Rivers* (1982), *A Desert Country Near the Sea: A Natural History of the Cape Region of Baja California* (1983), and *Downcanyon: A Naturalist Explores the Colorado River Through the Grand Canyon* (1995), which won the 1995 Western States Book Award for creative nonfiction.

However, Zwinger did not originally plan to be a naturalist. She studied and then taught art history while raising a family. Forced to move frequently because of her husband's assignments in the U.S. Air Force, it wasn't until 1960 that she was able to connect to a particular piece of land. At that time, she and her husband put down roots in Colorado Springs, Colorado, buying acreage there. Zwinger's first book, *Beyond the Aspen Grove* (1977), reflects her experiences on that land. (Knowles 1992; Trimble 1995)

See also Burroughs, John; *Downcanyon;* Nature Writing; Thoreau, Henry David.

BIBLIOGRAPHY

Abbey, Edward. 1968. *Desert Solitaire*. New York: McGraw-Hill.

———. 1975. *The Monkey Wrench Gang*. Philadelphia: Lippincott.

Abrahamson, Dean Edwin, ed. 1989. *The Challenge of Global Warming*. Washington, D.C.: Island Press.

Ackerman, Diane. 1995. *The Rarest of the Rare*. New York: Random House.

Adamson, George. 1988. *My Pride and Joy*. Boston: GK Hall.

Adamson, Joy. 1986. *Born Free*. New York: Pantheon Books.

———. 1962. *Forever Free*. New York: Harcourt, Brace, and World.

———. 1961. *Living Free*. New York: Harcourt, Brace, and World.

Allaby, Michael. 1989. *A Guide to Gaia: A Survey of the New Science of Our Living Earth*. New York: E. P. Dutton.

Allee, W. C., et al. 1949. *Principles of Animal Ecology*. Philadelphia and London: W. B. Saunders.

Asimov, Isaac, and Frederik Pohl. 1991. *Our Angry Earth*. New York: Tor.

Attenborough, David. 1979. *Life on Earth*. Boston: Little, Brown.

Bailes, Kendall E., ed. 1985. *Environmental History: Critical Issues in Comparative Perspective*. Lanham, New York, and London: University Press of America and American Society for Environmental History.

Bailey, E. B. 1963. *Charles Lyell*. Garden City, NY: Doubleday.

Bailey, Ronald. 1993. *Eco-Scam: The False Prophets of Ecological Apocalypse*. New York: St. Martin's Press.

Bates, Marston, and Philip S. Humphrey, eds. 1957. *The Darwin Reader*. London: Macmillan.

Beagon, Mary. 1992. *Roman Nature: The Thought of Pliny the Elder*. New York: Oxford University Press.

Becker, Lucille Frackman. 1996. *Pierre Boulle*. New York: Twayne.

Berry, Wendell. 1972. *A Continuous Harmony: Essays Cultural and Agricultural*. New York: Harcourt Brace Jovanovich.

———. 1986. *The Unsettling of America: Culture and Agriculture*. San Francisco: Sierra Club Books.

Bibby, Cyril. 1972. *Scientist Extraordinary; The Life and Scientific Work of Thomas Henry Huxley, 1825–1895*. New York: St. Martin's Press.

Bilsky, Lester J., ed. 1980. *Historical Ecology*. Port Washington, NY, and London: Kennikat Press.

Blair, Henry Alexander, ed. 1967. *Biological Effects of External Radiation*. New York: Hafner.

Bolsche, Wilhelm. 1906. *Haeckel: His Life and Work*. London: T. F. Unwin.

Bookchin, Murray. 1982. *The Ecology of Freedom: The Emergence and Dissolution of Hierarchy*. Palo Alto, CA: Cheshire Books.

———. 1980. *Toward an Ecological Society*. Montreal: Black Rose Books.

———. 1994. *Which Way for the Ecology Movement?* San Francisco: AK Press.

Botkin, Daniel B. 1995. *Our Natural History: The Lessons of Lewis and Clark.* New York: G. P. Putnam.

Botting, Douglas. 1973. *Humboldt and the Cosmos.* London: Joseph.

Boulle, Pierre. 1963. *Planet of the Apes.* New York: Signet.

Bowler, Peter J. 1996. *Charles Darwin: The Man and His Influence.* London: Cambridge University Press.

———. 1993. *The Norton History of the Environmental Sciences.* New York and London: W. W. Norton.

Boynton, Holmes, ed. 1948. *The Beginnings of Modern Science: Scientific Writings of the 16th, 17th, and 18th Centuries.* Roslyn, NY: Walter J. Black.

Brand, Stewart. 1986. *The Essential Whole Earth Catalogue.* Garden City, NY: Doubleday.

Buffon, George Louis Leclerc. 1831. *A Natural History of the Globe, of Man, of Beasts, Birds, Fishes, Reptiles, Insects, and Plants.* Ed. John Wright. Boston: Gray and Bowen.

Bulloch, David K. 1989. *The Wasted Ocean.* New York: Lyons and Burford (an American Littoral Society Book).

Burroughs, Edgar Rice. 1946. *The Land That Time Forgot.* Garden City, NY: Nelson Doubleday.

Butler, Samuel. 1923. *Erewhon.* New York: E. P. Dutton.

Callicott, J. Baird. 1987. *Companion to A Sand County Almanac: Interpretive and Critical Essays.* Madison: University of Wisconsin Press.

Carson, Rachel L. 1961. *The Sea Around Us.* Rev. ed. New York: Oxford University Press.

———. 1962. *Silent Spring.* Boston: Houghton Mifflin.

Caufield, Catherine. 1989. *In the Rainforest.* New York: Alfred A. Knopf.

Caulfield, Patricia. 1970. *Everglades: Selections from the Writings of Peter Matthiessen.* San Francisco: Sierra Club Books.

Chambers, Robert. 1994. *Vestiges of the National History of Creation and Other Evolutionary Writings.* Ed. James A. Secord. Chicago: University of Chicago Press.

Chase, Alston. 1987. *Playing God in Yellowstone: The Destruction of America's First National Park.* San Diego, New York, and London: Harcourt Brace Jovanovich.

Christopher, John. 1970. *Gilbert White and His Selbourne.* London: Kimber.

Cohen, Daniel. 1987. *Carl Sagan: Superstar Scientist.* New York: Dodd, Mead.

Collard, Andrée, with Joyce Contrucci. 1988. *Rape of the Wild.* London: The Women's Press.

Commoner, Barry. 1971. *The Closing Circle: Man, Nature, and Technology.* New York: Alfred A. Knopf.

Cooper, Susan Fenimore. 1968. *Rural Hours.* Introduction by David Jones. Syracuse, NY: Syracuse University Press.

Cousteau, Captain J. Y., with James Dugan. 1963. *The Living Sea.* New York: Harper and Row.

Cox, Donald W. 1971. *Pioneers of Ecology.* Maplewood, NJ: Hammond.

Crèvecoeur, J. Hector St. John. 1957. *Letters from an American Farmer.* New York: E. P. Dutton.

Crichton, Michael. 1990. *Jurassic Park.* New York: Alfred A. Knopf.

Curtis, Jane. 1982. *The World of George Perkins Marsh: America's First Conservationist and Environmentalist.* Woodstock, VT: Countryman Press (published for the Woodstock Foundation).

Darwin, Charles. 1972. *The Voyage of the Beagle.* Introduction by Walter Sullivan. New York: Signet (New American Library).

Dashefsky, H. Steven. 1993. *Environmental Literacy.* New York: Random House.

De Terra, Helmut. 1979. *Humboldt: The Life and Times of Alexander von Humboldt, 1769–1859.* New York: Knopf.

Devall, Bill, and George Sessions. 1985. *Deep Ecology: Living as if Nature Mattered.* Salt Lake City, UT: Peregrine Books.

Dillard, Annie. 1974. *Pilgrim at Tinker Creek.* New York: Harper's Magazine Press (published in association with Harper and Row).

———. 1982. *Teaching a Stone to Talk: Expeditions and Encounters.* New York: Harper and Row.

Dobson, Andrew. 1991. *The Green Reader.* San Francisco: Mercury House.

Dowie, Mark. 1995. *Losing Ground: American Environmentalism at the Close of the Twentieth Century.* Cambridge: MIT Press.

Doyle, Sir Arthur Conan. 1959. *The Lost World.* New York: Looking Glass Library.

Dreyer, J.L.E. 1953. *A History of Astronomy from Thales to Kepler.* New York: Dover Publications.

Easterbrook, Gregg. 1995. *A Moment on the Earth.* New York: Viking Penguin.

Eckholm, Erik P. 1982. *Down to Earth.* New York: W. W. Norton.

Editors of *The Ecologist,* including Edward Goldsmith, et al. 1972. *Blueprint for Survival.* Boston: Houghton Mifflin.

Ehrlich, Paul. 1986. *The Machinery of Nature: The Living World Around Us—and How It Works.* New York: Simon and Schuster.

Ehrlich, Paul R., and Anne H. Ehrlich. 1981. *Extinction: The Causes and Consequences of the Disappearance of Species.* New York: Random House.

———. 1990. *The Population Explosion.* New York: Simon and Schuster.

———. 1995. *The Stork and the Plow: The Equity Answer to the Human Dilemma.* New York: Grosset/Putnam.

Eiseley, Loren. 1971. *The Night Country.* New York: Charles Scribner's Sons.

Eller, Vernard. 1973. *The Simple Life: The Christian Stance Toward Possessions.* Grand Rapids, MI: Eerdmans.

Evans, I. O. (Idrisyn Oliver). 1966. *Jules Verne and His Work.* New York: Twayne Publishers.

Fellows, Otis E., and Stephen F. Milliken. 1972. *Buffon.* New York: Twayne.

Finch, Robert, and John Elder. 1990. *The Norton Anthology of Nature Writing.* New York: W. W. Norton.

Fitter, Richard Sidney Richmond. 1959. *Six Great Naturalists: White, Linnaeus, Waterton, Audubon, Fabre, Huxley.* London: H. Hamilton.

Fitzpatrick, T. J. 1982. *Rafinesque: A Sketch of His Life with Bibliography.* Weston, MA: M and S Press.

Fontenrose, Joseph Eddy. 1964. *John Steinbeck: An Introduction and Interpretation.* New York: Barnes and Noble.

Foreman, Dave. 1991. *Confessions of an Eco-Warrior.* New York: Harmony Books.

Forster, John Reingold. 1778. *Observations Made During a Voyage Around the World.* London: G. Robinson (facsimile made by University Microfilms International of Ann Arbor, MI, 1986).

Fossey, Dian. 1983. *Gorillas in the Mist.* Boston: Houghton Mifflin.

Frederick, John T. 1972. *William Henry Hudson.* New York: Twayne.

French, Roger, and Frank Greenaway, eds. 1986. *Science in the Early Roman Empire: Pliny the Elder, His Sources and Influence.* Totowa, NJ: Barnes and Noble.

French, Warren. 1975. *John Steinbeck.* Boston: Twayne Publishers.

Fuller, R. Buckminster. 1969. *Utopia or Oblivion: The Prospects for Humanity.* Toronto, New York, and London: Bantam Books.

Fumento, Michael. 1993. *Science Under Siege: How the Environmental Misinformation Campaign Is Affecting Our Laws, Taxes, and Our Daily Life.* New York: Quill/William Morrow.

Furbank, Philip Nicholas. 1976. *Samuel Butler, 1835–1902.* Folcroft, PA: Folcroft Library Editions.

Glass, H. Bently, O. Temkin, and W. L. Straus, eds. 1968. *Forerunners of Darwin: 1745–1859.* Baltimore: Johns Hopkins Press.

Glotfelty, Cheryll, and Harold Fromm, eds. 1996. *The Ecocriticism Reader: Landmarks in Literary Ecology.* Athens: University of Georgia Press.

Goldsmith, Edward, et al. (*The Ecologist*). 1972. *A Blueprint for Survival.* Harmondsworth, England: Penguin.

Goodall, Jane. 1971. *In the Shadow of Man.* Boston: Houghton Mifflin.

Gore, Al. 1992. *Earth in the Balance: Ecology and the Human Spirit.* Boston and New York: Houghton Mifflin.

Gottlieb, Robert. 1993. *Forcing the Spring: The Transformation of the American Environmental Movement.* Washington, DC: Island Press.

———. 1988. *A Life of Its Own: The Politics of Power and Water.* San Diego: Harcourt Brace Jovanovich.

Gould, Stephen Jay. 1993. *Eight Little Piggies: Reflections in Natural History.* London: Jonathan Cape.

———. 1980. *The Panda's Thumb.* New York: W. W. Norton.

Granger, Margaret, ed. 1983. *The Natural History Prose Writings of John Clare.* New York: Oxford University Press.

Greenberg, Martin. 1997. *Michael Crichton Companion.* New York: Ballantine.

Hardin, Garrett, and John Baden, eds. 1977. *Managing the Commons.* San Francisco: W. H. Freeman.

Harding, Walter Roy. 1965. *The Days of Henry Thoreau.* New York: Knopf.

———. 1959. *A Thoreau Handbook.* New York: New York University Press.

Harris, J. F. 1977. *Samuel Butler, Author of Erewhon: The Man and His Work.* Norwood, PA: Norwood Editions.

Harrison, Harry. 1979. *Make Room! Make Room!* Boston: Gregg Press.

Hassler, Donald M. 1973. *Erasmus Darwin.* New York: Twayne.

Hatch, Alden. 1974. *Buckminster Fuller: At Home in the Universe.* New York: Crown.

Haverstock, Mary Sayre. 1973. *Indian Gallery: The Story of George Catlin.* New York: Four Winds Press.

Hawkes, Jacquette. 1991. *A Land.* Boston: Beacon Press.

Hay, John. 1969. *In Defense of Nature.* Boston: Little, Brown.

Helvarg, David. 1994. *The War Against the Greens: The "Wise Use" Movement, the New Right, and Anti-Environmental Violence.* San Francisco: Sierra Club Books.

Heuer, Kenneth. 1987. *The Lost Notebooks of Loren Eiseley.* Boston and Toronto: Little, Brown.

Holt, Lee E. 1964. *Samuel Butler.* New York: Twayne Publishers.

Holtsmark, Erling B. 1986. *Edgar Rice Burroughs.* Boston: Twayne.

Hudson, W. H. 1922. *Afoot in England.* New York: Alfred A. Knopf.

Huth, Hans. 1972. *Nature and the American: Three Centuries of Changing Attitudes.* Lincoln: University of Nebraska Press.

Ibsen, Henrik. 1978. *Eleven Plays of Henrik Ibsen.* Ed. H. L. Mencken. New York: Modern Library/Random House.

Jevons, W. Stanley. 1906. *The Coal Question.* New York and London: Macmillan.

Johnson, Josephine W. 1969. *The Inland Island.* New York: Simon and Schuster.

Kaufman, Polly Wells. 1996. *National Parks and the Woman's Voice.* Albuquerque: University of New Mexico Press.

Kaufman, Wallace. 1994. *No Turning Back: Dismantling the Fantasies of Environmental Thinking.* New York: BasicBooks (HarperCollins).

Knowles, Karen, ed. 1992. *Celebrating the Land: Women's Nature Writings, 1850–1991.* Flagstaff, Arizona: Northland Publishing.

Kroeber, Karl. 1994. *Ecological Literary Criticism.* New York: Columbia University Press.

Krutch, Joseph Wood. 1950. *Great American Nature Writing.* New York: William Sloane Associates.

Lamarck, Jean Baptiste. 1984. *Philosophie zoologique.* Trans. Hugh Elliott as *Zoological Philosophy.* Chicago: University of Chicago Press, 1984.

Larson, James L. 1971. *Reason and Experience: The Representation of Natural Order in the Work of Carl von Linne.* Berkeley: University of California Press.

Leakey, Louis. 1953. *Adam's Ancestors.* London: Methuen.

Leakey, Richard. 1994. *The Origin of Humankind.* New York: BasicBooks (HarperCollins).

Leakey, Richard, and Roger Lewin. 1995. *The Sixth Extinction: Patterns of Life and the Future of Humankind.* New York: Doubleday.

LeGuin, Ursula. 1971. *The Lathe of Heaven.* New York: Avon Books.

Leopold, Aldo. 1966. *A Sand County Almanac.* New York: Oxford University Press.

Loehr, Raymond C. 1974. *Agricultural Waste Management: Problems, Processes, and Approaches.* New York: Academic Press.

Lorbiecki, Marybeth. 1996. *Aldo Leopold: A Fierce Green Fire.* Helena, Montana: Falcon Press.

Lucretius. 1975. *De Rerum Natura.* Boston: Harvard University Press.

Lurie, Edward. 1960. *Louis Agassiz: A Life in Science.* Chicago: University of Chicago Press.

Lyell, Charles. 1872. *Principles of Geology.* New York: D. Appleton.

Lyon, Thomas J. 1989. *This Incomperable Lande: A Book of American Nature Writing.* Boston: Houghton Mifflin Company.

MacKaye, Benton. 1928. *The New Exploration: A Philosophy of Regional Planning.* New York: Harcourt, Brace.

Maclean, Norman. 1992. *A River Runs Through It, and Other Stories.* New York: Pocket Books.

Malthus, T. R. 1976. *An Essay on the Principle of Population: Text, Sources, and Background, Criticism.* Ed. Philip Appleman. New York: Norton.

Manes, Christopher. 1990. *Green Rage: Radical Environmentalism and the Unmaking of Civilization.* Boston: Little, Brown.

Masumoto, David Mas. 1995. *Epitaph for a Peach: Four Seasons on My Family Farm.* San Francisco: HarperSanFrancisco.

Matthew, William Diller. 1939. *Climate and Evolution.* New York: New York Academy of Sciences.

Matthiessen, Peter. 1991. *African Silences.* New York: Random House.

———. 1987. *Wildlife in America.* New York: Viking.

Mayr, Ernst E. 1982. *The Growth of Biological Thought: Diversity, Evolution, and Inheritance.* Cambridge, MA: Belknap Press.

McHenry, Robert, ed. 1972. *A Documentary History of Conservation in America.* New York: Praeger.

McKibben, Bill. 1989. *The End of Nature.* New York: Random House.

McPhee, John. 1989. *The Control of Nature.* New York: Farrar Straus Giroux.

Meadows, Donella H., et al. (The Club of Rome). 1983. *The Limits to Growth.* London: Pan Books.

Meine, Curt. 1988. *Aldo Leopold: His Life and Work.* Madison: University of Wisconsin Press.

Miles, Josephine. 1964. *Ralph Waldo Emerson.* Minneapolis: University of Minnesota Press.

Mills, Stephanie. 1989. *Whatever Happened to Ecology?* San Francisco: Sierra Club Books.

Mitchell, John G., ed., with Constance Stallings. 1970. *Ecotactics: The Sierra Club Handbook for Environmental Activists.* New York: Pocket Books.

Mowat, Farley. 1963. *Never Cry Wolf.* Boston and Toronto: Atlantic Monthly Press.

———. *Sea of Slaughter.* 1984. Boston and New York: Atlantic Monthly Press.

———. 1972. *A Whale for the Killing.* Boston and Toronto: Little, Brown.

———. 1987. *Woman in the Mists: The Story of Dian Fossey and the Mountain Gorillas of Africa.* New York: Warner Books.

Muir, John. 1917. *Our National Parks.* Boston and New York: Houghton Mifflin.

Munson, Richard. 1989. *Cousteau: The Captain and His World.* New York: Morrow.

Nader, Ralph, et al. 1981. *Who's Poisoning America: Corporate Polluters and Their Victims in the Chemical Age.* San Francisco: Sierra Club Books.

Naess, Arne. 1989. *Ecology, Community, and Lifestyle.* Trans. David Rothenberg. Cambridge: Cambridge University Press.

Nash, Roderick Frederick. 1989. *The Rights of Nature: A History of Environmental Ethics.* Madison: University of Wisconsin Press.

Nash, Roderick, ed. 1976. *The American Environment: Readings in the History of Conservation.* Reading, MA: Addison-Wesley.

Netzley, Patricia. 1998. *Environmental Groups.* San Diego: Lucent Books.

Oelschlaeger, Max. 1991. *The Idea of Wilderness: From Prehistory to the Age of Ecology.* New Haven and London: Yale University Press.

Osborn, Fairfield. 1948. *Our Plundered Planet.* Boston: Little, Brown.

Pearce, David W., Anil Markandya, and Edward B. Barbier. 1989. *Blueprint for a Green Economy.* London: Earthscan.

Pepper, David. 1996. *Modern Environmentalism: An Introduction.* London and New York: Routledge.

Pinchot, Gifford. 1910. *The Fight for Conservation.* Garden City, NY: Harcourt, Brace.

Pohl, Frederik. 1987. *Chernobyl: A Novel.* New York: Bantam Books.

Ponting, Clive. 1991. *A Green History of the World: The Environment and the Collapse of Great Civilizations.* New York: St. Martin's Press.

Poynter, Margaret. 1997. *The Leakeys: Uncovering the Origins of Humankind.* Springfield, NJ: Enslow.

Rathje, William, and Cullen Murphy. 1992. *Rubbish! The Archaeology of Garbage.* New York: HarperCollins.

Ray, Dixy Lee, with Lou Guzzo. 1993. *Environmental Overkill: Whatever Happened to Common Sense?* New York: HarperPerennial.

Reich, Charles. 1970. *The Greening of America.* New York: Random House.

Reisner, Marc. 1986. *Cadillac Desert: The American West and Its Disappearing Water.* New York: Viking Penguin.

Ridley, Mark. 1996. *Evolution.* Cambridge, MA: Blackwell Science.

Roosevelt, Theodore. 1986. *Wilderness Writings.* Ed. Paul Schullery. Salt Lake City, UT: Peregrine Smith Books.

Rothenberg, David. 1993. *Is It Painful To Think?* Minneapolis: University of Minnesota Press.

Ruland, Richard, ed. 1968. *Twentieth-Century Interpretations of Walden: A Collection of Critical Essays.* Englewood Cliffs, NJ: Prentice-Hall.

Sagan, Carl, and Richard Turco. 1990. *A Path Where No Man Thought: Nuclear Winter and the End of the Arms Race.* New York: Random House.

Salyer, Gregory. 1997. *Leslie Marmon Silko.* New York: Twayne Publishers.

Sanborn, Franklin Benjamin. 1968. *The Life of Henry David Thoreau.* Detroit: Gale Research.

Schatt, Stanley. 1976. *Kurt Vonnegut Jr.* Boston: Twayne.

Schneider, Stephen Henry. 1989. *Global Warming: Are We Entering the Greenhouse Century?* San Francisco: Sierra Club Books.

Schubnell, Matthias. 1985. *N. Scott Momaday: The Cultural and Literary Background.* Norman and London: University of Oklahoma Press.

Schumacher, E. F. 1974. *Small Is Beautiful.* London: Abacus.

Science Action Coalition, with Albert J. Fritsch. 1980. *Environmental Ethics: Concerned Choices for Concerned Citizens.* Garden City, NY: Anchor Press/Doubleday.

Shabecoff, Philip. 1993. *A Fierce Green Fire: The American Environmental Movement.* New York: Hill and Wang.

Shi, David. 1985. *The Simple Life: Plain Living and High Thinking in American Culture.* New York: Oxford University Press.

Sikes, Edward Ernest. 1971. *Lucretius: Poet and Philosopher.* New York: Russell and Russell.

Simple Living Collective, American Friends Service Committee, San Francisco. 1977. *Taking Charge: Achieving Personal and Political Change Through Simple Living.* New York: Bantam Books.

Slovic, Scott. 1992. *Seeking Awareness in American Nature Writing: Henry Thoreau, Annie Dillard, Wendell Berry, Barry Lopez.* Salt Lake City: University of Utah Press.

Smardon, Richard C., ed. 1983. *The Future of Wetlands: Assessing Visual-Cultural Values.* Totowa, NJ: Allanheld, Osmun.

Snyder, Gary. 1990. *The Practice of the Wild.* San Francisco: North Point Press.

———. 1974. *Turtle Island.* New York: New Directions.

Spangenburg, Ray, and Diane K. Moser. 1993. *The History of Science from the Ancient Greeks to the Scientific Revolution.* New York: Facts on File.

———. 1993. *The History of Science in the Eighteenth Century.* New York: Facts on File.

Spivack, Charlotte. 1984. *Ursula K. LeGuin.* Boston: Twayne Publishers.

Steinbeck, John. 1986. *The Log from the Sea of Cortez.* New York: Penguin Books.

Steuding, Bob. 1976. *Gary Snyder.* Boston: Twayne.

Stickley, Gustav. 1909. *Craftsman Homes.* New York: Craftsman.

Stokes, William Lee. 1966. *Essentials of Earth History: An Introduction to Historical Geology.* Englewood Cliffs, NJ: Prentice-Hall.

Stone, Roger D. 1990. *The Voyage of the Sanderling.* New York: Alfred Knopf.

Stover, Leon. 1990. *Harry Harrison.* Boston: Twayne (G.K. Hall).

Teale, Edwin Way. 1954. *The Wilderness World of John Muir.* New York: Houghton Mifflin.

Thomson, James O. 1948. *History of Ancient Geography.* Cambridge University Press.

Thoreau, Henry David. 1965. *Walden, or Life in the Woods and On the Duty of Civil Disobedience.* New York: Harper and Row.

Trimble, Stephen. 1995. *Words from the Land.* Reno, Las Vegas, and London: University of Nevada Press.

Van Lawick–Goodall, Jane. 1971. *In the Shadow of Man.* Boston: Houghton Mifflin.

Verne, Jules. 1965. *A Journey to the Center of the Earth.* New York: Scholastic Books.

Vonnegut, Kurt. 1963. *Cat's Cradle.* New York: Delacorte Press.

Warming, Eugenius. 1909. *Oecology of Plants: An Introduction to the Study of Plant Communities.* Trans. P. Groom. Oxford: Clarendon Press.

Whalley, Joyce Irene. 1982. *Pliny the Elder, Historia Naturalis.* London: Sidwick and Jackson.

Whicher, Stephen E. 1957. *Selections from Ralph Waldo Emerson.* Boston: Houghton Mifflin.

White, Gilbert. 1880. *The Natural History of Selbourne, with Observations on Various Parts of Nature and the Naturalist's Calendar.* London and New York: G. Routledge and Sons.

Wild, Peter. 1993. *Ann Zwinger.* Boise, Idaho: Boise State University Press.

Wiley, Farida A. 1967. *John Burroughs' America: Selections for the Writings of the Hudson River Naturalist.* New York: Devin-Adair.

Wilson, Edward O. 1992. *The Diversity of Life.* New York and London: W. W. Norton.

Wilson, Leonard G. 1972. *Charles Lyell, the Years to 1841: The Revolution in Geology.* New Haven: Yale University Press.

Wood, James Playsted. 1965. *The Man Who Hated Sherlock Holmes: A Life of Sir Arthur Conan Doyle.* New York: Pantheon Books.

Woodberry, George. 1968. *Ralph Waldo Emerson.* New York: Haskell House.

Woodward, Horace B. 1911. *History of Geology.* New York and London: G. P. Putnam's Sons.

Wyndham, John. 1964. *The John Wyndham Omnibus.* London: Michael Joseph.

Yamashita, Karen Tei. 1992. *Brazil-Maru.* Minneapolis: Coffee House Press.

Zakin, Susan. 1993. *Coyotes and Town Dogs: Earth First! and the Environmental Movement.* New York: Penguin Books.

Zwinger, Ann Haymond. 1995. *Downcanyon: A Naturalist Explores the Colorado River Through the Grand Canyon.* Tucson: University of Arizona Press.

INDEX